Race, Crime and Criminal Justice

Race, Crime and Criminal Justice

International Perspectives

Edited by

Anita Kalunta-Crumpton
Texas Southern University, USA

First published 2010 by
PALGRAVE MACMILLAN

Palgrave Macmillan in the UK is an imprint of Macmillan Publishers Limited,
registered in England, company number 785998, of Houndmills, Basingstoke,
Hampshire RG21 6XS.

Palgrave Macmillan in the US is a division of St Martin's Press LLC,
175 Fifth Avenue, New York, NY 10010.

Palgrave Macmillan is the global academic imprint of the above companies
and has companies and representatives throughout the world.

Palgrave® and Macmillan® are registered trademarks in the United States,
the United Kingdom, Europe and other countries.

ISBN-13: 978-0-230-22029-4 hardback

This book is printed on paper suitable for recycling and made from fully
managed and sustained forest sources. Logging, pulping and manufacturing
processes are expected to conform to the environmental regulations of the
country of origin.

A catalogue record for this book is available from the British Library.

Library of Congress Cataloging-in-Publication Data
Race, crime and criminal justice : international perspectives / edited by
    Anita Kalunta-Crumpton.
        p.   cm.
    Summary: "This book provides a focused and critical international
    overview of the intersections between race, crime perpetration and
    victimisation, and criminal justice policy and practice responses to
    crime perpetration and crime victimisation"—Provided by publisher.
    Includes bibliographical references and index.
    ISBN 978-0-230-22029-4 (hardback)
    1. Crime and race—Case studies.   2. Discrimination in criminal justice
    administration—Case studies.   I. Kalunta-Crumpton, Anita, 1962–
    HV6191.R33 2010
    364.2'56—dc22   2009046205

10   9   8   7   6   5   4   3   2   1
19 18 17 16 15 14 13 12 11 10

Printed and bound in Great Britain by
CPI Antony Rowe, Chippenham and Eastbourne

Contents

Part III   Beyond Europe: Is There Race in Crime and Criminal Justice?

Part IV   Conclusion

List of Tables and Figures

Tables

Figures

Foreword

To *Race, Crime and Criminal Justice: International Perspectives*, edited by Anita Kalunta-Crumpton (forthcoming Palgrave Macmillan 2010).

By Michael Tonry (Michael Tonry is Professor of Law and Public Policy, University of Minnesota, and Senior Fellow, Netherlands Institute for the Study of Crime and Law Enforcement, Amsterdam).

* * * *

Interactions among race, ethnicity, immigration, and crime present difficult social and political challenges in every country. The challenges are the same – assuring equality before the law for all people, providing levels of security that allow individuals to choose the lives they want to live, and respecting the human rights of victims and offenders. And the challenges are different, varying with the particular histories of particular places and changing over time.

In the long term, decent people everywhere look forward to a day when cultural and ethnic difference is respected, when state institutions accord equal respect to all individuals, and when xenophobia, racial bias, and invidious stereotyping are rare events universally acknowledged to be wrong. The lion, however, has nowhere as yet lain down with the lamb, and everywhere credible allegations are made of racial and ethnic profiling by the police, unwarranted disparities in sentencing and punishment, and generally unfair treatment of members of some groups.

Anita Kalunta-Crumpton's *Race, Crime and Criminal Justice: International Perspectives* examines these subjects in general and in a broad range of countries. Issues of race, ethnicity, and crime are conceptualized differently in different places. In Australia, Canada, and New Zealand, the issues most often discussed and studied and made the subjects of government policy processes relate to Aborigines. In the United States, the overwhelming focus is on the experience of non-immigrant black people, with increasing but far less attention being paid to the experiences of Hispanics and immigrants. In England and Wales, the experiences of people of Afro-Caribbean background are front and center. In most of continental Europe, relatively recent immigrants and – in some countries – Roma and Sinti people receive greatest attention from politicians and the media.

So far as I know, no one has systematically examined why these problems are conceptualized in different ways in different places in different times. In the United States, for example, for 50 years beginning in the 1890s the primary problems were encapsulated in the phrase 'crime and the foreign-born.' People writing and worrying today focus mostly on 'race and crime,' even though the percentage of foreign-born residents in the United States is at historic highs and the number of first- and second-generation immigrants exceeds the number of black people. Australia, Canada, and New Zealand have all long been immigrant countries with first- and second-generation population fractions far higher than anywhere in Europe. And yet, those countries are preoccupied by the problems presented and faced by relatively small population fractions of Aborigines, while in many European countries crime by immigrants is a salient and contentious political and policy issue. Makes you wonder.

Some of the surface reasons seem straightforward (though they probably are not). The American civil rights movement, coupled with a history of slavery and legalized racism, might seem to suffice to explain recent decades' focus on blacks. So might liberal guilt about the treatment of Aboriginal populations in predominantly white former British colonies. So might European countries' seemingly (but for most not actually) new experience as destinations for immigrants. And so inexorably does post-Apartheid Africa's concentration on crime and criminal justice in relation to its preponderantly black and overwhelmingly disadvantaged population.

Studying race, ethnicity, immigration, and crime is exceedingly difficult, especially cross-nationally and comparatively. Nowhere have criminal justice data systems been designed to monitor the differential experiences of minority group members. In continental European countries, and Canada, laws forbid maintenance of data on race or ethnicity. Only nationality is possible and that often camouflages as much as it reveals. People categorized, for example, as Iraqis (the legal, 'nationality' category), may be Kurds, Yadziki, Turkmens, Armenians, Shiites, or Sunnis (the illegal but socially more salient 'ethnic' categories). In countries such as France or the Netherlands in which it is relatively easy to obtain citizenship, recent but naturalized immigrants count as citizens and unnaturalized immigrants as non-citizens. They thus appear in both the numerator and the denominator when imprisonment rates for non-citizens are calculated. Non-citizen rates are undercounted. By contrast, in countries like Switzerland, Austria, and, until recently, Germany where citizenship is not easily obtainable, non-citizen rates are exaggerated: they include fully acculturated second- and third-generation descendants of immigrants.

A century-old literature on immigration and crime, confirmed in Italy and Germany for post–World War II intra-European immigrants and in the USA in this century for Mexican immigrants, shows that self-selected economic migrants typically have lesser involvement in crime than residents of the destination country, but their second- and third-generation descendants have higher rates. More recently, although that model has been confirmed, we know it is incomplete. Why people migrate matters. Traumatized refugees typically have a much harder time than economic migrants and sometimes their levels of crime involvement are higher. Who migrates matters. The traditional literature was based on the experiences of late 19th- and early 20th-century European migrants to North and South America. More recent work shows that immigrant groups from ancient literate Asian societies (for example, China, Japan, India, and Korea) have low crime rates in the first and in subsequent generations. And social policy toward immigrants matters. Countries such as Sweden which have targeted programs and resources on helping immigrants assimilate have lower levels of immigrant crime than is found in other countries. And, finally, legal status matters. Illegal immigrants, cut off from social services and access even to police services (from fear of deportation), face much harder lives and stronger criminal temptations than do legal immigrants.

Within the resident non-immigrant populations of individual countries, the research problems are only slightly less difficult. One or more minority groups in every country is characterized by higher crime and imprisonment rates than the majority population. Those groups are always characterized by social and economic disadvantage and usually suffer from discrimination and negative stereotyping. Sometimes they are recent immigrant groups which, as happened with Eastern Europeans in the USA after 1930 and Italians in Germany and Switzerland after 1970, will in due course assimilate into the general population and lose their high-crime label (no one has referred to a 'Croatian crime problem' or a 'Jewish crime problem' in New York City for 75 years, although 100 years ago the terms were in common usage). Sometimes they are indigenous groups, though that problem seems much more acute in former British colonies than in Scandinavian countries. Sometimes, as in the United States and Britain, they are black people whose ancestors and predecessors suffered from explicit racism and discriminatory legal systems.

All of these problems, all of these issues, all of these groups, all of these countries are discussed in this wide-ranging survey of knowledge concerning race, crime, and criminal justice on five continents (giving Australia, unlike in other realms, Pluto, the benefit of the doubt). Readers will find much here of value.

M.T. 2009.

Preface

Nurturing this freshly written collection of essays through to completion was a very challenging task, not least because it leaped over language barriers to tap into non-English-speaking societies for their invaluable resource on a subject that many may view as 'sensitive'. These factors, among others, may account for why this very important topic has not made significant entry into the international scene even in this era of burgeoning globalization.

For the purpose of discussing the role of race (linked to distinct physical differences of the human species, primarily skin color) in contemporary crime and criminal justice issues as it relates to various societies, this book covers perspectives from 13 countries. In alphabetical order, the countries are: Australia and New Zealand, Brazil, Britain, Canada, France, Germany, Italy, The Netherlands, Portugal, South Africa, Spain, and the United States. These countries were not selected randomly. Rather, they were deliberately handpicked based on one main criterion: their history of relations between whites (those of European descent) and non-whites (those of non-European descent). This 'history' dates as far back as the 15th century and it is on its premise that our current thinking of the whole notion of race is rendered salient, and present-day white and non-white relations in these countries may be comprehended. For example, the current 'old' or 'new' populations of certain non-white racial groups in each of the Western countries under discussion seem to be a reproduction of the historical relationship between the racial group/s and the country.

Doubtless, the 13 countries do not represent an exhaustive list of countries which have centuries-long historical foundation for alluding to present-day race relations in a domestic setting. There are other countries in the Americas where the populations of Europeans, the indigenous minorities, and the descendants of African slaves are a reminder of the European imperialist expansion of the 15th century and onward. However, of the countries in the Americas, the United States, Canada, and Brazil are relatively prominent on both historical and contemporary issues of race, although they are much more prominent in the United States.

Across the Atlantic, there is one notable country missing from the list of selected European countries despite her significant historical link to Africa: Belgium. This omission is not by the editor's choice; rather, it is a reflection of a commonality that readers will find running through most of the European chapters – that of the non-existence of the concept of 'race' in popular usage and in official data. 'Race' is a sensitive subject and as such not a familiar concept in Belgium, the editor was informed during her search for a suitable scholar to address race, crime, and criminal justice situation in contemporary Belgium. Like Belgium, most of the European chapters (France, Germany, Italy, The Netherlands, Portugal, and Spain) in this book have replaced the visibility of race with concepts of nationality, immigrant, ethnic minority, and similar 'non-race' labels, and through such expressions have interpreted differences in offending, criminal victimization, and criminal justice approaches to offending. In this way of assessing crime and criminal justice, 'invisible' ethnicities or nationalities become an integral part of the discourse of differences in offending behavior, criminal victimization experiences, and how the criminal justice system responds to people who come before it as suspects and offenders.

Like me, the authors of the chapters in question show awareness of the problematic of locating and debating race in a country where the concept is non-existent – at least in principle. Despite this situation, which I consider an issue of relativism, I hope that readers are able to gauge the visibility of race from those chapters and, as such, can deduce differences and similarities in the ways in which whites and non-whites are represented in the conceptualization and contextualization of crime and criminal justice. Very importantly, the inclusion of 'invisible' ethnicities in some of the accounts is a much appreciated and refreshing approach to deliberating race, crime, and criminal justice, a subject which traditionally has tended to prioritize the circumstances of particular non-white racial/ethnic groups to the exclusion or marginalization of the white population.

Structure of the book

The book is structured in four parts. Part I is home to only one chapter: Chapter 1. This chapter is one of my two chapter contributions to the collection. It stands alone in terms of its primary focus on *history*. The chapter serves to alert the reader to the background and central interest of the book on race by tracing this concept and its practical application back through history. In this chapter, my focus on history is deliberate as I constantly remind myself that every *present* is born out of its *past*, and I have a strong belief that recalling the *history* allows us to make informed and logical connection to the *contemporary*. On this note, this background chapter takes us back to the historical periods of the trans-Atlantic slave trade, slavery, and colonialism with the primary purpose of outlining the ideologies that initiated and sustained these historical events, and how those ideologies informed race relations in theory and practice during and beyond these historical situations. My concentration on these events may seem overwhelming and perhaps out of touch with current concerns but it is worth noting that every country covered in this book is connected to this history, and in some of the chapters this historical background is revisited in the discussion as a useful tool for alluding to contemporary relationships between race, crime, and criminal justice.

Part II is made-up of Chapters 2–8 and comprises discussions on the seven European countries respectively. The European chapters are arranged in alphabetical order of countries, and commence with Bankole Cole's contribution in Chapter 2 with reference to Britain. Cole incorporates Scotland into the discussion, thereby positing a point of departure from the traditional focus of British studies on England and Wales for literature on race and crime issues. In this collection, Britain is the only European country in which race as a variable is recognized in official data, including crime data. This fact is evident in Cole's detailed assessment of variations in rates of offending and criminal victimization according to racial groups. Juxtaposed alongside his analysis of the race–crime–criminal justice nexus, Cole makes a very refreshing addition to the literature through his critical evaluation of the race implications in a range of national and local policy and practice initiatives to tackle offending and victimization in Britain.

In Chapter 3, Pamela Irving Jackson examines the race, crime, and criminal justice issue as it applies to France. Even in the absence of systematic race-based official crime data, Jackson's discussion provides useful insights into the statistical representation of minority populations in offending, and experiences of hate crimes. Prominent in this chapter is Jackson's analysis of the externalization of immigrants and minorities through processes of racialization and criminalization that are not only embraced in French discourses of crime but also illustrated in policy and practice toward immigration and crime.

Similar to France, immigration is integral to Germany's discourses of the crime problem. Hans-Jörg Albrecht's discussion of the German situation in Chapter 4 locates the construction of the relationship between immigration and crime in Germany within broader socio-economic and political changes in Europe. To an extent, Germany's law enforcement policies and their application are reflective of changes in the level and nature of immigration and invariably changes in domestic interpretations of and policy responses to immigration. Albrecht goes on to assess the position of immigrants in offending, victimization, and encounters with the criminal justice system.

In Chapter 5, Vincenzo Ruggiero examines Italy's migrant population's involvement in crime and contact with the criminal justice system. In so doing, Ruggiero sheds light on how human variations intersect with levels and patterns of offending as well as exposure to law enforcement attack on criminality. Drawing on Sutherland's idea of the influence of acculturation on immigrant criminality, Ruggiero explores migrant criminality in Italy within the economic context of migration and its implications for criminality, and within the structure of the criminogenic nature of Italy. Based on this general framework, Ruggiero discusses the situation of migrants as offenders and crime victims, and taps into the notions of institutional racism and relative deprivation to assess the representation of migrants in crime figures.

Chapter 6 is authored by Josine Junger-Tas, who draws heavily on her recent quantitative self-report study of the delinquency of young migrants in The Netherlands to explore the influence of ethnicity on offending. The chapter moves beyond the juvenile population to also debate the issue of ethnicity as it impacts on experiences of criminal victimization and encounters with the criminal justice system among the adult population of The Netherlands.

Manuela Ivone Cunha, in Chapter 7, offers differing perspectives from which to understand the intersections of nationality and ethnicity with crime and criminal justice in Portugal. Cunha points to the roles of class and gender in these intersections. Her analysis of the ways race/ethnicity and class in particular interact with crime and law enforcement practices are illustrated in her ethnographic study of an adult female prison where drug offences constituted the main reason for women's imprisonment.

The last – but not the least – of the European chapters is Josh Goode's exploration of the *past* and *present* of race and crime issues in Spain in Chapter 8. The chapter's depth of history complements the content of Chapter 1. Goode details the formation of racial thought, the racialization of differences, and the association of race with criminality in Spain's history. In contemporary Spain, similar processes of racialization and criminalization surface within the discourses of immigration, minorities, and Spain's crime problem. Goode describes how the unwelcoming discursive responses to immigration and minority presence in Spain translate into social and economic segregation, racially motivated hate crimes, and the racial profiling of minority groups.

Part III of the book contains the respective discussions beyond Europe. It is made up of Chapters 9, 10, 11, 12, and 13, structured in alphabetical order of countries. The first discussion in this section of the collection, Chapter 9, is co-authored by Samantha Jeffries and Greg Newbold. The chapter focuses on the Australian and New Zealand state of affairs. The chapter directs its interest to the situations of the native peoples of Australia and New Zealand in respect of offending, victimization, and relations with the criminal justice system. The authors' reflections on the historical colonization of Australian Aboriginals and the New Zealand Maori present very interesting background information for interpreting the current position and experiences of the native populations of these countries in relation to crime and criminal justice.

In Chapter 10, Ignacio Icano, Ludmila Ribeiro, and Elisabet Meireles rely on their quantitative research on racial bias in penal sentencing practices in Brazil to analyze the connection between race, crime, and criminal justice in Brazil. The authors' research into this aspect of the criminal justice process seems to be a useful addition to existing Brazilian studies on race and sentencing – a topic which the authors claim is under-researched. Despite this focus, the authors acknowledge the pre-court process in their assessment of race and criminal justice in Brazil.

Canada's perspective on the issue of race, crime, and criminal justice is explored by Clay Mosher and Taj Mahon-Haft in Chapter 11. In this chapter, there is detailed account of the position of the Aboriginal population in crime perpetration and offender–criminal justice relations. In the account, the authors tapped into Canada's history of colonization to analyze current Aboriginal relations with the Canadian criminal justice system. A welcome addition to this chapter is the examination of the location of black people and Asians in the discursive, policy, and practice responses to crime in Canada. In addition to the chapter's concern with offending, criminal victimization, particularly in relation to hate crimes, is articulated.

Chapter 12 is Kgomotso Bosilong and Paulin Mbecke's discussion of the relationship between race, crime, and criminal justice in South Africa. The authors' account of offending and experiences of criminal victimization is illustrative of how race in itself and also in interaction with class inform the levels and nature of offending and victimization. And notably mirrored in the discussion is the legacy of South Africa's Apartheid regime in determining how the main racial groups are situated in the socio-economic arena, in crime, and in interactions with the criminal justice system in post-Apartheid South Africa.

Daniel Georges-Abeyie's contribution in Chapter 13 with reference to the United States finalizes the chapters in Part III of the book. The author utilizes a range of racially categorized official data to debate the issue of race, crime, and criminal justice in the United States. Despite his reservations about the incomprehensiveness of race-based data in capturing ethnicities within racial categories, Georges-Abeyie's chapter illuminates how various racial groups feature in offending and criminal victimization statistics.

Each of the chapters described above provides very interesting narrative in its own and unique right. Some are explicitly race-specific and others are not. Yet in the midst of their differences, they share a number of similarities. And I take pleasure in drawing out their areas of divergence and convergence in Part IV – home to the final and concluding chapter of this book.

I now hope that this collection will be appreciated within and beyond the international coverage of the book.

Anita Kalunta-Crumpton
Texas Southern University, USA

Acknowledgements

The birth of *Race, Crime and Criminal Justice: International Perspectives* is attributed to the contributions of the 17 authors whose interesting and stimulating analyses have quenched much of my thirst for an edited collection on how human variations impact on crime and are negotiated at the point of criminal justice across continents and countries. It was a long and winding road to get to the completion of this book. To each one of the authors, I express my deep gratitude for their commitment to the project and, above all, for their positive response to my editorial demands. I very much thank Michael Tonry for his highlights, in the Foreword, on some of the complexities and challenges surrounding the subject topic of this book.

My 9-year-old daughter chose the cover image for this book. Her recognition of pictorial creativity must not go unnoticed. Ezinwa, I truly and deeply appreciate your eagerness to understand my work and to be able to demonstrate your understanding in your choice of a captivating cover image. My special and warmest thanks go to Ezinwa, to my 6-year-old son Nkemjika, and to David for their unlimited patience with me while I was devoted to bringing this collection to fruition.

As always I owe *all* to God!

Anita Kalunta-Crumpton

Notes on Contributors

Hans-Jörg Albrecht is Professor, and Director at the Max Planck Institute for Foreign and International Criminal Law in Freiburg/Germany. He teaches criminal law, criminal justice, and criminology at the University of Freiburg. Dr. Dr. Albrecht is guest professor at the Center for Criminal Law and Criminal Justice of the China University of Political Science and Law, Beijing; Law Faculty of Hainan University; the Law Faculty of Renmin University of China, Beijing; the Law Faculty of Wuhan University; and the Law Faculty of Beijing Normal University. He holds life membership of Clare Hall College at Cambridge University, UK, and professorship and permanent faculty membership at the Faculty of Law of Qom High Education Center, Teheran/Iran. His research interests are in various legal, criminological, and policy topics such as sentencing theory, juvenile crime, drug policies, environmental crime, and organized crime, evaluation research and systems of criminal sanctions. He has published, co-published, and edited books on various topics, including sentencing, day-fine systems, recidivism, child abuse and neglect, drug policies, research on victimization, and white-collar-crime.

Kgomotso Pearl Bosilong is Researcher at the Council for Scientific and Industrial Research (CSIR) in the Safety and Security Division, South Africa. She has been working in the areas of violence and social crime prevention for the past 6 years. She is part of a team that focuses on technology-based interventions that will improve the effectiveness of the criminal justice system and particularly aspects of the physical and social environment which can reduce crime and the fear of crime. Much of this work is aimed at providing support at local and metropolitan levels and at empowering communities and law enforcement structures with regards to the creation of safer living environments. She has a Bachelor of Arts in Communications degree from University of North West in North West Province, and a Diploma in Project Management.

Ignacio Cano received his PhD in Sociology at the Universidad Complutense de Madrid (Spain) in 1991. From 1991 to 1993, he worked for the United Nations in El Salvador on issues relating to human rights and refugee assistance. Between 1993 and 1996 he developed a post-doctoral research program at the universities of Surrey (UK), Michigan, and Arizona (USA), focusing mainly on research methodology and programme evaluation. Since 1996, he has been based in Rio de Janeiro, working for NGOs and teaching at several universities. He is currently a lecturer in research methods in the Department of Social Sciences at the Universidade do Estado do

Rio de Janeiro. His main areas of research and teaching include violence, public security, and human rights; public policies and program evaluation; and research methodology. Since 2001, he has been leading a line of research on racial bias in the criminal justice system in Brazil.

Bankole A. Cole is Reader in Criminology at the University of Northumbria at Newcastle, UK. Prior to this, Dr Cole was Lecturer in Criminology and Director of the Centre for Criminology and Criminal Justice at the University of Hull, UK. His main publications and research are in the areas of comparative criminal justice, international and comparative policing, crime and justice in 'developing' and 'transitional' countries, the local delivery of criminal justice, and 'race' and criminal justice in the UK. His publications include *Hidden from Public View? Racism against the UK's Chinese Population* (with G. Craig et al.) (2009); 'Working with ethnic diversity' in Green, Lancaster and Feasey (eds), *Addressing Offending Behaviour* (2008); *Globalisation, Citizenship and the War on Terror* (ed. with M. Mullard) (2007), 'Black and Asian men on probation: social exclusion, discrimination and experiences of criminal justice' (with A. Wardak) in S. Lewis et al. (eds), *Race and Probation* (2006); 'Post-colonial systems' in R.I. Mawby (ed.), *Policing Across the World* (1999); and 'Rough justice: Criminal proceedings in Nigerian magistrates courts', *International Journal of the Sociology of Law*, 18(3), 1990.

Manuela Ivone Cunha is Professor of Anthropology and teaches at the University of Minho, Portugal. Dr Cunha is a member of CRIA-UM (Portugal) and of IDEMEC (France). She has conducted extensive fieldwork in a major women's prison and in a psychiatric hospital in Portugal. Her research focuses on prisons and total institutions, informal processes, and the comparative structure of drug markets. She is currently developing a research project on vaccination and the social administration of the body. Alongside her edited volumes and journal articles, she is the author of *Malhas que a reclusão tece. Questões de identidade numa prisão feminina* (1994), and *Entre o Bairro e a Prisão: Tráfico e Trajectos* (2002). The latter book was awarded a prize for the social sciences.

Daniel E. Georges-Abeyie is a Professor of Administration of Justice at Texas Southern University. He was awarded his PhD from the Maxwell School, Syracuse University. Dr. Georges-Abeyie is of Afro-Caribbean-Gullah-Geechee maroon parentage. He specializes in the study of social distance and Petit Apartheid within the USA criminal justice and juvenile justice systems (i.e., the transmutation of discretion into discrimination); forensic psychology with special interest in personality disorders, which result in violent criminal behavior; terrorism and homeland security; the impact of race and ethnicity on criminal justice and juvenile justice; the impact of race and ethnicity as alleged criminogenics; the spatial analysis of criminogenics and the US criminal justice and juvenile justice systems; defensible space; and human rights law. Dr. Georges-Abeyie has authored or edited more than 65 scholarly publications and has served on 20 different editorial boards for scholarly publications. He has served at the very highest level within the *pro bono* leadership structure of Amnesty International USA for which he has received the very highest honors and awards issued by Amnesty International USA. He also serves as a consultant in regard to defensible space; police–community relations; hostage negotiation and hostage survival; and the reduction of violence in correctional and detention settings.

Joshua Goode is a Visiting Assistant Professor in the History and Cultural Studies Departments at Claremont Graduate University in Claremont, California, USA. Dr. Goode is also the author of *Impurity of Blood: Defining Race in Spain, 1870–1930* (2009). His current research focuses on the role that national history and memory play in shaping contemporary European political and social debates about immigration, citizenship, and pluralism. One particular aspect of this work considers the role that the Holocaust and Spain's wartime alliances have played in shaping current Spanish attitudes toward ethnic and national identity.

Pamela Irving Jackson is Director of the Justice Studies Program and Professor of Sociology at Rhode Island College, USA. She holds a Brown University PhD, and served 3 years as Associate Editor of the *American Sociological Review*. Her book, *Minority Group Threat, Crime and Policing: Social Context and Social Control*, examines and explains variations in collective support for social control. Her research focuses on issues of social control and minority status, including comparative analysis of the integration of Muslims in Western societies. She is the recent recipient of two Fulbright grants on this topic, and has worked with international groups of scholars at the *Institut National d'Etudes Demographiques* (INED) in Paris, France; the German Institute for International and Security Affairs (SWP) in Berlin, Germany; and the Center for European Studies (ZEI) at the University of Bonn, Germany. She has published in several professional journals, including the *American Sociological Review*, *Criminology*, *Justice Quarterly*, and *Democracy and Security*.

Samantha Jeffries is a lecturer in the School of Justice at the Queensland University of Technology, Australia. Dr. Jeffries' current research areas include projects investigating the sentencing of Indigenous Australians and gay men's experiences of domestic violence. She has also published and continues to be interested in: alternative criminal court practices (e.g., problem-solving courts), the sex industry, and relationships between gender, crime, and criminal justice.

Josine Junger-Tas is Visiting Professor at the University of Utrecht, the Netherlands. Dr Junger-Tas has worked at the Research Institute of the Dutch Ministry of Justice as special Adviser and Director of the Research Unit on juvenile crime, and as Director of the Institute. She was active in the Council of Europe. From 1984–1989, she chaired an Expert Committee on Juvenile Delinquency which produced two reports with recommendations for member states. She wrote several basic documents for the Council of Europe and in 1992 was appointed member of its Scientific Council. She was also active in the United Nations where she carried out preparatory work for the UN Criminology congresses, and served as an expert on juvenile delinquency for Central European and Middle Eastern states. In 1989, she received the Sellin-Glueck Award from the American Society of Criminology for her 'Contributions to Criminology'. She has written a great number of articles, books and reports. In 1994 she was appointed Professor of Youth Criminology at the University of Lausanne in Switzerland. She taught Self-report methodology at the University of Cambridge for three years. In 2000, she took the initiative – with several close colleagues – to launch the European Society of Criminology. Together with Prof. Killias, she organized the first ESC conference in Lausanne during which she was elected the ESC President. In November 2007, she received the Distinguished International Scholar Award from the American Society of Criminology.

Anita Kalunta-Crumpton received a PhD from Brunel University, West London, United Kingdom. She has taught at a number of universities in England, United Kingdom. She is currently Associate Professor of Administration of Justice at Texas Southern University, USA. Her main research and teaching interests are in the areas of race, crime, and criminal justice; drug use and trafficking; and comparative criminology/criminal justice. She has published extensively and her publications have appeared in a wide range of scholarly journals including the *British Journal of Criminology*, *Social Justice*, the *International Journal of the Sociology of Law*, and the *International Journal of Offender Therapy and Comparative Criminology*. She is the author of *Race and Drug Trials: The Social Construction of Guilt and Innocence* (1999), *Drugs, Victims and Race: The Politics of Drug Control* (2006), and the editor (with Biko Agozino) of *Pan-African Issues in Crime and Justice* (2004).

Taj Mahon-Haft is currently a PhD candidate in Sociology at Washington State University, Vancouver, USA. His recent criminological research has focused on drug use, drug treatment programs, and inequalities in the criminal justice system. He has also extensively studied research methods, authoring numerous reports for NSF and the Census Bureau (with Don Dillman and Nick Parsons) and an article in the *Journal of Official Statistics* (with Don Dillman and Arina Gertseva). He has also conducted research in the areas of culture, work/organizations, and law.

Paulin Mbecke is Senior Researcher in the Crime Prevention Research Group, a division of the Council for Scientific and Industrial Research (CSIR Safety and Security), South Africa. His field of expertise includes child abuse, neglect, and exploitation prevention; development and implementation of local crime prevention strategies; project management, crime prevention research, policy analysis, and the monitoring and evaluation of crime prevention projects. In addition to his crime prevention expertise, Paulin has an extensive experience in matters relating to migration, refugees, and asylum seekers. Between 1997 and 2002, he worked for Jesuit Refugee Service (JRS) Johannesburg as an Advocacy/Information/Policy Officer and Deputy Project Director. He is currently the chairman of the Refugee Children's Project (RCP) Board. He volunteers for the Global Initiative for Peace and African Development (GIPAD) as Executive President; Young Entrepreneurs for NEPAD (YENEPAD) as Director of Human Development; and the Group of Refugees Without Voice (GRWV) as Chairman of the Board. Internationally, he is a member of CARE International and the American Refugee Committee (ARC). Paulin is currently a PhD Candidate in Public and Development Management at the University of the Witwatersrand, Johannesburg.

Elisabet de Sousa Meireles received a Bachelor's degree and Master's degree in psychology from the Federal University of Rio de Janeiro. She was a research assistant in several projects funded by official Brazilian research agencies, such as FAPERJ and CNPq. She has been an applied researcher for more than 14 years, participating in numerous research projects and applying various quantitative and qualitative techniques, including surveys, focal groups, and in-depth interviews. In many of these projects she has acted as a field coordinator or a supervisor. Since 2004, she has had a permanent position as a psychologist in the municipality of Japeri, Rio de Janeiro, Brazil.

Clayton J. Mosher received his PhD in Sociology from the University of Toronto, and is currently an Associate Professor and Associate Chair in the Department of Sociology at Washington State University, Vancouver, USA. His research focuses on issues of inequality in the criminal justice system; racial profiling; and drug use, drug treatment, and drug policies. His work has been published in several Sociology and Criminology journals, and he is author of a number of books including *Discrimination and Denial*, *The Mismeasure of Crime* (with Terance Miethe and Dretha Phillips), and *Drugs and Drug Policy: The Control of Consciousness Alteration* (with Scott Akins).

Greg Newbold is an Associate Professor of Sociology at the University of Canterbury, New Zealand, where he specializes in corrections. Dr. Newbold is the author of seven books and more than 50 scholarly articles. He is frequently consulted as an expert advisor on crime and criminal justice policy by New Zealand government ministries.

Ludmila Ribeiro has a PhD in Sociology, a BA and MA in Public Administration, and a BA in Law. She has experience in policy development and analysis, especially in public security and the criminal justice system. She helped develop prison policies for the state of Minas Gerais, Brazil, and was also involved in the evaluation of their impact in terms of recidivism. In 2008, she worked for Viva Rio, an international NGO, developing public policies at the municipal level to prevent and reduce victimization. Her areas of research interest are criminal justice in Brazil, and crime victimization and political culture in Latin America. She is currently the regional representative of Altus Global Alliance in Brazil and is also a lecturer at Candido Mendes University in Rio de Janeiro.

Vincenzo Ruggiero is Professor of Sociology at Middlesex University in London, United Kingdom. Dr Ruggiero has conducted research on behalf of a number of international agencies, including the European Commission and the United Nations. His most recent books are *Social Movements: A Reader* (2008); *Understanding Political Violence* (2006); *Crime in Literature: Sociology of Deviance and Fiction* (2003); *Movements in the City* (2001); and *Crime and Markets* (2000). He is currently completing a book on penal abolitionism.

Michael Tonry is professor of law and public policy and director of the Institute on Crime and Public Policy at the University of Minnesota Law School. He has been a senior fellow of The Netherlands Institute for the Study of Crime and Law Enforcement, Amsterdam, since 2003, and a visiting professor in the Faculty of Law, University of Lausanne, since 2001. From 1999 to 2005, he was director of the Institute of Criminology, University of Cambridge. He also edits *Crime and Justice – A Review of Research*; the two Oxford University Press series *Studies In Crime and Public Policy*, and *Oxford Handbooks on Criminology and Criminal Justice*; and *Criminology in Europe*, the newsletter of the European Society of Criminology.

Part I
History

1
History: Race Relations and Justice

Anita Kalunta-Crumpton
Texas Southern University, USA

Introduction

This overview of race relations in a historical setting aims to provide a background framework for comprehending contemporary relations between white (European descent) and non-white (non-European descent) racial groups in the domestic settings of societies with populations that are significantly racially diverse. In the context of the subsequent chapters of this book, an explanatory overview of history is particularly vital for making sense of how white and non-white relations interact with offending behavior, experiences of criminal victimization, popular and official discourses of crime, and policy and practice approaches to crime. It is worth noting, however, that despite the evidence of racial diversity in many Western countries, some countries, for known or unknown reasons, may seem on face value to have embarked on cloaking the ideology of race by overtly adopting 'non-physical' identities to differentiate between peoples. This strategy has seen some white ethnic groups encompassed in the discourses of differences. This is not a new phenomenon. White ethnicities such as the Irish and Sicilians were at some point a part of the historical process of racialization. Much later in history, the ideology of racial hygiene in parts of the West affected sections of the white population that fell victim to the applied eugenics of the 20th century. But at least as far as the global reach of the racialization process was concerned, white ethnicities were never placed on the same level as non-white groups.

Contemporarily, the use of 'non-biological' identification models in some European countries embraces implicitly a negotiation of interactions characterized by elements that precipitated and subsequently sustained the social construction of human differences in its biological framework. As specific chapters in this collection either explicitly or implicitly illustrate in their coverage of Western and non-Western societies, there is hierarchical structuring of human populations and this combines with distribution of socio-economic and power resources to illuminate the circumstances of people of European and non-European descent. In whatever forms that differing group identities are propagated in the contemporary hierarchical arrangement of peoples, there is some evidence that it resonates with the historical forms of structuring human variations and upon which racial identification (and racialization) in its current mode found origin.

This chapter engages with history and, in doing so, places an emphasis on two interrelated historical events and accounts – the trans-Atlantic slave trade and the European colonization of non-white territories – that fostered and shaped the most influential ideological and pragmatic construction of human variations. In the historical narrative, we will find clear instances of an overlap in dates and periods as they relate to the slave trade and colonialism, and this can be explained logically by virtue of the fact that both historical events complemented each other. As is shown from the sections below, the trans-Atlantic slave trade was an outcome of European overseas expansion that was motivated by economic interests. Related to this, there were instances of European colonial presence in the Americas and parts of Africa prior to and during the European engagement in the African slave trade. Invariably, both the slave trade and colonization constituted a part of the European imperialist project, which carried on into the latter part of the 19th century, and the 20th century.

Notwithstanding this chapter's narratives of these historical situations, its essence is to draw attention to the thinking that facilitated and sustained European imperialism during and beyond these historical settings. In so doing, it centralizes the role of the concept of race in the creation and functioning of imperialism before, during, and after the slave trade. Centuries of imperialism were underpinned by various interpretations of the notion of race in which essentially distinguishing physical characteristics were linked to biological ancestry and within these frameworks of comprehending race, demarcations were drawn between inferior and superior racial groups. This chapter commences its historical journey from the era of the trans-Atlantic slave trade and concludes by transporting the reader to a snapshot of contemporary reflections of historical race relations.

Theorizing race for the trans-Atlantic slave trade

A more accurate label for the trans-Atlantic slave trade is the African slave trade. It was a trade that was not premeditated; rather, it was preceded by a chain of African and European relations that ultimately gave birth to its existence. Notable eras in the history of European presence in Africa seemingly started with the Portuguese pioneer adventure in Africa. The adventure was instigated by a combination of economic, religious, and military interests to foster Portuguese trading endeavors in Africa and Asia, engage in the conversion of Africans to Christianity, and wage military attack on Maghreb Muslims whose territory they needed to pass in order to access the West African gold trade (Onyeozili 2004). The Portuguese, followed by the Spanish, had contact with Africa long before the 16th century when the English had their first encounters with Africans on the coast of Africa (Jordan 1968). Prior to the Portuguese and Spanish colonization of the Americas from the late 15th century, the Portuguese were engaging in the importation of African slaves to Lisbon and from Lisbon many of the slaves entered Spain. With the colonization of the Americas, Congo and Angola became slave forts for the Portuguese transportation of larger numbers of African slaves to the Americas (Landers and Robinson 2006). While the organized trade in African slaves was pioneered by the Portuguese, there are claims that the initial contact that the Portuguese and the Spanish had with Africans involved some missionary-based relationship which aimed to convert Africans into Christians. As Wade (1997) notes, the Portuguese exploration of Africa was partly motivated by the search 'for the legendary Christian Kingdom of Prester John'. In contrast to the Portuguese and the Spanish, the earliest English voyagers of the 16th and 17th centuries were guided mainly by interests in adventure and trading in Africa rather than an engagement in religious endeavors. However, turning African humans into a trading commodity was not an initial part of the agenda of the early English voyagers (Jordan 1968). With reference to the Kingdom of Benin (that is, Nigeria), Onyeozili (2004) observes how the exchange of material goods between English traders and the *Oba* (King) of Benin was negotiated on 'equal terms and on mutual respect'.

However, one by-product emerging from what seemed to be a straightforward trading relationship that placed Africans on a par with their European counterparts was the second-hand reports about Africans produced by European travelers and traders. African blackness was seemingly the most striking feature of European–African difference that fed extensively into European discourses of Africans. In English descriptions of their earliest meetings with Africans there was a particular fascination with skin color. This was probably because they were encountering the really black-skinned peoples of West Africa – unlike their Portuguese and Spanish counterparts who had over the centuries come into contact with the generally lighter-skinned Africans located in North Africa (Jordan 1968). The negative meanings that the English ascribed to African blackness were consistent with already existing conceptualizations of blackness and its opposite, whiteness, in English vocabulary prior to the English contact with Africans. Whilst blackness ultimately came to represent every symbol of the 'devil incarnate' exemplified in its ugly and evil characteristics, whiteness, in contrast, was inscribed in English ideology as a symbol of godliness evidenced in a range of positive attributes such as beauty and purity. At this time, theoretical thinking about physical differences was grounded in a pre-Enlightenment or pre-modern worldview and as such drew substance from the basic religious understanding that all creations and differences were the act and will of God.

From the perspectives of the English and other Europeans, causal explanations for African blackness prioritized two key accounts: one alluded skin color to Africans' exposure to the hot climatic condition of the sun, and the other subscribed to a religious interpretation that posited African skin color as a curse from God (Husband 1982). The former explanation, although significant, was gradually discredited as illogical since it failed to explain why all groups of people in hot regions were not black or blackened by the sun. The later account prevailed under the auspices of the Old Testament which, according to Banton (1980), was at least up to the 18th century the primary framework for assessing differences between peoples. It was within this religious paradigm that African skin color was viewed as God's curse on Africans – an explanation which clearly denoted white skin color as God's blessing on Europeans. God's supposed curse on Africans is also encapsulated in the Old Testament account of Noah's curse on Ham's son, Canaan, and his descendants (Ham was believed to be black) that they will be inferior and servants to Noah's other sons Shem and Japheth – both mythically representing the white race. According to myth, the consequences of this curse were manifested in the 'evil', criminal, and deviant behaviors of the Canaanites and – by extension – the black race (Banton 1980). Whatever forms the religious explanation took, they pointed toward ideological constructions of differences in quality between black and white racial groups with the former signifying inferiority and the latter superiority. Like their physical features, African non-physical features amazed the English and other European travelers and traders. African language, mannerisms, morals, religion, and social customs were dissected and judged against European standards which were perceived as superior.

These observations, inter alia, were invaluable to the justification of the African slave trade during its growth in the 17th and 18th centuries. The slave trade itself was propelled by the discovery of the 'new world' and marked by the substantial shift from European trading in material goods to trading in human beings from Africa. Spain and Portugal established colonies in the 'new world' for the purpose of producing sugar, cotton, and tobacco. And in order to meet the huge labor demands of the plantation economy, which the supply of poor whites and native Indians alone could not satisfy, the trade in Africans became a viable option. This move was also facilitated by the belief that Africans in Portuguese colonies in Africa were stronger and sturdier than Native Indians – who were nevertheless being exterminated gradually as a consequence of the colonists' brutal forms of enslavement, and the diseases brought from Europe (Finger 1959). The discovery of the 'new world' began the competitive scramble for African slaves between the Portuguese, Spanish, French, Dutch, Danes, and English.

The forcible transportation by Europeans of millions of Africans from Africa to the 'new world' marked the beginning of the extensive enslavement of Africans in colonies in the Americas and elsewhere between the 16th and 19th centuries. Notwithstanding the involvement of a range of European nations in the trans-Atlantic slave trade, the lead role in this economic project during the 18th century was taken by Britain. This followed her establishment of colonies in North America and the Caribbean in the early 17th century, in addition to securing a contract from France under the 1713 Treaty of Utrecht to supply the Spanish colonies with African slaves from her Caribbean colonies (Hiro 1992). Britain's central position in the 'triangular trade' marked her as the main slave trader for other European colonists in the Americas. Britain made profits on all three parts of the 'triangular trade' by shipping trading goods to West Africa, transporting African slaves to Europe and the 'new world', and shipping back produce such as cotton and sugar from the colonies to Europe (ibid.).

Justifying the slave trade became imperative, particularly for the British. For the purpose of doing so, Jordan (1968) notes that those 16th-century discoveries previously embraced by the English in almost harmless wonderment, curiosity, and interest were in the 18th century elaborated upon and popularized in very negative contexts. Racial stereotypes were relayed in reports of the discoveries and made easily available to the European audience through various communication media such as periodicals. The Africans' physical appearance, in terms of skin color, hair texture, flat nose, and fleshy lips, was likened to that of apes. Similarly, they began to be described through the use of terms such as 'filthy', 'unclean', 'smelly', 'wickedness', 'stupidity', 'ignorance', in which offered further justification of the slave trade and slavery (Hill 1967; Walvin 1973; File and Power 1981). African moral standards were described as ape-like and beastly. Perhaps, the issue of morality is best exemplified in the Englishman's popular narrative of African sexuality. Like other related themes, narratives of African sexuality essentially judged African standards of morality against what Europeans considered to be the superior forms found only amongst Europeans. African sexuality during the period of slavery was portrayed via literature as a characteristic symptomatic of an incurable black immorality (Barker 1978). In various ways, African sexuality was conceived in both cultural and biological terms. African nakedness was visualized as an indication of sexual abnormality and as clear evidence of cultural inferiority. Biological interpretations of African sexuality are illustrated in the descriptions of Africans as libidinous, naturally promiscuous with uncontrollable sexual appetite, and whose response to sexual desires is animalistic in nature (Walvin 1973; Barker 1978; Caplan 1987). Polygamous relationships in Africa and the colonies, and the alleged presence of public prostitution in Africa, were explained in terms of Africans' excessive sexual desires. In all, Africans were described as having a peculiar sexual morality that was greatly inferior to European sexual morals (Caplan 1987). In his 1774 book *History of*

Jamaica, Edward Long offers his own stereotypical description of African sexuality:

> They are libidinous and shameless as monkeys, or baboons...if lust can prompt such excesses (in England)...despite all the checks which national politeness and refined sentiment impose, how freely will it operate in the more genial soil of Africa...where passions rage without any control; and the retired wilderness presents opportunity to gratify them without fear of detection.
>
> (Cited in Walvin 1971: 131).

Slavery had also thrived on notions of white racial superiority articulated by European philosophers of the Age of Reason (Eze 1997). The views of Enlightenment philosophers were paramount in shaping the popular belief in the physical and mental inferiority of Africans and invariably in the practical demonstration of this belief in the subjugation of Africans. For example, in 1753 the Scottish philosopher and historian David Hume, who also worked in the British government as the Under-Secretary of State dealing with colonial affairs, did not mince his words in a racist rationalization of the enslavement of Africans:

> I am apt to suspect the negroes and in general all the other species of men (for there are four or five different kinds) to be naturally inferior to the whites. There never was a civilized nation of any other complexion than white, nor even any individual eminent either in action or speculation. No ingenious manufactures amongst them, no arts, no sciences.... Not to mention our colonies, there are NEGROE slaves dispersed all over EUROPE, of which none ever discovered any symptoms of ingenuity.... In JAMAICA indeed they talk of one negro as a man of parts and learning; but 'tis likely he is admired for very slender accomplishments, like a parrot, who speaks a few words plainly.
>
> (Bracken 1973/2001: 174)

The belief that intelligence, reason, and civilization could be found only among Europeans justified the subjection of Africans to hostile and savage labor since, as was perceived, their stupidity, lack of intelligence, and indolence meant that they were not suited to activities requiring the application of reason (Walvin 1971, 1973; Fryer 1984). Africans were described as sub-human and barbaric and so to the advocates of slavery transporting them to the 'new world' was an opportunity to expose Africans to Christian doctrines, civilization and tranquility of the 'new world', and away from African barbarism. It was on the premise of the racially loaded justifications for the treatment of African slaves as a commodity and as beasts of burden – rather than human beings – that the justice system operated. Accordingly, the protection of African slaves was non-existent in slave societies. Slavery and the oppressive treatment of slaves were codified into law as a way of guaranteeing the continuance of the unpaid enslavement of Africans for labor, and simultaneously restricting their freedom in order to keep them tied to their slave status. This meant that the slaves had no legal rights to freedom, to defend, and to protect themselves from slave owners and the wider white population. As Russell (1998: 15) states with reference to the United States, '...the hardest criminal penalties were reserved for those acts that threatened the institution of slavery' – as, for instance, in the event of a slave rebellion. Crimes were interpreted and punished differently along racial lines whereby justice for the enslaved hardly existed (see, for example, Hiro 1992; Browne-Marshall 2007). Rape or attempted rape stands out as one such crime that incurred wide racial distinction in the administration of justice: the rape of a black woman by a white male constituted 'no crime' whereas black male-on-white female rape or attempted rape was punishable by death or castration (see, for example, Higginbotham and Jacobs 1992).

This pattern of slave trade and slavery was abolished in the 19th century, but the global process took several decades. For example, the chief trading nation, Britain, abolished the slave trade in 1807 and the institution of slavery in 1834, whereas in the Portuguese colony of Brazil, slavery carried on until 1888. In the United States, the end to slavery came at the conclusion of the 1861–1865 Civil War between the North and the South. But as will be demonstrated in the following section of this chapter, the ethnocentric ideology of white superiority that developed with the birth of the slave trade carried over into the next stage of European imperialist domination.

Theorizing race for the imperialist project of the 19th century and beyond

Implicit in the preceding section is evidence of colonialism that pre-dates the existence of the slave trade. Nevertheless, this section begins with an explicit snapshot of instances of the pre-19th century colonial project to give a clearer base for considering the philosophy behind the colonization agendas of the 19th century and beyond. First, there was the founding of and the setting up of colonies in the 'new world' pre-19th century. This project is, in plain language, the European invasion of the Americas and the related subjugation of the native peoples in the forms of enslavement, extermination, or displacement. In the context of the 'new world' discovery, much of the Americas belonged to Spain; Brazil belonged to Portugal; other European nations such as Britain and France had colonies in the Americas, with the British becoming the dominant force in the West Indies. This European approach to the acquisition of territories was relevant to the colonization and treatment of native peoples in these territories, and, later, in Australasia from the 18th century.

In relation to Africa, it has already been noted that the European presence in Africa was spearheaded by the Portuguese. Their lead presence in Africa culminated in the establishment of colonial administration in a number of countries in East Africa in the 16th century (Onyeozili 2004). Economic interests propeled the Dutch to West Africa in the 17th century and subsequently to South Africa. The Dutch and German occupation of South Africa in the 17th and 18th centuries brought with it an apartheid policy later adopted by the English in the 19th century following their permanent occupation of the Cape region (ibid.) which they took over from the Dutch. Despite years of conflicts between the Afrikaners (descendants of early Dutch settlers) and the British as best illustrated in the 1899 South African War, British rule of South African territories including the Cape region was ratified under the 1902 Peace Treaty (ibid.). The Congo came under the sole control of King Leopold of Belgium who gained this part of Africa as a huge investment for himself and whose legal right to the Congo was recognized at the European Conference on the partition of Africa held in Berlin in 1885 (Onyeozili 2004). It was the ratification of King Leopold's claim on the Congo at this conference that encouraged other European countries, and in particular Britain and France, to scramble for and partition the African continent. The French had established business investment in Africa as early as the 17th century and by the 20th century had, through the use of militarized coercion, colonized territories in West, North, and Equatorial Africa (ibid.). Britain's cunning, forceful, and coercive strategy in the African slave trade manifested itself in her colonial domination of countries in Africa. As Onyeozili (2004: 226) states, Britain's colonial presence in Africa 'took the same systematic pattern of introduction of trade, religious pacification and finally military decapitation of opposition'. In line with their competing European neighbours, Spain, Germany, and Italy also made territorial claims in Africa.

The colonization of countries in Asia was propeled by Europe's agenda of overseas expansion. The search for the sea route to the Indian subcontinent in order to exploit the riches of India was a significant factor in the Portuguese presence in West Africa and the subsequent trans-Atlantic trading of Africans by Europeans. Similarly, the need to protect the sea route to India drove the British to take over the Cape region from the Dutch. The discovery of India by the Portuguese in the 15th century later brought the British and other Europeans into the territory. The seed for Britain's subsequent colonization of India was planted at this point, starting with the use of military support for its trading interests. Following Britain's defeat in the American War of Independence in 1781 and the resulting loss of her American colonies, India became an increasing focus in her global economic and political expansion. By the mid-19th century, the Indian subcontinent was under the control of the British (Hiro 1992). Economic interests in Asia culminated in European control of other parts of the continent during the

19th century – for example, Hong Kong was colonized by Britain, and France took over Indo-China.

It is clear from the above accounts that the imperialist colonial project has developed in a series of phases. This section is more concerned with the era of imperialism that is often associated with post-slave trade European acquisition and the occupation of territories. The start of this post-slave trade era is located in the mid- and late 19th century. In any case, Snyder (1962/2001) locates this phase of the European imperialist project in the latter part of the 19th century. He refers to this era as a period of the 'New Imperialism', which was underlined by a 'revival of neo-mercantilism' involving European nations whose search for economic expansion amounted to a new scramble for economically viable territories in Africa, Asia, and elsewhere, and inevitably led to the subordination of non-whites in those territories. The 'New Imperialism' is characterized by the abolition of the slave trade and the simultaneous need to establish a permanent access to industrial raw materials in territories in Africa and Asia in order to substitute the economic benefits previously gained from the slave trade. Prior to the 19th century, colonization and imperialism by European nations had revolved around the discovery of the 'new world', the establishment of colonies in the 'new world', and the slave trade. As already indicated, it was during this 'old' era of Western overseas expansion that native peoples in the Americas and Pacific Islands became victims of European acquisition of their territories.

Irrespective of the different phases in the process of European territorial acquisition, they collectively embodied a common project, which introduced Western ideals, discourses, and practices that were intended to marginalize and subjugate the natives of the colonized territories. Like their African counterparts, the subjugation of Native Indians in the Americas derived rationalizations from the stereotypical views that this group was inferior (Clarke 1992). By extension, the scramble for empire in the 19th century drew heavily on the racially fueled representations of the slavery period to justify this wave of imperial colonial expansion. Asians were exposed to the same racial thinking advanced by Europeans to legitimize their 'rights' to colonize non-Europeans. Hiro (1992: 5, 6) provides instances of such racist themes in British discursive representation of Indians:

> By 1792, Charles Grant, a British Historian, was calling the Indian people 'a race of men lamentably degenerate and base, retaining but a feeble sense of moral obligation ... governed by a malevolent and licentious passion ...' And this 'race of men' was by then commonly referred to by the British as 'blacks'. Another term which had its origins in African slavery – nigger – was also freely applied to Indians. By the 1850s, Indians had been described as 'the barbarians, indifferent to human life ... yet free, simple as children, brave, faithful to their masters' by the Historian Herbert

Edwards. This could well have been a general description of African slaves by their masters.

By the latter part of the 19th century, the 'new imperialist' project had become linked principally to the notion of trusteeship – an idea that was simultaneously embedded within the philosophy of colonial domination by the 'superior' race. According to this concept, Europeans presented themselves as having moral obligations as the civilized race to oversee the uncivilized non-European nations with a view to instill civilization into them. With this guiding concept of 'trusteeship', came the revival of racist discourses of the savage 'black' and 'yellow' races whose progress toward civilization can only be effected under the superior direction of Europeans. At that point, Snyder (1962/2001: 92) notes:

> . . . it became necessary to show that weaker races should die out to make room for the stronger. To substantiate this view, any argument became acceptable. Racialism became more and more irrational. The only important thing was to prove the inferior races as 'outsiders', a kind of racial proletariat meant to be kept in subjugation. False pseudo-scientific myths were used to justify the control of one people by another. . . race differences were widely held to account for important cultural or economic differences and were used to excuse politically repressive actions.

As exemplified in the works and views of David Hume, Charles Grant, Edward Long, and Friedrich Blumenbach (a German physiologist and anthropologist who in 1795 categorized races into five types), by the late 18th century the Enlightenment had established solid grounds for treating race as a subject of 'scientific' analysis. Such contributions strengthened the notion of distinctions between the 'naturally' superior European race and the 'naturally' inferior non-European races. They served the slave trade and slavery, and laid the foundation for the 19th-century science from which the 'new imperialism' drew further credence. The writings of this period not only provided validation for colonialism outside of Western societies, but also they conditioned the racially based hierarchical relations between whites and non-whites in Western societies beyond the 19th century.

Ethnological writers such as the Frenchman Joseph Arthur Gobineau preached the philosophy of innate white supremacy in his pseudo-scientific ideology of the natural inequality of human races. His 1854 work, *Essai sur l'Inégalité des Races Humaines* (The Inequality of Human Races), claimed exclusive control of superiority in intelligence and civilization in the domain of the Aryan race. He related the supposed God-given Aryan superiority to innate physical differences found in skull and brain size and shape, hair texture, skin color, and so forth (Ellis 1915). While Gobineau associates virtues of intelligence, strength, and beauty with the white race, his conception of non-whites is encapsulated in his negative descriptions of the 'black' and 'yellow' races. In relation to the former, he states:

> the animal character, that appears in the shape of the pelvis is stamped on the negro from birth and foreshadows his destiny...mental faculties are dull or even non-existent...has an intensity of desire, and kills willingly, for the sake of killing.
>
> (Cited in Bowling and Phillips 2002: 2)

The 'yellow' race, according to Gobineau, have 'little physical energy and inclined to apathy...desires are feeble...tends to mediocrity in everything...has a love for utility and respect for law and order. His whole desire is to live in the easiest way possible' (ibid.). For Gobineau, 'no history is possible' as far as 'black' races and 'yellow' races are concerned. 'They did not create anything, and no memory of them has survived...History results only from the mutual contact of the white races'. (cited in Malik 1996: 83–4)

One of the most influential scientific contributions to the imperialist agenda of the 19th century and beyond is attributed to Charles Darwin, an English naturalist whose theory of evolution through natural selection paved the way for the social interpretation of Darwin's theory. In his later edition of *On the Origin of Species* (1869), Darwin's theory of biological evolution adopts Herbert Spencer's notion of the 'survival of the fittest' to describe the natural selection process of the fittest species and the disintegration of the weaker ones. Social Darwinists extended these ideas and concepts in their intellectual interpretations and ranking of human societies. According to the framework of social Darwinism, there is a natural and inevitable divide between races that is consistent with firstly, differences in physical characteristics. Secondly, social Darwinists' interpretations of the physical differences posit races in terms of their superior and inferior quality with the former attributed to whites and the latter linked to non-whites and, in particular, people of African descent. On the strengths of the concepts of the 'survival of the fittest' and 'natural selection', it denounces contact between the superior and inferior races for fear of contamination of the former. Thus for the 'superior' race to maintain its purity and superiority, it must resist any possible threats of racial degeneration (Kalunta-Crumpton 2004).

Darwin's theoretical contribution to the popular interpretations of the social progress of human societies at the time influenced the development of the eugenics movement toward the latter part of the 19th century. Founded by the British scientist Francis Galton (1822–1911), the movement, with its underlying aim to maintain white domination, promoted the notion of racial purity. Related to this mission was the need to prevent racial degeneration. Galton's definition of eugenics as 'the science of improving stock' encapsulated his intention, which was to ultimately purify the genetic stock of the white race. His ideas, mapped out in *Hereditary Genius* (1869), argued the existence of variations in hereditary qualities such as 'intelligence' across social groups in society, and he proposed that those with negative hereditary characteristics would cause a decline in the mental and physical racial qualities of the West. The eugenics movement's scientific approach to its fear of an imminent threat to the human race argued for strategies that would cause the extinction of social categories with negative hereditary qualities through selective breeding. Criminals, alcoholics, and the lower classes are among the social categories defined as unfit and undesirable. Arguably, their reproduction rates were far higher than those of the biologically and mentally 'fit' and the 'desirable'. Eugenicists therefore campaigned for policy interventions that aimed either to eliminate or at best to control the reproduction of the 'inferior' stock.

By the 20th century, eugenics ideology had begun to manifest itself in other aspects of human behavior, including the area of criminality. In his publication, *The English Convict*, Charles Goring (1913 cited in Garland 2002: 36) suggested that the eugenic preventive solution to criminality was to 'modify opportunity for crime by segregating the unfit' as well as to 'regulate the reproduction of those constitutional qualities – feeblemindedness, inebriety, epilepsy, deficient social instinct, insanity, which conduce to the committing of crime'; otherwise, 'crime will continue to exist as long as we allow criminals to propagate'. Herein, we begin to witness the embodiment of criminological thinking within the auspices of eugenic ideologies of the innately 'unfit' whose biological constitution, as overtly argued by eugenicists in particular, was synonymous with racial degeneration. While the definition of the 'unfit' in the eugenic vocabulary seemed to embrace an amalgam of categories ranging from the 'inebriate', the 'feeble-minded', the 'drunkard', the 'epileptic', and the 'vagrants' to the 'prostitute' (see Garland 1985), the eugenic ideology nevertheless retained a common theme which brought together notions of physical and mental degeneracy, criminality, and racial deterioration.

Credence for establishing an explicit link between biology and criminality is owed notably to Cesare Lombroso (1835–1909). Based on empirical data, Lombroso conducted a 'scientific' study of criminals on the basis of which he claimed that criminal behavior was biologically determined. In *Criminal Mind*, Lombroso (2006 first published in 1876) linked crime to physical characteristics and thereafter concluded that criminals were genetic throwbacks to the primitive forms of human species on the evolutionary ladder. In his observation, the primitive throwbacks – referred to as atavistic – were identified by many anatomical similarities which they shared with savages and non-white races. On the premise of his viewpoint that races were hierarchically structured in order of their superiority and inferiority, Lombroso's innovative paralleling of white criminals with non-whites essentially marked the abnormality in biological constitution found in the white criminals, and not their non-white counterparts whose biological make-up, in the views of Lombroso, was normal by virtue of its abnormality. Thus, as Lombroso (1876/1911: 140 cited in Gabbidon 2007: 11) claimed 'the frequency of homicide in Calabria, Sicily, and Sardinia is fundamentally due to African and Oriental elements'. Explicit portrayals of the supposed inferiority of Africans and other non-white groups and the view of a relationship between the primitive stocks and criminality donned the writings of Lombroso and his proponents (Lombroso and Ferrero 2004 first published in 1893; Ferrero 1900; Henderson 1901).

In essence, those 'scientific' differentiations between the 'fit' and the 'unfit', the 'criminal type', and the 'noncriminal' type reinforced assumptions of superior and inferior races. They were beneficial to Europe's move toward the post-slave trade colonization of the supposedly inferior non-white races. With reference to India, Hiro (1992: 7) cites Lord Kitchener, who was the British Army's Commander-in-Chief in India from 1902 to 1909, as stating: 'it is this consciousness of inherent superiority of the Europeans which has won for us India'. In his book *Black Peril, White Virtue*, McCulloch (2000) narrates how the race relations between white colonialists and Africans in colonial Southern Rhodesia between 1902 and 1935 reproduced patterns previously found in slave societies. Colonial Southern Rhodesia's mining and farming economy was heavily reliant on the exploitation of African male labor by white employers. And in order to maintain white domination and gain black compliance, black male employees were subjected to various forms of savage beatings which at best included flogging and kicking and at worst often resulted in the brutal killing of black employees. The injustices experienced by the African majority were marginalized by the criminal justice system – a multi-faction institution united toward a common agenda to protect the economic and political interests of white settlers (also see Kalunta-Crumpton 2001). A key justification of the oppressive colonial regime toward Africans was found in the invocation of moral panics around the perceived sexual threats that black men were believed to pose to white women. Referred to as 'black peril', the moral panics reproduced those racist notions of black sexual immorality, violence, indolence, and similar stereotypes that found favor in the legitimization of the slave trade. These assertions subsequently rationalized the blatant biased law enforcement policies and practices against Africans.

Also worth noting is that the moral panics in Southern Rhodesia were linked to miscegenation, an issue which was integral to the eugenics concerns expressed in Europe and North America. Opposition to miscegenation on grounds of the threat of the racial degeneration of the superior white race meant that miscegenation was legislated against in colonized societies such as South Africa and Southern Rhodesia. Within Western societies, concern about miscegenation is known to have drawn support from European 'scientific' interpretations of racial differences. In the United Kingdom, for example, the views of the eugenics society on the subject of miscegenation in the mid-20th century is captured in the words of Bertram (1958 cited in Gilroy 1991: 81) whose fear of the dangers of West Indian immigration on miscegenation warned that 'special consideration should be given before immigrants are allowed to enter the country having measurable and largely inheritable, physical attributes below the average for the United Kingdom'.

The 20th century also witnessed applied eugenics in North America and Europe. In the United States, the eugenics attack is exemplified in the program of involuntary sterilization practiced in many southern states. The program was aimed at preventing the reproduction of 'inferior' stocks, and included in the eugenicists' list of clients were African–Americans (Miller 1997). This racial group, according to the British eugenicist Rentoul, needed to be sterilized if the United States was to retain her superior mental capacity (Black 2003). In line with the influence of the Lombrosonian ideology on eugenics, the movement and its application also drew a great deal of strength from the growing interest in the connection between crime and intelligence in the early 20th century literature. Such literature posited intelligence as biological, fixed, and directly or indirectly related to criminality (see, for example, Goddard 1912, 1914). In practice, intelligence quotient scores were utilized to justify the incarceration of the 'unfit' as part of the applied eugenics initiative in the United States.

The United States' method of applied eugenics was highly influential in facilitating similar approach to eugenics in Canada and Europe. One notable example was Nazi Germany, where a more elaborate applied eugenics was adopted which, in comparison to the United States, was seemingly more severe in its hostility, barbarity, and scale. The German approach went beyond large-scale forced sterilization to include large-scale 'euthanasia'. Through legislation such as the 1933 Law for the Prevention of Hereditarily Diseased Progeny, the need to enforce racial hygiene and purity of people of German origin was legitimized within the law. Between 1933 and 1939, more than 360,000 people were compulsorily sterilized (see Evans 2005) and contrary to the popular Nazi rhetoric that forced sterilization was targeted at biological or genetic defects, the actual recipients of this form of applied eugenics encompassed a wide range of social groups regardless of whether or not members of such social groups had hereditary defects. Their common categorization as 'asocial' meant that anyone remotely perceived as a social deviant was likely to fall victim to forced sterilization. Juxtaposed alongside the sick, the feeble-minded, the criminal, and the insane on the target list of coerced sterilization were, amongst others, 'the underclass, beggars, prostitutes, vagrants, people who did not want to work, graduates of orphanages and reform schools...' (Evans 2005: 510). By 1939, the ideology of ridding Germany of all traces of the 'unfit' had amounted to the false notion of 'euthanasia' programs exemplified in mass killing of adult and children asylum patients through various killing strategies such as gassing and starvation. While the overall composition of the 'asocial' tended to cut across racial or ethnic groups in the sense that people of German origin were also vulnerable, the singling out of particular racial or ethnic groups of people for the eugenic attack was apparent in its own right. The Nazi genocide in which millions of Jews and other minority ethnic groups such as the Poles, Russians, Roma, and Sinti were killed during World War II represent perhaps the classic case of an extermination approach that was defended on the basis of the constructed eugenic ideologies of racial hygiene. There was the sterilization of African–Germans and their children – a racial group popularly described as 'Rhineland bastards' – and who like the Jews, Roma and Sinti were classed as aliens of inferior racial quality (see Burleigh and Wippermann 1991; Campt 2005).

Many historical examples illustrate how race thinking was embedded in Western policies and practices of the 20th century. Some of these will be dealt with in subsequent chapters, where for example, the discussion on South Africa is a reminder of how white power structures in colonial Africa operated on an ethnocentric concept of race; and in Canada, the racial injustice that pervaded relations between whites and colonized native peoples on the premise of the same ideology of white superiority is implicit in the narratives of contemporary race relations and approaches to crime in this country.

Conclusion: From history to contemporary

To conclude this chapter, I reflect, in brief and by way of examples, on how contemporary relations between whites and non-whites may seem to bear resemblance to the historical accounts above. By 'contemporary', I refer to post–World War II periods during which colonialism in its traditional sense 'officially' came to an end in many countries across the globe. Although it can be claimed that native peoples in Australasia and parts of the Americas are still under colonial administration, colonized countries in Asia, Africa, and most of the Caribbean gained their 'official' independence at differing periods from the 1940s onward, but most notably in the 1960s. Until the latter part of the early 1990s, South Africa was probably the most glaring example of colonial white suppression of non-whites in contemporary times. The U.S. Jim Crow laws are also worth noting as an example of a 20th-century open segregationist regime – similar to the system of segregation in apartheid South Africa. The Jim Crow structure of segregation was legally codified in the southern states from the late 19th century to the mid-20th century, and like its counterpart in South Africa, was based on the rationale of white superiority and imperialist domination.

Slavery and colonialism, in their traditionally manifest forms, may now have disappeared but the social thinking that created and sustained centuries of blatant subjugation of non-white races did not seem to disappear with these historical regimes. The deep influence that the centuries-long race thinking can have on contemporary ways of negotiating 'race' in concept and context is captured by Snyder (1962/2001: 92) when he states:

> Today, racialism, while scientifically outmoded and fallen from intellectual respectability, retains considerable historical importance. Systematic racial thought had strong influence on the growth and conduct of peoples in the Age of Imperialism. Our contemporary world took its political shape when racialism was at its height.

Since Snyder's observation, race thinking has continued to surface in various spheres of relations between whites and non-whites both within and outside the West, and in recent years it has tended to take an increasingly covert form. In some Western countries, there has been a paradigm shift from the traditional pseudo-scientific racism which preaches racial superiority and inferiority on grounds of biological differences to a 'new' form of racism based on cultural differences. For example, in Britain the 'new racism' is seen in how the cultural distinctiveness of the *Other* finds significance in official discourses to explain behavioral patterns (including offending) that supposedly deviates from the British way of life. Thus, the discursive emphasis on cultural differences invokes questions of national and cultural identity as crucial to segregated relations between the indigenous white community and non-whites (see Gilroy 1991). In the face of the anti-racist ethos of a democratic society, the 'new racism' allows political and media discourses to freely espouse the protection of British national identity against the threat of non-white presence. Yet, what seems to be a transition from the 'old' to the 'new' racism is merely a continuation of the 'old' manifested in a more subtle form. Culture is linked to race and the language in which the notion of differences in culture (or, in other words, cultural superiority versus cultural inferiority) is couched draws out, albeit subtly, the racist themes upon which the 'old' racism is based (Kalunta-Crumpton 2006). Despite the seemingly dominant culturalization of race rooted in the 'new' racism, the 'old' racism still lingers alongside the 'new'. Through organized racist groups such as the British National Front, racist ideologies of white superiority and supremacy based on pseudo-scientific theories are paraded openly.

In other parts of Europe, we have continued to be reminded of the 'old' racism through neo-Nazi and fascist movements and so forth, and across the Atlantic, the Ku Klux Klan in the United States exemplifies a key carrier of the philosophies of traditional racism. That said, the 'old' racism is not restricted to extreme right groups which have stood out by virtue of their practical application of their racist views, for example, through their use of violence. Racial differences in human behavior based on innate differences have also featured in scholarly writings of the mid- and latter part of the 20th century – as exemplified in works on intelligence tests (Jensen 1969; Eysenck 1971; Hirschi and Hindelang 1977; Wilson and Herrnstein 1985). Intelligence quotient scores were employed to make the claim that European–Americans had, on average, greatly superior intelligence than their African–American counterparts largely because of genetic differences between the two racial groups. And differences in crime rates between the two racial groups were explained within this intelligence–biology framework, with the recorded high crime rate for African–Americans attributed to the perceived low IQ among this group (Gordon 1976; Hirschi and Hindelang 1977).

Notwithstanding challenges to the scientific validity of the race–biology connection, and controversial debates and criticisms that surrounded studies of the IQ–race–crime nexus (see, for example, Rose et al. 1984; Kamin 1977), this subject was resurrected toward the end of the 20th century in the widely read book by Herrnstein and Murray, *The Bell Curve* (1994). In this book, Herrnstein and Murray signifies intelligence as a biological element, associates differences in IQ scores to differences in class and racial origins, and links crime and delinquency to low IQ. As Bracken (1973/2001) rightly observed, the 20th-century IQ study of the relationship between race and intelligence in the name of science is simply an extension of the 'scientific' project of 19th-century craniologists and their study of racial differences based on the size and shape of the skull.

If we move away from the West to explore the effects of the *past* on the *present* in non-Western societies, doubtless we will find that past centuries of slave trade and colonialism have had deep and lasting negative impacts on the subjugated territories. The underdevelopment of Africa socially, economically, and politically as a result of the trading in human beings and the effects of colonialism is well documented (see, for example, Rodney 1972; Nkrumah 1968). Like Africa, the continent of Asia has its own share of the legacy of Western colonization. Domestically, both continents share similar experiences of political, social, and economic instability exemplified in political tension, corruption, and endemic poverty.

At the global level, in the past few centuries the global economy and politics has seen the domination of the West and the subjugation of non-Western nations. This relationship continues to thrive, albeit subtly, on the dynamics of racial hierarchy rooted in a European ethnocentric view of the world. Racial hierarchy is the key navigator of various forms of racially based discrimination and as Jennings (2000: 80) observes, it 'involves a pervasive system of caste based on race...and reflects a "vertical" order of domination'. It differs from what Jennings refers to as the 'horizontal' structures of relations in which 'bigotry and discrimination' are reflected. Jenning notes that while 'legality is far more effective in resolving horizontal relations....', it is '...often ineffective in resolving vertical structures of domination based on race' (ibid.). This interpretation of racial hierarchy from its 'vertical' position illuminates the broader structure of racial injustice and can be illustrated in various macro-level relationships through which racial inequality is maintained. For example, Western foreign policies are known to be implemented to serve the interest of the West to the detriment of non-Western nations (see, for example, Henry 2000).

Within the context of the seemingly indirect way of practicing racial domination, it is no longer politically correct to, for instance, refer to Africa as 'the dark continent' or to openly describe African nations as backward. Instead, terms such as 'developing countries' have come into popular usage in global politics as an appropriate phrase for lumping many non-Western countries into one category. In whichever way the phrase 'developing' is interpreted, it nevertheless denotes the 'inferiority' of the non-Western countries that are categorized as such.

What we witness in contemporary times in terms of thinking and practicing race in various settings may indicate a continuation of history. And as such, an in-depth understanding of present-day crime and criminal justice issues as they relate to race in any society requires taking a very long step back through history. I have argued elsewhere that

> one of the striking aspects of studying race and criminal justice has been the location of interpretations within contemporary context of the postwar periods. Not only does this trend of analysis portray a false image of a new problem at hand, but it also limits the scope of our comprehension of the issue by failing to sufficiently examine its historical context.
>
> (Kalunta-Crumpton 2001: 104)

References

Banton, M. (1980) 'The idiom of race: A critique of presentism', *Research and Race Relations*, vol. 2, pp. 21–40.

Barker, A. (1978) *The African Link: British Attitudes to the Negro in the 17th and 18th Centuries*, Frank Cass: London.

Bertram, G. (1958) *West Indian Immigration*, The Eugenics Society: London.

Black, E. (2003) *War against the Weak: Eugenics and America's Campaign to Create a Master Race*, Thunder's Mouth Press: New York.

Bracken, H. (1973) 'Essence, accident, and race', Reprinted in E. Cashmore and J. Jennings (eds) (2001) *Racism*, Sage: London.

Bowling, B. and Phillips, C. (2002) *Racism, Crime and Justice*, Pearson Education: Essex.

Browne-Marshall, G. (2007) *Race, Law, and American Society: 1607 to Present*, Routledge: New York.

Burleigh, M. and Wippermann, W. (1991) The racial state: Germany, 1933–1945, Cambridge University Press, Cambridge.

Campt, T. (2005) Other Germans: Black Germans and the politics of race, gender, and memory in the Third Reich, University of Michigan Press, Michigan.

Caplan, P. (ed.) (1987) *The Cultural Construction of Sexuality*, Tavistock: London.

Clarke, H. (1992) *Christopher Columbus and the African Holocaust*, A & B: New York.

Ellis, G. (1915) 'The psychology of America race prejudice', *The Journal of Race Development*, vol. 5, no. 3, pp. 297–315.

Evans, R. (2005) *The Third Reich in Power 1933–1939*, Penguin Books: London.

Eysenck, H. (1971) *Race, Intelligence and Education*, Temple Smith: London.

Eze, E. (1997) *Race and the Enlightenment*, Blackwell: Oxford.

Ferrero, G. (1900) 'Savages and Criminals', Reprinted in D. Horton (ed.) (2000) *Pioneering Perspectives in Criminology*, Copperhouse Publishing: Nevada.

File, N. and Power, C. (1981) *Black Settlers in Britain 1555–1958*, Heinemann: London.

Finger, B. (1959) *Concise World History*, Philosophical Library: New York.

Fryer, P. (1984) *Staying Power*, Pluto: London.

Gabbidon, S. (2007) *Criminological Perspectives on Race and Crime*, Routledge: New York.

Garland, D. (1985) *Punishment and Welfare: A History of Penal Strategies*, Gower: Aldershot.

——— (2002) 'Of crimes and criminals: The development of criminology in Britain', in M. Maguire, R. Morgan and R. Reiner (eds) *The Oxford Handbook of Criminology*, 3rd edn, Oxford University Press: Oxford.

Gilroy, P. (1991) *There Ain't No Black in the Union Jack*, Chicago Press: Chicago.

Goddard, H. (1912) *The Kallikak Family: A Study in the Heredity of Feeble-Mindedness*, Macmillan: New York.

——— (1914) *Feeblemindedness*, Macmillan: New York.

Gordon, R. (1976) 'Prevalence: the rare datum in delinquency measurement and its implications for the theory of delinquency', in M. Klein (ed.) *The Juvenile Justice System*, Sage: California.

Goring, C. (1913) *The English Convict: A Statistical Study*, HMSO: London.

Henderson, C. (1901) *Introduction to the Study of Dependents, Defective, and Delinquent Classes*, D.C. Heath: Boston.

Henry, C. (ed.) (2000) *Foreign Policy and the Black (Inter)National Interest*, SUNY Press: Albany, NY.

Herrnstein, R. and Murray, C. (1994) *The Bell Curve: Intelligence and Class Structure in American Life*, Free Press: London.

Higginbotham, A. and Jacobs, A. (1992) 'The law as an enemy: The legitimization of racial powerlessness through the colonial and antebellum criminal laws of Virginia', *North Carolina Law Review*, vol. 70, pp. 969–1070.

Hill, C. (1967) *How Coloured Prejudiced is Britain?*, Panther: London.

Hiro, D. (1992) *Black British, White British: A History of Race Relations in Britain*, Paladin: London.

Hirschi, T. and Hindelang, M. (1977) 'Intelligence and delinquency: A revisionist review', *American Sociological Review*, vol. 42, pp. 572–87.

Husband, C. (ed.) (1982) *Race in Britain*, Hutchinson and Co. Publishers: London.

Jennings, J. (2000) 'The international convention on the elimination of all forms of racial discrimination: Implications for challenging racial hierarchy', in C. Henry (ed.) *Foreign Policy and the Black (Inter)national Interest*. Albany, New York: State University of New York Press.

Jensen, A. (1969) 'How much can we boost IQ and scholastic achievement?', *Harvard Educational Review*, vol. 39, pp. 1–123.

Jordan, W. (1968) *White Over Black: American Attitudes to the Negro, 1550–1812*, University of North Carolina Press: North Carolina.

Kalunta-Crumpton, A. (2001) 'Race and injustice: A global phenomenon', *International Criminal Justice Review*, vol. 11, pp. 104–19.

——— (2004) 'Criminology and orientalism', in A. Kalunta-Crumpton and B. Agozino (eds) *Pan-African Issues in Crime and Justice*, Ashgate: Aldershot.

——— (2006) The Importance of Qualitative Research in Understanding Black Disproportionate Presence in UK Crime Figures', *African Journal of Criminology and Justice Studies*, 2/2, pp. 1–32.

Kamin, L. (1977) *The Science and Politics of IQ*, Penguin: Harmondsworth.

Landers, J. and Robinson, B. (eds) (2006) *Slaves, Subjects, and Subversives: Blacks in Colonial Latin America*, University of New Mexico Press: New Mexico.

Lombroso, C. (2006 first published in 1876) *Criminal Mind*, Duke University Press: Durham, NC.

Lombroso, C. and Ferrero, G. (2004 first published in 1893) *Criminal Woman, the Prostitute, and the Normal Woman*, Duke University Press: Durham, NC.

Malik, K. (1996) *The Meaning of Race: Race, History and Culture in Western Society*, Macmillan Press: London.

McCulloch, J. (2000) *Black Peril, White Virtue: Sexual Crime in Southern Rhodesia, 1902–1935*, Indiana University Press: Bloomington.

Miller, J. (1997) *Search and Destroy*, Cambridge University Press: Cambridge.

Nkrumah, K. (1968) *Neo-Colonialism: The Last Stage of Imperialism*, Heinmann: London.

Onyeozili, E. (2004) 'Gunboat criminology and the colonization of Africa', in A. Kalunta-Crumpton and B. Agozino (eds) *Pan-African Issues in Crime and Justice*, Ashgate: Aldershot.

Rodney, W. (1972) *How Europe Underdeveloped Africa*, Bogle-L'Ouverture: London.

Rose, S., Lewontin, R. and Kamin, L. (1984) *Not in Our Genes: Biology, Ideology and Human Nature*, Penguin: London.

Russell, K. (1998) *The Color of Crime: Racial Hoaxes, White Fear, Black Protectionism, Police Harrassment, and Other Macroaggressions*, New York University Press: New York.

Snyder, L. (1962) 'The idea of racialism: Its meaning and history', Reprinted in E. Cashmore and J. Jennings (eds) (2001) *Racism*, Sage: London.

Wade, P. (1997) *Race and Ethnicity in Latin America*, Pluto: London.

Walvin, N. (1971) *The Black Presence*, Orbach and Chambers: London.

—— (1973) *Black and White*, Penguin: London.

Wilson, D. and Herrnstein, R. (1985) *Crime and Human Nature*, Simon and Schuster: New York.

Part II

Europe: Is There Race in Crime and Criminal Justice?

2
Race, Crime and Criminal Justice in Britain

Bankole A. Cole
University of Northumbria in Newcastle, United Kingdom

Introduction

The racial composition of Britain has become significantly diversified in recent years, a trend that has accelerated since the expansion of the European Union (EU).The relaxation of border controls between the United Kingdom and new EU countries has led to an influx of other white ethnicities into the country, principally as migrant workers. In addition, deteriorating political situations in countries all around the world have led to further influxes of peoples into the country as refugees and asylum seekers. This chapter looks at the importance of 'race' in the discussion of crime and victimisation in Britain, focusing on the three countries that constitute Great Britain, namely Scotland, England and Wales. (Northern Ireland is not discussed in the chapter – it is a country outside Britain but within the United Kingdom.) The intention of the chapter is not to racialise crime and victimisation but to explore the role that 'race' has on offending and victimisation rates in Britain. The question is whether 'race' is the most important variable in white and non-white involvement in the criminal justice system in Britain or whether there are other competing or even more significant factors.

Racially coded data

In the 2001 Census, Britain introduced a new 16+1 ethnic classification for the national population. Prior to 2001, ethnically coded crime and victimisation data had been recorded using a standard 4+1 classification, namely: white, black, Asian, Other (including Chinese) and Unknown (+1). The 16+1 categorisation expands each of these key ethnic groups into ethnic sub-groups and introduces a new ethnic category of mixed 'races' or mixed heritage groups. Thus the white ethnic category is now divided into three sub-groups: white British [W1], white Irish [W2] and any other white background [W9]. The black category becomes black or black British incorporating black Caribbean [B1], black African [B2] and any other black background [B9]. The Asian group also becomes Asian or Asian British incorporating Indian [A1], Pakistani [A2], Bangladeshi [A3] and any other Asian background [A9]. The Chinese or Other ethnic group was separated into Chinese [O1] and Other [O9]. The mixed heritage groups consist of racial mixtures of white, black and Asian in the following manner: white and black Caribbean [M1], white and black African [M2], white and Asian [M3] and any other mixed background (possibly including mixtures with Chinese or other ethnic groups) [M9]. The +1 category is the 'Not Stated' ethnic group, consisting of persons whose ethnicity is not known or those who have refused to declare membership of any particular ethnic group.

In Scotland, further divisions were created within the white ethnic group, allowing those who so wished to define themselves distinctly as white Scottish, white English, white Irish and white Welsh. In addition, there were three other ethnic groups used in the Scottish census but not listed separately in the British data sets. These were occupational traveller, gypsy traveller and 'other traveller'. A new census will be held in 2011. In that census, there will be four white ethnic categories in England and Wales, namely white English/ Welsh/Scottish/Northern Irish; white Irish (Republic of Ireland); Gypsy or traveller; and any other white background. In Scotland, the white English, Welsh, Scottish, Northern Irish and British will be listed separately and there will be an additional 'Polish' category. In addition, Scotland proposes to allow non-whites who feel strongly that they are Scottish to identify themselves as such. There will therefore be separate categories of Pakistani Scottish, Indian Scottish, Bangladeshi Scottish, Chinese Scottish, African Scottish, Caribbean Scottish and black Scottish listed amongst the Asian/ Asian British and African/Caribbean/black categories (see Scottish Government and the General Register Office for Scotland, 2008). In both Scotland and England and Wales, for the first time 'Arab' will be used as a distinct ethnic group (Office of National Statistics, 2009). It would seem that the attempt to make a clear distinction between racial/ethnic groups will be endless until, perhaps, all the world's ethnic groups are listed separately! However, these developments cannot be underestimated. They represent recognition of the diversity that exists within perceived main 'racial' groups and the fact that there are people who would prefer not to classify themselves as belonging to any particular ethnic group or 'race'.

The use of ethnically or racially coded statistics in Britain has been problematic since their first introduction by the London Metropolitan Police in the 1970s. There have been allegations of miscategorisation as visual identification is allowed, especially for non-whites, people of mixed heritage and those placed in the 'other' ethnic categories. All the criminal justice agencies in Britain currently record their crime and victimisation statistics using the 16+1 categorisation. However, the publication of criminal justice statistics for the public is presented differently. Police data (for example, on stop and search and arrests) are published in the 4+1 classification of white, black,

Asian, Other (including Chinese, Arabs and so on) and 'Not known' or 'Not recorded'. The mixed heritage groups are not shown in published police data. They are merged with the black or Asian categories depending on the nature of the 'mixture', whereby white and black Caribbean and white and black African become 'black'; white and Asian becomes Asian; and 'any other mixed backgrounds' becomes 'other'. Published British Crown Prosecution Service (CPS) data simply follow the police classification of black, white, Asian 'other' and 'unknown', and so do court sentencing data. In other words, in Britain, mixed heritage people are invisible in published criminal justice statistics from stop and search to court sentence. However, official criminal justice statistics in relation to young offenders (10–17 years old) are classified by self-defined ethnicity and are published using the 5 + 1 ethnic categories of white, mixed, black or black British, Asian or Asian British, Chinese or other and 'unknown'. Similarly, statistics on adults on probation or community penalties and prison statistics (including deaths in prison) are published using the 5 + 1 ethnic categories (see Ministry of Justice, 2008).

The aim of this chapter is to examine whether there are significant differences in offending and victimisation rates of the non-white and white populations in Britain. As the discussion above shows, this racial distinction will have to be broad. For this chapter, the term 'white' will be used to refer only to those defined in the census data and crime and victimisation survey statistics as white British [W1].[1] In other words, the white category is used in this chapter to refer only to those within the local population who are British Caucasians. White Irish [W2] and any other white background [W9] ethnic groups are excluded from the discussion. The term 'non-whites' is used in the discussion to include those listed in the census data under blacks, Asians, Chinese and mixed heritage ethnic groups. However, the Chinese and mixed heritage peoples will be discussed separately, wherever possible. This leaves the question of where to place the 'other' category which may include a variety of 'white and non-white ethnic groups who are local or from any part of the world'. Ethnic groups currently in the 'other' category include Arabs, Jews, Polish, Kashmiri, Eastern Europeans, Sikh, Kurdish, Vietnamese, Turkish/Turkish Cypriot and Iranians (see Gardener and Connolly, 2005). The extremely diverse nature of this group makes it impossible for it to be discussed as either a white or a non-white group. For this reason, the 'other' ethnic category is also excluded. This is a shortcoming as this group includes asylum seekers, refugees and migrant workers from Europe, the defunct Soviet Union and elsewhere who, in recent years, have featured as both offenders and victims of crimes in Britain (Cooper, 2009).

Offending and criminal justice

The main sources of data on offending in Britain are the official police statistics, which are collected locally by all 39 county police forces in England, the four police forces in Wales and the eight police forces in Scotland. Police statistics are available for wards, counties (local government areas) and police force areas.[2] Other sources of crime data include survey data and findings from studies that record the self-reporting of offences. The main sources of survey data in Britain are the British Crime Survey (BCS) and the Scottish Crime and Victimisation Survey (SCVS). Each of these sources of data has its own particular advantages and limitations. Police statistics are subject to police discretion in law enforcement and recording practices. They are also affected by the public's crime reporting practices. Crime and victimisation surveys have relatively small samples of respondents which, in spite of booster samples for non-whites, could not be said to be truly representative of the total population. However, crime and victimisation survey data and findings from self-reporting studies provide information on crimes that have not been reported to the police, often referred to as the 'dark figures' of crime. In combination these sources provide a reasonably comprehensive picture of the current crime situation in Britain.

Section 95 of the Criminal Justice Act 1991 and Section 306 of the Criminal Procedure (Scotland) Act 1995 both require the Secretaries of State of England and Wales and Scotland, respectively, to publish such information as they see fit to assist those engaged in the criminal justice system to avoid discrimination against persons on the grounds of 'race', sex or any other improper grounds. This has led to the publication of racially coded criminal justice statistics on a national basis by all the criminal justice agencies in Britain. In England and Wales, these are often referred to as section 95 statistics on 'race' and the criminal justice system. Since 1992, the Home Office (and now the Office of Criminal Justice Reform in the Ministry of Justice) have been publishing documents and statistics on 'race' and criminal justice system in England and Wales.[3] The statistics cover all stages of the criminal justice system – from stop and search to imprisonment.[4] At the present time, Scotland produces no racially coded crime statistics on offenders and victims in the criminal justice system from stop and search to sentencing. However, it does produce racially coded figures on persons on community penalties and in prisons (Scottish Government, 2008b, 2008c).

Statistical evidence points to the fact that, in general, rates of crime in Britain have been falling since 1995. Recent police recorded crime figures and findings from the BCS and the SCVS all show that there has been a downward trend in the level of crime recorded in the country (Kershaw et al., 2008; Scottish Government, 2008a; Scottish Government Social Research, 2007).

However, police crime data are recorded differently in Britain. In Scotland, crimes are recoded under the following broad categories: Non-sexual crimes of violence (which includes robbery); crimes of indecency (sexual crimes generally); crimes of dishonesty (property-related crimes generally, including fraud and vehicle-related thefts); and a variety of other/miscellaneous offences (including drug-related offences and the handling of an offensive weapon) (see Scottish Government, 2008a). In England and Wales, police recorded crimes are classified as follows: violence against the person (including racially or religiously aggravated offences, harassments and possession of weapons); sexual offences; property crimes (including robbery and vehicle-related thefts); drug offences; and various other miscellaneous offences. The BCS does not have crime data on fraud, but it does collect additional crime data on mugging (robbery plus snatch) and domestic violence (Jansson et al., 2008). Broadly speaking, the three main categories of crime are property crimes (or crimes of dishonesty), sexual crimes (or crimes of indecency) and crimes against the person, including violent crimes. It is against this background of crime classifications that offending rates between whites and non-whites will be discussed.

Criminal justice statistics in Britain have shown consistently that non-whites are more likely than whites to have contact with the criminal justice system as offenders. This has often been interpreted as implying that non-whites in Britain commit more crimes than whites. The statistics show differential offending rates between whites and non-whites for different types of crimes or groups of crimes. For the purpose of this chapter, a prison sentence will be used as an indicator of offending rates.[5] Over 90 percent of criminal cases are tried in the lower courts in Britain. However, in England and Wales, in 2006 only 20 percent of all magistrates' courts sentencing records contained the 'race'/ethnicity of defendants. This makes magistrates' courts data unreliable for the purpose of comparison of whites and non-whites offending in England and Wales. In contrast, during the same year, the 'race'/ethnicity of offenders was recorded in 82 percent of cases tried in the Crown Courts (Ministry of Justice, 2008). Thus Crown Court data, although consisting of relatively smaller numbers of (usually serious) cases, is the best that could be used for assessing white and non-white offending rates in England and Wales.[6] At the time of writing, Scotland does not publish the ethnic origins of offenders sentenced in any of its courts. However, as mentioned above, it publishes ethnically coded prison statistics. The 2001 census figures revealed the percentage of non-whites in Scotland as roughly 2 percent of the population (Office of the Chief Statistician, 2004), but, in 2007, non-whites accounted for 3.4 percent of the prison population in Scotland (Scottish Government, 2008c). This could be taken as a slight over-representation in offending by non-whites in Scotland.

In England and Wales, court sentencing data in 2006 showed that a higher proportion of non-whites (blacks and Asians) than whites received immediate custody for crimes of violence against the person and sexual offences. For example, 55 percent of black and 53 percent of Asian offenders charged with violent crimes against the person were imprisoned while 80 percent of blacks charged with sexual offences also received custodial sentences, but the percentage of whites imprisoned for sexual offences (71 percent) was slightly higher than that for Asians (68 percent). In the case of robbery, 83 percent of white offenders prosecuted for the offence were sent to prison, compared with 80 percent of blacks and 76 percent of Asians. Non-whites had the highest numbers of custodial sentences for fraud and forgery with up to 81 percent of blacks and 69 percent of Asian offenders charged with the offence being imprisoned, compared with 47 percent of whites. Similarly, non-whites had the highest custody rates for drug offences (75 percent of blacks and 71 percent of Asians compared with 57 percent of whites) and thefts and handling (50 percent of blacks and 47 percent of Asians, compared with 45 percent of whites) while whites had the highest custody rates for burglary (68 percent of whites compared with 61 percent of blacks and 59 percent of Asians) and criminal damage (41 percent of whites compared with 36 percent of blacks and 33 percent of Asians) (see Ministry of Justice, 2008 for details). Where an offence was racially or religiously aggravated, the offenders in England and Wales were mainly whites (Jansson, 2006; Ministry of Justice, 2008). Similarly, in Scotland, 95 percent of the perpetrators of racially motivated offences were also whites (Times Online, 2009).

Notwithstanding the fact that court sentencing statistics are incomplete, they do, however, indicate that non-whites, on the one hand, are more likely to be involved in violent and sexual crimes, fraud and forgery, theft and handling and drugs offences than whites; and that whites, on the other hand, are more likely to commit offences of burglary, robbery and criminal damage than non-whites. Overall, the figures indicate higher offending rates for non-whites than whites. This is interesting as non-whites account for roughly 11 percent of the total population in England and Wales (Office of National Statistics, 2004a).

However, these sentencing and prison figures are contradicted by findings from self-report studies. For example, the results of the 2003 Offending Crime and Justice Survey (OCJS) (Home Office, 2005)[7] revealed that whites were more likely to say that they had 'ever' and in the 'last year' offended compared with non-whites. This pattern was repeated across all offence categories (including drug offences) as well as for serious and frequent offending.

Variations in offending rates are also found in crime data for young people. In 2006–2007, more than 70 percent of crimes dealt with by the British Youth Offending Teams were committed by white youths. This figure relates to all offence categories (violence against the person and property crimes), with the exception of robbery where the offending rates were both similar at 50 percent (Ministry of Justice, 2008). These figures are supported by findings from the 2003 OCJS which showed that young white males were far more likely than non-whites to say that they had committed an offence in the past year (Home Office, 2005). However, there were slight variations by police area. For example, in Leicestershire, West Midlands and the London Metropolitan Police area, offending rates of non-whites for robbery were higher than those of whites. Offending rates for drugs offences were also higher for non-whites than whites in the London Metropolitan Police area (Ministry of Justice, 2008).

In contrast, pre-court decision figures in 2006–2007 showed that mixed heritage and black youths were more likely to have a final warning with intervention and Asian and Chinese youths more likely to receive a police reprimand while white youths were more likely to be given a final warning without intervention (Ministry of Justice, 2008). Similarly, sentencing decisions during the same period showed that non-whites received disposals at the higher end of the sentencing tariffs than whites. For example, offences committed by mixed heritage and black youths were more likely to attract a custodial order than offences committed by white youths. Chinese, black and mixed heritage youths were also more likely to receive a community sentence than white youths (Ministry of Justice, 2008). The above figures show that the offending rates of white and non-white youths did not tally with the sentences imposed. White youths are generally more likely to be involved in crime but more likely to receive lower sentences or a more lenient pre-sentence disposal.

Drivers of criminality, and crime figures

The causes of criminality are, indeed, many and varied. Engaging in crime is an individual decision or choice. Every offender has a reason for offending and the reason may be quite different from that of another offender who has committed the same crime. Greed, selfishness, a lack of consideration for others, differential exposure to criminal opportunities or even sheer hedonism explain many acts of criminality. While there is yet no strong evidence of a biological explanation of criminality, factors such as age and gender have been used to explain differential rates of offending. Furthermore, it is generally believed that living in a deprived area or exposure to deprivation has a significant effect on offending. In this regard, the age and gender composition of different ethnic groups and differential exposure to deprivation will be used to explain the offending rates of whites and non-whites in Britain.

National crime and victimisation survey results and police recorded crime data indicate that crime is not evenly distributed across Britain. Some counties or regions have higher crime rates than others whilst some have higher crime rates in particular crimes but lower rates in others. In 2007–2008, Yorkshire and the Humber region, the North West and the East Midlands had higher than average crime rates for burglary and vehicle-related crimes. During the same period, the East Midland and Yorkshire and the Humber also had higher than national average crime rates for thefts. The West Midland, North-East, North-West and Yorkshire and the Humber all had higher than average crime rates for criminal damage, with the North-East having the highest figures in the country. The South-East, West Midlands and Yorkshire and the Humber all had average crime rates for violent crimes. Wales and the East of England had the lowest crime rates for all recorded and BCS crimes in England and Wales during this period (Kershaw et al., 2008).

In 2007–2008, crime figures recorded for the 32 county areas of Scotland showed that the highest crime rates for all types of crimes occurred in the area of Glasgow City Council. Edinburgh City also recorded a high rate of non-sexual violent crimes. Aberdeen City, Dundee City, Fife, Edinburgh City, Glasgow City and North and South Lanarkshire all had high rates for crimes of dishonesty (property crimes). Generally, crime in Scotland is concentrated in Central Scotland (incorporating the Strathclyde, Central and Lothian and Borders police areas), and the North-East, mainly Aberdeen City, Dundee City and Fife (incorporating the Grampian, Tayside and Fife police areas). The lowest crime rates were recorded in the Scottish Islands and north of the country. Viewed in terms of police force areas, the London Metropolitan Police had the highest number of recorded crimes in the whole of Britain in 2007–2008. Outside the London Metropolitan Area, the highest recorded crime figures in England and Wales were within the Greater Manchester Police Area. Over the same period, the Strathclyde Police Area had the highest crime figures in Scotland (Kershaw et al., 2008; Scottish Government, 2008a).

In Britain, crimes are generally higher in urban areas than in rural areas, with areas classified as cities recording the highest overall crime rates. London has the highest crime figures in the United Kingdom. Outside London, the cities with the highest crime figures in England and Wales are Bristol (South-West), Manchester (North-West), Leicester and Nottingham (East Midlands), Birmingham (West Midlands), Sheffield and Leeds (Yorkshire) (Bangs et al., 2008; Home Office RDS, 2008). In Scotland, the highest crime figures, as mentioned above, were recorded in Glasgow, Edinburgh, Aberdeen and Dundee (Scottish Government, 2008a).

The figures in the 2001 Census show that the highest populations of non-whites are to be found in urban areas, with the majority residing in large cities. For instance, nearly half (45 percent) of non-whites in Britain live in London. In England and Wales, the largest population of non-whites live in the West Midlands (13 percent), followed by the South-East (8 percent), the North-West (8 percent) and Yorkshire (7 percent) (Office of National Statistics, 2004a). Large numbers of non-whites are also known to reside in the East Midlands (for example, in Leicester) and the South-West (for example, in Bristol) (see Office of National Statistics, 2001). Thirty-one percent of non-whites in Scotland live in Glasgow City, followed by Edinburgh City (18 percent), Aberdeen City (6 percent) and Dundee City (5 percent). Glasgow City's neighbouring counties (East Renfrewshire, North Lanarkshire, East Dunbartonshire, Renfrewshire and South Lanarkshire); and the counties of West Lothian and Fife also have non-white populations that are higher than the Scottish non-white percentage of roughly 2 percent. The above statistics show that non-whites in Britain are more likely to live those parts of the country with high crime rates.

Although the causal links, if any, between criminality and community deprivation have yet to be proven, several authors have reported an association between crime and the quality of the social environment. Communities with the highest crime rates also have a higher concentration of poor families, high unemployment rates, substandard or poor housing, poor health, high levels of school exclusion, truancy or dropouts from school and generally low levels of educational attainment (see Bradshaw et al., 2004). British cities and counties with high proportions of non-whites also happen to be amongst those with high levels of deprivation.[8] In 2007, over half of London boroughs (19 out of 33) are in the top 30 percent most deprived in England. Four out of the eight most deprived local authorities in England with the highest levels of multiple deprivations are in London. They are Hackney, Tower Hamlets, Newham and Islington (Government Office for London, 2007). These are areas of London with high populations of non-whites. The other parts of England with high concentrations of deprived areas are located in the North-West (21 percent), the West Midlands (15 percent), Yorkshire and the Humber (14 percent), the North-East (9 percent) and the East Midlands (ibid.). Cardiff (18 percent), Rhondda Cynon Taf (15 percent) and Swansea (10 percent) contained the most deprived areas in Wales (Welsh Assembly Government, 2008). These are also areas with reasonably large proportions of non-whites.

In Scotland, the most deprived areas are found in Glasgow City, which contains more than half of Scotland's 5 percent most deprived areas and a third of Scotland's 15 percent most deprived areas. Some of the most deprived wards in Glasgow have high percentages of non-whites – for example, Pollokshields East (48 percent non-whites), Maxwell Park (24 percent), Woodlands (23 percent) and Strathbungo (21 percent). Other local authority areas with a considerable share of Scotland's 15 percent most deprived zones are North Lanarkshire (9 percent), City of Edinburgh (7 percent), South Lanarkshire (6 percent), Dundee City (5 percent) and Fife (5 percent) (Scottish Executive, 2006). Generally, non-whites in Britain are more likely to live in areas characterised as 'low income' than whites (Home Office, 2005).

The crucial question is: why is it that Britain's non-whites have come to be living in disproportionate numbers in the deprived crime-prone areas of the country? The answers can be found in the history of immigration in Britain, the discrimination and disadvantage that Britain's non-whites have faced over the decades, in relation, for example, to education, employment and housing (see Bowling and Phillips, 2002). This has been worsened by negative media images of non-whites as 'problem' and confused political messages on multiculturalism, social inclusion and the value of immigration to Britain's society and the economy (Adamson et al., 2009), all of which had led to further blocked opportunities for non-whites in Britain.

'Race' and socio-economic variables are known to intersect with demographic factors of gender and age in explanations of crime figures. Young people (those aged 10–17) and men are known to more frequently and persistently offend compared to adults and females. According to the 2001 Census statistics, non-whites generally have higher percentages of males and a younger age structure than whites, with the mixed heritage groups having the youngest age structure in the country (50 percent were under the age of 16 years in 2001; 44 percent in Scotland alone) (Office of the Chief Statistician, 2004; Office of National Statistics, 2004b). Statistically, the levels of offending are slightly higher amongst young people in deprived areas than their adult counterparts. Deprivation and exclusion are more likely to affect young people more significantly than adults as it affects them both as individuals and members of families living in deprived areas. Research has shown that young non-whites are more likely than their white counterparts to have low educational achievements because of disproportional school exclusion and truancy that are often the result of bullying (see Bradshaw et al., 2004). Non-whites are also more likely to report school experiences as negative or irrelevant to their needs and expectations (Cooper, 2002; Cole and Wardak, 2006). This differential disadvantage is not reflected in the offending rates of young whites and non-whites outlined in the preceding section.

While Britain's non-whites live disproportionally in deprived areas, the high offending rates in official statistics cannot simply be explained as a consequence of that, as whites in the same places are also exposed to the same criminogenic factors. Studies have shown that British non-whites than whites have less confidence in the fairness of the criminal justice system (Clancy et al., 2001a, 2001b; Mirrlees-Black, 2001; Confidence Unit, 2003; Page et al., 2004; Pepper et al., 2004). Non-whites are more likely than whites to state that they will be treated unfairly by criminal justice agencies (particularly the police) than whites (Ministry of Justice, 2008). The non-whites' fears are supported by various studies that have shown that non-whites are discriminated against within the criminal justice system generally and by the police in particular (see Hood, 1992; Cook and Hudson, 1993; Bowling and Phillips 2002; Feilzer and Hood, 2004; Kalunta-Crumpton, 2005; Webster, 2007; Bhui, 2009).

Studies have shown that crime and prison figures are the results of the selective over-policing of deprived areas where non-whites predominantly live and the systematic targeting of non-whites by the police for stop and search and arrests (Bowling and Phillips, 2002). Section 95 statistics in 2007–2008 show that non-whites are more likely than whites to be stopped and searched and are more likely to be arrested (Ministry of Justice, 2008). While arrest figures do not automatically translate into sentencing or prison figures, they increase the likelihood of being processed through the criminal justice system. This has raised an important issue that the high sentencing rates and disproportionate prison figures for non-whites in general may not necessarily be the result of greater involvement in offending. They may, perhaps, be due to discriminatory pre-trial practices which have led to non-whites being more likely to be arrested and processed through the criminal justice system than whites. Furthermore, the findings from the aforementioned OCJS self-report study (Home Office, 2005) indicate that the dark figures of crime are more likely to consist of crimes committed by whites than non-whites. Lord Macpherson, in his report of inquiry into the death of black teenager Stephen Lawrence (Macpherson, 1999), concluded that the criminal justice system generally and the police in particular are, in fact, institutionally racist.

The issue of non-white offending and the research evidence of the influence of racism in the criminal justice system on non-white crime rates have continued to generate differing viewpoints in official and academic circles. Notwithstanding the apparent divergence in viewpoints, these debates have set the scene for developments in the criminal justice system to tackle offending behaviour. The implications of such policy and practice developments for 'race' are discussed in the section below.

Policy and practice response to offending

The official response to 'race' issues in offending could be judged on two grounds: first, on the extent to which policies to address crime clearly identifies 'race' as an issue and second, the extent to which professional practice prioritises 'race' in the approaches that are taken to address offending during sentence.

Since coming to power in 1997, the Labour government has pursued a policy of being 'tough' on crime and 'tough' on the causes of crime. This has been reflected in the publication of a series of policy documents on crime and justice, including various public service agreement (PSA) targets, government vision statements and strategic plans to address crime and the causes of crime. The current PSA targets cover a variety of issues such as making communities safer (PSA 23); tackling social disadvantage and exclusion (PSA 16), housing (PSA 5) and employment (PSA 8); addressing the disadvantage that individuals experience because of their gender, 'race', disability, age, sexual orientation or religious beliefs (PSA 15); building more cohesive, empowered and active communities (PSA 21); reducing the number of children in poverty (PSA 9), raising educational achievement especially for children from disadvantaged backgrounds (PSA 10 and 11); increasing the number of children on the path to success and reducing the number of first entrants into the youth justice system (PSA 14); improving the health, wellbeing and safety of children and young people (PSA 12 and 13); reducing the harm caused by alcohol and drugs (PSA 25); and ensuring that the criminal justice system is fairer, effective and transparent, that offences are brought to justice and that the problems of disproportionality and confidence in the criminal justice system are tackled effectively (PSA 24).

In 2003, Local Criminal Justice Boards (LCJBs) were set up in all 43 counties of England and Wales.[9] The boards are to be the principal vehicles for the frontline delivery of the governments' policies and vision on criminal justice at the local level. Specifically, they are to provide strategic direction for the delivery of key government PSA targets locally and to agree values and principles (OCJR, 2008). However, while the government sets the overall targets and standards for the Criminal Justice System at the national level, LCJBs have some leeway, working within the government framework, to drive forward reforms and changes, taking into account the specific needs, circumstances and priorities identified by their local communities (OCJR, 2007, 2008).

There is yet to be a full evaluation of the LCJBs' overall performance. Instead, reports exist on the performance of individual LCJBs on specific issues relating to their work on 'race' issues (see Cole et al., 2005; Adamson and Cole, 2008). However, it may be argued that the significant reduction in crime mentioned in the previous section is attributable to the relentless efforts of government to tackle crime and its causes. Crime data still insinuate that non-whites are still disproportionately involved in crime, and this means that the root causes of non-white offending is yet to be tackled fully. With regard to professional response to offending post-sentence, 'race' was not a key issue until the 1990s. Policies and approaches to tackling offending and re-offending have, traditionally, adopted a 'one-hat-fits-all' approach, the underlying assumption being that the factors that propel a person towards offending are generally the same, irrespective of 'race'.

The recognition of 'race' as an issue in the official response to offending began as part of the New Labour government's 'what works' with offenders agenda. The drive, however, was towards identifying what could 'work' with non-white offenders within the framework of what is offered generally to all offenders to help them deal with their offending behaviour. This move was based, most probably, on the results of the pilot works on working with black offenders that were being carried out by the probation service in London in the early 1990s. These early efforts relate mainly to how to improve the quality of offender work with non-whites as well as promote anti-racist practice generally; they do not address the causes of offending that could be due to 'race' (Williams, 2006). In fact, the main bulk of polices and practice documents on work with offenders have focused much on how to eliminate discrimination and ensure that all offenders are treated fairly within the penal system, irrespective of 'race' (see Criminal Justice System, 2005).

Thus, the major development in relation to offender management relates to how to deliver mainstream offender programmes and initiatives to non-whites, having regard to accessibility and the principles of responsivity, the main aim being to match the delivery of offender programmes to the personal characteristics of individual offenders and make them more relevant to non-whites. Therefore, the bulk of efforts in policy and practice has been focused on the training of correctional staff to address diversity issues in the delivery of offender programmes to offenders and the adaptation of offender programme materials to meet the needs of offenders from different cultural backgrounds (National Probation Service and HM Prison Service, 2002; Calverley et al., 2004). But the assessment tools currently used to determine appropriate offender intervention such as the Offender Assessment System (OASys) place far too much emphasis on individual pathology than the contextual and institutional factors that explain offending (see Home Office, 2001). There is little clarity in the offender assessment instruments about the issue of how 'race' is to be approached; much is left to personal development of the professionals, 'experience' and structured professional judgement (SPJ).

However, some positive developments have taken place in the introduction of offender programmes specifically for non-whites, although these programmes are not available to offenders in prison but only those on community penalties. Examples include a number of black 'empowerment' offender programmes that are offered by some probation areas in England and Wales (see Powis and Walmsley, 2002). Another example, the Think First Black and Asian Offender programme (TFBAO), run by Greater Manchester Probation, offered black and Asian offenders the opportunity to undertake the Think First offence-focused group work from their own (cultural) perspectives (see Home Office, 2004).

There is still much debate, as to whether offender programmes that prioritise 'race' are effective in addressing offending behaviour. According to Dell and Boe (2000), such an attempt assumes that offending behaviour arises more from racial experience than from shared common life histories. Dell and Boe continued:

> Criminological research that forefronts offender race may also need to account for individual life histories, acknowledging potential similarities across racial groupings. Individuals differ due to their racialized experiences but they also resemble one another due to common life experiences. The overall implication is that caution must be exercised in focussing research exclusively on race. With the current trend in research focusing on cultural heterogeneity, the lack of attention to similarity across racial categories may result in overlooking or minimizing elements of individual shared life histories that may contribute to understanding and identifying criminogenic factors (risk and needs).
>
> (Del and Boe, 2000: iv)

In contrast, Cole (2008) argued that, in practice, there is a tendency to overemphasise the 'similarities across racial categories' and undermine the 'racialised experiences'. Cole (2008) maintained that the experience of racism is a significant factor in the understanding of the offending behaviour of non-whites. As far back as the 1980s, Green (1989) had argued in relation to probation service practice, that the racist context in which the offending behaviour of black and minority ethnic people took place is ignored in the report to the courts and in criminal justice response to their offending behaviour. In addition, research in England and Wales has shown that the most frequent form of explanation offered to account for offending by black and Asian offenders is racism in school, society and within the criminal justice system (Denney, 1992; Bhui, 1999; Cole and Wardak, 2006). Cole's (2008) position is that the risk of re-offending is high where offenders are confronted by racism after the completion of a sentence (see also Calverley et al., 2004).

The question remains as to how the issue of racism should be approached in the delivery of offender programmes to non-whites. As Williams (2006) rightly pointed out, there is very little that correctional establishments can do to change the social environments within which offenders live, other than to 'assist them through the exploration of self-identity and self-conceptualisation to change their views about the choices available within those environments' (Williams, 2006: 149). This is the core principle behind the black empowerment offender programmes mentioned earlier. Consequently, offender programmes are not used in Britain to tackle 'race' issues in offending but to provide the individual non-white offender with:

> an opportunity to identify strategies for coping with events that influence his/her lifestyle but for which he/she does not have ultimate control for change.
>
> (Duff, 2002: 10, cited in Williams, 2006: 151)

Crime victimisation and criminal justice

Research has shown that most victims share the same demographic and socio-economic characteristics as their offenders. Lea and Young (1984) have argued that crime is broadly intra-racial and intra-class. Most victims are more likely to know their attackers, either personally or as people who live within the same neighbourhood. However, there appears to be an increase in the number of victimisations by total strangers. Very few victims are 'totally innocent' victims; many are very likely to have 'precipitated' their own victimisation either through negligence, carelessness, lifestyle or simply because of their gender, ethnicity or religion. However, very few cases of victimisation are provoked. It may be argued that everybody is a potential victim of a crime. Crimes against the environment, serious financial crimes or state crimes, for example, directly or indirectly affect everybody; but some people are more victim-prone than others. This section looks at victimisation rates amongst whites and non-whites with regard to violent, sexual and property crimes.

The main sources of victimisation data in Britain are the British Crime Survey (BCS) and the Scottish Crime and Victimisation Survey (SCVS). The police also collect victimisation data, but these are not normally published. However, the BCS and SCVS only record personal victimisation; they do not cover commercial victimisation such as theft from shops and the vandalism of business premises.

Available data show that young people are more likely to be victims of violent crimes than adults; men more likely than women (Ministry of Justice, 2008). Generally, adults experience more crimes than young people. Men, and in particular young men, are at the greatest risk of being victims of violent crimes, with the exception of domestic violence where the risk for women are significantly higher than for men. Men are also more likely than women to be victims of stranger violence but are less likely than women to have experienced a sexual assault (including attempts) in the previous 12 months (ibid.). Generally, men do not only have a higher risk of violent crime victimisation; they are also most likely to be the offenders. Eighty-seven percent of violent incidents in 2007–2008 involved men as offenders and 71 percent of robbery offences were committed by 16–24-year-old males (Hoare and Povey, 2008; Jansson et al., 2008).

The BCS[10] statistics in 2007–2008 have also shown that the risks of victimisation are higher in urban areas than in rural and suburban (affluent) areas and higher in deprived neighbourhoods than in less deprived ones (Bangs et al., 2008). Unemployed people had a higher risk of becoming victims of violence compared with employed or economically active people; offences involving knives are more common in urban than rural areas and the risk of becoming a victim of burglary is higher for households where the occupants are unemployed than for households where the occupants are employed or economically active. Burglary rates are also much higher in deprived areas. Furthermore, households with young residents (16–34 years) are more likely to be victims of car-related crimes than households with older residents (for example, those aged 55 years and above). Households in deprived areas are also more likely to be the victims of car-related crimes. Young people are generally more likely than adults to be victims of other thefts including muggings, and victims of vandalism are most likely to live in deprived areas (ibid.).

Specifically, the results of the 2007–2008 British Crime Survey show that whites are more likely to be victims of assaults and domestic violence than non-whites, who are more likely to be victims of robbery and mugging (robbery and snatch theft) (Kershaw et al., 2008; Povey et al., 2009). Findings from the Crime and Justice Survey (2003) show that this pattern is also reflected in the victimisation of young people: White young people are more likely to have been victims of assault than black and minority ethnic young people but are less likely to have been victims of robbery (Home Office, 2005).

In addition, the 2007–2008 BCS data show that non-whites are more likely to be assaulted or attacked by a stranger while attackers of whites are more likely to be an acquaintance. White women are more likely to suffer sexual assaults than non-white women. Overall, non-whites are more likely to be the victims of any form of violence than whites. With regard to property crimes (burglary and car crimes), non-whites also have a higher rate of victimisation than whites. Furthermore, non-whites are more likely to experience crime in their local areas than whites. Thus, non-whites have a higher level of fear of crime and actual experience of crime than whites (Kershaw et al., 2008).

There is growing concern in Britain about victimisations that are racially or religiously aggravated, especially where they occurred between whites and non-whites. The BCS data for England and Wales show that harassment (which does not involve physical injury to the victim) accounted for 25 percent of police recorded violence against the person in 2007–2008 and that 11 percent of harassment offences were racially or religiously aggravated (Ministry of Justice, 2008). Statistics and research findings in Britain have shown that racially or religiously aggravated crimes are generally disproportionately committed by whites and against non-whites than whites (Jansson, 2006; Scottish Government, 2009). For example, in Scotland, police recorded data (2004–2008) showed that non-whites were more likely than whites to be victims of racist incidents (Scottish Government, 2009). The Crown Prosecution Service *Hate-Crime Report 2007–2008* revealed a similar picture for England and Wales (Crown Prosecution Service, 2008). Furthermore, the results of the 2006 (SCVS) and the BCS showed that non-whites were much more likely to worry that they would be attacked because of their skin colour, ethnic origin or religion than whites (Salisbury and Upson, 2004; Scottish Government Social Research, 2007).

Specifically, research has shown that Chinese people are more likely than any other minority ethnic group to be subject to racial harassment and racially motivated property damage. The Fourth National Survey of Ethnic Minorities found that 16 percent of Chinese people in the UK encountered more racial abuse and insulting behaviour in the past year and that this figure is higher than that for any other ethnic minority group (Modood et al., 1997; Virdee, 1997).

A recent national study of Chinese victims of crime in England and Wales (Adamson et al., 2009) revealed that the experience of racially motivated crimes by Chinese people is possibly much more than is recorded in official statistics and reports of victims' surveys. This was found to be due to many reasons, including the fact that Chinese victims are less likely than other ethnic groups to report instances of victimisation to the police.[11] There are many reasons for this, but the majority relate to communication problems and lack of confidence in the police and the criminal justice system that resulted from past experiences when they believed that they were treated unfairly by the police. Non-reporting has meant that many of such victims suffer multiple and repeat victimisations in silence.[12] Official statistics confirm that victims of racially motivated offences are more likely than other victims to be repeatedly victimised (Kershaw et al., 2008).

Studies have also shown that Chinese people in Britain are more likely than other ethnic groups to experience commercial victimisation, including vandalism or criminal damage of their restaurants and takeaway shops (Bowling, 1998; Law, 2004; Chan et al., 2004; Adamson and Cole, 2006a). Adamson et al. (2009) argued that considering the very low population of Chinese people in Britain and the extent of their racial harassment, attacks and abuse, they are possibly the most disproportionately racially victimised ethnic group in the country. A media report in 2005 suggested that, unlike most crimes, the likelihood of being the victim of a racially or religiously motivated attack is far greater in rural areas than in urban areas (ibid.: 29). More recent studies have shown that since the September 11 terrorist attack in New York and the July 7 London bombings, racial hatred and victimisation of Muslims (mainly non-whites) in Britain have increased (see Spalek et al., 2009).

The above discussions show that there are demographical factors that determine victimisation or victim-proneness, but there is no clear explanation in terms of 'race' except where the victimisation is racially or religiously aggravated. Possible explanations of victimisation in Britain include an escalating culture of violence and aggression, gender inequalities, lack of respect for diversity, a growing intolerance of difference and change, peer pressure, increase in problems of alcohol and drug misuse and a decreasing fear of authority (see Law, 2007). Differential exposure to these factors is more important in explaining victimisation than 'race'.

Policy and practice response to victimisation

Until the 1990s, the British government's criminal justice response to victims had been poor and patchy. Victim participation was minimal and victim issues were generally handled by state-sponsored charitable organisations such as Victim Support. Charity organisations still carry out much of the work done with victims in the country, including local work that prioritises 'race' issues. It was largely through the relentless efforts of these organisations that Britain's Victim's Charter was published by the government in 1990. This Charter sought to empower victims and states standards of service for victims of crime. One significant development is the provision in the 1996 edition of the Charter of a Victim Impact Statement scheme.

This scheme grants a victim the right to participate in the criminal justice decision-making by providing a written statement to the court explaining how the crime had affected them. However, the Victim Statement could be introduced only after the defendant has been found guilty, not before, and it is not expected to influence sentencing.

The Victims' Charter does raise the hopes of victims in respect of what they are to expect from the police and the criminal justice system when victimised. However, statistics continue to show that victims of crime in Britain are far less likely to report their victimisation to the police. As shown above, non-whites are disproportionately represented in these figures. The main reason for non-reporting is the general perception that the police do not take certain crimes seriously or that reporting would not achieve anything. Studies of non-white victims have shown a general lack of confidence in the police to treat them fairly, and a general dissatisfaction with the service provided which many attributed to the fact that they are non-whites (Yarrow, 2005). Specific complaints relate to dissatisfaction with police follow-up or the police not keeping victims adequately informed about the investigation of the crime and a general lack of satisfaction about the way in which they were treated by the police. The study of Chinese people in Britain (Adamson et al., 2009) revealed an additional allegation or concern on the part of Chinese victims that they were treated like suspects rather than victims. Thus, many reported crimes only if they thought that it was serious or unbearable (for example, in the case of repeat victimisations).

Chinese victims in particular are more likely than other ethnic groups to seek emotional support and practical help from their relatives (Chan et al., 2007a, 2007b). The same situation was found with young black victims of crime (Yarrow, 2005). There is an issue, therefore, that in spite of the relentless efforts by Victim Support and other charities to publicise their services, the level of contact by victims, especially non-white victims, are still generally low. This was particularly the case with non-English-speaking non-whites. It has been a topic of much debate as to whether the problem lies with these groups' inability to communicate in English or the inability of the service providers to provide services that fully understand and meet the needs of non-English speaking non-whites (Adamson et al., 2009).

However, it must be said that there have been significant developments in terms of policy and practices relating to victims. In addition to the efforts of Victim Support,[13] individual criminal justice agencies (for example, the police) have developed specialist victims units and support teams, and there is a growing use of multi-agency and inter-agency groups or partnerships for specific victim work. Victim work is now extended to support when victims attend court as witnesses. A witness service system exists in both Scotland and England and Wales. The Scottish Court Service (SCS) provides a range of services to vulnerable witnesses and has embarked on a scheme of adapting the courts and improving services to meet the needs of victims and witnesses (Scottish Executive Social Research, 2006). Similar services exist in England and Wales. In recent years, there has been a growth in victim empowerment work. This includes the introduction of restorative justice schemes. Scotland also has structures in place to support victims of repeat victimisation (Scottish Executive Social Research, 2006).

Most importantly, The 'Justice for All' PSA framework 24 states the government's vision for the criminal justice system as that which 'puts victims at its heart and in which the public are confident and engaged' (HM Government, 2007: 3) This vision is reiterated in the government's Strategic Plan for Criminal Justice 2008–2011 in which the government stated that one of the aims for 2011 is to deliver a fair and effective criminal justice service that puts the victims of crime and law-abiding citizens first (OCJR, 2007). The government accepts that there is a need to improve the services that are currently being offered to crime victims and vowed to treat people of all 'races' equally (OCJR, 2007: 2).

A significant government-driven improvement is in the area of policy and directives to criminal justice agencies on how to deal with racist victimisations and support victims of racially or religiously motivated crimes. Inspired mainly by the recommendations of the Macpherson report (1999), police forces and criminal justice agencies in Britain have developed schemes for dealing with racially motivated crimes and their reporting, such as the establishment of third-party reporting centres. In addition, criminal justice agencies have established accountability mechanisms for ensuring that decisions taken in such cases are fair to victims. In the latter category is the establishment of independent Scrutiny Panels (such as the Crown Prosecution Service Scrutiny Panels in England and Wales) to review decisions taken in racially motivated crime investigations and prosecution in order to verify their consistency and fairness (Adamson and Cole, 2006b). However, studies are still showing that much needs to be done for victims of racially motivated crimes, especially those that are 'hidden from public view' such as Chinese people, asylum seekers, migrant workers and refugees (Adamson et al., 2009; Cooper, 2009).

A crucial question still remains concerning the extent to which 'race' is prioritised in work with victims and the availability and quality of service that are offered to non-white victims. In Scotland, it was found that almost half of the services available to non-white victims are located in Glasgow City and its surrounding local authorities. Thus, non-whites who live in other areas (for example, rural areas of Scotland) are unlikely to be able to gain access to specialist support providers but only mainstream ones such as Victim Support (Clark and Moody, 2002; Scottish Executive Social Research, 2006). This is a crucial issue for non-white victims. The majority of specialist support for non-whites is provided locally and by groups run largely by non-whites. In the case of Chinese victims, for example, specialist support to victims is provided by the local Chinese organisations and other charities such as

Min Quan and the Monitoring Group (Adamson et al., 2009). Unfortunately, these organisations are poorly funded.

In the face of an increasingly competitive environment and the future reduction in public funding, small and local organisations are not in a good position to compete with larger ones. Large organisations and those who can provide 'broad' services in a 'cost-efficient' manner because they already have the experience and structures in place to deliver to government targets are more likely to be successful in bidding for funding than smaller organisations, no matter how relevant or innovative the ideas of the smaller organisations might be. There is no such thing as a fair and transparent market, competitive neutrality or a 'level playing field'. It is all market-driven politics (cf Leys, 2003). Favoured organisations are more likely to be national, large and based in urban areas; but organisations that provide specialist services on the basis of 'race' are more likely to be local and small. They cannot compete with larger organisations who claim to be able to provide for 'all types' of victims. Unfortunately, in public funding language, size matters.

Voluntary and community organisations that are rooted in the local neighbourhood are more likely to understand the 'local' victim population better than national organisations that work from a distance, but are simply physically located in the community. Work with non-white victims is more likely to be more effective in dealing with their needs and circumstances if it is delivered by organisations that are set up by locals and rooted in the community. The argument here is that there is a need to encourage and support local initiatives for victims that identify with particular ethnic groups. This will move policy and practice closer to respecting diversity in the delivery of services to victims of crime.

Conclusion

There is clear evidence of differences in the offending of whites and non-whites in Britain. While it could be said that no crime is ethnically pure, British non-whites are disproportionally represented in some crimes than others, and vice versa. There are many causes of offending. It is clear that the geographical factor of area deprivation is a key issue in explaining offending in Britain, thus probably prioritising social class and general social inequalities above 'race'. However, from the history of immigration in Britain and the discrimination that studies have shown that non-whites in Britain have experienced and still experiencing, it is no doubt that they disproportionately live in deprived areas and experience the criminogenic factors that could propel one into offending more than whites. More significant, perhaps, are the studies that have found non-white offending in Britain to be the by-product of racism within the criminal justice system. The statistics on stop and search, arrests and even sentencing have all revealed that non-whites are discriminated against within the British criminal justice system.

In this regard, the importance of Lord Macpherson's' definition of the 'British criminal justice system' as institutionally racist cannot be underestimated.

Victimisation figures also showed differences in terms of 'race' but, other than the impact of area as discussed with regard to offending, there is no clear evidence that 'race' is a key factor in victimisation. However, there is an exception with regard to racially motivated crimes, where 'race' or religion is a key factor and non-whites are more likely to be victims.

The British government has been relentless in its efforts to address crime and victimisation. However, there is no clear evidence that 'race' is given much priority in these developments. Instead, there is recognition of the need to be fair to all 'races' but there appears to be an underlying political drive to meet stated targets and possibly satisfy election promises on crime and justice than meet criminal justice needs solely on the basis of 'race'. Although the British government appears to be moving slowly away from a 'one-hat-fits-all' method and is recognising the need to adopt a 'grounded' approach to issues, it will be some time yet before Britain can lay claims to a truly diversity-focused and 'race'-sensitive criminal justice system.

Notes

1. Including those who are defined in the Scottish data sets as white Scottish, white English and white Welsh.
2. A police force area may cover more than one county.
3. Section 95 publications also include analysis of data from the British Crime Survey (BCS).
4. Section 95 publications are also available on gender and crime.
5. However, in the discussion on youth offending, sentence to a community order was also used as an indicator.
6. These figures do not include cases that were discontinued by the Crown Prosecution Service, withdrawn during court hearing or administratively finalised.
7. The 2003 OCJR consisted of a sample of 10,079 respondents aged from 10 to 65 living in private houses in England and Wales. The sample included a booster sample of young people up to half of the total sample (4574).
8. The indicators of deprivation used in Britain varied slightly and the time when the surveys were conducted also varied. A survey was conducted in Scotland in 2006; England had a survey conducted in 2007 and a Welsh survey was conducted in 2008 (Scottish Executive, 2006; Government Office for London, 2007; Welsh Assembly Government, 2008). Seven indicators of deprivation were used in all three surveys namely: Income, Employment, Health, Education, Housing, Access to Services and Crime or community safety. An additional indicator of the living or physical environment was used in the English and Welsh surveys.
9. An LCJB is normally made up of all the chief officers of the local criminal justice agencies and other local agencies that work with offenders and victims of crime.
10. Murders are not included in victim-based surveys. 'Victimless' crimes such as drug-use are also excluded.
11. BCS statistics in 2007–2008 showed that more than half (58 per cent) of crimes are not reported to the police. Thefts and burglaries are more likely to be reported

than interpersonal violent crimes and vandalism. The most frequently mentioned reasons for not reporting incidents were that the victims perceived them to be trivial, personal or private and the general belief that the police would or could not do much about the crime.

12. 'Multiple victimisation' is defined in BCS statistics as the experience of being a victim of more than one crime in a year, or the same of different types. Repeat victimisation is a subset of multiple victimisation and is defined as being a victim of the same type of crime more than once in the last 12 months. BCS statistics on repeat victimisation also shows that victims of domestic violence and vandalism are more likely to be repeatedly victimised than victims of other violent, sexual or property crimes.

13. Victim Support provide a variety of services to victims including emotional and psychological support to victims, counselling, provision of information on how the criminal justice system works and victims' rights within it, practical advice on personal safety and security, help with obtaining financial compensation and witness support.

References

Adamson, S. and Cole, B. (2006a) *The UK Chinese and Racially-Motivated Crime.* Working Paper in Social Sciences and Policy No. 16. Hull: The University of Hull.

Adamson, S. and Cole, B. (2006b) *Evaluation of the West Yorkshire Crown Prosecution Service Scrutiny Panel: Final Report.* Hull: The University of Hull.

Adamson, S. and Cole, B. (2008) *Review of Greater Manchester Local Criminal Justice Board (LCJB)'s Policies, Procedures and Practices on BME Community Engagement and Confidence in the Criminal Justice System.* Manchester: Greater Manchester Criminal Justice Board.

Adamson, S., Cole, B., Hussain, B., Smith, L., Law, I., Lau, C., Chan, C.K. and Cheung, T. (2009) *Hidden from Public View? Racism against the UK Chinese Population.* London: The Monitoring Group.

Bangs, M., Roe, S. and Higgins, N. (2008) 'Geographical patters of Crime' in C. Kershaw, S. Nicholas and A. Walker (eds), *Crime in England and Wales 2007/08,* Home Office Statistical Bulletin 07/08. London: HMSO.

Bhui, H.S. (1999) 'Race, Racism and Risk Assessment: Linking Theory to Practice with Black Mentally Disordered Offenders', *Probation Journal* 46(3): 171–81.

Bhui, H.S. (ed.) (2009) *Race and Criminal Justice.* London: Sage.

Bowling, B. (1998) *Violent Racism Victimization, Policing and Social Context.* Oxford: Oxford University Press.

Bowling, B. and Phillips, C. (2002) *Racism, Crime and Justice.* London: Longman.

Bradshaw, J., Kemp, P., Baldwin, S. and Rowe, A. (2004) *The Drivers of Social Exclusion: A Review of the Literature for the Social Exclusion Unit.* York: Social Policy Research Unit, University of York.

Calverley, A., Cole, B., Kaur, G., Lewis, S., Raynor, P., Sadeghi, S., Smith, D., Vanstone, M. and Wardak, A. (2004) *Black and Asian Offenders on Probation,* Home Office Research Study 277. London: Home Office.

Chan, C.K., Bowpitt, G., Cole, B., Somerville, P. and Chen, J.Y. (2004) *The UK Chinese People: Diversity and Unmet Needs.* Nottingham: Nottingham Trent University.

Chan, C.K., Cole, B. and Bowpitt, G. (2007a) 'Beyond Silent Organisations: A Reflection on the UK Chinese People and Their Community Organisations', *Critical Social Policy,* 27(4): 509–33.

Chan, C.K., Cole, B. and Bowpitt, G. (2007b) 'Welfare state without dependency: The case of the UK Chinese people', *Social Policy and Society*, 6(4): 503–14.

Clancy, A., Hough, M., Aust, R. and Kershaw, C. (2001a) *Ethnic Minorities' Experience of Crime and Policing: Findings from the 2000 British Crime Survey*, Research Findings No. 146, London: Home Office.

Clancy, A., Hough, M., Aust, R. and Kershaw, C. (2001b) *Crime, Policing and Justice: The Experience of Ethnic Minorities – Findings from the British Crime Survey*, Home Office Research Study 223, London: Home Office.

Clark, I. and Moody, S. (2002) *Racist Crime and Victimisation in Scotland*. Edinburgh: Scottish Executive.

Cole, B. (2008) 'Working with Ethnic Diversity', in S. Green, E. Lancaster and S. Feasey (eds), *Addressing Offending Behaviour*, Cullompton Willan.

Cole, B. Davidson, N., Adamson, S. and Murtuja, B. (2005) *Black and Minority Ethnic People's Confidence in the Criminal Justice System in West Yorkshire*. Leeds: West Yorkshire Criminal Justice Board.

Cole, B. and Wardak, A. (2006) 'Black and Asian Men on Probation: Social Exclusion, Discrimination and Experience of Criminal Justice', in S. Lewis, P. Raynor, D. Smith and A. Wardak (eds), *Race and Probation*. Cullompton: Willan.

Confidence Unit (2003) BME Confidence in the criminal justice system (Briefing Paper), Home Office.

Cook, D. and Hudson, B. (1993) *Racism and Criminology*. London: Sage.

Cooper, Charlie (2002) *Understanding School Exclusions: Challenging Processes of Docility*. Hull: University of Hull.

Cooper, C. (2009) 'Refugees, Asylum Seekers and Criminal Justice', in H.S. Bhui (ed.) *Race and Criminal Justice*. London: Sage.

Criminal Justice System (2005) Fairness *and Equality in the CJS: Toolkit to Help Local Criminal Justice Boards Increase the Confidence of the Black and Minority Ethnic (BME) Community they Service*. London: Home Office.

Crown Prosecution Service (CPS) (2008) *Hate Crime Report 2007–2008* CPS Management Information branch. London: CPS.

Dell, C.A. and Boe, R. (2000) *An Examination of Aboriginal and Caucasian Women Offender Risk and Needs Factors*. Ottawa: Research Branch. Correctional Services of Canada.

Denney, D. (1992) *Racism and Anti-Racism in Probation*. London: Routledge.

Duff, D. (2002) *A Programme for Change and Rehabilitation: Black Self-Development Groupwork Manual*. London: LPA.

Feilzer, M. and Hood, R. (2004) *Differences or Discrimination – Minority Ethnic Young People in the Youth Justice System*. London: Youth Justice Board.

Gardener, D. and Connolly, H. (2005) *Who are the 'Other' Ethnic Groups?* London: Office of National Statistics.

Green, R. (1989) 'Probation and the Black Offender', *New Community*, 16(1): 81–91.

Government Office for London (2007) *Indices of Deprivation*. Corporate Information and Analysis Team. London: Government Office for London.

Hoare, J. and Povey, D. (2008) 'Violent and Sexual Crimes', in C. Kershaw, S. Nicholas and A. Walker (eds), *Crime in England and Wales 2007/08*, Home Office Statistical Bulletin 07/08. London: HMSO.

HM Government (2007) *PSA Delivery Agreement 24: Deliver a More Effective, Transparent and Responsive Criminal Justice System for Victims and the Public*. London: HMSO.

Home Office (2001) *Offender Assessment System OASys User Manual*. London: Home Office.

Home Office (2004) *Black and Asian Offenders Pathfinder: Implementation Report.* London: Home Office Development and Practice Report.

Home Office (2005) *Minority Ethnic Groups and Crime: Findings from the Offending, Crime and Justice Survey 2003*, 2nd edn. Home Office Online Report 33/05. London: HMSO.

Home Office RDS (2008) *Crime and Disorder Reduction Partnership Areas: Recorded Crime for Seven Key Offences and BCS Comparator 2006/07 to 2007/08.* London: HMSO.

Hood, R. (1992), *Race and Sentencing.* Oxford: Clarendon Press.

Jansson, K. (2006) *Black and Minority Ethnic Groups' Experiences and Perceptions of Crime, Racially Motivated Crime and the Police: Findings from the 2004/05 British Crime Survey.* London: Home Office.

Jansson, K., Robb, P., Higgins, N. and Babb, P. (2008) 'Extent and Trends', in C. Kershaw, S. Nicholas and A. Walker (eds), *Crime in England and Wales 2007/08*, Home Office Statistical Bulletin 07/08. London: HMSO.

Kalunta-Crumpton, A. (2005) 'Race, Crime and Youth Justice', in T. Bateman and J. Pitts (eds), *The RHP Companion to Youth Justice.* Dorset: Russell House Publishing.

Kershaw, C., Nicholas, S. and Walker, A. (eds) (2008) *Crime in England and Wales 2007/08* Home Office Statistical Bulletin 07/08. London: HMSO.

Law, I. (2004) *Household Needs, Public Services and Community Organisations.* Chinese Action Research Project Final Report. Leeds: Centre for Ethnicity and Racism Studies, University of Leeds.

Law, I. (2007) *The Racism Reduction Agenda: Building the Framework, Signposting Good Practice and Learning the Lessons.* Leeds: Centre for Ethnicity and Racism studies University of Leeds.

Lea, J. and Young, J. (1984) *What is to be Done about Law and Order?* London: Penguin Books Ltd.

Leys, C. (2003) *Market Driven Politics: Neoliberal Democracy and the Public Interest.* London: Verso.

Macpherson, W. (1999) *The Stephen Lawrence Inquiry: Report of an Inquiry by Sir William Macpherson.* London: HMSO.

Ministry of Justice (2008) *Statistics on Race and the Criminal Justice System – 2006/7: A Ministry of Justice Publication under Section 95 of the Criminal Justice Act 1991.* London: HMSO.

Mirrlees-Black, C. (2001) *Confidence in the Criminal Justice System: Findings from the 2000 British Crime Survey*, Research Findings No. 137, London: Home Office.

Modood, T., Berthoud, R., Lakey, J., Nazroo, J., Smith, P., Virdee, S. and Belshon, S. (1997) *Ethnic Minorities in Britain: Diversity and Disadvantage.* London: Policy Studies Institute.

National Probation Service and HM Prison Service (2002) *Offending Behaviour Programmes: Diversity Review Report on Cognitive Skills Programmes.* London: Home Office.

Office of Criminal Justice Reform (OCJR)(2007) *Working Together to Cut Crime and Deliver Justice: A Strategic Plan for Criminal Justice 2008–2011: An Overview.* London: HMSO.

Office of Criminal Justice Reform (OCJR) (2008) *Working Together to Cut Crime and Deliver Justice: The Criminal Justice System Business Plan 2008–09.* London: HMSO.

Office of National Statistics (2001) *Neighbourhood Statistics* http://www. neighbourhood.statistics.gov.uk/ Accessed 16 March 2009.

Office of National Statistics (2004a) *Ethnicity and Identity: Geographic Distribution* http://www.statistics.gov.uk/cci/nugget.asp?id=457. Accessed 13 February 2009.

Office of National Statistics (2004b) *Ethnicity and Identity: Age/Sex Distribution* http://www.statistics.gov.uk/cci/nugget.asp?id=456. Accessed 13 February 2009.

Office of National Statistics (2009) *Information Paper: Deciding Which Tick-Boxes to Add to the Ethnic Group Question in the 2011 England and Wales Census.* London: Office of National Statistics.

Office of the Chief Statistician (2004) *Analysis of Ethnicity in the 2001 Census: Summary Report.* Edinburgh: Scottish Executive.

Page, B., Wake, R. and Ames, A. (2004) *Public Confidence in the Criminal Justice System,* Research Findings No. 221, London: Home Office.

Pepper, S., Lovbakke, J. and Upson, A. (2004) 'Confidence and the Criminal Justice System', in S. Nicholas and A. Walker (eds), *Crime in England and Wales 2002/2003: Supplementary Volume 2: Crime, Disorder and the Criminal Justice System – Public Attitudes and Perceptions,* Home Office Statistical Bulletin 02/04, London: Home Office, Chapter 1.

Povey, D., Coleman, K., Kaiza, P. and Roe, S. (2009) *Homicides, Firearm Offences and Intimate Violence 2007/08 (Supplementary Volume 2 to Crime in England and Wales 2007/08), Third Edition.* Home Office Statistical Bulletin 02/09. London: HMSO.

Powis, B. and Walmsley, R.K. (2002) *Programmes for Black and Asian Offenders on Probation: Lessons for Developing Practice.* Home Office Research Study 250. London: Home Office.

Salisbury, H. and Upson, A. (2004) *Ethnicity, Victimisation and Worry About Crime: Findings from the 2001/02 and 2002/3 British Crime Survey.* Home Office Research Findings No. 237. London: Home Office Research Development and Statistics Directorate.

Scottish Executive (2006) *Scottish Index of Multiple Deprivation 2006: General Report.* A Scottish Executive National Statistics Publication. Edinburgh: Scottish Executive.

Scottish Executive Social Research (2006) *Provision of Support to Victims and Witnesses of Crime in Scotland.* Edinburgh: Scottish Executive Social Research.

Scottish Government (2008a) *Recorded Crime in Scotland 2007/08.* Statistical Bulletin Crime and Justice Series. Edinburgh: Scottish Government National Statistics.

Scottish Government (2008b) *Criminal Justice Social Work Statistics 2007–08.* Statistical Bulletin Crime and Justice Series. Edinburgh: Scottish Government National Statistics.

Scottish Government (2008c) *Prison Statistics Scotland 2007/08.* Statistical Bulletin Crime and Justice Series. Edinburgh: Scottish Government National Statistics.

Scottish Government (2009) *Racist Incidents Recorded by the Police in Scotland, 2004/05 to 2007/08.* Statistical Bulletin Crime and Justice Series. Edinburgh: Scottish Government.

Scottish Government and the General Register Office for Scotland (2008) *Scotland's New Official Ethnicity Classification.* Edinburgh: Scottish Government.

Scottish Government Social Research (2007) *2006 Scottish Crime and Victimisation Survey: Main Findings.* Crime and Justice. Edinburgh: Scottish Government.

Spalek, B., Lambert, R. and Baker, A.H. (2009) 'Minority Muslim Communities and Criminal Justice: Stigmatized UK Faith Identities Post 9/11 and 7/7', in S. Bhui (ed.), *Race and Criminal Justice.* London: Sage.

Times Online (2009) 'Rise in Race Crime Against Non-whites: Around Half the Victims of Race Crimes in Scotland Were of Asian Origin and 95 Percent of the Perpetrators Whites' March 31. London: The Times.

Virdee, S. (1997) 'Racial Harassment', in T. Modood, R. Berthoud, J. Lakey, J. Nazroo, P. Smith, S. Virdee and S. Belshon (eds), *Ethnic Minorities in Britain: Diversity and Disadvantage.* London: Policy Studies Institute.

Webster, C. (2007) *Understanding Race and Crime.* London: Open University Press.

Welsh Assembly Government (2008) *Welsh Index of Multiple Deprivation (WIMD) 2008: Local Authority Analysis.* Cardiff: Welsh Assembly Government.

Williams, P. (2006) 'Designing and Delivering Programmes for Minority Ethnic Offenders', in S. Lewis et al. (eds), *Race and Probation.* Cullopmton: Willan.

Yarrow, S. (2005) *The Experiences of Young Black Men as Victims of Crime.* London: Criminal Justice System Race Unit and Victims and Confidence Unit.

3
Race, Crime and Criminal Justice in France

Pamela Irving Jackson
Rhode Island College, USA

Introduction

Discussion of "race" and "visible ethnicity" in France continues to be limited by the extension of the nation's Republican ideal to the collection of official data. In the official census those who are French citizens are not differentiated in terms of race, religion or ethnicity (National Institute of Statistics and Economic Studies (INSEE)) or criminal justice statistics gathered by the Ministry of Justice, National Police or Gendarmerie (Jackson, 1995, 1997; Bleich, 2003; Laurence and Vaisse, 2006: 17). Nonetheless, appreciation of the current French criminal justice landscape requires recognition of the racial and ethnic distinctions not only among non-citizens (*étrangers*, who may be immigrants or born in France), asylum seekers and refugees, but also among French citizens. Both the non-citizen and citizen populations in France include members of the racialized Muslim ethnic groups (of Algerian, Moroccan, Tunisian and Turkish backgrounds) that are disproportionately represented at all levels of the French criminal justice system.

Étrangers (who may reside permanently in France, but are not French citizens) constitute just under 6 percent of the total French population. About 40 percent of the foreign born in France have obtained French citizenship (Migration Policy Institute (MPI), 2007). About 8 percent of the French population is foreign born (a figure roughly comparable to that for the United Kingdom (8 percent) and Germany (9 percent)). Recent efforts by the French census (INSEE) have sometimes adopted a broader definition of foreign ancestry than usually permitted in French statistics, including those with one or more immigrant parents, grandparents or great-grandparents, yielding a figure of 14 million people of foreign ancestry living in France (Tribalet, 1995; Institut National Etudes Demographiques (INED), 2006), more than one-fifth of the French population. Of these, 21 percent trace their origins to North Africa. Since the post-1978 economic restructuring and associated "disappearance" (Wilson, 1987, 1996) of factory work in France, it is this group of people – North Africans invited after the Second World War from

51

former French colonies to work in the factories in France – who are perceived as the "crime problem".

According to Olivier Roy (2006: xi), the "constant association of Islam and immigration in the mind[s] of the public and of politicians... continues to have a negative effect...". Other scholars agree. Virginie Guiraudon (2006: 145), for example, notes that "electoral debates and policy discourses call into question the legitimacy of the presence of immigrants on French soil: immigration is linked to crime and insecurity and, in the case of North Africans, their loyalty to France is questioned because of their adherence to Islam."

Minority integration in France

Étrangers of color and from a non-Christian background are often criticized for their failure to integrate fully into French society, and there are several indicators of difference between these groups and French citizens who do not have foreign ancestry. Native-born French citizens, for example, averaged 9 percent unemployment between 2003 and 2005, while the figures for foreign-born French citizens and foreigners without French citizenship were about 16 percent and 26 percent, respectively (Migration Policy Institute, 2007: 5). About 5 percent of the civilian labor force in France is made up of people who are not French; Algerians and Moroccans each make up about 12 percent of the non-French labor force (Migration Policy Institute, 2007: 5). The unemployment rate among immigrants from North Africa or Turkey is more than twice that of French citizens (Laurence and Vaisse, 2006: 34), and the fertility rate of "Maghrebian" (North African) and Turkish women in France is greater than that of native or naturalized French women (Laurence and Vaisse, 2006: 29). However, immigrant women are as likely to work as French women, and immigrants who live outside of the housing projects (known as *banlieues*) socialize with both foreigners and native French (Laurence and Vaisse, 2006: 34).

Despite these indicators of progress, however, considerable evidence points to discrimination in employment. The 2004 University of Paris French Monitoring Center on Discrimination's study, which "sent out different standard *curricula vitae* in response to 258 job advertisements for a sales person... found that a person from the Maghreb had five times less chance of getting a positive reply" (European Monitoring Center (EUMC), 2006: 45).

Minorities of Muslim religious orientation in France are especially likely to find difficulty in establishing themselves as both "Muslim and French" (Killian, 2008; Stewart, 2008; Jackson and Parkes, 2008a). In its report examining *Muslims in the European Union: Discrimination and Islamophobia*, for example, the European Monitoring Center on Racism and Xenophobia (EUMC, 2006: 48) reports that in France, "institutionalized responses to religious and cultural diversity are rare, reflecting the secular republican tradition." Official regulations in 2005 "defined the limits of expression of religious identity in the workplace, especially in public services..." Foreigners' "cultural or religious rights" are not explicitly provided for in the diversity charters signed by the major trades unions (EUMC, 2006: 49). Research by Point and Singh (2005), indicating that diversity initiatives put forward by companies in France do not address religion, is also cited by the EUMC (2006: 49).

Discrimination, social background, language, residential segregation, religious and cultural differences are among the "other factors" mentioned later in the report as alternative explanations for the noted "differences in the educational attainment of various ethnic groups" (EUMC, 2006: 51, 52). An examination of ethnic segregation in schools in France, for example, found that "40 per cent of pupils with migrant descent concentrate in 10 per cent of middle schools"; another study cited by the EUMC (2006: 52), examining Priority Education Zones in France, indicated "that parents often try to avoid these schools." The resulting concentration of minority youth in a small number of schools impedes the erosion of social barriers between the children of immigrant origin and native French. Further exacerbating the barriers between minority and majority youth is the fact that, "[i]ndependent Muslim schools...are increasingly being established in a number of EU states, including...France, Netherlands...and the UK" (EUMC, 2006: 54).

A census report on France (INSEE, 2005) is referenced by EUMC (2006: 57) as highlighting the problems of "overpopulated households" and circumscribed residential mobility for "migrant households, particularly from the Maghreb". The *National Observatory of Sensitive Areas* (*Observatoire national des zones urbaines sensibles*, 2003, 2004, noted in EUMC, 2006: 57) found "twice as many foreign households... resident in such areas, while 51.5 percent of foreign households occupied social housing in comparison to 31.7 percent of French households." The French Council for Integration (*Haut Conseil à l'Integration*, 2005) is cited as having acknowledged the "precarious conditions" of many "retired migrant workers," including their significantly lower life expectancy (EUMC, 2006: 57).

Conditions in the highly segregated housing projects, or *banlieues*, on the outskirts of Paris provided an incendiary foundation for the 2005 riots. These housing projects were established near the factories of the industrial era, but now lack both employment opportunities and direct transportation links to major cities. The segregated, high unemployment minority communities that have developed in the *banlieues* are characterized by high rates of both crime and victimization. The development of *educational priority zones*, *community policing priority zones* (Zauberman and Levy, 2003), and use of the term *sensitive urban zones*, all underscore institutional recognition of specific problems of inclusion to be addressed in minority communities, even though current official policy does not provide for these communities to be singled out demographically for statistical analysis based on race and ethnicity.

Geographic distribution of racialized groups

Étrangers are unevenly distributed throughout the administrative districts in France. There are 22 designated *régions* in what is officially referred to as "Metropolitan France" (the French mainland and Corsica). Each *région* is divided into a number of smaller administrative units termed *départements* – there are a total of 95 of these units. The *Haut Conseil à l'Integration* (High Council on Integration), in its 2001 report, *L'Islam dans la Republique*, noted that four in ten *étrangers* reside in one *région*, the Île-de-France (which includes the Paris *département*, along with seven others). In fact, just three administrative *régions* are home to 60 percent of the nation's *étrangers*. In addition to Île-de-France (in which 39.9 percent of *étrangers* live in eight *départements*), these include Rhône-Alpes (where 11.2 percent of French *étrangers* live in eight *départements*) and Provence-Alpes-Côte d'Azur (PAC) (where 8.7 percent of French *étrangers* are located in six *départements*). Each of the other *régions* of France (Metropole) contains less than 5 percent of the *étranger* population. The size and "visibility" of the "minority" population in the 22 *départements* included within Île-de-France, Rhône-Alpes and PAC are likely to have stimulated both public attention and institutionally sponsored programmatic efforts to improve their situation (Jackson and Carroll, 1981; Jackson, 1989, 1995, 1997). Table 3.1 provides data on these *départements* to illustrate the links among race, crime and criminal justice. These data are utilized below as indicative of factors shaping French perceptions of minority offending.

Minority offending: Perceptions and reality

French police statistics show that in 2007 just under half (46 percent) of *étranger* criminal suspects came to the attention of authorities for having violated the rules governing foreigners. These are minor offenses (*délits*, typically judged by a correctional tribunal, as opposed to *crimes*, which are major offenses requiring a jury trial), and this percentage was 4 percent higher than the figure for 2006 (42 percent). The *délits*, or minor offenses, typically recorded for *étrangers*, include violation of their conditions of entry and residence, and assisting foreigners to illegally enter, travel or stay in the country. *Étrangers*, as expected, constitute over 97 percent of suspects in the category of *délits à la police des étrangers* (Direction Centrale de la Police Judiciaire, 2007: 61).

While *étrangers* (who make up about 6 percent of the French population) comprised about 21 percent of criminal suspects in 2007, very few of their offenses involved crimes against persons. *Étrangers* were about 13 percent

Table 3.1 Departments in the three regions containing 60 percent of *Étrangers* in France: official nationally comparative levels of *Étranger* suspects and minor suspects

Region Department	Percent national *Étranger* population in the region*	Level *Étranger* suspects**	Level minors suspects***
Île-de-France	40		
Paris		1	2
Seine-et-Marne		4	4
Yvelines		3	4
Essonne		4	4
Haute-de-Seine		3	3
Seine-Saint-Denis		4	4
Val-de-Marne		4	3
Val-d'Oise		4	3
Rhône-Alpes	11		
Ain		3	3
Ardeche		1	3
Drome		2	4
Isere		2	3
Loire		2	4
Rhone		4	3
Savoie		4	3
Haute-Savoie		4	3
Provence-Alpes-Côte d'Azur	9		
Alpes-de-Hautes Provence		3	4
Hautes-Alpes		1	3
Alpes-Maritimes		4	2
Bouches-du-Rhone		4	3
Var		2	3
Vaucluse		3	3

Haut Conseil à l'Integration (2001), pp. 169–70.
**Direction Centrale de la Police Judiciaire (2007), p. 59.
**(1 =< 10%; 2 = 10–15%; 3 = 15–20%; 4 => 20%).
***Direction Centrale de la Police Judiciaire (2007), p. 54.
***(1 =< 15%; 2 = 15–18%; 3 = 18–20%; 4 => 20%).

of those arrested for minor or major personal crimes (Direction Centrale de la Police Judiciaire, 2007: 59). Their involvement in crime varies considerably by offense category. For example, only 10 percent of those suspected of street crime are *étrangers*. By contrast, of those picked up for white-collar offenses, including fraudulent checking, about 17 percent were *étrangers*, as were about 30 percent of those suspected of "other infractions". This last category includes drug infractions (for which *étrangers* make up under just 8 percent of suspects) and those minor offenses involving the policing of *étrangers* (for which *étrangers* constitute over 97 percent of suspects) discussed above.

Young people (minors) are seen as a major source of the crime problem in those *départements* that contain the highest proportions of minorities (*étrangers*). While the percentage of minors among the criminal suspects (those *mis en cause*) for minor and major offenses in these 22 *départements* ranges between 11 and 23 percent, the statistical average is 18 percent, which is also the overall average for the nation as a whole. The official statistical publication providing crime data for the administrative units of France (Direction Centrale de la Police Judiciaire, 2007: 54) categorizes *départements* along a four-point comparative scale according to the percentage of suspects (for *crimes* or *délits*) who are minors. This comparative "ranking" is provided in Table 3.1. Of the 22 *départements* in the three *régions* that contain 60 percent of the nation's *étranger* population, 13 have suspect populations that are 18–20 percent minors, and in seven *départements* the suspect populations are over 20 percent minors. The remaining two *départements* fall within the 15–18 percent range for minors in the suspect population.

A similar categorization is provided for the proportion of *étrangers* among criminal suspects in the departments (Direction Centrale de la Police Judiciaire, 2007: 59). Table 3.1 indicates that 10 of the 22 *départements* in the three regions that contain 60 percent of the *étranger* population in France have suspect populations that are more than 20 percent *étranger*; in five of the *départements*, the suspect population is 15–20 percent *étranger*. Four of these *départements* have suspect populations that are 10–15 percent *étranger*, or non-citizens, the only designation of "minority" available in official statistics in France. In three of the *départements*, the suspect population is less than 10 percent *étranger*.

In both cases – with regard to minority and youth representation among criminal suspects – the proportion of those *mis en cause* (suspects) in these *départements* would be expected to reflect the disproportionate distribution of *étrangers* among the *régions* of France. Nonetheless, the confluence of high minority and youth criminal involvement and minority visibility in these *départements* has criminalized the image of minority youth.

In Clichy-sous-Bois, a commune about ten miles east of Paris, in the department of Seine-Saint-Denis, approximately 50 percent of the population are under 25 years of age. In October 2005, it was the location of riots that later spread to other major urban locations in France. While almost two-thirds (64 percent) of Clichy-sous-Bois residents were born in "Metropolitan" France, 28 percent were born outside the EU-15. The juxtaposition of youth, rioting and a visible non-European immigrant population has promoted the view that immigrant youth are to blame for the levels of crime and unrest in France (see, for example, Bohlen, 2007).

A research study of the Grenoble *département* – conducted by Sebastian Roche and Monique Dagnaud – was reported by Nathalie Guilbert in the

French newspaper, *Le Monde* (April 16, 2004). Guilbert's newspaper report (cited in Laurence and Vaisse, 2006: 42) indicated that "two-thirds of juvenile delinquents are of foreign origin." Laurence and Vaisse (2006: 42) summarize the results of this study as indicating that:

> integration problems are partly to blame for elevated crime rates but also that crimes involving young Muslims are prosecuted more vigorously than those of their peers, which leads to a slight distortion of the available statistics. The study's authors concluded that 'we are faced with a justice system that concentrates its energies on youth of foreign origin'.

President Sarkozy named two ministers of North African heritage to help initiate public policy efforts directed at suburbs such as Seine-Saint-Denis, where problems of minority exclusion are unofficially recognized. The position of Secretary of State for Urban Affairs went to Fadela Amara, of Algerian parentage; the Minister of Justice position was filled by Rachida Dati, whose parents immigrated from Algeria; and the office of Secretary of State for Human Rights was assumed by the Senegalese-born Rama Yade. However, improvements in both the objective conditions of minorities and in minority identification with the state have been slow to emerge.

Anti-minority sentiment

The widespread belief that immigrants are an illegitimate presence on French soil and that there are clear links between crime, Islam, immigration and terrorism cannot be ignored in any examination of public policy implementation and electoral politics in France (Roy, 2006: xi; Guiraudon, 2006: 145). Feldblum's (1999: 31) analysis of the politicization of "citizenship in French immigration politics" from 1983 to 1998 underscores the catalyzing effect of French immigrant Muslims' religio-ethnic identity. The 1989 "headscarf affair" raised the question of whether " 'Franco-Maghrebis' were a critical challenge to the 'French model' of immigrant integration" (Feldblum, 1999: 130). Hollifield (1999: 67) cites a " 'crisis of control' and national identity" that led French political discussion to move from President Mitterrand's 1991 declaration of the importance of a "threshold of tolerance" for immigrants to Interior Minister Charles Pasqua's 1993 goal of "zero immigration" (Hollifield, 1999: 74). The redefinition of the French principle of *laïcité*, or secularism, as a "boundary between culture and religion" (Kastoryano, 2006: 61), has been central to this crisis.

In this restrictive political environment, several new policies have led to increased police scrutiny of those who are – or appear to be – foreigners in France. For example, Brice Hortefeux, who was appointed French Minister of Immigration, Integration, National Identity and Codevelopment in 2007, introduced a plan to "tackle illegal immigration" (Prime Minister's electronic *Portal Du Gouvernement* (Portal), accessed November 21, 2008) and "ferret out networks of illegal migrant workers." According to a statement on the French Prime Minister's electronic Portal (2008), the number of people expelled at the borders increased by 140 percent between 2002 and 2006. Brice Hortefeux was quoted in *Le Figaro* (May 6, 2007, noted on Prime Minister electronic Portal, 2008) as "aiming for 25,000 expulsions" in 2007. He also underscored the "need to tackle abuse of political asylum" (Prime Minister's electronic Portal, 2008). On January 15, 2009, President Sarkozy replaced Minister Hortefeux with the former Socialist Eric Besson. (Hortefeux assumed the position of Minister of Social Affairs.) *The New York Times* (January 16, 2009: A7) reported that Minister Hortefeux "whose hardline behavior toward immigrants has been strongly criticized by the left, ended 19 months at the head of the Immigration Ministry by saying that nearly 30,000 illegal migrants were expelled last year, a 29 percent increase from 2007 and more than the 26,000 that Mr. Sarkozy had requested."

A reception and integration contract, implemented in 2006 for individuals, and proposed for family members seeking to immigrate to France, was highlighted on the Prime Minister's Portal Web site just months before Hortefeux was replaced by Besson at the Ministry of Immigration, Integration, National Identity and Codevelopment. Such integration contracts have been adopted by other Western European states, including Germany and the Netherlands. Joppke (2007: 5) examines the new civic integration policies, which increasingly require that some level of knowledge of the host country's language and culture be demonstrated before immigration from non-Western, less developed nations. He argues that the policies are a "tool of migration control, helping states to restrict especially the entry of unskilled and non-adaptable family migrants." Guiraudon (2006: 146) also discusses the political implications of integration contracts, citing the view (advanced by Professor Blandine Kriegel, head of the 2002 French High Council on Integration) that integration contracts broke with "the logic of [societal] guilt and discrimination," placing the obligation to integrate on the shoulders of immigrants. Integration contracts for migrants can also be seen as a form of cultural securitization (Huysmans, 2000) through which immigrants are screened or educated to prevent threats to the cultural traditions of the host nation.

Immigration securitization and minority incarceration

Examination of the data in Table 3.2 for adult suspects (those *mis en cause*) demonstrates the link between the securitization of immigration policy and incarceration. The number of *étranger* suspects (*mis en cause*) per 1,000 *étrangers* increased from 28 to 79 between 1990 and 2007. Scrutiny of immigrants (*étrangers*) was clearly much greater in the 21st century than in the last three decades of the 20th century – during which the rate remained

Table 3.2 France: percentage *étranger*, *étranger* suspects per thousand *étranger* population, percentage incarcerated who were *étrangers*, 1970–2007

Year	Percentage *étranger*[*]	*Étranger* suspects per 1000 *étrangers*[**]	Percentage incarcerated who were *étrangers*[***]
2007	6	79	19
2005	6	80	20
1990	8	28	30
1980	7	24	20
1970	5	20	15

All figures rounded.

Sources: *INSEE; Jackson (1995: 352); *Direction Generale de la Police Nationale* (1990: 125).
**Direction Centrale de la Police Judiciaire (2007, 2005).
 Jackson (1995: 352); Tournier and Robert (1991: 67–8).
***Kensey and Tournier (1997); Kensey (2000); World Prison Brief (2007).
 Council of Europe Annual Penal Statistics, SPACE (2006).
 Jackson (1995: 352); Tournier and Robert (1991: 103).

at less than half of its 2007 level. Data provided by the French Ministry of Justice (Kensey, 2000; Jackson, 1995, 1997; World Prison Brief, 2007; Jackson and Parkes, 2008b), demonstrate a continuing decline in the proportion of French prisoners who are "foreigners," from a high of 31 percent in the early 1990s, to the 2007 figure of 19.2 percent (Jackson and Parkes, 2008b). This decline may be explained in part by the more aggressive efforts to expel *étrangers* at the border, as well as by the greater numbers of French minorities who have now become naturalized.

But the decline in *étrangers* among the prison population does not reflect a decline in the racialization of the prison population. In his examination of the French prison population of 60,775 inmates, Farhad Khosrokhavar (2004), professor of sociology at Ecole des Hautes Etudes en Sciences Sociales, estimated that 70 percent were French Muslims. Since prison populations, like crime rates, are not reported by ethnic or religious groups (only by nationality of non-citizens, *étrangers*), Khosrokhavar was forced to estimate on the basis of the prisoner's father's place of birth, attendance at Friday prayers and requests for meals without pork (where the prisoner did not identify as Jewish). Muslims comprise only 8.5 percent of the 18–24-year-old age group in France, but 39.9 percent of the prisoners in this age group. Similarly, 75 percent of 18–24-year-olds in France have a French father, whereas only 38.8 percent of prisoners within that age range have a French father. Similarly, there are nine times as many prisoners with a North African father as with a French father in the 18–29-year-old age group, and six times as many in the 30–39-year-old age group (Khosrokhavar, 2004: 280 cited in Laurence and Vaisse, 2006: 41).

Table 3.3   Policing of *étrangers* in France: comparative increase in incidents over 1990

Year	Entry and stay infractions	Total foreigner ('*Papers*') regulation infractions
2007	338	301
2006	295	266
2005	223	207
2004	185	174
2003	168	161
2002	166	155
2001	133	128
2000	127	124
1999	127	125
1998	113	113
1997	118	127
1996	110	127
1995	120	144
1990	100*	100**

All figures rounded.

*1990 (Base) Figure, 30,681 *"Infractions conditions generales entrée et soujour."*
  Etrangers responsible for 99% of the total.
**1990 (Base) Figure, 37,113 Infractions concerning policing of *etrangers*.
  Etrangers responsible for 98% of the total.
Source: Direction Centrale de la Police Judiciaire (2004: 16, 2005: 39, 2006: 63, 2007: 61).

Despite the fact that the French prison population per capita (99 prisoners per 100,000 population in France) is much lower than that found in either the USA (700 per 100,000 population) or Great Britain (135 per 100,000), the situation in French prisons has been termed "explosive" (Guilbert, 2003 cited in Laurence and Vaisse, 2006: 279).

Given the data in Table 3.3, and the effort to increase expulsions at the border indicated on the French Prime Minister's Portal, police scrutiny of visible minorities is the likely reason for the increase in the rate of *étranger* suspects – from 28 per thousand in 1990 to 79 per thousand by 2007, even while the proportion incarcerated who were *étrangers* decreased from 30 percent in 1990 to 19 percent in 2007 (as indicated above in Table 3.2). Table 3.3 allows for the examination of the infractions regarding entry and stay (for which *étrangers* were responsible for 99 percent of the total in 1990), and for examination of the broader category of infractions involving the policing of foreigners (for which *étrangers* were responsible for 98 percent of the total in 1990). These data were obtained from the Direction Centrale de la Police Judiciaire (2004, 2005, 2006, 2007), which provided (in its 2004 volume) a numerical comparison, using 1990 as a base. This comparative system indicates, for example, that for each 100 incidents of entry and stay violations in 1990, there were 185 in 2004. (This system can be updated with later volumes using the data provided on entry and stay and foreigner regulation infractions.)

By 2007, the number of entry and stay infractions for each 100 in 1990 was 338. Examination of foreigner regulation infractions overall provides similar findings. For each 100 infractions in 1990, there were 174 in 2004 (calculation provided in Direction Centrale de la Police Judiciaire, 2004: 16), and by 2007 the number of foreigner regulation infractions was 301 for every 100 infractions in 1990,meaning that for each set of infractions, three times as many offenses were recorded in 2007 as in 1990, and more than twice as many by 2005. The increase cannot be explained by the growth in the proportion of *étrangers* in France, as this group fell from approximately 8 percent of the French population in 1990 to about 6 percent in 2007.

Criminalization of immigrants extends to minorities

In 2004, France had the highest level of asylum applications (50,547) of any EU nation (Eurostat, 2006–2007: 78–9). It also had a higher rate of rejection of these applications (91 percent) than some of its European neighbors, including Germany (where the rejection rate was 62 percent in 2004) and the United Kingdom (with a 2004 asylum application rejection rate of 83 percent) (Eurostat, 2006–2007: 79).

Widely regarded as undeserving, bogus and dangerous, asylum seekers in France who resist the order of deportation are sentenced to detention in one of 23 *centres de retention administrative* (CRA), or in *locaux de retention administrative* (LRA). Ninety-five percent are held at the centers at Roissy Charles de Gaulle airport, "where 96–98 per cent of asylum claims are lodged" (Welch and Schuster, 2005: 340). Welch and Schuster (2005: 340) note that in two reports, the *Association Nationale d'Assistance aux Frontières pour les Étrangers* (ANAFE, 2003a, 2003b) provides documentation of "hundreds of acts of violence perpetrated by the border police against asylum seekers in the centres, particularly at . . . de Gaulle airport," and explicit refusals to allow asylum seekers to register their claims, obtain information about their rights or disembark when they arrive. The work of NGOs seeking to assist asylum seekers is deliberately hampered; and those asylum seekers who do not speak French receive the worst treatment.

The French law on Immigration and Integration passed on July 24, 2006, known as Sarkozy Law II, is seen as an "effort to open France to high-skilled immigration, stem illegal immigration, restrict family migration, and promote integration into French society" (MPI, 2007: 6). The law provided for the establishment of a list of economic sectors in which foreign labor would be beneficial ended automatic amnesty to unauthorized immigrants with 10 years of residence in France (and set up a system requiring each

request to be heard individually). The law also tightened family reunification requirements, and required immigrants seeking a residency permit to
sign a Welcome and Integration Contract (*Contrat d'accueil et d'integration*
(CAI)) agreeing to "respect and uphold the laws and values of France and to
take civic and, if deemed necessary by the government, language courses"
(MPI, 2007: 6).

The provisions of Sarkozy Law II both reflect and project a negative view of
immigrants as illegitimate, unnecessary and unreceptive to French culture.
Wacquant (1999: 216) argues that these supposed attributes of foreigners
have been extended to the "quasi-foreigners" in France and other Western
European states:

> so-called 'second-generation' immigrants – who precisely are not
> immigrants – of non-Western extraction and persons of color, who are
> known to figure among the most vulnerable categories both on the
> labor market and vis-à-vis the public assistance sector of the state, owing
> to their lower class distribution and to the multiple discriminations
> they suffer, who are massively over-represented within the imprisoned
> population....

Wacquant (1999: 217) explains that the percentage of foreigners (*étrangers*)
in French prisons:

> does not take account of the pronounced 'carceral over-consumption' of
> nationals perceived and treated as foreigners by the police and judicial
> apparatus, such as the youth born to North African immigrants or come
> from France's predominantly black overseas dominions and territories.
> This is tantamount to saying that the cells of France have grown distinctly
> 'colored' these past years since two-thirds of the 15,000-odd foreign pris-
> oners officially recorded in 1995 originated from North Africa (53 percent)
> and Sub-Saharan Africa (16 percent).

According to Tournier (1996, cited in Wacquant, 1999: 218), France has
made a "deliberate choice to repress illegal immigration by means of imprisonment." Rather than reflecting the delinquency of foreigners, Wacquant
(1999: 218) notes, "the growing share of foreigners in the prison population
of France is due exclusively to the tripling in 20 years of incarcerations for
violations of immigration statutes."

Jackson and Parkes' (2008b: 47) comparison of the incarceration of immigrants in France, Germany and Britain in the period 1970–2003 noted the
high point of *étranger* incarceration in France to be 1993, with 31.4 percent foreigners among the total French prison population, compared with
the 1973 figure of 14 percent. This increase occurred despite the fact that
the percentage of "legally resident foreigners" in the French population

remained in the range of 5–8 percent. *Étrangers* were incarcerated during this period of increase largely for *délits* (less serious offenses), especially for immigration and drug violations (Jackson, 1997). Kensey and Tournier (1997) have demonstrated that in the 1991 restrictionist immigration period in France, prison sentences were at least twice as likely to be given to foreigners as to French nationals for offenses involving drug possession, the use of illegal drugs and the handling of stolen goods (Jackson and Parkes, 2008b: 48).

As attention turned to the limitations on entry and to the removal of foreigners from France, and as those of foreign background attained citizenship in greater numbers, the proportion of foreigners in the French prison population has declined noticeably in the 21st century, but, as is indicated by recent examination (cf. Khosrokhavar, 2004; Beckford, Joly and Khosrokhavar, 2005) of the French prison population, "quasi-foreigners" – that is those of North African ancestry and Muslim religious orientation – predominate.

Victimization of Muslims: Islamophobia and racist violence

The 2005 French RAXEN report, 'National Analytical Study on Racist Violence and Crime', states in its executive summary (RAXEN Focal Point for France, 2005: 3) that:

> [i]t seems that forms of 'religious' violence in the public sphere will now be taken into account. 'Islamophobia' and anti-Semitism are seen as antagonistic, but some intellectuals, such as the philosopher Etienne Balibar, observe that they derive from convergent social and cultural factors, and that they may both illustrate a rejection of the Oriental, now the 'Other' *par excellence* in France.
>
> (Balibar, 2002, cited in RAXEN Focal Point for France, 2005: 3)

The RAXEN report discusses Alain Finkielkraut's (2003) analysis of a new "judeophobia" and anti-Semitism "originating from frustrated Arab Muslim youth living in suburban housing projects who seize the Palestinian cause to nourish a discontent with their own social and economic disenfranchisement in French society" (RAXEN Focal Point for France, 2005: 27). The report reviews the problems of minority youth with the police and the establishment of the 'National Council of French Muslims (CFCM),' which began operation in 2003, and plans toward development of the 'Immigration Memorial and Resource Center' (RAXEN Focal Point for France, 2005: 35), which opened in 2007. By and large, however, the 2005 National Focal Point report on France presents a picture of Muslims as a group to be controlled in France, rather than a group to be protected. Their impact on the growth of anti-Semitism in France is considered in the report at greater length than are the development and impact of "Islamophobia."

The EUMC (2006: 60) "bases its approach to identifying the phenomenon of Islamophobia and its manifestations on internationally agreed standards on racism and the ongoing work of the Council of Europe and United Nations." The EUMC cites the definition of racism put forward by the European Commission on Racism and Intolerance (ECRI) (General Policy Recommendation number 7): "the belief that a ground such as race... colour, language, religion, nationality or national or ethnic origin justifies contempt for a person or a group of persons, or the notion of superiority of a person or a group of persons" (EUMC, 2006: 60, fn. 137). The ECRI General Policy Recommendation number 5 "recognizes that Muslim communities are subject to prejudice" (EUMC, 2006: 60), and the EUMC (2006: 61) uses the term "Islamophobia" (despite recognition of the criticism it incurs) in reference to racism and racial discrimination toward Muslims and prejudice toward Islam.

The EUMC (2006: 60–90) reviews the official (criminal justice) data and other data (e.g. from surveys, NGO reports, research and media reports) relevant to the examination of the victimization of Muslims in France. The general inadequacy of available data for the 2006 EUMC report and a previous related EUMC (2005b) report, 'Racist Violence in 15 EU Member States', is first recognized by the EUMC (2006: 63).

The *Système de Traitement des Infractions Constatées* (STIC) (cf. Cotteret and Giquel, 2009) police database in France contains official complaints of racist violence and crime. Though it has been in development (and the subject of controversy) for some time, it was not yet fully operational at the time of the EUMC (2006: 73) report. Complaints reported to STIC are eventually published in the annual report of the *Commission Nationale Consultative des Droits de l'Homme* (CNCDH). For 2005, 266 threats and 64 violent acts against "North African or Muslim people/targets" were reported (EUMC, 2006: 73). A list of some of the incidents reported in 2004 is provided by EUMC (2006: 74). These include mosque and Muslim tomb desecrations, as well as aggression toward an imam and attempted murder of an imam.

The report, 'Policing Racist Crime and Violence', prepared on behalf of the EUMC, describes the purpose in France of gathering statistical data on racism. The report (EUMC, 2005a: 15) notes that from its inception in 1978 "by the Central Board of the security branch of the French police force of the Ministry of the Interior... [s]uch collection aims at giving the government information on racist phenomena, and also on their evolutions, in order to prevent social unrest." Data gathered from the regional police offices of the Ministry of the Interior throughout France include a broad range of incidents, "from attacks (which can kill people) to racist graffiti." These incidents are categorized either as "actions" involving serious crimes against the person or resulting in other serious consequences, or "'threats' (*'voies de fait et menaces'*)", which may be as minimal as insults. Legislation in 2003 and 2004 provided for more severe sentencing for racist offenses, but EUMC (2005a: 17) indicates that police in France at that time did not yet have complete instructions as to how to categorize a crime as racially motivated.

The recording of "ethnicity" is illegal in France, and while a victim's nationality may be recorded, there is not an effective system in place to require this to be done (EUMC, 2005a: 20). The EUMC (2005a: 22) identified police as "gatekeepers" in determining "whether criminal incidents will be subsequently recorded and then investigated as racially-motivated. Whether and how effectively this is done will determine whether the element of racial motivation can be presented in court as an 'aggravating factor' for the purposes of sentencing." France is categorized in the EUMC (2005a: 26–7) report as having "partial recognition" of the need for police training "to help them deal with racist crime and violence," including the problem of "repeat victimization" and the issue of racism in society and within the police force. The failure by the Higher Police Academy to provide training on the subject of racism was specifically noted by the EUMC, on the basis of observations by the National Focal Point (NFP) for France.

While specialist in-service training dealing with racist crime and violence was not identified in France, such a program had "been ordered" following an increase in racist incidents (EUMC, 2005a: 28). According to the EUMC (2005a: 33), "it was stated that racism in the police is considered too sensitive an issue to be dealt with directly in the police academies and training centres." The French National Focal Point (NFP-France) had provided information to EUMC (2005a: 35) about police engagement with "civil society when responding to racism, crime and violence", minority group reporting of such incidents, related police work with minority NGOs and communities, public availability of information on such initiatives and on the satisfaction of victims of racist crime and violence. Subsequently, the EUMC (2005a: 36) indicates that the NFP-France report:

> stated that no attempt is made by the police to encourage the representatives of associations of vulnerable social groups to increase the number of complaints filed. This is because of the French republican principle prohibiting public services from granting special treatment to certain users in view of their origins, cultural group, religious beliefs or nationality.

Further underscoring the complications of protecting and assisting targets of racist violence in light of the French national policy that it is unconstitutional to recognize minority groups within the citizenry of the state, EUMC (2005a: 40) described efforts by French police to work with (primarily) Jewish anti-discrimination NGOs as follows.

In France, the police and gendarmes work regularly and in a variety of ways with a large number of anti-racism or human rights NGOs with local branches or representation, particularly the CRIF (...Council of Jewish Institutions in France) in the case of anti-Semitism. However this form of cooperation depends on the legal skills of the NGOs and not the fact that they may be representative of populations particularly exposed to racist violence, especially foreigners or persons of foreign extraction. The police do not therefore recognize these associations as being representative of vulnerable groups but as partners that assist them with their mission and who are specialized in the catering for and follow-up of victims of racist crimes or acts.

In singling out an NGO focused on preventing and assisting the victims of anti-Semitism, and in publicly clarifying that police worked with this NGO because of its legal skills, rather than its representation of a group more likely to be victimized by racist violence and crime, EUMC (on the basis of the NFP-France report to it) has provided an illustration that highlights the discomfort in France in focusing on the problems and concerns of specific racial or cultural groups. The history of the Holocaust has engendered widespread agreement that anti-Semitic incidents must be prevented, in contrast to the less well-shared recognition that those of color or of Muslim background deserve similar protection by police. Yet even the efforts to protect those of a Jewish religious background from anti-Semitic violence and related offenses cannot be discussed in France as a specific focus of police work even when Jewish social service groups are involved, because of the French Republican principle requiring that institutions of the state be blind to minority groups.

Conclusion: Impact of the culture of control on minorities in France

Both French cultural and constitutional traditions and current public policy initiatives figure prominently in the "visibility" of racial and ethnic groups in France. The "asylum issue" combines "concerns about economic migrants, illegal immigrants and the spectre of terrorist activities" (Malloch and Stanley, 2005: 53) throughout Western Europe. Public attitudes toward minorities in France and perceptions of their criminality reflect a widely shared view that they are "foreign" to French society, and represent both a cultural and hard-security threat. A negative and threatening image of visibly non-Christian minorities is reflected in several characteristics of the French structural and immigrant policy situation. These include the strict interpretation of *laïcité*; the imposition of more restrictive criteria for regularization of immigrants' status with the Immigration and Integration Law of July 24, 2006; limitations on family reunification; the "Welcome and

Integration Contract" (CAI) implemented in 2007; pronouncements on the Prime Minister's electronic Portal indicating the 140 percent increase in entrants expelled at the borders between 2002 and 2006 and specifying a numerical goal for expulsions (25,000 in 2007); and the high rate of asylum application rejections in France (91 percent).

By and large, the minorities who can be examined in French crime statistics, *étrangers* (non-citizens), are involved in less serious non-violent offenses. Nonetheless, as French police stepped up their scrutiny of visible minorities in their effort to "ferret out networks of illegal migrant workers" and "abuse of political asylum" (Prime Minister's electronic Portal, 2008), the increase in recorded infractions for immigration violations served to "criminalize" the identity of visible minorities. Their concentration in three administrative *régions* of France (Île de France, Rhône-Alpes and Provence-Alpes-Côtes d'Azur) makes their involvement in crime appear threatening, even where these crimes are primarily immigration violations and misdemeanors. The involvement of youths indicted for such violations in departments with large minority populations exacerbates the perception problem, suggesting the presence of a new generation of troublemakers who do not fit into the French mainstream and who refuse to respect its laws. The "color" (Wacquant, 1999: 217) and religious orientation (Khosrokhavar, 2004; Laurence and Vaisse, 2006) of the French prison population reflect what Wacquant (1999: 218) describes as a "confinement of differentiation or segregation, aiming to keep a group separate and to facilitate its subtraction from the societal body...".

The crisis of xenophobia created by the high unemployment rates among French minorities and the problem of integrating Muslims into secular France have shaped efforts to prevent threats to the nation's security and culture. The resulting securitization of French (and European) immigration policies has disrupted the already difficult process of religious minorities' integration into French society (and those of other European states). It is difficult to be precise about the nature of these disruptions because the French tradition of *laïcité* has been interpreted as preventing the designation and collection of data on minorities among the citizens of France. This approach is not exclusive to France. Jocelyne Cesari (2004: 44) describes the "ideological function" of secularization in Europe, noting that it "manifests itself as an element of European identity in a variety of political and cultural narratives." From this vantage point, she explains, "Islam is perceived as a potential threat to this cultural norm...". Understanding of policies and data relating to race, crime and criminal justice in France must be based on recognition of the contradictions imposed by strict ideological secularism in a religiously diverse society with historically Christian roots. Indirect data indicate that policies implementing the securitization of immigration target minorities through the social, cultural and political forces described by Garland (2001) as a culture of control. Official data collection practices, however, prevent precise analysis of the impact of these policies on specific groups of French minorities.

The parameters of the French situation are not immutable. The European Monitoring Center on Racism and Xenophobia, for example, has clarified the limits of legislative and constitutional barriers to the collection of data on ethnicity and religion. The EUMC (2006: 25) notes that the use of data on ethnicity and religion where the subject cannot be identified is permitted by Directive 95/46/EC of the European Parliament and Council (On the Protection of Individuals with Regard to the Processing of Personal Data or the Free Movement of Such Data). The EUMC (2006: 25) explains that "a wealth of information" could be obtained about the "social situation of Muslim communities" without identifying the individual. The European Parliament Committee on Benchmarking Integration (European Parliament Committee on Civil Liberties, Justice and Home Affairs, 2007: 197, 101) similarly notes the importance of such data. At present, however, widespread public concern over "the asylum question" and terrorism presents a political climate with little support for the development of data permitting direct examination of the situation of racial and religious minorities in France.

Acknowledgements

Dr Jackson would like to thank the Fulbright Program and the Rhode Island College Faculty Research and Development Funds for their support of this project. This chapter reflects the author's views, not necessarily those of her institution. A paper derived from this chapter was presented at the 2009 annual meetings of the American Sociological Association.

References

ANAFE (2003a) (*Association Nationale d'Assistance aux Frontières pour les Etrangers*), *Violences policieres en zone d'attente*, Paris: ANAFE.

ANAFE (2003b), *Zone d'attente: 10 ans après, les difficultes persistent*, Paris: ANAFE.

Balibar, E. (2002) 'Transformations de l'antisemitisme', *Liberation*, July 9.

Beckford, J. A., Joly, D. and Khosrokhavar, F. (2005), *Muslims in Prison*, New York: Palgrave Macmillan.

Bleich, E. (2003), *Race Politics in Britain and France*, Cambridge: Cambridge University Press.

Bohlen, C. (2007), 'Letter from Europe: In Suburbs Near Paris, Simmering Frustration', *International Herald Tribune*, 25 September.

Cesari, J. (2004), *When Islam and Democracy Meet: Muslims in Europe and in the United States*, New York: Palgrave Macmillan. *Commission Nationale Consultative des Droits de l'Homme* (CNCDH) (2005), Annual Report, http://www.cncdh.fr/rubrique.php3?id_rubrique=27.

Cotteret, J. M. and F. Giquel (2009), *Conclusions du Controle du Systeme de Traitment des Infractions Constatees (STIC): Commission nationale de l'informatique et des libertes*. Paris.

Council of Europe Annual Penal Statistics, SPACE (2006) (accessed 11/5/09), http://www.coe.int/t/e/legal_affairs/legal_co-operation/prisons_and_alternatives/statistics_space_i/pc-cp%20(2007)%2009%20rev3%20-%20e%20(SPACE%202006)%2023-01-08.pdf.

Direction Centrale de la Police Judiciaire (2004), *Criminalité et Delinquance Constatées en France. Tome 1. Données Générales. Nationales, Régionales, Départementales*, Paris, France: La Documentation Francaise.

Direction Centrale de la Police Judiciaire (2005), *Criminalité et Delinquance Constatées en France. Tome 1. Données Générales. Nationales, Régionales, Départementales*, Paris, France: La Documentation Francaise.

Direction Centrale de la Police Judiciaire (2006), *Criminalité et Delinquance Constatées en France. Tome 1. Données Générales. Nationales, Régionales, Départementales*, Paris, France: La Documentation Francaise.

Direction Centrale de la Police Judiciaire (2007), *Criminalité et Delinquance Constatées en France. Tome 1. Données Générales. Nationales, Régionales, Départementales*, Paris, France: La Documentation Francaise.

European Monitoring Centre on Racism and Xenophobia (EUMC) (2005a), *Policing Racist Crime and Violence: A Comparative Analysis*, Vienna: European Union Agency for Fundamental Rights (successor to the European Monitoring Center for Racism and Xenophobia).

European Monitoring Centre on Racism and Xenophobia (EUMC) (2005b), *Racist Violence in 15 EU Member States*, Vienna: European Union Agency for Fundamental Rights (successor to the European Monitoring Center for Racism and Xenophobia).

European Monitoring Centre on Racism and Xenophobia (EUMC) (2006), *Muslims in the European Union: Discrimination and Islamophobia*, Vienna: European Union Agency for Fundamental Rights (successor to the European Monitoring Center for Racism and Xenophobia).

European Parliament Committee on Civil Liberties, Justice and Home Affairs (2007), *Setting Up a System of Benchmarking to Measure the Success of Integration Policies in Europe*, Brussels: European Parliament.

Eurostat (2006–2007), *Europe in Figures: Eurostat Yearbook 2006–7*, Luxembourg: European Commission.

Feldblum, M. (1999), *Reconstructing Citizenship*, New York: SUNY Press.

Finkielkraut, A. (2003), *Au non de l'Autre, reflexions sur l'Antisemitisme qui vient*, Paris: La Decouverte.

Garland, D. (2001), *The Culture of Control*, Chicago: University of Chicago Press.

Guilbert, N. (2003), 'The Situation in the Prisons is "explosive," According to Guards', *Le Monde*, July 18.

Guilbert, N. (2004), 'Study by Sebastian Roche and Monique Dagnaud', *Le Monde*, April 16.

Guiraudon, V. (2006), 'Different Nation, Same Nationhood: The Challenges of Immigrant Policy', in P. D. Culpepper, P. A. Hall and B. Palier (eds), *Changing France*, New York: Palgrave Macmillan, pp. 129–49.

Haut Conseil à l'Integration (2001), *L'Islam dans la Republique*, Paris: La Documentation Francaise.

Haut Conseil à l'Integration (2005) *Vieux_trav_migrants.doc* (accessed 11/21/08), http://www.premier-ministre.gouv.fr/IMG/doc.

Hollifield, J. F. (1999), 'Ideas, Institutions and Civil Society: On the Limits of Immigration Control in France', in G. Brochmann and T. Hammar (eds), *Mechanisms of Immigration Control*, New York: Oxford, pp. 59–96.

Huysmans, J. (2000), 'The European Union and the Securitization of Migration', *Journal of Common Market Studies*, 38(5): 751–77.

Institut National Etudes Demographiques (INED) (2006), *Repartition socio-demographique des immigres en metropole: Enquetes annuelles de recensement de 2004 a 2006*. http://www.ined.fr/.

National Institute of Statistics and Economic Studies (INSEE) (2005), *Official Census in France*, http://www.insee.fr/en/bases-de-donnees/default.asp?page=recensements.htm.

Jackson, P. I. (1995), 'Minority Group Threat, Crime, and the Mobilization of Law in France', in D. F. Hawkins (ed.), *Ethnicity, Race, and Crime*, New York: SUNY Press, pp. 341–59.

Jackson, P. I. (1997), 'Minorities, Crime, Criminal Justice in France', in I. H. Marshall (ed.), *Minorities, Migrants and Crime*, Thousand Oaks, California.: Sage, pp. 130–50.

Jackson, P. I. (1989), *Minority Group Threat, Crime and Policing*, New York: Praeger.

Jackson, P. I. and Carroll, L. (1981), 'Race and the War on Crime', *American Sociological Review*, 46: 290–305.

Jackson, P. I. and Parkes, R. (2008a), 'Parallel Societies, Cultural Tolerance and Securitization: Muslims and Anti-immigrant Sentiment in Western Democracies', *Journal of Social and Ecological Boundaries*, 3(1): 7–42.

Jackson, P. I. and Parkes, R. (2008b), 'The Securitization of Immigration Policy, Shifts in National Immigrant Integration Models and the Incarceration of Immigrants in Germany, France and Britain 1970–2003', *Humboldt Journal of Social Relations*, 31(1): 39–82.

Joppke, C. (2007), 'Beyond National Models: Civic Integration Policies for Immigrants in Western Europe', *West European Politics*, 30(1): 1–22.

Kastoryano, R. (2006), 'French Secularism and Islam: France's Headscarf Affair', in T. Modood, A. Triandafyllidou and R. Zapata-Barrero (eds), *Multiculturalism, Muslims and Citizenship: A European Approach*, London: Routledge, pp. 57–69.

Kensey, A. (2000), *Detention and Foreigners in French Prisons*, Internal document available from author at the French Ministry of Justice, Paris.

Kensey, A. and Tournier, P. (1997), *French Prison Population*, Paris: Ministère de la Justice, Direction de l'administration penitentlare.

Khosrokhavar, F. (2004), *L'Islam dans les Prisons*, Paris: Balland.

Killian, C. (2008), 'Covered Girls and Savage Boys: Representations of Muslim Youth in France', *Journal of Social and Ecological Boundaries*, 3(1): 69–90.

Laurence, J. and Vaisse, J. (2006), *Integrating Islam: Political and Religious Challenges in Contemporary France*, Washington, DC: Brookings Institution Press.

Malloch, M. S. and Stanley, E. (2005), 'The Detention of Asylum Seekers in the UK', *Punishment and Society*, 7(1): 53–71.

Migration Policy Institute (MPI) (2007), *Immigration and the 2007 French Presidential Election*, http://www.migrationpolicy.org/.

Observatoire national des zones urbaines sensibles (2003) *Rapport. La Documentation Francaise*, www.ladocumentationfrancaise.fr/rapports-publics.

Observatoire national des zones urbaines sensibles (2004) *Rapport.* www.ladocumentationfrancaise.fr/rapports-publics.

Point, S. and Singh, V. (2005), 'Defining and Dimensionalizing Diversity: Evidence from Corporate Websites across Europe', *European Management Journal*, 21(6): 750–61.

Prime Minister's *Portal Du Government*, France (May, 2008) (accessed 11/21/08), http://www.premierministre.gouv.fr/en/information/latest_news_97/controlling_immigration_56561.html.

RAXEN Focal Point for France (2005), *National Analytical Study on Racist Violence and Crime*, European Monitoring Center on Racism and Xenophobia, http://fra.europa.eu/fraWebsite/home/home_en.htm.

Roy, O. (2006), 'Forward', in J. Laurence and J. Vaisse (eds), *Integrating Islam: Political and Religious Challenges in Contemporary France*, Washington, DC: Brookings Institution Press, pp. ix–xv.

Stewart, M. (2008), 'L'Esquive and the Art of Indirection: *cinema de banlieue* in the New Republic', *Journal of Social and Ecological Boundaries*, 3(1): 43–68.

Tournier, P. (1996), 'La délinquance des étrangers en France: analyse des statistiques pénales', in S. Palidda (ed.), *Délit d'immigration/immigrant delinquency*, Brussels: European Commission.

Tribalet, M. (1995), *Faire France: une grande enquete sur les immigrés et leurs enfants*, Paris: La Decouverte.

Wacquant, L. (1999), 'Suitable Enemies: Foreigners and Immigrants in the Prisons of Europe', *Punishment and Society*, 1(2): 215–22.

Welch, M. and Schuster, L. (2005), 'Detention of Asylum Seekers in the US, UK, France, Germany and Italy: A Critical View of the Globalizing Culture of Control', *Criminal Justice*, 5: 331–55.

Wilson, W. J. (1987), *The Truly Disadvantaged*, Chicago: University of Chicago.

Wilson, W. J. (1996), *When Work Disappears*, New York: Knopf.

World Prison Brief (2007), *Prison Brief for France*. http://www.kcl.ac.uk/depsta/law/research/icps/worldbrief/.

Zauberman, R. and Levy, R. (2003), 'Police, Minorities and the French Republican Ideal', *Criminology*, 41(4): 1065–1100.

4
Race, Crime and Criminal Justice in Germany

Hans-Jörg Albrecht
Max Planck Institute for Foreign and International Criminal Law, Freiburg, Germany

Introduction: Race, crime and criminal justice – concepts and contexts

In Germany, as in other countries of continental Europe, race is not a category which is used in political and scientific discourses on crime, victimization and criminal justice. In accounts on crime and criminal justice it is rather immigration and its links to crime, criminal justice and criminal victimization which continue to receive widespread attention. The topic 'immigration and crime' figures prominently in German internal and European Union politics and has an increasing impacts on election campaigns, which emphasize crime control and security. Recently, in addition to demands to strengthen criminal law, strict immigration control and the effective enforcement of deportation orders and requests for better integration policies are voiced. The social integration of immigrants has become a particularly salient and ambiguous issue in political and public debates as deficits in social integration are perceived to be the root cause of an outstanding crime problem among groups of young immigrants. In Germany (and elsewhere in Europe), the process of immigration has so far led to the re-emergence of cultural, ethnic and religious divides in society and, ultimately, has triggered the question of how social and political integration can be achieved under conditions of ethnic and religious diversity. An ongoing discussion on the rise of a "parallel society" (Halm and Sauer 2006)[1] points in particular at Muslim immigrants who are sometimes criticized for their apparent refusal to integrate with mainstream society.

Evidently, the particular German approach to political integration, that is a federal state with a careful balance between the federal and the state level, is not well-suited to make an effective response to problems of social cohesion and integration in the face of substantial groups of immigrants who bring with them ethnic, cultural and religious differences. Federalism was, just like the French tradition of secular Republicanism or the British approach of community-oriented pluralism, a reasonably efficient approach to identity building and social cohesion in the 19th and 20th centuries, but does not seem to provide adequate solutions to some of the social problems in the new millennium.

Post-war Germany has experienced a comparatively short history of immigration, the process beginning around 1960 and significant changes in immigration patterns occurring in subsequent decades. The ethnic composition of immigrants has changed significantly over the last 50 years. In the 1960s, the most important sources of immigrant labor were the countries of South-Western European countries (Italy, Spain and Portugal). From the end of the 1960s onward, these were replaced by workers from South-Eastern European countries and Turkey. This change is reflected in the official statistics: At the beginning of the 1960s, approximately two-thirds of Germany's foreign population came from countries (Italy, Spain, Portugal and Greece) that are now members of the European Community. By the 1990s, their share has dropped to less than 30 percent. In present-day Germany, Turkish immigrants and immigrants from the former Yugoslavia account for almost half of the resident immigrant population.

Furthermore, since the second half of the 1980s immigrants from developing countries in Africa and Asia have begun made up substantial proportions of the immigrant population inn Germany. In the 1990s, the complete abolition of schemes set up for hiring workers abroad and severe restrictions on work permissions for non-European Community nationals in Germany led to larger numbers of foreigners applying for asylum (which until amendments to the German constitution and the introduction of the immigration law in 1993 had the effect of granting a preliminary permission to stay on German territory awaiting the final decision on asylum). One immigration phenomenon that is unique to the country concerns ethnic Germans whose ancestors emigrated to Poland, Russia, Romania and who are entitled to be re-naturalized (under the condition that they can provide evidence relating to their German origins). Between the early 1950s and the early 2000s, 4.5 million ethnic Germans have been re-naturalized (Sachverständigenrat für Zuwanderung und Integration 2004),[2] the majority of whom had immigrated to Germany since the second half of the 1980s (Bayerisches Staatsministerium für Arbeit und Sozialordnung 2008)[3] making them the most important (immigrant and ethnic) minority in quantitative terms. After reunification in 1990, ethnic Germans migrating to Germany come mostly from the countries of the former Soviet Union and they face increasingly problematic conditions of integration into the labor market. The number of migrants from the former Soviet Union is decreasing significantly, however, due also to more restrictive admission rules (Currle 2004).[4]

While the debate in the 1960s and 1970s emphasized the concept of 'guest-workers' (migrant workers who it is assumed will return to their home countries after a more or less extended period of work in Germany), the 1990s saw a growing recognition that in fact immigration had taken place (Bade 2006).[5] Legal and institutional changes in respect of immigration have come slowly in Germany with the traditional concept of a policing-oriented immigration law (Ausländergesetz) and its focus on risk control and prevention replaced only recently by a new immigration law. The amended immigration law (Gesetz zur Steuerung und Begrenzung der Zuwanderung und zur Regelung des Aufenthalts und der Integration von Unionsbürgern und Ausländern) came into force in 2005. This legislation places more weight on naturalization and integration. The title of the new law combines restriction and regulation of immigration on the one hand and the integration of European Union citizens and foreign nationals on the other hand. The focus switched (though not completely) from a rather restrictive approach to naturalization to an approach that seeks to facilitate integration through a reduction in the length of stay before naturalization can be applied for, accepting to a certain extent dual citizenship and providing for increased protection against deportation.

Part of the overhauling of the normative framework of immigration came with the introduction of new institutions, including an ombudsman for immigration (Ausländerbeauftragter), the Council of Experts on Immigration (Sachverständigenrat für Zuwanderung und Integration) and a new concern for the collection of basic information relating to the economic and social situation of immigrants (Sachverständigenrat für Zuwanderung und Integration 2004).[6] In 2006, the Federal Ministry of the Interior founded the 'German Islamic Conference' which seeks to initiate a dialog between Islamic associations and state institutions as well as civil society (www.deutsche-islam-konferenz.de).[7] These changes have been encouraged by the obvious social problems that are visible in growing inner-city ghettos and concerns about the emergence of "parallel societies". The changes have also been driven by human rights perspectives that were expressed in particular in the reports produced by the Council of Europe and non-governmental organizations (NGOs) supported by the United Nations which emphasize the particular problems experienced by immigrants in Germany (European Commission against Racism and Intolerance 2004).[8]

The history of ethnic and racial minorities in 20th-century Germany is overshadowed by the murderous terror regime German Nazism exerted in Europe during the 1930s and 1940s (Bade 2006).[9] As a consequence, information on race and ethnicity was eliminated from official data systems. Official statistics, including crime or judicial statistics as well as general population statistics, do not account for the racial or ethnic characteristics of citizens. Only very rough estimates are available, for example, on the number of black or Afro-Germans (thought to range between 40,000 and 50,000) or on the size of the (gypsy) groups of Sinti and Roma (Forbes and Mead 1992).[10] The above estimates for black or Afro-Germans apply to German

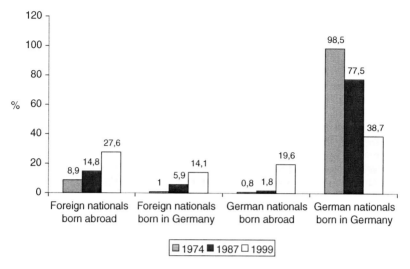

Figure 4.1   Ethnicities in German youth prisons (%)
Source: Jugendstrafvollzugsanstalt Adelsheim.

nationals with at least one parent of African or Afro-American origin. Most of these are the offspring of German mothers and Afro-American members of the US military forces.

The only information which is collected on a regular basis in adminis-trative processes is related to nationality. The problems that arise from the lack of valid data on ethnicity, race or a background of immigration and the use of nationality when interpreting official, and in particular crime-related statistics, become apparent when looking, for example, at changes in inmate structures in German youth prisons. Data from the state of Baden-Wuerttemberg demonstrate that over a period of some 25 years the structure of youth prison inmates has changed completely. In the mid-1970s virtually all inmates were German citizens, whereas in 1999 young German nationals accounted for less than 40 percent of prison inmates. If reliance was placed solely on the variable of nationality, it would not be noticed that today immigrant youth in fact constitute the majority of prison inmates.

The first micro census study to consider the share of immigrants in Germany was carried out in 2005 and revealed quite interesting data. In the micro census immigrants were defined according to particular German conditions:

Immigrant 1: Persons entering Germany (and staying) after 1949, these persons may be foreign nationals (for example a Turkish national living today in Berlin and having arrived in Berlin in 1965, or, an ethnic German coming in 1985 from Romania or Poland or Kazakhstan and adopting immediately German nationality)

Immigrant 2: German nationals, born in Germany, with at least one parent entering Germany after 1949 (that parent may now be a German national)

Immigrant 3: German nationals, born in Germany to a family with at least one parent of foreign nationality (for example a man of Turkish descent, having adopted German nationality who was born as a child of parents of Turkish nationality).

(Statistisches Bundesamt d: Bevölkerung und
Erwerbstätigkeit 2008a, 2008b).[11]

While on the basis of nationality or citizenship the proportion of immigrants was approximately 9 percent of the (resident) population in 2007 (Statistisches Bundesamt 2008b),[12] the share of immigrants (defined according to the criteria mentioned above) amounts to 18.6 percent in 2005 (Statistisches Bundesamt 2008a)[13] and 18.7 percent in 2007 (Statistisches Bundesamt 2008a).[14]

According to the data available from the micro census 2005, and shown in Table 4.1, in present-day Germany the two main immigrant groups are ethnic Germans and Turkish. Immigrants are disproportionally affected by

Table 4.1   Selected characteristics of immigrant groups

Region of Origin	%	Median age	% under 15 Years	Unemployed %	School not completed %	Dependent on social security %
Ethnic German	4.7	37	17.7	15	3	13
Turkish	3.4	27	27.7	23	30	16
Southern Europe	1.8	34	17.6	17	17	10
Former Yugoslavia	1.4	32	19.6	19	14	18
Far East	0.9	29	20.6	17	18	14
Near East	0.6	27	25.6	35	17	34
Africa	0.6	28	28.6	26	25	24
European Union	2.3	35	27.5	13	3	9
German	81	44	12	10	1	8

Source: Institut für Bevölkerung und Entwicklung: Ungenutzte Potenziale. Zur Lage der Integration in Deutschland. Berlin 2009 (micro census data 2005).

unemployment with unemployment rates ranging between 13 and 35 percent along various groups of immigrants (Statistisches Bundesamt 2008a).[15] The immigrant population is also significantly younger, with a median age well below that of the German population. In many aspects immigrants display characteristics of the lower working class, as can be seen, for instance, in relation to housing (Harrison and Law 2005),[16] social security dependency, education and income levels (Anhut and Heitmeyer 2000; Tiemann 2004).[17] A particularly precarious situation is found among young immigrants. For them, research on educational achievements and integration in the labor market displays significant differences compared to German young people (Anhut and Heitmeyer 2000; Tiemann 2004; Statistisches Bundesamt 2004).[18] The emergence of profound social inequality is driven by a system of education and professional formation which evidently does not cater to the particular needs of young immigrants (Gomolla and Radtke 2002).[19]

A look at the spatial distribution of immigrants across Germany reveals significant regional differences. The majority of immigrants are drawn to the western part of Germany. In 2007, the share of immigrants at the population of the 'New Bundesländer' (the former German Democratic Republic with some 16 percent of the total population of Germany) amounts to 2.4 percent (Statistisches Bundesamt 2008a).[20]

The complete neglect of ethnic or racial information in official statistics and censuses has been criticized recently by the Committee on the Elimination of Racial Discrimination (Report of the Committee on the Elimination of Racial Discrimination 2008).[21]

The economically and socially precarious situation of immigrants may be explained in part by social and economic changes in recent decades that have worked, in general, to the disadvantage of immigrants. The disappearance of low-skilled work and the transformation of industrial societies into service and information societies with an increasing dependence on high-skilled workers have led to rapid changes in labor markets and with that the basic framework of conventional mechanisms of social integration (which have always been based around the issues of education, labor and employment). Shadow economies, black markets and low-paid jobs, particularly in metropolitan areas, now offer only precarious employment opportunities for newly arrived immigrants and also for the second- and third-generation of immigrants who lack the educational achievements and professional skills required to enter the labor market. Political changes in Europe then have contributed to affect the legal status of immigrants considerably through changing the statutory framework of immigration as well as enforcement policies. While in the 1960s and 1970s the majority of immigrants entered Germany legally (as labor immigrants or on the grounds of family reunification), today, the legal status of new arrivals focuses around illegality or the precarious status of asylum seekers and refugees who are subject to strict administrative controls and threatened by serious risks of criminalization (if, for example, not complying with administrative rules assigning a place of residence).

Immigration and crime

The process of constructing immigration as a crime problem and of young immigrants as persons particularly at risk of chronic offending has gained momentum following the socio-political and economic changes in the east of Europe and the opening of the once tightly controlled borders between Western and Central European countries. The focus then turned to the question of whether some immigrant groups, in particular Turkish immigrants, have segregated themselves into "parallel societies" which preserve their own culture and language, resist offers of integration and create particular problems for immigrant children and juveniles. The discourse reflects the dominant understanding of social integration and an acceptance of basic values of German society as a fundamental civil duty. As a consequence, in 2004, the immigration law was amended in a number of ways, including the introduction of integration courses for immigrants (Integrationskursverordnung vom 13. Dezember 2004).[22] The law stipulates that immigrants in need of integration may participate in German language courses as well as courses offering aspects of basic knowledge relating to German culture, history and the German political system. The law also provides that under certain conditions participation in such courses becomes mandatory. The mandatory participation clause is aimed in particular at parents with young children who are not capable of communicating with youth welfare and educational institutions and are as a result exposing their offspring to a serious risks of failure in the educational system. This law has been created to address concerns about the large proportion of immigrant youth who are chronic and repeat offenders and the view that school failure and subsequent unemployment are among the root causes of crime. In fact, in 2008, the Bavarian government proposed a clarification of the mandatory participation clause by introducing special integration courses for immigrant youth at risk of entering a criminal career (BR-Drs. 154/08).[23] Behind the efforts to strengthen integration are also concerns for "home grown terrorism" which see in "parallel societies" a fertile ground for radicalization and recruitment.

Rates of police recorded foreign suspects have increased continuously in the second half of the 20th century in Germany, giving a fairly accurate reflection of the increasing numbers of immigrants. In 1953, when the first post-war police statistics were published, the rate of foreign suspects amounted to just 1.7 percent (Albrecht 1997).[24] Figure 4.2 contains data on the resident foreign population in Germany and on the rates of foreign suspects between 1961 and 2007. It is evident from these data that foreign nationals are disproportionally represented in police crime statistics.

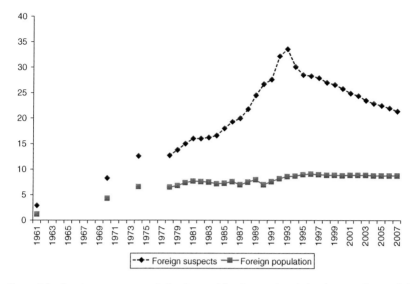

Figure 4.2 Foreign suspects and the share of foreign nationals in the population (%) 1961–2007

Sources: Bundeskriminalamt (ed.): Polizeiliche Kriminalstatistik 1961–2007. Wiesbaden 1962–2008; Statistisches Bundesamt: Bevölkerung und Erwerbstätigkeit. Bevölkerungsfortschreibung 2007. Wiesbaden 2008, table 1.2.

However, it is also clear that the significant changes in the rates of foreign national suspects are independent of the rate of the resident foreign population. Although the proportion of foreign nationals in the resident population at large does not change between the beginning of the 1990s and 2007, the rate of foreign suspects drops by approximately one-third during the same period. This drop reflects the drastic decrease in the number of asylum seekers from 1993 onward (when the German constitution in respect of the right of asylum was amended and applications for asylum were placed under far-reaching restrictions). The decrease is especially marked in the area of small property crimes (essentially shoplifting).

The analysis of police recorded data reveals that crime rates (see Table 4.2 below) among foreign nationals are approximately double the rates observed for German nationals. Police recorded data also show that in a comparison of various categories of violent crime significant differences emerge between foreign and German nationals.

However, some immigrant groups display either the same degree of crime involvement or even lower rates of participation in crime than is observed in the majority group. First-generation immigrants of the 1950s and 1960s have much lower levels of involvement in crime than the second- or third-generation immigrants and immigrants who arrived in the 1980s and 1990s.

Table 4.2 Crime rates (100.000) in selected German cities 2004

	Berlin		Hamburg		Cologne		Frankfurt		Stuttgart	
	German	Foreign	German	Foreign	German	Foreign	German	Foreign	German	Foreign
All Crime	3860	7782	3657	8417	3219	6706	3674	10024	3898	7377
Rape	12	49	9	38	14	49	12	52	11	46
Robbery	97	356	92	334	68	247	70	314	45	133
Aggravated Assault	288	810	213	650	239	596	241	900	251	653
Theft	944	2253	892	2164	828	1927	773	2266	770	1472

Source: Landeskriminalamt Berlin: Polizeiliche Kriminalstatistik – Langzeitvergleich Städtedaten – 1995–2004. Berlin 2005.

What is common to most immigrant groups is a position of socially and economical disadvantage. However, cultural differences between groups in similar social groups can result in rather different crime patterns, different in terms of both, the structure of crime involvement and the magnitude of crime involvement. Cultural differences found between immigrant groups concern the capacity for community building and for the preservation of the cultural and ethnic homogeneity of the immigrant group.

Over the past two decades the discussion around immigration and crime has emphasized particular problems of young immigrants (belonging to the second and third generations). As Figure 4.3 shows, data from the Freiburg Cohort Study (Grundies, Höfer, and Tetal 2002)[25] confirm that the risk of contacts with police (suspicion of a criminal offence) is far higher among foreign youth and that the risk of police contacts is increasing for younger birth cohorts. Data relating to ethnic German youth (those who have arrived from Russia) show that the risk of police contacts for the 1970 birth cohort is fairly close to that of German youth. However, the birth cohorts for 1973, 1975 and 1978 display an increasing risk of police contacts with prevalence rate for the 1978 cohort as high as that observed for foreign nationals. These changes certainly reflect a drastic increase in problems of integration as ethnic German youth immigrating from the former Soviet Union from the late 1980s onward have lower language skills and face greater difficulties in completing school education and accessing the labor market.

Among groups of young immigrants, violence and chronic offending as well as gang activities are assumed to play a significant role. The relevance

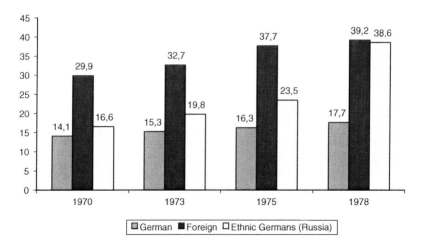

Figure 4.3 Prevalence of police contacts in 4 birth cohorts (1970, 1973, 1975, 1978) at the age of 17
Source: Freiburg Cohort Study.

of violent crime and group violence is underlined by an in-depth analysis of police crime data from the city of Berlin. According to these figures, approximately 45 percent of youth violent crimes committed in groups are linked to young immigrants (PKS 2006).[26] However, police recorded crime data bring two problems: they identify immigrants through the variable of nationality (which may lead to an underestimation of crime participation rates) and they do not account for those crimes that go unreported by victims. The crime participation rate of immigrants will be underestimated when using 'foreign nationals' as a proxy for 'immigrants' because many immigrants (for example, those coming from the East of Europe or Kazakhstan or Turkey) have adopted German nationality and are therefore no longer classified as foreign nationals. To put it the other way, the adoption of German nationality by immigrants is leading to an overestimation of the rate of crime participation among the indigenous population.

Over the past two decades numerous self-report studies have been carried out with the aim of testing assumptions of disproportional crime involvement of young immigrants. Most of the self-report surveys have been implemented in the form of (local) school surveys (focusing on 15–17-year-olds) (Naplava 2002).[27] These surveys found that overall crime participation rates do not differ significantly between young Germans and various groups of young immigrants (Naplava 2002),[28] in particular similar participation rates in property crime and drug use are noted.

To date, all of the studies carried out confirm the disproportional involvement in violent crime such as assault and (street) robbery by young Turkish immigrants and by young immigrants from the South-East of Europe (principally those countries from the former Yugoslavia) (Heitmeyer 1995; Tillmann et al. 2000; Enzmann and Wetzels 2000; Oberwittler et al. 2001).[29] Young immigrants from a Turkish background are also more likely to resort to violence in conflict situations when controlling for the extent of inter- and intra-ethnic conflicts (Müller 2000).[30] The greater role of violence for Turkish boys is explained through their strong connection to gang culture and the particular importance of honor within Turkish communities (Müller 2000).[31] Moreover, young immigrants report greater experience of corporal punishment and abuse in their childhood, something that is assumed to initiate "cycles of violence" (Baier et al. 2009).[32] If emphasis is placed on the role of honor in the interpretation and explanation of violence among young Turkish males (Gesemann 2004),[33] it should also be considered that this refers to classic themes in research on subcultures and gangs (Miller 1979; Graham and Wells 2003).[34] The violence exerted by young males is associated with motives such as "male honor" and a "desire for violence" (Graham and Wells 2003).[35] These motives are embedded in systems of group loyalty/solidarity and the search for social status.

In the explanation of youth violence, chronic offending and the increase of youth violence a special emphasis is laid on the disappearance of unskilled labor and the growing importance of qualifications and training as pre-requisites for access to the labor market. This is believed to lead to a growing concentration of problem youth in disadvantaged inner-city neigh-borhoods and processes of social exclusion and economic marginalization. In addition, an increase in formal complaints of assault and robbery and a lower reliance on informal mechanisms of conflict resolution have been observed. The exchange of control mechanisms to the disadvantage of informal mechanisms is interpreted also as reflecting a deep change in the risk management of children and juveniles (Oberwittler and Köllisch 2004).[36]

Immigrants, law enforcement and criminal justice

Statistics on law enforcement, prosecution, adjudication, sentencing and criminal corrections make no account either of ethnicity or race or of the immigration background of those coming into contact with criminal justice institutions or detained. As stated earlier, the only variable used in official justice and correction statistics concerns nationality. Information on dis-play in Figure 4.1 has demonstrated that the variable nationality does not provide a reliable account of the size of the immigrant youth prison popu-lation; rather, it results in a significant underestimation. If nationality alone were used to break down the prison population, then German nationality would dominate in youth prisons; if data on the immigration status are col-lected, then it would become clear that the indigenous/autochthon group of prisoners represents a minority.

Studies into the criminal justice responses to criminal offenses committed by foreign nationals (and immigrants) have been carried out from a perspec-tive of (systematic) discrimination introduced to explain the disproportional share of immigrants among suspects recorded by the police. Theoretical approaches to the issue of discrimination and of biased law enforcement can be broken down into assumptions related to the emergence of immigrant crime as a significant social problem and into hypotheses related to the role of the immigration variable for decision-making in the administrative and criminal justice system. Recently, increasing attention has been paid to the attitudes and perceptions of immigrants (and other minorities) toward law enforcement institutions and their practices. This line of research addresses the questions of the legitimacy of criminal law and criminal justice and the extent of trust and acceptance that can be observed among immigrant groups.

With respect to the role of police in initiating criminal investigations it should be noted that the German police is not entitled to formal decision-making on arrest. German police, when receiving a complaint about a criminal event, investigate the case and, after the completion of their inves-tigation, forward the case to the public prosecutors' office where the decision is made about whether or not to bring the case to court (or arrest, in the case of pre-trial detention).

Some of the studies have dealt with the question of whether immigrants are more likely to be reported to police by victims or witnesses (LKA Nordrhein-Westfalen 2006).[37] The empirical evidence is not conclusive; however, it seems that inter-ethnic crime is associated with a somewhat higher probability of being reported to police. Research then shows that the probability of being suspected of a criminal offence is fairly the same for foreign nationals and offenders of German nationality. The probability of being suspected of a criminal offence is extremely low in the case of most offences anyway and police investigations are guided principally by the characteristics of the offence, and especially its seriousness. It has been hypothesized that higher rates of suspects among immigrants could be the consequence of a more negative initial encounter with the police. However, research does not lend support to this assumption. In general, immigrant suspects appear to be even more co-operative when interrogated by the police. Further on in the criminal process, the findings do not lend support to the assumption of a larger risk of immigrant suspects being formally charged and indicted with a criminal offence (Kubink 1993).[38]

However, in some areas, including drug law enforcement, law enforcement strategies adopt ethnic profiling and target selected ethnic minorities (those involved in street drug distribution networks). This points to structural problems in the relationship between immigrants and police. Immigrants (in particular, immigrants who have arrived since the 1990s) are placed in disadvantageous conditions. High levels of unemployment and the problem of access to the labor market are associated with high participation rates in shadow economies. This is, in particular, true for illegal immigrants (Albrecht 2006).[39] High participation rates in drug markets or other informal economies expose immigrants to a high rate of encounters with law enforcement. Street-level drug distribution networks in large cities such as Frankfurt, Berlin and Hamburg are operated by (young) people coming from various ethnicities (or immigrant groups). West Africans (Nigerians, Senegalese) and Turkish/Kurdish are involved in small-scale heroin distribution; Maghreb immigrants (Algerians, Moroccans) are participating in cocaine, crack and cannabis distribution in some areas; and Lebanese and other Arab immigrants are, for example, active in the drug markets of Berlin (cannabis and heroin). The involvement in street drug distribution depends partially on the drug trafficking routes. Since the 1980s, West Africa has been an important hub for heroin and cocaine, along with Turkey and the Near and Middle East. In many European countries this has led to the participation of many West Africans in local drug distribution. Furthermore, the Maghreb has always been an important drug-producing region which has meant that, in France, Germany and the Netherlands, large numbers of immigrants from Algeria and Morocco have become involved in cannabis distribution.

While there are no available data on the use of force in general or police practices as regards stop and search, the incidence of firearms use is provided in information collected by the Ministries of the Interior. These data do not, however, distinguish between immigrants and other groups as regards victims of police force. Longitudinal data on the use of deadly force by police reveal that the number of persons killed or injured by police firearms is stable (and tentatively on the decline) as is the use of guns against persons in general (Innenministerium Baden-Württemberg 2005).[40] Over the past two decades the police have used firearms against individuals an average of 60–70 times per year. These instances resulted in ten deaths and some thirty injuries. Although no in-depth study of these cases has been carried out, it appears that almost all of the instances that involved the deadly use of firearms did not display any potential to further fuel ethnic tensions.

Studies of the level of trust in the police as an institution reveal that the differences between German youth and various immigrant groups are not particularly marked. While approximately one-quarter of West German youth, Italian youth and Greek youth declare that they have a general distrust of police, 37 percent of Turkish youths and 33 percent of East German youths express distrust toward police. Levels of trust and mistrust in the police might therefore be explained not by the particular status of an immigrant but by the general feeling of belonging to a marginalized and deprived social group. The differences, however, are not particularly marked when looking at the groups as a whole. Differences become more pronounced following the introduction of variables such as gender, education and place of residence. Mistrust in police is particularly high in the metropolitan area of Berlin, where some 84 percent of young Turkish interviewees declare that they have either no or only limited trust in the police (Gesemann 2003).[41] This shows a clear ethnic divide: the corresponding rate of distrust among the group of German young people is only around 30 percent. An explanation may be found in a process of spatial segregation and the emergence of inner-city ghettos and inner-city ethnic communities which – also as the result of the substantial population of immigrants of Turkish origin – in Berlin have gained significant momentum (Groenemeyer and Mansel 2003).[42] The mistrust in police in metropolitan areas may be fueled also by the frequency of (arrest-related) contacts between police and immigrant youth which is especially marked in large cities.

A higher risk of being held in pre-trial detention has been observed with respect to foreign suspects. Decision-making with regard to pre-trial detention considers first and foremost the likelihood that the suspect will leave the country to avoid prosecution. In addition, a number of other variables are also considered, such as: the possible size of the criminal penalty which can be expected; the nature and the intensity of bonds to society; and the territory of the jurisdiction in which the criminal trial will be held. So, in the

Table 4.3   Non-prosecution rates* (%) in two birth cohorts (birth cohorts 1970, 1980 at age 16, male)

	German			Ethnic German			Foreign		
	1st Offender		2nd	1st Offender		2nd	1st Offender		2nd
	1985	1995	1995	1985	1995	1995	1985	1995	1995
Theft	60	82	77	61	85	82	54	81	82
Aggravated Theft	22	37	22	20	49	14	18	27	17
Violence	32	49	37	38	24	9	32	28	18
Total	55	76	60	55	78	60	50	71	66

*Non-prosecution refers to cases dismissed by the office of the public prosecutor on grounds of expediency.

case of foreign suspects legal conditions of pre-trial detention are more likely to be established than in other offender populations (Albrecht 1997).[43]

Data from the Freiburg Cohort Study (Grundies, Höfer, and Tetal 2002)[44] reveal then that non-prosecution rates at large do not differ for first offenders and recidivist youth when comparing German, ethnic German and foreign youth offenders in 1985 and 1995 (see Table 4.3 below). Non-prosecution rates increased between 1985 and 1995, a finding that is consistent with the adoption of juvenile crime policies stressing diversion from juvenile court proceedings. However, there are differences in non-prosecution rates for violent offences. Foreign juvenile offenders of the 1980 birth cohort are less likely to have their cases dismissed. This may reflect the growing political concern for violent immigrant youth offenders in the 1990s.

Rather small effects of the immigration variable on sentencing can be observed. Foreign nationals run a somewhat higher risk of receiving prison or custodial sentences and are somewhat less likely to receive suspended sentences or probation (Steinhilper 1986).[45] But, in general, ethnic and minority variables add only very modestly to any explanation of the variation in sentencing (Greger 1987; Albrecht 1994).[46] This holds true not only in the case of adult criminal sentencing but also for dispositions in juvenile criminal cases (Albrecht and Pfeiffer 1979; Oppermann 1987; Geißler and Marißen 1990; Wernitznig 2002).[47] It is especially noteworthy that differences in dispositions are virtually non-existent in the case of violent crimes and sexual offences. As ethnicity is a diffuse status variable, it can be assumed that its impact on sentencing is less pronounced or even non-existent in cases where a consistent set of offense and offender-related characteristics (e.g. seriousness of the offence, prior record) or an obvious need for adopting tariffs in sentencing (petty cases) or administrative convenience points to rather obvious dispositional strategies (Unnever and Hembroff 1988).[48] Therefore, only an inconsistent particular set of characteristics may be assumed to trigger

Table 4.4 Rates of (sentenced) foreign prisoners in Germany (% of age brackets) between 1971 and 2007

	14–17	18–20	21–24	25–30	31–40	41–50	51–60	>60
1971	2.3	3.2	4.3	3.2	2.9	5.3	4.6	3.0
1975	4.9	4.3	6.3	7.3	4.7	5.5	8.4	2.7
1981	11.9	6.9	7.0	8.1	9.6	6.9	8.9	5.5
1985	17.9	10.0	8.7	10.0	11.1	8.0	7.6	7.1
1990	35.5	22.5	14.4	13.5	13.0	9.9	8.4	10.2
1995	31.9	33	33.6	25.3	20.2	15.2	10.5	10.2
2004	25.2	21.5	20.8	26.7	26.5	15.4	12.2	8.3
2007	28.1	19.6	20	23.5	28.6	17.9	14.7	10.3

Source: Statistisches Bundesamt: Strafvollzug. Demographische und kriminologische Merkmale der Strafgefangenen zum Stichtag 31. 3. Wiesbaden 1972, 1976, 1982, 1986, 1991, 1996, 2005, 2008.

effects of ethnicity or nationality on sentencing. It has been hypothesized that the relatively minor effect of ethnic variables on sentencing outcomes might be due to the fact that the majority of serious personal crimes committed by immigrant offenders also involve an immigrant victim. The effect might be more pronounced if only those crimes committed by immigrant offenders on victims from the majority group were counted. However, such information is not presently available.

Prisoner rates for immigrants cannot be computed as prison statistics only account for the number of foreign nationals in correctional institutions. Table 4.4 contains information on the proportion of foreign nationals among various age brackets of the prison population. However, the figures also include illegal immigrants and foreign nationals entering Germany as tourists or for other purposes (which excludes them from being counted as residents). The prison statistics reflect a mix of influences that lead to the over- and underestimation of the share of the immigrant prison population. However, from Figure 4.1 it can be concluded that imprisonment rates for young immigrants are approximately three times the average of the general population. These high rates of imprisonment are explained by the high levels of participation in violent crime (which attracts longer prison sentences). The increase in the rates of foreign prisoners over recent decades is partially accounted for the increased sentences for drug trafficking.

Immigrants and victimization

To date the relationship between immigration and victimization has not received the same attention as the active participation of immigrants in crime in Germany. While police statistics account for the nationality of suspects, they do not account for nationality (or the immigration status) of victims. Only on rare occasions have Victim surveys carried out in Germany included immigrant populations on a systematic basis. From the perspective of immigration research, in particular research on illegal immigration, the issue of victimization did not play a role either (Eichenhofer 1999).[49]

The victim perspective with respect to immigrants during the last two decades has been influenced by several issues and different political interests that also, to a certain extent, reflect their assumed potential for creating conflicts and violence due to segregation and cultural 'otherness'.

At the beginning of the 1990s, it was the issue of hate violence (or xenophobic violence) which attracted attention due to a rise in right-wing extremism and a number of large-scale violent attacks on asylum seekers and other immigrants. A second issue that was placed prominently on political agendas relates to the issue of honor killings. A third issue addresses the cycle of violence with allegations that the high levels of domestic violence found among immigrant (in particular Turkish) families have a negative impact on children, making them prone to become violent youth and young adults (Baier et al. 2009).[50] Finally, victims of trafficking have been made a topic of concern. Here, several sensitive social problems are confounded: prostitution, illegal immigration and organized crime (Albrecht 2007).[51]

The foreign nationals' risk of becoming victims of crime was – on the basis of police recorded crime – for the first time studied thoroughly in the 1990s in Bavaria (Luff and Gerum 1995).[52] From this study it is known that the share of foreign national victims accounts for some 11 percent of all victims registered in police statistics. For various nationalities the rate of violent victimization is between two and five times the rates observed among German nationals (Luff and Gerum 1995).[53] A separate study of four police districts found a share of 54 percent of foreign national victims of homicide/murder and an elevated rate of foreign national victims for rape and assault (close to 30 percent of rape and assault victims are foreign nationals) (Luff and Gerum 1995).[54] It can be assumed also that the reporting of crime by foreign nationals is strongly influenced by the immigration status as illegals account for 0.5 percent of all crimes reported by foreign victims (Luff and Gerum 1995)[55] and settled labor migrants were over-represented among victims coming to the attention of the police.

For the first time data from the 2005 European Crime Survey (see Figure 4.4) provide information on victimization rates for a national and representative sample which includes immigrants. According to these data ($N = 2000$, telephone survey) victimization rates across a selection of property and personal criminal offenses are broadly the same for immigrants and non-immigrants.

Germany has developed and implemented devices aimed at counting racist (xenophobic, anti-Semitic) crime and thereby providing a way of assessing the extent of racist crime. Summarizing the available evidence on racial violence, the following can be concluded. First, the general problem of

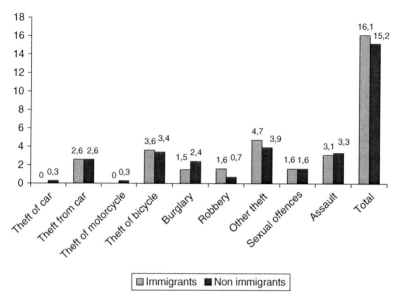

Figure 4.4 Prevalence of victimization (last 12 months) among immigrants and non-immigrants in Germany
Source: European Crime Survey (2005).

all police registered crime data, namely that they are dependent on reporting by victims and by resources invested in investigating (victimless) crime (such as incitement to racial hatred through the Internet or other propaganda crime), has a particular effect on hate crimes where the specific problem of establishing a motive creates additional uncertainties. No police data are available at all on racially motivated violence perpetrated by certain professions, such as the police themselves or prison/correctional staff. (As regards problems of data collection in this field see in particular Jobard 2001; Busch 2000).[56] Information in this field comes almost exclusively from NGO reports as well as the media (Aktion Courage 1999; www.amnesty.org).[57] No police data are available on situations of racist violence amounting to pogroms or other forms of collective, though not necessarily organized violence.

The structure of the racist crime registered by the police reflects the respective definitions as well as the data collection procedures. However, in general police statistics show that the majority of racist offenses comprise propaganda crimes and crimes of harassment. What appears to be evident in the case of Germany is an increase in racial violence, which seemed to occur at the beginning of the 1990s. The increase seems to be related to the rise of extremist political parties and organizations as well as the political discourses on 'asylum problems' and immigration. The course of racist violence evidently is subject to a rise and fall of waves of violence which may be explained tentatively by violent campaigns initiated by various extremist groups, the mobilizing effects of international violent conflicts and 'copy cat' behavior. Key events in terms of spectacular and extreme violence at the beginning of the 1990s (Rostock/Lichtenhagen and Hoyerswerda for example) (Esser 1999)[58] are assumed to have been generated by a media–politics–violence reinforcement process that served to embed xenophobic violence in a framework of legitimating discourses (on asylum politics) (Lüdemann 1992; Ohlemacher 1998).[59] Rostock/Lichtenhagen and Hoyerswerda were pogrom-like attacks on homes for asylum seekers. These events resulted in the fire bombing of asylum seekers' homes, leading to the destruction of homes and numerous people being assaulted and seriously injured.

The above-mentioned European Crime Survey (2005) included for the first time variables that aim to identify hate crime. Respondents were asked, where possible, to identify the motive of the offender(s). From this survey it can be concluded that official accounts of racial violence seriously underestimate the extent of racial violence. Although victimization rates at large do not differ between immigrants and non-immigrants, a significantly larger share of victimizing events is perceived by immigrants to be motivated by hate (see Figure 4.5 below).

Racially motivated crime has a stronger impact than 'ordinary' crime on feelings of safety, community life and individual adjustment and coping

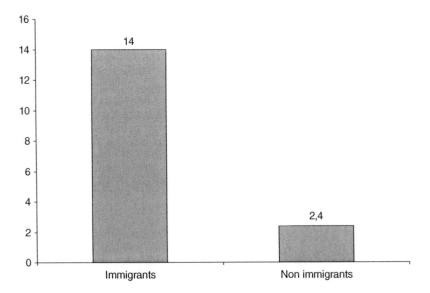

Figure 4.5   Prevalence of hate crimes (last five years)
Source: European Crime Survey (2005).

strategies. The particular concern linked to such crimes comes evidently from their being committed against individuals solely because they belong to a visible group in society and the potential for escalation of social conflicts as well as for the disturbance of public peace and social order.

Conclusions

In Germany no account is taken of race or ethnicity in crime, court or prison statistics. In principle, the variable nationality may be used as a proxy for an immigration background of police recorded suspects, convicted and sentenced offenders and prisoners. However, recent micro census data show that the use of the variable nationality will lead to a serious underestimation of offenders with an immigration background.

Germany has experienced large-scale immigration during recent decades. Substantial numbers of immigrants live in precarious economic and social conditions that expose them to disproportional unemployment rates and also to other problems. The immigrants communities are concentrated in large cities and the integration of these populations into the mainstream ranks high on the political agenda. It is assumed that parts of the immigrant population segregate into "parallel societies", creating particular problems for the younger generation in the school and educational system.

On the basis of police statistics high participation rates in crime, in particular among groups of young immigrants, can be observed. Violent crime and chronic offending have been made particular topics of political concern. Self-report studies show in general that young immigrants differ little from their autochthon counterparts with respect to property crime. However, over time serious violence has been shown to be more prevalent among some groups of young immigrants in general – and particularly prevalent among Turkish youth. Levels of Trust in the police (and other institutions) are not significantly different from those found among other immigrant youth and German youth. One exception is to be found in the city of Berlin, where segregation is most visible and the level of distrust in police is most pronounced. High rates of imprisonment among immigrant groups are explained by high participation rates in violent crimes which attract longer prison sentences. Studies of prosecution, adjudication and sentencing show that immigration status (or nationality) does not add significantly to the explanation of variation in prosecution rates and sentencing severity.

Notes

1. Halm and Sauer (2006: 1–2, 18–24).
2. *Sachverständigenrat für Zuwanderung und Integration: Migration und Integration – Erfahrungen nutzen, Neues Wagen. Jahresgutachten 2004.* Berlin 2004, p. 62.
3. Bayerisches Staatsministerium für Arbeit und Sozialordnung, Familie und Frauen: Statistik Spätaussiedler und deren Angehörige 2007. München 2008.

4. Currle (2004: 55–8).
5. Bade (2006: 3–6, 40–1).
6. *Sachverständigenrat für Zuwanderung und Integration: Migration und Integration – Erfahrungen nutzen, Neues Wagen. Jahresgutachten 2004.* Berlin 2004, p. 396.
7. www.deutsche-islam-konferenz.de.
8. European Commission against Racism and Intolerance: Third Report on Germany. Adopted on 5 December 2003. Strasbourg 2004; Report of the Committee on the Elimination of Racial Discrimination: Seventy-second session (18 February–7 March 2008), Seventy-third session (28 July–15 August 2008), General Assembly, Official Records, Sixty-third session, Supplement No. 18 (A/63/18), p. 38.
9. Bade (2006: 3–6, 40–1).
10. Forbes and Mead (1992: 39).
11. Statistisches Bundesamt: Bevölkerung und Erwerbstätigkeit. Bevölkerung mit Migrationshintergrund – Ergebnisse des Mikrozensus 2007 – Wiesbaden 2008, p. 6.
12. Statistisches Bundesamt: Bevölkerung und Erwerbstätigkeit 2007. Wiesbaden 2008, table 1.2.
13. Statistisches Bundesamt: Bevölkerung und Erwerbstätigkeit. Bevölkerung mit Migrationshintergrund – Ergebnisse des Mikrozensus 2005 – Wiesbaden 2007, p. 7.
14. Statistisches Bundesamt: Bevölkerung und Erwerbstätigkeit. Bevölkerung mit Migrationshintergrund – Ergebnisse des Mikrozensus 2007 – Wiesbaden 2008, p. 32.
15. Statistisches Bundesamt: Stand und Entwicklung der Erwerbstätigkeit 2004. Wiesbaden 2005; see also micro census data on unemployment among immigrants Statistisches Bundesamt: Bevölkerung und Erwerbstätigkeit. Bevölkerung mit Migrationshintergrund – Ergebnisse des Mikrozensus 2007 – Wiesbaden 2008, p. 236.
16. Harrison, Law and Phillips (2005).
17. Anhut and Heitmeyer (2000: 17–75, 22); Tiemann (2004: 37).
18. Anhut and Heitmeyer (2000: 17–75); Tiemann (2004: 37; Statistisches Bundesamt: Strukturdaten und Integrationsindikatoren über die ausländische Bevölkerung in Deutschland 2002. Wiesbaden 2004.
19. Gomolla and Radtke (2002).
20. Statistisches Bundesamt: Bevölkerung und Erwerbstätigkeit 2007. Wiesbaden 2008, table 3.3.
21. Report of the Committee on the Elimination of Racial Discrimination: Seventy-second session (18 February–7 March 2008), Seventy-third session (28 July–15 August 2008), General Assembly, Official Records, Sixty-third session, Supplement No. 18 (A/63/18), p. 40.
22. Integrationskursverordnung vom 13. Dezember 2004, BGBl. I, p. 3370.
23. Entwurf eines Gesetzes zur Erleichterung ausländerrechtlicher Maßnahmen bei der Bekämpfung von Jugendgewalt und Jugendkriminalität (BR-Drs. 154/08).
24. Albrecht (1997: 31–99).
25. For an introduction to the Freiburg Cohort Study see Grundies, Höfer and Tetal, Basisdaten der Freiburger Kohortenstudie. Prävalenz und Inzidenz polizeilicher Registrierung. Freiburg 2002.
26. Der Polizeipräsident in Berlin: Polizeiliche Kriminalstatistik 2006. Berlin 2007, p. 87.

27. See for a summary Naplava, T., Freiburg, 2002.
28. Naplava (2002: 14).
29. Heitmeyer (1995); Tillmann, Holler-Nowitzki, Holtappels, Meier and Popp (2000); Enzmann and Wetzels (2000: 146–52); Oberwittler, Blank, Köllisch and Naplava (2001: 79); Baier et al. (2009: 43).
30. Müller (2000: 257–305, 283).
31. Ibid., p. 284.
32. Baier et al. (2009).
33. See Gesemann (2004: 67–8).
34. Miller (1979: 339–59); Graham and Wells (2003: 546–66).
35. Graham and Wells (2003: 560).
36. Oberwittler and Köllisch (2004: 144–7).
37. Landeskriminalamt Nordrhein-Westfalen: Das Anzeigeverhalten von Kriminal- itätsopfern. Einflussfaktoren pro und contra Strafanzeige. Düsseldorf 2006, pp. 13–16.
38. Kubink (1993: 60).
39. Albrecht (2006: 60–80).
40. Innenministerium Baden-Württemberg: Schusswaffengebrauch der Polizei. Stuttgart, Pressestelle Innenministerium 2005.
41. Gesemann (2003: 203–28, 211).
42. Groenemeyer and Mansel (eds) (2003).
43. Albrecht (1997).
44. For an introduction to the Freiburg Cohort Study see Grundies, Höfer and Tetal (2002).
45. Steinhilper, U.: Definitions- und Entscheidungsprozesse bei sexuell motivierten Gewaltdelikten. Konstanz 1986.
46. Greger (1987: 261–77); Albrecht (1994).
47. Geißler and Marißen (1990: 663–87); Oppermann (1987: 83–95); Albrecht and Pfeiffer (1979); Wernitznig (2002: 251).
48. Unnever and Hembroff (1988: 53–82).
49. See, for example, Eichenhofer (ed.) (1999).
50. Baier et al. (2009).
51. Albrecht (2007: 39–71).
52. Luff, J. and Gerum (1995: 48).
53. Ibid., p. 176.
54. Ibid., p. 172.
55. Ibid., p. 126.
56. As regards problems of data collection in this field see in particular Jobard (2001) and Busch (2000: 49–53). Reports of the Anti-Torture Commission of the Council of Europe have pointed repeatedly to the risk of detained persons being mal- treated and abused during detention, see, for example, Comité de prevention de la torture: Rapport au gouvernement de la République française relatif a la visite effectuée par le C.P.T en France du 27 octobre au 8 novembre 1991. Strasbourg: Conseil de l'Europe 1991; Feltes (2006: 539–56).
57. Aktion Courage – SOS Rassismus: Polizeiübergriffe gegen Ausländerinnen und Ausländer. Dokumentation. November 1999, Bonn; AI Report 2001 – Germany (www.amnesty.org).
58. For an overview see Esser (1999: 48–55).
59. Ohlemacher (1998: 319–32); Lüdemann (1992: 137–53).

References

Albrecht, H.J. (1994) *The Sentencing of Serious Crimes*. Berlin: Duncker and Humblot.
Albrecht, H.J. (1997) 'Ethnic Minorities, Crime and Criminal Justice in Germany', in M. Tonry (ed.), *Crime and Justice: A Review of Research*, vol. 21. Chicago: University of Chicago Press.
Albrecht, H.J. (2006) 'Illegality, Criminality and Security', in J. Alt and M. Bommes (eds), *Illegality: Limits and Opportunities for Migration Policy*. Wiesbaden: VS Verlag für Sozialwissenschaften.
Albrecht, H.J. (2007) 'Trafficking in Humans and Human Rights', in S. Parmentier and E. Weitekamp (eds), *Crime and Human Rights: Sociology of Crime, Law and Deviance*, vol. 9. Amsterdam: JAI Press.
Albrecht, P.A. and Pfeiffer, C. (1979) *The Criminalization of Young Migrants: Findings and Reactions from Control Authorities*. Munich: Juventa.
Anhut, R. and Heitmeyer, W. (2000) 'Disintegration, Conflict and Ethnicization', in W. Heitmeyer and R. Anhut (eds), *Endangered Urban Societies: Social Disintegration and Ethnic-Cultural Conflict Constellations*. Weinheim, Munich: Juventa.
Bade, K. (2006) *Integration and Politics – Learning from History? From Political and Contemporary History Nr. 40, 2006*. Berlin: Bundeszentrale für Politische Bildung.
Baier, D., Pfeiffer, C., Simonson, J. and Rabold, S. (2009) *Juveniles in Germany as Victims and Offenders of Violence*. Hannover: BMI.
Busch, H. (2000) Different Countries – Similar Customs. Police Assault and Control in Great Britain and France, in CILIP 67. http://www.cilip.de/ausgabe/67/gb-fr.htm (last accessed 18.01.2010).
Currle, E. (2004) *Migration in Europe: Data and Background Information*. Stuttgart: Lucius and Lucius, *Bürgerrechte & Polizei/CILIP 67 (3/2000)*.
Der Polizeipräsident in Berlin (2007) Police Criminal Statistics 2006. Berlin.
Eichenhofer, E. (ed.) (1999) *Migration and Illegality*. Osnabrück: Universitätsverlag Rasch.
Enzmann, D. and Wetzels, P. (2000) 'Violent Crime amongst Young Germans and Foreigners', *Kölner Zeitschrift für Soziologie und Sozialpsychologie*, 52.
Esser, F. (1999) 'The Effect of the Media on Racial Violence: A Longitudinal Analysis from 1991 to 1996' in Federal Department for Harmful Media (ed.), *From 'Anti-Semitism' to 'Xenophobia': Right-wing Media in Germany*. Bonn: Bundesamt für Verfassungsschutz.
Feltes, T. (2006) 'Legitimate and Illegitimate Use of Force by the Police', in W. Heitmeyer and M. Schröttle (eds), *Violence: Descriptions, Analysis and Prevention*. Bonn: Bundeszentrale für politische Bildung.
Forbes, I. and Mead, G. (1992) *Measure for Measure: A Comparative Analysis of Measures to Combat Racial Discrimination in the Member States of the European Community*. Southampton, England: University of Southampton.
Geißler, R., and Marißen, N. (1990) 'Crime and Criminalization of Young Foreigners: The Ticking Social Time-bomb – An Artefact of Criminal Statistics', *Kölner Zeitschrift für Soziologie und Sozialpsychologie*, 42: 663–87.
Gesemann, F. (2003) ' "It Doesn't Matter If You Are A Foreigner – Everyone Needs the Police": Perceptions of the Police amongst Young Migrants', in A. Groenemeyer and J. Mansel (eds), *The Ethnicization of Everyday Conflicts*. Opladen: Leske and Budrich.
Gesemann, F. (2004) *Young Immigrants and Crime in Berlin – Cause, Analysis and Prevention*. Berlin: Der Beauftragte des Senats für Integration und Migration.
Gomolla, M. and Radtke, F.O. (2002) *Institutional Discriminations: The Establishment of Ethnic Differentiation in School*. Opladen: Leske and Budrich.

Graham, K. and Wells, S. (2003) ' "Somebody's Gonna Get Their Head Kicked in Tonight." Aggression among Young Males in Bars – A Question of Values?', *British Journal of Criminology*, 43: 546–66.

Greger, R. (1987) 'The Sentencing of Sexual Assaults', *Monatsschrift für Kriminologie und Strafrechtsreform*, 70: 261–77.

Groenemeyer, A. and Mansel, J. (eds) (2003) *The Ethnicization of Everyday Conflicts*. Opladen: Leske and Budrich.

Grundies, V., Höfer, S. and Tetal, C. (2002) *Basis Data from the Freiburg Cohort Study: Prevalence and Incidence of Police Registration*. Freiburg: Edition Iuscrim.

Halm, D. and Sauer, M. (2006) *Parallel Societies and Ethnic Stratification: From Political and Contemporary History*. Bonn: Bundeszentrale für politische Bildung.

Harrison, M., Law, I. and Phillips, D. (2005) *Migrants, Minorities and Housing: Exclusion, Discrimination and Anti-Discrimination in 15 Member States of the European Union*. Leeds, England: University of Leeds.

Heitmeyer, W. (1995) *Violence*. Weinheim: Juventa.

Höfer, S. and Tetal, C. (2002) *Basis Data from the Freiburg Cohort Study: Prevalence and Incidence of Police Registration*. Freiburg: Edition Iuscrim.

Jobard, F. (2001) *L' usage de la force par la police*. Paris: Edition la Découverte.

Kubink, M. (1993) *Understanding and Impact of Foreigner Crime: An Analysis of the Constitution of Social Problems*. Pfaffenweiler: Centaurus-Verlag.

Lüdemann, C.H. (1992) 'The "Contagion-Effect" of Violence against Foreigners – Application of a Threshold Model of Collective Behaviour', *Soziale Probleme*, 3: 137–53.

Luff, J. and Gerum, M. (1995) *Foreigners as Victims of Crime*. Munich: KFG.

Manchin, R., Van Dijk, J., Kury, H., Schaber, G. (2007) International Crime Survey in the EU (EU ICS) 2005. Brussels. http://www.nrc.nl/redactie/binnenland/Misdaad.pdf.

Miller, W.B. (1979) 'The Culture of the Underclass as a Milieu for the Emergence of Gangs', in F. Sack and R. König (eds), *Criminal Sociology*, 3rd edn. Wiesbaden: Akademische Verlagsgesellschaft.

Müller, J. (2000) 'Youth Conflicts and Violence with an Ethnic-Cultural Background', in W. Heitmeyer and R. Anhut (eds), *Endangered Urban Societies: Social Disintegration and Ethnic-cultural Conflict Constellations*. Weinheim, Munich: Juventa.

Naplava, T. (2002) *A Comparison of Delinquency among German and Immigrant Adolescents: Secondary Analysis of Student Surveys from 1995–2000*. Freiburg: Kriminologisches Forschungsinstitut Niedersachsen.

Oberwittler, D., Blank, T., Köllisch, T. and Naplava, T. (2001) *Social Life and Delinquency amongst Youths*. Freiburg: Max-Planck-Institut für ausländisches und internationales Strafrecht.

Oberwittler, D. and Köllisch, T. (2004) 'Not Youth Violence, But Rather Its Registration by Police Has Increased: Results of a Comparative Study after 25 Years', *Neue Kriminalpolitik*, 14: 144–7.

Ohlemacher, T. (1998) 'Xenophobia and Right-wing Extremism: Media Coverage, Public Opinion and the Interaction with Xenophobic Violence, 1991–1997', *Soziale Welt*, 49: 319–32.

Oppermann, A. (1987) 'Delinquent Young Foreigners: Crime and Social Stress Conditions', *Bewährungshilfe*, 34: 5–31.

Steinhilper, U. (1986) *Definitions and Decision Making Processes in Sexually Motivated Violent Offences*. Konstanz: Universitätsverlag.

Tiemann, S. (2004) *The Integration of Islamic Migrants in Germany and France: A Comparison of Selected Populations*. Berlin: WOSTOK.

Tillmann, K.J., Holler-Nowitzki, B., Holtappels, H.G., Meier, U. and Popp, U. (2000) *School Violence as a School Problem: Causal Conditions, Forms and Educational Treatment Perspectives*. Weinheim, Munich: Juventa.

Unnever, J.D. and Hembroff, L.A. (1988) 'The Prediction of Racial/Ethnic Sentencing Disparities: An Expectation States Approach', *Journal of Research in Crime and Delinquency*, 25: 53–82.

Wernitznig, B. (2002) *Sentencing of German and Foreign Juveniles and Adolescents: An Investigative Example Using the Crime of Burglary*. Konstanz: University of Konstanz.

Statistics

Aktion Courage – SOS Rassismus: Polizeiübergriffe gegen Ausländerinnen und Ausländer. Dokumentation. November 1999, Bonn; AI Report 2001 – Germany (www.amnesty.org).

Bayerisches Staatsministerium für Arbeit und Sozialordnung, Familie und Frauen (2008) Ethnic German Immigrants and their Relatives 2007. München.

Bundeskriminalamt (ed.) (2009) *Police Criminal Statistics 1961–2007*. Wiesbaden.

Der Polizeipräsident in Berlin (2007) *Police Criminal Statistics 2006*. Berlin.

Der Polizeipräsident in Berlin: Polizeiliche Kriminalstatistik 2006–2007. Berlin.

European Commission (2005) European Crime Survey 2005–2006. Brussels.

European Commission against Racism and Intolerance (2004) *Third Report on Germany*. Adopted on 5 December 2003. Strasbourg.

European Commission against Racism and Intolerance (2008) *Report of the Committee on the Elimination of Racial Discrimination: Seventy-second session* (18 February–7 March 2008); *Seventy-third session* (28 July–15 August 2008); General Assembly, Official Records, *Sixty-third session, Supplement No. 18* (A/63/18).

Innenministerium Baden-Württemberg (2005) *Use of Firearms by the Police*. Stuttgart: Pressestelle Innenministerium.

Institut für Bevölkerung und Entwicklung (2009) *Untapped Potential. A Review of Integration in Germany*, Micro Census Data 2005. Berlin.

Landeskriminalamt Berlin (2005) *Police Criminal Statistic: A Longitudinal Comparison of City Data 1995–2004*. Berlin.

Landeskriminalamt Nordrhein-Westfalen (2006) *The Likelihood of Victims to Press Charges: Factors For and Against Criminal Charges*. Düsseldorf.

Report of the Committee on the Elimination of Racial Discrimination (2008) *Seventy-second session* (18 February–7 March 2008); *Seventy-third session* (28 July–15 August 2008); General Assembly, Official Records, *Sixty-third session, Supplement No. 18* (A/63/18), p. 40.

Sachverständigenrat für Zuwanderung und Integration (2004) *Migration and Integration: Learning from Past Experiences, Annual Report 2004*. Berlin.

Statistisches Bundesamt (1972, 1976, 1982, 1986, 1991, 1996, 2005, 2008) *Sentencing. Demographic and Criminological Characteristics of Prisoners as at March 31st*. Wiesbaden.

Statistisches Bundesamt (2004) *Structural Data and Integration Indicators for the Foreign Population of Germany 2002*. Wiesbaden.

Statistisches Bundesamt (2005) *Status and Development of Employment 2004*. Wiesbaden.

Statistisches Bundesamt (2007) *Population and Employment. Populations with an Immigrant Background – Results from the 2005 Micro Census*. Wiesbaden.

Statistisches Bundesamt (2008a) Population and Employment. *Populations with an Immigrant Background: Results from the 2007 Micro Census*. Wiesbaden.

Statistisches Bundesamt (2008b) *Population and Employment 2007*, Table 1.2. Wiesbaden.

Statistisches Bundesamt (2008c) *Population and Employment. Populations with an Immigrant Background:-Results from the 2007 Micro Census.* Wiesbaden 2008.

Statistisches Bundesamt (2008d) *Population and Employment 2007*, Table 3.3. Wiesbaden.

Statistisches Bundesamt (2008e) *Population and Employment: Population Update 2007*, Table 1.2. Wiesbaden.

Statistisches Bundesamt (2008f) *Micro Census Data on Unemployment among Immigrants: Populations with an Immigrant Background – Results from the 2007 Micro Census.* Wiesbaden.

5
Race, Crime and Criminal Justice in Italy

Vincenzo Ruggiero
Middlesex University, London, United Kingdom

Introduction

As a necessary premise to this contribution, it should be borne in mind that debates around 'race', in Italy, would be deemed racist. Likewise, 'race' or 'ethnicity' are not important social categories in official crime statistics where crime and victimisation rates are generally classified, first, along the lines of two broad groups of Italian residents such as 'Italian' and 'non-Italian' and, secondly, by nationality. Even those who are indeed racist, therefore, prefer to adopt terms such as foreigners or immigrants, while most would designate the newcomers by their country of origin. This does not mean that stereotypes are avoided. On the contrary, naming people by nationality may become a shortcut leading to their faster labelling. Thus, 'Rumanian' may evoke notions of theft, 'Albanian' violence and 'Nigerian' prostitution (Monzini, 2005; Uba and Monzini, 2007). Nationalities, in brief, may become synonyms for specific illegal activities.

A widely used word like 'extra-comunitari', which describes all those whose origin is outside of the European Union, contains a subtler racist element. The word seems to imply that those who are not part of the 'community' of Europe are, in fact, outsiders in the human community itself, interlopers in civilisation. Their role, at best, is to fill in the temporary vacancies in the labour market and to disappear as soon as they are no longer required. The word 'nationality', although incorporating race and ethnicity, allows those using it to escape accusations of racism. Nationality, on the other hand, allows for an expansion of stereotypes and labelling processes. Africans who reach the southern island of Lampedusa, for example, undergo the same degrading ceremonies and humiliating treatment experienced by Poles employed as tomato pickers or Moroccans working on building sites (Guzzetti, 2006; Massari, 2006).

Given the 'anomaly' in the perception of the issue of 'race' in Italy, this chapter implicitly integrates the theme of the book within the focus of its discussion on immigrants, criminality and criminal justice in Italy. This focus draws upon the academic literature on migration and crime, where little attention has been given to a research tradition which would overturn much of the current debate. I am thinking of some of the work conducted by Sutherland (1924), who rejected the automatic association between immigrants and criminality, observing that, at most, the criminality of non-nationals increases along with their growing integration within the society of the host country. In this perspective, increased acculturation into the country chosen by new settlers explains why second-generation migrants are more likely to engage in illicit activities than their first-generation counter-parts. The process of acculturation, moreover, translates into criminal careers for first-generation migrants who lack a criminal background in their country of origin. Scholars who have followed this tradition of research have noted, for example, that Hispanic–American residents in the USA for 16 years are three times more likely to receive a custodial penalty than those who have been resident in the USA for 5 years (Rumbaut and Ewing, 2007). Similarly, readers of the *New York Times* were disconcerted when, after elaborating available data, Sampson (2006) suggested that the drop in crime that began in the USA in the early 1990s might be explained partly by a simultaneous increase in immigration. Moreover, the decline of violent crime, in its turn, may be a consequence of a surge in the arrival of increasing numbers of new, peaceful, family-oriented, and hard-working migrants (Lee and Martinez, 2000; Martinez, 2006; Hagan and Phillips, 2008). In brief, a growing body of research indicates that immigrants are, on average, not only healthier but also more law-abiding than the native born and in these ways contribute to positive trends in US society.

In this chapter, I will draw on this tradition of study and these research findings. But before attempting to assess to what extent such a tradition might be helpful for the analysis of non-nationals and crime in Italy, I would like to briefly examine the economic context in which migrants find hospitality in the country.

Economic context of migration and criminality

Italy needs the work of migrants; it does not need, or want, migrant workers. This paradox is pursued through the limitation of their expectations and the encouragement to become invisible. Let us see how these two injunctions are intertwined (Ruggiero, 2001).

In the post-war period, economic reconstruction required unskilled workers, particularly in the mass production of consumer durables, but also in the construction and service sectors. While the prospect of a job attracted people from the south to the north of the country, a variety of essential services and some forms of basic social rights favoured the permanent settlement of the new arrivals. The mobility of Italian Southerners came at a cost: the migrants were offered elementary guarantees in terms of work and assistance. In the current period, with the growing demand for flexible and occasional work, Italy (like other European countries) tries to reduce, or to eliminate totally, the social costs of labour. In many contexts, for instance, relatively stable migrants are being replaced by the newcomers, who are more flexible and marginalised, but also more suitable for today's style of production. In this way, the economy benefits from work without having to pay for its social costs such as training, education and social insurance.

In brief, so-called advanced countries, while becoming less attractive for migrants, put in place selective mechanisms so that only those who are prepared to accept the worst conditions are granted access to their territories. This lowering of the expectations is, in its turn, the result of the growing polarisation of the world economy, a polarisation which should perhaps be described as a manifestation of 'less global eligibility', whereby the deeper the poverty of countries, the lower the expectations of those who abandon them by migrating. To migrate, then, becomes a form of individual resistance adopted by those who are prepared to renounce the right enjoyed by the migrants who preceded them. Among such rights is the possibility to move freely from one country to another, a right totally enjoyed by all sorts of commodities.

It should be noted that the selection of migrant workers is also carried out through the imposition of a monetary contribution, a sum of money in exchange for the privilege to migrate. I am alluding here to the widespread phenomenon of illicit movement across borders, whereby it is not the developed countries but migrants themselves who pay the price of their mobility, thus showing in advance the modest demands they will put forward once turned into guest workers. The trafficking in human beings towards Italy describes, not only metaphorically, the invisibility that many migrants are forced to accept. This is also a unique example in which the cost for the transfer of a commodity (migrant labour) is not incurred by producers or consumers, but by the commodities themselves.

To accept one's illegal status in the country of destination is tantamount to accepting to 'disappear'. In this sense, we can remark that the strengthening of border control does not result in a decrease in migratory flows, but in an increase in the human and economic costs of migration. In this respect the US example is illuminating. See how, during the course of the 1990s, increased border enforcement in the South of the country pushed flows into more remote, inaccessible and dangerous areas, trebling the likelihood of death for those attempting to cross them (Massey, 2005). Similarly, see the fatal risks for those who intend to reach Italy illegally, with death being an additional entry cost into a labour market that simultaneously both attracts and rejects. In both the Italian and the US cases, it should be added, the growing harshness of border control has unforeseen consequences: if welcome migrants are mainly those who accept their role as seasonal workers, and leave without making any demands once they are no longer employable, those who manage to enter, due to the high costs they have paid, will be inclined to remain.

To hide oneself or to disappear, in Italy, amounts to seeking work in the irregular economies and markets, where goods are produced and distributed and services are delivered irrespective of their official designation as legitimate or illegitimate. The hidden economy and the criminal economy proper, in effect, are often adjacent, and end up overlapping considerably, including at times entrepreneurs and sectors of the workforce. In this occupational 'grey area', flexible labour and a variety of illegal activities mesh, thus making uncertain not only the confines between employment and unemployment, but also the boundaries between legality and illegality.

From what has been laid out so far, we may draw some initial conclusions. Particularly harsh legislations addressed to migrants have a considerable effect on their expectations, namely on those who, despite all of the obstacles in their way, manage to reach the desired destination. We are faced with legislations treating migrants as enemies (Caputo, 2007), encouraging them to become illegal, forcing them to join an economically and socially excluded group: migrants 'do not possess the right to have rights' (Ferrajoli, 2007: 353). The act of migrating itself is accompanied by a process of cultural and material devaluation which, while producing a notable reduction of expectations, makes migrants accept insecure, mean, badly paid, and, at times, illegal occupations. The hidden economy in Italy, the dimensions of which are unmatched in Europe, is the ideal candidate for the employment of such workers. In a vicious circle, in this way, the ideological conviction will take shape that, the more migrants are obliged to accept jobs which devalue their social position, the more they will be perceived as individuals of little value.

The relationship between the hidden economy and migration is also of concern to other scholars, who describe irregular or illegal occupational arenas as the receptacles of an extremely adaptable post-industrial labour reserve army, comprising labourers who are prepared to regard even the worst working conditions as a chance for social promotion. If we read the migratory dynamics exclusively from the point of view of the demand for labour, we might see 'in the flows of migrants and in their intense participation in the hidden economy the evidence of how much they are needed or, even, of how restrictive the admission policies are' (Cesareo, 2008: 23). The emphasis on the demand for labour, of course, benefits the employers, who are inclined to offload on society and the state the problems which arise when the labourers employed, suddenly, are no longer deemed necessary. Irresponsible employers, characteristically, aim at the extreme polarisation of the costs and the benefits of their enterprise: the social tensions caused by the sacking of the workers who are no longer wanted will be tackled by local welfare agencies or state agencies, such as the police. Migration, in this case, will turn into a law and order issue. To liberalise the circulation of labour without dealing with the hidden economy, it is therefore suggested, is 'an economically short-sighted and a socially imprudent choice' (ibid.: 23). It is also a manifestation of connivance with illegal markets which attract those workers who are periodically deemed redundant. As Cesareo (ibid.: 24) states:

> The international agencies themselves admit that employers are granted too much power to decide who and at what conditions can cross the national borders, to the point that governments are deprived of their own prerogative and sovereignty...This is the power to divert on today's and tomorrow's society the costs of dealing with the human 'scrap' regarded as unproductive.

This unproductive human 'scrap', in effect, once released by the semi-licit, hidden economy, might find opportunities in the criminal economy proper, which therefore acts as a temporary occupational arena for workers made redundant by the former. As we shall see below, unregistered migrants are statistically more involved in the criminal economy, but it is their illegal status which makes them particularly welcome in the hidden economy, where they become a source of very cheap labour. In a similar context one should ask why campaigns against unregistered migrants are not turned into campaigns against the firms employing them. Of course, to impose harsher control measures on such firms may be economically disadvantageous, and it is a fact that such measures are particularly weak in the sectors of construction and domestic work, namely where a higher presence of irregular migrants is observed. Finally, the hidden economy itself seems to be the prime beneficiary of the typically Italian anomaly whereby only 1 percent of those who are asked to leave the country does so and only 4 percent are arrested when they fail to comply with the order to leave (Sciortino, 2008).

Immigrants as offenders and victims

In Italy, like elsewhere, the hidden economy and the criminal economy share a number of characteristics, including work insecurity, an atmosphere hazardous to the health – and sometimes the very life – of those employed, the absence of a legal employment contract, the rejection of official labour norms and the refusal to comply with fiscal regulations. In other words, those who are employed in the hidden economy undergo a sort of 'training for illegality' which may incline them towards the choice of a criminal career. Such a choice may also result from the inadequacy of the hidden economy itself, which does not guarantee the standard of living which might be optimistically expected by those employed in it (Sbraccia, 2007). For migrants, as for other excluded groups, therefore, the criminal choice entails relatively limited costs: perceived as illegal in the first place, treated as enemies, rejected by prejudices and devalued by the legislation, migrants who choose to engage in crime simply fulfil the prophecies of those excluding them.

According to the hypothesis advanced so far, the relationship between migration and crime in Italy is fed by the illegal conditions characterising the firms and the labour market in some sectors of the economy. This hypothesis echoes Sutherland's notion that migrants' criminality is the result of their growing integration into the social system of the host country. I will return to this in the final part of the present chapter, where I will supplement Sutherland's idea with a consideration of some aspects that may be specific to the Italian system. It is now time to consider the country's official statistics on crime and migration.

In 2006, one in every three individuals charged with homicide was non-Italian, an increase on the previous years which reflects the corresponding increase in the number of non-Italian residents. (Fondazione ISMU, 2007). The incidence of non-Italians in criminal statistics, however, varies substantially according to the type of offence. For example, the rates for bank and post office robberies are rather low (3 percent and 6 percent, respectively), while those for theft, pick-pocketing and burglary are high (70 percent, 60 percent and 51 percent, respectively). In respect of other offences, the incidence of non-Italians is as follows: 45 percent of those charged with mugging, 19 percent of those charged with extortion, 29 percent of those charged with fraud and 38 percent of those charged with either theft from vehicles or shoplifting (Ministero Dell'Interno, 2007). It is worth noting that more than 90 percent of the Italian citizens murdered are murdered by their fellow citizens, while the reverse is true for non-Italians, with 74 percent being murdered by other non-Italians. As for the victims of robberies, 68 percent of Italians are victimised by other Italians, while 71 percent of non-Italians are victimised by other non-Italians.

Data show a significant increase in migrants brought to court in the North of Italy, which reflects their increased presence in that area of the country. On the other hand, the very modest growth of the migrant population in the South is coupled with a marked increase in the incidence of their criminality, as reflected in the statistics. If migrants are becoming the source of growing concern, it is argued, this is due to the fact that 20 percent of individuals charged with any type of offence are non-Italian, while the percentage leaps to 30 percent in the regions of the North and to as high as 40 percent in urban centres such as Bologna, Milan, Verona and Padua (Cesareo, 2008: 9).

In 2005, of all those receiving a penal sentence one in five was non-Italian, with a much larger incidence being found in the regions of Veneto and Lombardy. Non-Italians serving a prison sentence were over 30 percent of the population in custody (Di Nicola, 2008). The percentage of non-Italians among crime victims, however, was also high, particularly for violent crimes, including sexual violence (Ministero Dell'Interno, 2007). Victimisation data, of course, do not provide a complete picture, as non-Italians may be reluctant to report the violence suffered for fear of revealing their illegal status. Around 30 percent of the victims of homicide are non-Italian, 'as are 22 percent of the victims of sexual violence' (ibid.: 374). Finally, non-Italians are more likely to get injured or die at work. While, in general terms, accidents in the work place have declined by 1.3 percent, accidents affecting non-Italians have gone up by around 4 percent (Cesareo, 2008).

Over-representation: Institutional racism?

The categories and variables utilised in a quantitative study reveal the degree of civil sensitivity for certain specific issues in the country in which it is conducted. We have seen that data released by the Ministry of the Interior (Ministero Dell'Interno) include percentages of victimisation among the non-Italian population, both when the perpetrators are Italian and when they are not. One sensational absence from the official statistics pertains to the offences committed against non-Italians as 'foreigners'. I am alluding to the episodes of verbal and physical violence, the aggressions and the criminal raids targeting groups and communities which are regarded, for their mere presence in the Italian territory, as deserving of some form of punishment. I am thinking of hate crime, which targets individuals not in their capacity as individuals but as members of a despised group. This type of crime is monitored in many European countries, both by academics and institutional agencies. In England and Wales, for instance, for the year 2006, around 179,000 'racial incidents' were recorded (Home Office, 2007). If we are not prepared to believe in the adage that 'Italians are not racist', we will have to explain the reason why such crimes do not appear in the statistics. I have mentioned earlier that the degree of civil sensitivity in a context determines whether a conduct is perceived as unacceptable or criminal. It is for governments to give statistical meaning to certain conducts, not only in the form of specific legislations, but also in the form of guidelines for the police force and the judiciary. It is, then, for the police and the judiciary to implement those guidelines by classifying the charges involved and delimiting them into precise criminal categories. Finally, it is for the victims to report the incidents of a racial nature that they suffer. This is exactly what does not occur in Italy, where the legislative void in the area of hate crime is compounded by the reluctance of the victims to report it, both for lack of trust in the institutional agencies of the host country and for fear of being exposed as illegal migrants.

The figures summarised above are the result of a series of components which refer to a chain of acts and interactions. The criminal justice system is activated by an action/interaction consisting of a victim reporting an offence and, at times, accusing a perpetrator. It is hard to know, due to the particular emergency climate surrounding illegal migration in Italy, whether Italian victims of crime are more inclined to report incidents in which non-Italians are involved. A subsequent action/interaction consists of police activity in terms of control of the population. This is, in a sense, the crucial entry point for non-Italians into the criminal justice system. Official statistics do not reveal the choices made by the police regarding which groups and individuals to prioritise in their activity. The visibility of migrants, because of their skin pigmentation and perhaps even their clothing, should leave no doubt in this respect: like elsewhere, the other, the excluded and, in the Italian context, the 'probably illegal' are all the object of differentiated attention on the part of the police. Similarly, the choice of the urban area in which differentiated control is to be enacted is likely to be determined by the ethnic composition of its inhabitants, thus producing the paradoxical condition that can be observed in many contexts. Namely, the areas targeted by particularly intense policing become attractive to those who seek illicit goods or services. Statistics, in other words, describe police activity and its promotional effects in specific contexts, rather than the criminal activities carried out in those contexts (Hearnden and Hough, 2004).

At the subsequent stage, the interaction between migrants and the criminal justice system takes place when specific detective practices are adopted vis-à-vis migrants themselves. The percentage of non-Italians whose fingerprints are held by the police has grown consistently over recent years, particularly after 2002, when a law made it an obligatory legal requirement. The Italian police today hold the fingerprints of nearly 2 million registered migrants: 'In December 2005 there were 2,286,024 foreigners with a work permit and the finger prints of nearly all were kept by the police for their identification' (Ministero Dell'Interno, 2007: 360).

The over-representation of migrants in the criminal statistics is perhaps also the result of another circumstance: migrants may be charged more severely for the same offences committed by Italian citizens. Moreover, when brought to trial, migrants may lack adequate defence lawyers and the harshness of the sentence suffered may reflect their marginalised condition in society along with the perception that excluded individuals who commit crimes may be too difficult to reform. Their presence in custodial institutions, which testifies to yet another aspect of over-representation, may result from the reluctance of the judiciary to give non-custodial sentences to those who are excluded, because of their lack of the family and social networks which could help them in the process of reintegration. All of this could be regarded as a version of institutional racism, consisting in a sum of actions, events and choices which, against the backdrop of deep prejudices among the general population as well as in some components of the institutional agencies, determine the considerable over-representation of migrants in the criminal justice system (Marshall, 1997; Tonry, 1999; Palidda, 2001; Newburn et al., 2004).

Over-representation and unequal treatment intertwine with the process inappropriately described as 'criminalisation', that is to say a particular harshness displayed against migrants who, allegedly, are punished for crimes they have not committed or for crimes that, when committed by others, would be tolerated. On the contrary, I have described so far a number of stages, composed of choices, actions and interactions, which lead to a series of disadvantages for migrants who do commit crimes, not for migrants who do not. The choice of the illicit activity in which to engage, in its turn, deserves specific scrutiny, irrespective of the quantitative studies available and their credibility.

Over-representation: Relative deprivation

Observers who are prepared to acknowledge the existence of institutional racism may, nevertheless, reject any automatic association between ethnic background and crime. Some do not accept the idea that 'figures are perennially manufactured by a police service which is so irredeemably racist that it keeps fitting people up for crimes they didn't commit rather than pursue the real perpetrators' (FitzGerald, 2004: 22). I am thinking of authors who adopt the classical paradigm centred on relative deprivation, according to which the large presence of foreigners in criminal statistics is related to the social disadvantages that characterise their condition. Their very visibility, moreover, is also due to the specific activities available to them, which mainly take place on the street, thus exposing them to the routine action of control agencies. In this perspective, it might be pointless to ask why so many foreigners are stopped by the police; rather, the question should be why do so many foreigners spend so much time on the street?

The relationship between crime and social condition forms the core of the studies conducted by Tonry (1999), who distinguishes between first- and second-generation migrants, noting that the latter experience more severe assimilation problems and are more likely to offend because they feel more intensely the frustration for their unfulfilled expectations. If parents, as I have suggested above, are forced to drastically reduce their expectations, their children may not be prepared to accept a similar reduction, as they have grown up with the conviction that they have equal rights to the other natives. The successive generations, it is suggested, will show rates of criminality not different to those shown by the population in general.

Similarly, Marshall (1997) focuses his analysis on the disillusionment and the discrimination suffered by second-generation minorities, while the variable 'unfulfilled expectations' returns in post-colonial studies attempting to explain, for instance, the differences in the crime rates shown by Afro-Caribbean youths and young people of Asian descent. The decline in the social and economic conditions affecting specific minorities is deemed one of the factors leading to criminal conducts. Such factors include, among other things, dysfunctional families, paternal absenteeism, school failure and neighbourhood poverty: 'Serious offending is significantly more likely in the most disadvantaged neighbourhoods, particularly those experiencing high levels of concentrated poverty, weak residential stability and high transience of populations' (Webster, 2007: 65). In such urban environments, social disadvantage and exclusion are said to shape aggressive identities and masculine attitudes favouring criminal careers.

In research funded by the House of Commons in the UK, similarly, the point is reiterated that, when examining the data on ethnic minorities and crime, consideration should be given to the fact that minorities experience a number of disadvantages not only in the occupational sphere, but also in education and housing, and all of these 'are in part predictive of offensive behaviour and general involvement in the criminal justice process' (House of Commons, 2007: 38). In brief, official analyses of the crime–minorities nexus adopt the notion of relative deprivation and use it as an explanatory tool for the over-representation of minorities in criminal statistics. While this is associated with discriminatory practices by the police, an important role is given to socio-demographic factors, to the presence of minorities in the streets, their lifestyle and visibility, particularly in certain zones targeted by control agencies. It is also argued that crime investigation makes supplementary efforts when faced with reports of offences committed by foreigners and minorities, on whom agencies hold a significant array of information (Home Office, 2005). This is even more the case in Italy, where as I have mentioned the near totality of non-Italians with a permit to stay are obliged to deposit their fingerprints at police stations.

If, on the one hand, the international literature does not offer a conclusive answer with respect to the different crime rates of minorities as opposed to majorities (Bowling and Phillips, 2002), on the other hand, the studies I have just mentioned focus on the poverty–crime nexus, rather than on processes of criminalisation. Inspired by the ecological tradition of the 1920s, such studies propose a notion of 'deviant zones' as a key instrument for the explanation of the larger incidence of certain conducts in specific urban areas. Among the factors examined are population density, marginalisation, unemployment rates and demographic instability. 'In brief, as neighbourhoods provide differential opportunity structures and differential motivations for crime and deviance, they simultaneously attract deviant and crime-prone people while they repel the least deviant as mechanisms of social control are diminished in presence and impact' (Barak, 1998: 198).

In conclusion, higher crime rates among minorities are due in large measure to the type of urban area in which they reside, rather than their ethnic background or the institutional agencies' responses that are elicited by their criminality. This hypothesis, as I have noted, constitutes an extension of the analyses produced by the Chicago sociologists between the 1920s and 1930s, who identified 'transitional areas' in the urban environment where the most visible 'social pathologies' were concentrated. The new migrants who intended to join their family members or acquaintances, it was argued, were attracted to areas whose social conditions and prevailing subcultures determined the perpetuation of illegality. This analysis, however, deserves to be updated decisively. With the expansion of migratory flows and, simultaneously, of illicit economies, the variable 'urban area of residence' loses part of its explanatory value, because illicit goods and services, even when delivered by minorities, reach layers of the population which transcend the specific communities and their ethnic composition. In this respect, authors who adopt a post-colonial perspective pay more attention to class differences, to structural exclusion and oppression perceived by foreigners (Tatum, 2000) which 'result in higher levels of alienation and in higher inter- and intra-personal levels of crime and violence' (Barak, 1998: 209). I would like to start from these considerations and address the relationship between foreigners and crime from another angle.

Immigrants, crime and vulnerability

In the study I referred to, conducted by the Italian Ministry of the Interior, a preliminary distinction is drawn between instrumental offences, which aim to achieve material benefits, and expressive offences, which are determined by passion and conflicts. Although useful, such a distinction should be complemented with categories which establish the costs and benefits of the individual offences in order to ascertain whether some groups of offenders are led to adopt criminal conducts characterised by an unfavourable balance between costs and benefits.

The argument I am going to present could benefit from the insights offered by a classical African–American novelist: Richard Wright. His characters, even when involved in crime, are self-destructive, unable to control the effects of their criminality and to change, though illegality, their social condition. Even when violent, theirs is the violence of the violated (Ruggiero, 2003). In this respect, some observations relating to freedom and choice, and their highly differentiated distribution among individuals and groups may be extremely important. Each person is offered a range of choices and a series of instruments to predict their effects. Social disadvantage, in this perspective, coincides with a limited variety of available options, but also with an inadequate perception of the expected outcomes of those options. In sum, migrants, who are offered limited opportunities in the official labour market, face a similarly limited range of choices in the illegitimate labour market. This is a less visible form of 'criminalisation'; it consists of a differentiated distribution of criminal opportunities which affects migrants and minorities, who are left with the most risky criminal tasks, those tasks which are, simultaneously, less remunerative and more exposed to institutional intervention. If, as I have noted, the cost of the deviant and criminal choice for migrants is relatively low, it is the effects of this choice which imply extremely high costs. In other words, if the condition of marginality facilitates the access to adjacent social areas, where illicit businesses operate, once gained access to such areas migrants find that the choices available to them are profoundly unfavourable in terms of their costs and benefits.

The data I have listed briefly in the previous pages indicate that bank and post office robberies, perhaps the offences with the most favourable added value, are virtually precluded to migrants, who are mainly involved in pick-pocketing, theft and burglary. These offences yield relatively low profits. Even mugging, despite the high emotional costs incurred by victims, does not produce substantial financial benefits for offenders. The data reveal a repertoire of minor crimes which are extremely stigmatised, easily detectable and scarcely remunerative. The statistics also testify to the high victimisation rates among migrants themselves: both intra- and inter-ethnic types of vic-timisation. What the data do not reveal is the incidence of what I would term self-inflicted crimes. I am alluding, for instance, to the trafficking in human beings which, when perpetrated by foreigners, victimises the very ethnic minorities forming the traffickers' clientele. Prostitution, in its turn, victimises minority women and it is rare for migrant criminal entrepreneurs to manage to recruit Italian sex workers, who are more inclined to operate in the more protected and up-market sections of the sex industry. When migrants operate protection rackets in Italian cities, their greatest impact is generally felt by other migrants; indeed, it is likely that the victimisation of Italians would not be tolerated by local organised criminal groups. As already mentioned, even violent offences, when not committed by Italians against migrants, are perpetrated within minority enclaves (Ruggiero, 2000). In respect of homicide, when committed by migrants who do not belong to well-structured criminal groups, the vulnerability of the offenders is reflected in the high probability that they will be arrested. By contrast, the use of professional assassins, as is common among Italian organised groups, pro-tects the masterminds and results in very low rates of both detection and arrest. It is exactly in relation to their involvement in structured criminal organisations that the position of migrants offers an unclear and nuanced outlook.

In the literature on organised crime, when there is any examination of the involvement of migrants, images and judgements recur which are often based on opinions, hypotheses and moral panics. Some studies set off with the premise, reiterated and transmitted without corroboration from one commentator to the next, that organised crime formed by foreigners 'is characterised by particular forms of aggression and violence and the fast growth of their capacity to operate in different criminal areas' (Di Nicola, 2008: 193). It is very hard to establish the precise nature of this 'particular-ity', especially in Italy, where the violence and expansive force of indigenous organised crime is a well-known fact: but, of course, foreigners are always more violent than us! A more useful strategy, perhaps, consists of focusing on some specific types of criminal activity, or on some specific geographical area, and observing the interactions that organised criminal groups formed by migrants establish with the new or traditional Italian organised groups.

In a tentative manner, pending further substantiation, we might suggest that in some Italian regions foreign organised crime is independent from Italian criminal groups, because the latter are by now engaged in productive, entrepreneurial and financial activities. Other specific criminal sectors may have undergone a process of 'succession', whereby foreign groups occupy the space vacated by Italian groups who have moved on to operate elsewhere. In some cases, however, the succession is accompanied by the request by Italian groups of a percentage on the profits made by the new operators (Becucci and Massari, 2001; Becucci, 2006). In other areas, partnerships can be formed between Italian and non-Italian groups, with a division of labour based on the respective power and on the capacity of the latter to access and distribute illicit goods . In yet other areas, non-Italian groups are subordinate to Italian ones, particularly in contexts in which the demand for illicit goods and services is traditionally high. Finally, if we prefer to focus on the specific criminal activity in which the different groups specialise, we might want to investigate, for instance, whether the illegal transfer of people carried out by Rumanians is to be associated with the demand for labour by the Italian hidden economy; whether the supply of African prostitutes is fostered by the increasing number of Italian customers in the sex industry; whether the ability of Russian groups to infiltrate the official economy is due to the proven willingness by official actors to facilitate illicit infiltration; and, finally, whether the predominance of Chinese groups in the importation of forged goods is the effect of the particular prosperity of this illicit economic sector in Italy. In brief, the criminality of migrants in Italy should perhaps be analysed against the background of the criminogenic characteristics of the country. This is what I will attempt to do in the final section of this chapter.

Criminogenic Italy

The perception that foreigners constitute a threat to Italian identity and culture is spreading quickly. I propose to overturn this by examining the criminality of migrants from their own perception of that cultural identity that many believe is being threatened. Before doing this, let us return briefly to Sutherland's suggestion from which I have started. Migrants in Italy, as we have seen, commit less serious offences, while for particularly remunerative offences the percentage of migrants charged 'is very low and at times lower than for Italian citizens' (Ministero Dell'Interno, 2007: 371). The figures tell us that registered migrants commit more serious crimes: murder, smuggling, extortions, violent crimes and sexual violence and prostitution rackets. If we assume that registered migrants have had more opportunities and time to familiarise themselves with criminal markets, to refine their ability to supply illegal goods and to establish forms of cohabitation with the indigenous criminality, then Sutherland's notion of acculturation undeniably finds a degree of validation. The process of 'acculturation' allows migrants to slowly learn the ways operations are to be conducted, the techniques for stimulating demand and the principles that regulate illicit markets. Acculturation also permits them to acquire the necessary flexibility, in some cases, to share the market with competitors, and in other cases to dissuade them through the use of violence. Pre-existing illicit markets play a crucial role in the acculturation of migrants. But there is a final aspect of this process which makes the acculturation of foreigners in Italy as unique and anomalous as the country itself.

Reputations travel, and Italy's reputation as a country where rules are outflanked or ignored, and where agreed-upon principles of legality are hard to establish, travels through the international media, within Europe as well as across the world. The choice of migrating to Italy may not be triggered by fallacious dreams of prosperity revolving around images of fast cars and stylish clothes. The country is attractive less for the occupational opportunities it offers than for its widespread, diffuse illegality. Those who seek an occupation in Italy receive tips and information, hearsay and concrete proof that describe the country as land of tax evasion and the commodification of rights. They know that the authorities, unable as they are to impose rules upon employers, will be equally unable to impose rules upon them. In the perception of many, and in the experience of some, visas, letters of employment, work permits and similar documents can be either bought or forged. The country offers some of the advantages of its own bad reputation, and elicits comments based on a mixture of reality and prejudice. Its political representatives, one may remark, have one trait in common: they all have a criminal record; its white collars are renowned all over the world for their corrupt practices and their illegal adventurism in the financial world.

The other characteristics of the country, be these assumed or proven, include the following: the impunity of its deviant entrepreneurs; the dexterity of its institutional fraudsters and cheats, in the areas of both sport and fashion; its exasperating nepotism, in show business as well as among the top professions; its criminals who have been on the run for decades while living very close to their official residence; and its dangerous prisoners on remand being freed due to the incapacity of judges to conduct quick trials. There is a widespsread feeling that in Italy violation of the norms is itself part of the country's customs, if not even a source of pride. Some regard the violations themselves as one of the causes of the apparent Italian prosperity, which in its turn is ostentatious. The power of organised crime in Italy, whether or not it is overestimated, feeds the perception that, due to the inefficiency of the state apparatus, there exist in the country vicarious forms of social mobility and success. The longevity of Italian organised crime not only renders the ineptitude of state control agencies manifest, but also suggests that illegal activities of all sorts are tolerated, or even encouraged by an elastic demand which transcends the legal or illegal nature of the goods and services supplied. The overflowing level of illegality in the country makes migrants believe that, if not the official, then the criminal economy may offer job opportunities, along with ready-made techniques of rationalisation. I am, of course, referring to the observations made by Sykes and Matza (1957), according to whom crime not only entails the appropriate use of abilities and technical tools, but also requires a range of 'neutralisations' which help perpetrators live with their offence vis-à-vis public reprobation and their own conscience. 'Condemning the condemners' is the ideal technique of neutralisation for migrants who engage in crime: how can a country where everything is illegal discriminate against, and single out, their own illegality?

Conclusion

To conclude on an optimistic and sarcastic note, one might consider that the acculturation process of migrants in Italy is at present only in its infancy. The criminal groups formed by non-Italians are not yet able to establish partnerships with deviant entrepreneurs or corrupt politicians, nor are they yet capable of directly designating their own public administrators and political representatives who could boost their criminal careers. Some classics of the sociology of deviance note that successful criminal careers imply some form of alliance or even symbiosis between criminal groups and members of the elite from the political or economic arena (Cloward and Ohlin, 1960; Chambliss, 1978; Block, 1980; Ruggiero, 2000). In this way, organised crime, white collar crime, business deviance and state crime blend together in a variety of inextricable forms of crimes of the powerful. Unlike Italian criminal groups, groups formed by migrants are, for the time being, excluded from such a symbiosis and seem destined to engage in the hidden economy and in the labour market of conventional criminal activity. One has to hope that their acculturation will not reach completion too quickly.

References

Barak, G. (1998), *Integrating Criminology*, Boston: Allen & Bacon.

Becucci, S. (2006), *Criminalità multietnica: I mercati illegali in Italia*, Rome/Bari: Laterza.

Becucci, S. and Massari, M. (2001), *Mafie nostre, mafia loro*, Turin: Edizioni di Comunità.

Block, A. (1980), *East Side–West Side: Organizing Crime in New York 1930–1950*, Cardiff: University of Cardiff Press.

Bowling, B. and Phillips, C. (2002), *Racism, Crime and Justice*, Harlow: Longman.

Caputo, A. (2007), 'Irregolari, criminali, nemici: Note sul "diritto speciale" dei migranti', *Studi sulla Questione Criminale*, II(1): 45–63.

Cesareo, V. (2008), 'Migrazioni 2007: Uno sguardo d'insieme', in Fondazione ISMU, *Tredicesimo rapporto sulle migrazioni 2007*, Milan: Franco Angeli.

Chambliss, W. (1978), *On the Take: From Petty Crooks to Presidents*, Bloomington: Indiana University Press.

Cloward, R.A. and Ohlin, L.E. (1960), *Delinquency and Opportunity: A Theory of Delinquent Gangs*, New York: Free Press.

Di Nicola, A. (2008), 'Criminalità e devianza degli immigrati', in Fondazione ISMU, *Tredicesimo rapporto sulle migrazioni 2007*, Milan: Franco Angeli.

Ferrajoli, L. (2007), *Principia iuris. Teoria della Democrazia*, vol. 2, Rome/Bari: Laterza.

FitzGerald, M. (2004), 'Understanding Ethnic Differences in Crime Statistics', *Criminal Justice Matters*, 55: 22–3.

Fondazione ISMU (Iniziative e Studi sulla Multietnicità) (2008), *Tredicesimo rapporto sulle migrazioni 2007*, Milan: Franco Angeli.

Guzzetti, L. (2006), 'Il linguaggio dei corpi: lager, gulag e Cpt', *Conflitti Globali*, 4: 39–50.

Hagan, J. and Phillips, S. (2008), 'Border Blunders: The Unanticipated Human and Economic Costs of the US Approach to Immigration Control, 1986–2007', *Criminology & Public Policy*, 7: 83–94.

Hearnden, I. and Hough, M. (2004), *Race and the Criminal Justice System: The Complete Statistics*, London: Home Office.

Home Office (2005), *Minority Ethnic Groups and Crime: Findings from the Offending Crime and Justice Survey 2003*, London: Home Office.

Home Office (2007), *British Crime Survey*, London: Home Office.

House of Commons (2007), *Select Committee on Home Affairs. Second Report*, London: House of Commons.

Lee, M.T. and Martinez, R. (2000), 'Social Disorganization Revisited: Mapping the Recent Immigration and Black Homicide Relationship in Northern Miami', *Sociological Focus*, 35: 363–80.

Marshall, I. (ed.) (1997), *Minorities, Migrants and Crime*, London: Sage.

Martinez, R. (2006), 'Coming to America: The Impact of the New Immigration on Crime', in R. Martinez and A. Valenzuela (eds), *Coming to America: Immigration, Ethnicity and Crime*, New York: New York University Press.

Massari, M. (2006), *Islamophobia: la paura e l'Islam*, Rome: Laterza.

Massey, D. (2005), *Backfire at the Border: Why Enforcement without Legalization Cannot Stop Illegal Immigration*, Washington: Center for Trade Policy Studies.

Ministero Dell'Interno (2007), *Rapporto sulla criminalità in Italia*, Rome: Ministero Dell'Interno.

Monzini, P. (2005), *Sex Traffic: Prostitution, Crime and Exploitation*, London: Zed Books.

Newburn, T, Shiner, M. and Hayman, S. (2004), 'Race, Crime and Justice? Strip Search and the Treatment of Suspects in Custody', *British Journal of Criminology*, 44: 677–94.

Palidda, S. (2001), *Devianza e vittimizzazione tra i migranti*, Quaderni ISMU, Milan: Franco Angeli.

Ruggiero, V. (2000), *Crime and Markets*, Oxford: Oxford University Press.

Ruggiero, V. (2001), *Movements in the City*, New York: Prentice-Hall.

Ruggiero, V. (2003), *Crime in Literature: Sociology of Deviance and Fiction*, London: Verso.

Rumbaut, R. and Ewing, W.A. (2007), 'The Myth of Immigrant Criminality', http:// borderbattles.ssrc.org.

Sampson, R. (2006), 'Open Doors Don't Invite Criminals: Is Increased Immigration Behind the Drop in Crime?', *The New York Times*, 11 March.

Sbraccia, A. (2007), 'More or less eligibility? Prospettive teoriche sui processi di criminalizzazione dei migranti irregolari in Italia', *Studi sulla Questione Criminale*, II(1): 91–108.

Sciortino, G. (2008), 'Dopo l'allargamento: cambiamenti nella struttura e direzione dei flussi migratori irregolari', in Fondazione ISMU, *Tredicesimo rapporto sulle migrazioni 2007*, Milan: Franco Angeli.

Sutherland, E. (1924), *Criminology*, Philadelphia: Lippincott.

Sykes, G. and Matza, D. (1957), 'Techniques of Neutralization: A Theory of Delinquency', *American Sociological Review*, 22: 664–73.

Tatum, B. (2000), *Crime, Violence and Minority Youths*, Aldershot: Ashgate.

Tonry, M. (ed.) (1999), *Crime and Justice: A Review of Research*, vol. 25, Chicago: University of Chicago Press, 1999.

Uba, W. and Monzini, P. (2007), *Il mio nome è Wendy*, Rome: Laterza.

Webster, C. (2007), *Understanding Race and Crime*, Abingdon: Open University Press, 2007.

6
Race, Crime and Criminal Justice in the Netherlands

Josine Junger-Tas
University of Utrecht, the Netherlands

Introduction

All prosperous European countries have within their borders large groups of residents who have different ethnic origins. This is a relatively new phenomenon for those former non-immigrant countries who had originally received only students from their colonies, who came to Europe to complete their studies. According to a 1952 definition from the United Nation sub-commission for the Protection of Minorities, minorities are 'Non-dominant population groups with stable ethnic, religious or linguistic characteristics and traditions that distinguish them from the rest of the population and which they wish to conserve'.

The reasons for the presence of ethnic minorities are similar for all rich countries. They have always had a considerable demand for cheap labor. Some minority groups are the descendants of slaves, who were imported in earlier times for the purpose of working on plantations. In the Netherlands this is the case for immigrants from the Caribbean, Surinam and the Antilles. This population consists of a mix of different ethnic groups: Creoles make up about one-third of the total population, and they are the descendants of slaves who were brought from Africa, principally Ghana, between the end of the 19th century and the First World War; the Hindustani community comprises 37 percent of the population, and they are descendants of contract laborers from the Indian West coast brought to Surinam between 1890 and 1939; the Javanese, who were brought to Surinam as contract laborers from Java Indonesia, currently make up about 15 percent of the population; finally, there are the Bush Negroes, consisting of escapees from slavery who now live in the Surinamese jungle. The Creoles and Hindustani are the two groups who later immigrated to the Netherlands.

However, the largest category of immigrants now consists of labor migrants. Since 1950, 18 million persons have migrated to the United States, of which most are of a non-European background, while 15 million persons immigrated to Western Europe, usually as so-called 'guest workers'

(Yinger, 1994). Southern Europeans were recruited by Switzerland, Belgium and the Netherlands. In the 1960s and 1970s, Germany and the Netherlands recruited large numbers of Turkish and Moroccan workers. Another important category consists of immigrants from former colonies, who settled in the mother country, usually in search of work and a better future. These groups, for example the West Indians, Pakistani and Bangladeshi in the United Kingdom, and the Surinamese and Antilleans in the Netherlands, generally become nationals within the host country. To some extent, a similar position exists among Mexican immigrants in the United States and African immigrants in Europe, although many of these still have an illegal status. In this connection it is important to observe that, despite the imposition of increasingly strict immigration laws, economically motivated immigration is a slow but continuous process, leading to a growing – albeit hard to quantify – number of illegal or 'undocumented' residents in the Western world. Finally, there is a growing category of people who, for a variety of reasons, including oppression and military conflict, have fled their home country, hoping to build a new future for themselves and their children in Europe.

In sum, ethnic minority groups may be defined in the following ways:

- Their ethnic-cultural position differs from that of the original population;
- Their socio-economic status is usually low;
- The size of the groups is too small to have much (political) influence on policy making;
- This unfavorable situation may last for more than one generation.

In the 1970s, the Netherlands recruited large numbers of 'guest workers', mainly from Turkey and Morocco. They were needed for unskilled work in factories and in market gardening. These were followed by new waves of Surinamese immigrants who came to the Netherlands when their own country achieved independence. The overwhelming majority of these (approximately 97 percent) have Dutch nationality, which makes their legal position stronger than that of other migrant groups. Moreover, they are familiar with Dutch culture and speak the language. Antilleans came to the country in two waves. The first group, essentially middle class, arrived in the 1960s, mainly for study reasons. However, as a consequence of the Antilles's worsening economic situation in recent years, many young people, with low levels of education and speaking hardly any Dutch, immigrated to the Netherlands. In addition, many of them do not come with their parents; they are accommodated by family members and often have no fixed address. It is common for these young people to experience considerable difficulties integrating into mainstream Dutch society.

In recent years a growing number of asylum seekers have arrived in the Netherlands. many of them being refugees from war zones or dictatorships.

In addition, a proportion of these (new) immigrants come from countries with high levels of unemployment and great poverty, including the former Yugoslavia, Africa, Asia or the Middle East (Syria, Iraq, Iran) and also Central Europe. Finally, the country also contains a group of residents from neighboring Western countries as well as some from Canada, Australia and the United States.

This chapter deals with three issues, the first of which is the demographic and social situation of ethnic minorities in the Netherlands. Secondly, instead of dealing with crime in the adult population I choose to study the extent and nature of juvenile delinquency among ethnic minorities in comparison with the youth population of Dutch origin. A number of Dutch criminologists and cultural anthropologists have studied ethnicity and adult crime (De Kort and Korf, 1990; Etman et al., 1993; De Haan, 1993, 1997; Huls, 1995; Bovenkerk et al., 2000, 2003; Engbersen et al., 2007). And in this chapter, some discussions relating to ethnic minorities and criminal justice, and victimization are generic in approach and as such draw on the experiences of the adult population as well. However, I have been involved in an International Self-reported Delinquency Study (ISRD-2) and the Dutch sample of this study, which included 35 percent of ethnic minorities, produced recent and interesting findings on juvenile delinquency and experiences of victimization. Thus, this chapter presents some of the findings from this study. Third, an attempt is made to offer [in particular] some possible explanations for young migrants' involvement in delinquency, again as compared to Dutch young people. The choice to focus primarily on young people while drawing from the ISRD-2 is also motivated by the circumstance that Dutch criminal statistics include no reference to an offender's ethnicity. This is a consequence of the fact that during the Second World War the occupying Nazi forces made considerable use of the Dutch Registry of Births, Deaths and Marriages, which was kept in every community and made a careful note of every citizen's religion and address. This made it very easy for the occupants to find and arrest any Jewish citizens. After the war it was decided that population statistics should no longer be allowed to note the religious status or ethnicity of residents. Rather, nationality is registered and this means that the ethnic origin of some ethnic groups that have Dutch nationality and of those that are naturalized foreigners does not figure in any of the crime statistics. The result of this situation is that we have to rely on specific research efforts (such as self-report studies) for most of our knowledge about ethnic groups.

Social and economic position of ethnic minority groups

Some demographic data

As at January 1, 2005, approximately 1.7 million non-Western migrants[1] were living in the Netherlands, a figure that translates to about 10 percent of the total population of 16.5 million. About two-thirds of the non-Western migrants came from Turkey, Morocco, Surinam and the Antilles, and one-third migrated from so-called 'asylum' countries such as Iraq, Iran, Somalia and China. Forty percent of non-Western and 60 percent of Western migrants belong to the second generation, having been born in the Netherlands. Long-term estimates suggest that the share of the non-Western population will grow to 17 percent while the population of Dutch origin will decrease to about 70 percent of the total population (Bijl et al., 2005). Moreover, most of these migrants live in the four largest cities, forming 40 percent of the population in Amsterdam and Rotterdam, 30 percent in The Hague and 20 percent in Utrecht.

Table 6.1 (below) shows that the migrant population is, on average, considerably younger than either the population of Dutch origin or the Western migrants: The average age of migrants is between 25 and 30 compared to about 40 in the population of Dutch origin. Interestingly, the average of the Surinamese group is somewhat older than the others. This is the result of their relatively low birthrate, which is comparable to that of the native Dutch population. The Dutch population is shrinking slowly while the migrant population is still increasing in number, although one also notes among the latter a gradual decrease in the birthrate. Slowly they seem to be adapting their average family size to that of the host country. For example, the Somali group, which migrated to the Netherlands in the 1990s and raised large families, is the youngest population group while the Turkish and the Moroccans are already ageing populations.

In the meantime ethnic minority youth form a larger proportion of the total youth population than Dutch juveniles. For example, in a

Table 6.1   Age composition according to country of origin – 2005

Ethnicity	0–19 yr.	Average age	Increase since 1996
	%	Years	%
Population of origin	23.5	40	1.7
Turkish	38	27.5	3
Moroccans	42	26	2.5
Surinamese	31.5	31.5	3.5
Antilleans	36.5	28	2.5
Other N-western	37.5	27	1.5
Western	18	41.5	2
Total	24.5	39	1.5

Source: Bijl et al. (2005), Central Bureau of Statistics (CBS) and Research Centre of the Ministry of Justice (WODC).

representative study among Rotterdam youth aged between 14 and 15 years, 60 percent of the sample were members of one of the ethnic minority groups (Junger-Tas et al., 2003b). One of the consequences of the younger age pyramid of minorities than of the Dutch population is that the former is also stronger than the latter in their representation in the criminally most active age 14–18/20.

Minorities in the education system and in the labor market

Approximately 15 percent of the pupils in the Dutch education system are members of one or other of the minority groups. It has been reported that when these children are beginning their period of education – at age 4 – most of them are estimated to be about 2 years behind their Dutch schoolmates with respect to language skills and cognitive development (Gijsberts, 2003). As a consequence, throughout the whole of their school career their average level of achievement remains lower than that of Dutch children. Despite this situation, minority students will gradually close the gap on their Dutch schoolmates. The expectations are that their difficulties in mastering mathematics will be overcome in 10 years, while overcoming language problems will take another 10 years (Gijsberts, 2003, p. 63). At the end of the primary school stage Surinam pupils have the highest levels of achievement of the minority comunities. The gap in language skills of Turkish, Moroccan and Antillean pupils continues to be estimated at around 2 years, while that in mathematics is only 6 months.

Studies conducted by the Social Cultural Planning Office[2] (SCP) revealed that parents' education level, the language spoken at home and their level of Dutch language skills are the main causal factors for these gaps in school success. Unfortunately, many Moroccan and Turkish parents are illiterate and speak almost no Dutch, which explains one-third of the lag in school success at the end of Primary school. In those cases where the parents' education level is similar to that of Dutch parents, the disadvantage in mathematics of migrant children disappears, but part of the language deficit remains. This is said to be due to cultural factors, such as the interactions between parents and children as well as specific patterns in the raising of children.

The consequence of the disadvantageous position in the education system is that the majority of migrant children usually move on to technical schools that offer them vocational training[3] whereas in general Dutch children move on to medium- or higher-level schools. At the end of the High school phase, in the year that the final examination takes place, 36 percent of Dutch students participate in the higher-level examination, compared with only 21 percent of Surinamese and Antillean students, and only 14 percent of Turkish and Moroccan students. Furthermore, a higher proportion of Dutch students also go on to obtain a certificate that entitles them to enter higher professional education or go to university.

For the purposes of this study what is more important than the measure of school success is the number of young people that leave school without a diploma. In 1998, one-quarter of Turkish and Moroccan students dropped out of the Dutch education system without any certificate, whereas the figure was only 6 percent among Dutch students. Fortunately, this situation is improving: in 2002, the dropout rate was 21 percent among Turkish students, 17 percent among Moroccan youths and 10 percent among Surinamese and Antillean students. Actually, the dropout percentage continues to fall, in particular among Moroccan and Turkish girls, whose dropout percentages are falling faster than those of their brothers. The situation for Surinamese girls is even better: not only have they caught up with their male counterparts, but they currently score as highly as Dutch girls.

Overall, the level of education among migrant youths has increased at a faster pace than among Dutch students. They are gradually increasing their levels of participation in higher levels of secondary education and their enrollment in higher professional education as well as university is also increasing slowly (Gijsberts, 2004).

Within the labor market, migrants' position shows mixed levels of participation. The first-generation unskilled 'guest workers' were recruited in the 1970s for work in the industrial sector. The change from an industrialized society into a service society in the 1980s and 1990s hit them hard. Unemployment among them increased tremendously and most became dependent on social benefits. This situation relates to first-generation migrants as well as parts of the second generation. One possible explanation for this negative trend might be the economic slump during this period as well as the higher qualifications that employers came to demand from their employees in these new types of occcupation. Since many migrant groups still have relatively low levels of education and cannot satisfy the demand for higher qualifications, they tend to find themselves placed outside the regular labor market (Bijl et al., 2005, p. 39).

In 2003, the proportion of social benefits paid to migrant populations was indeed some two or three times that paid to the Dutch population as a whole, and the average spendable income of non-Western migrant families in 2004 was 28 percent lower than that of Dutch families (Central Bureau of Statistics (CBS), Statline, 2006). In addition, these families tend to live in deprived neighborhoods (Social Cultural Planning Office (SCP), 2003; CBS, 2004). However, the second generation immigrants show a greater rate of labor market participation and also a greater participation in social organizations. There is a remarkable development of small enterprises, in particular among migrants from Turkey, Morocco, Egypt, China, India and Pakistan, based on mutual support and social networking. However, this may also be a reaction to exclusion from and discrimination in the Dutch labor market (Bijl et al., 2005).

Juvenile crime

The next data are based on police statistics and are a reflection of the number of young people (aged 12–24)[4] who are suspected by the police of having committed a delinquent act. The different groups are standardized for age and sex so that the greater number of youth aged 12–18 in the migrant population as compared to the Dutch population does not play a role (Blom et al., 2005). Figure 6.1 (below) distinguishes first-generation from second-generation migrants, as well as second-generation kids with one parent born abroad from youth with two parents born abroad.

Several findings can be drawn from Figure 6.1. A first general observation is that most crime peaks between age 15 and 20 and subsequently decreases. The same has repeatedly been found in other European countries, in official statistics as well as in self-report studies (Rutter et al., 1998; Junger-Tas et al., 2003a; Bottoms and Dignan, 2004; Blokland, 2005). In this respect there is no difference between Dutch and migrant young people. A second observation is that, at all ages, the level of delinquency involvement of migrant youth is higher than that found among the population of Dutch origin. A final interesting observation is that children with two parents born abroad are considerably more delinquent than children of mixed marriages, with only one parent born abroad, suggesting that to the extent that the cultural gap to Dutch society is reduced juvenile delinquency decreases.

Table 6.2 illustrates the delinquency of the major population groups in the Netherlands. It is clear from Table 6.2 that Moroccans and Antilleans are the most delinquent groups, followed by recently arrived males from

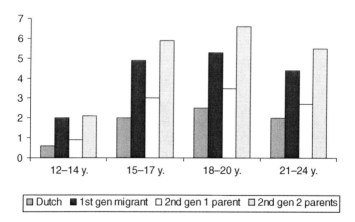

Figure 6.1 Percentage of young people suspected by the police by origin and age – 2002
Source: Blom et al., 2005, p. 46.

Table 6.2 Percentage suspected by the police by country of origin: age group and sex – 2002

	12–17 year		18–24 year	
	Males	**Females**	**Males**	**Females**
Netherlands	2.3	0.5	4.3	0.6
Ex-Yugoslav.	5.6	1.8	8.7	2.3
Morocco	12.1	2.2	19.5	2.4
Antilles	10.1	3.0	13.2	4.1
Somalia	9.4	1.8	11.9	1.9
Surinam	6.9	2.1	12.0	2.4
Turkey	5.7	0.6	9.0	0.7

Source: Bijl et al. (2006, p. 62).

Somalia and Surinam. The involvement in delinquent activity is particularly high among Antillean boys and girls. As stated earlier, these are also recently immigrated groups, who have often travelled to the Netherlands on their own. Migrating to the Netherlands because of massive unemployment in the Antilles, they have a low education level, speak hardly any Dutch and many of them no longer live with their own family. We found in an earlier random study of 14–15-year-old students in Rotterdam that half of the Surinamese and only one-third of the Antilleans lived in a family with two biological parents (Junger-Tas et al., 2003b, 2008). Raised only by their mother, who has to take care of the family income and has trouble in exercising control over her children, may explain in part the high delinquency rates among both boys and girls in the Antillean community.

Ex-Yugoslavia and Turkey have considerably lower delinquency rates and Turkish girls have rates that are no higher than are found among Dutch girls. This latter finding may be a reflection of the close-knit nature of the Turkish community, which is characterized by high levels of social cohesion and tight social controls on both boys and girls. In addition, the Turkish community is active in organizing leisure for the children, for example through sports activities and local festivities. All this might explain the under-representation of Turkish children in the Juvenile justice system as well as in the Youth protection system.

There is some variation in the nature of the delinquency activities in which young people are involved. Although migrant youths – in particular, those of the first generation – are usually more violent than Dutch juveniles, differences between groups are relatively modest. Moreover, second-generation migrants with only one parent born abroad do not differ a great deal from Dutch juveniles with respect to the nature of their delinquent behavior (see Figure 6.2 below).

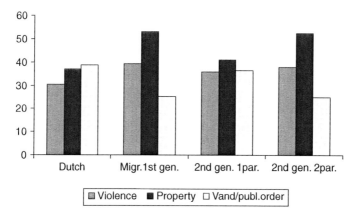

Figure 6.2 Percentage suspected by the police by ethnicity and nature of delinquent behavior – 2002
Source: Blom et al. (2005).

A remarkable fact is that first-generation immigrants and second-generation immigrants with two parents born overseas tend to commit property offenses at a much higher rate than the two other groups. Dutch young people commit relatively more vandalism and also more crimes against public order, which may include football hooliganism, a frequent offense among Dutch juveniles.

Victimization of ethnic minorities

The Dutch Central Bureau of Statistics (CBS) conducts regular victimization studies, including 16 personal offenses, on a representative sample of the Dutch resident population. The CBS victimization surveys distinguish between Dutch citizens and foreigners. They show that foreigners have considerably higher victimization rates than are found among the indigenous population. However, for reasons explained above the category 'Dutch' includes some ethnic groups, including most of the Surinamese, the Antilleans and those who are naturalized. In addition, most foreigners (and ethnic minorities) live in the larger cities where crime rates are higher than those found in the rest of the country. Finally, the members of ethnic minority groups are generally of a lower socio-economic status and live in poor, and relatively crime-ridden urban neighborhoods. This means that one should be cautious when interpreting official statistics. Some earlier studies were undertaken (Van Dijk and Mayhew, 1992) showing that men and young people are more often victimized than women, and older persons and higher educated more than those with little education.

However, most research suffers from bias by comparing victims of mainly lower socio-economic status and living in poor neighborhoods with random samples of people living in the large cities. In order to address this objection, another study (van Dijk and van Soomeren, 1993) compared a sample of Turks, Moroccans and Surinamese with a matched group of Dutch citizens who were living in the same neighborhood. Interestingly, this comparison showed no difference in victimization between the three ethnic groups and Dutch citizens. The study concluded that victimization risk is more strongly related to the degree of urbanization and neighborhood quality than it is to ethnicity. Junger (1990) found also that environmental factors were more important than ethnicity. Her study was carried out among a random sample of Surinamese, Turkish, Moroccan and Dutch boys living in the same neighborhood. Although Dutch boys were somewhat more often victims of property offenses and physical threats of assault than Turkish and Moroccan boys, differences were slight.

The following victimization data come from a large-scale self-report survey among 2,300 juveniles aged 12–15, based on a random sample of schools and school classes in large, middle-sized and small cities[5] (Junger-Tas et al., 2008). Data collection was completed in 2006, and the data include 35 percent ethnic minorities.

Figure 6.3 (below) shows that Dutch (18.4 percent) and Turkish (15.9 percent) young people are the least likely victims of theft while the other groups have higher rates ($p < .002$). Robbery also shows a significant difference in victimization between the ethnic groups, with Western migrants and Surinamese juveniles being victims more often than the other groups, but general victimization prevalence of both robbery and assault is low. Victims of bullying behavior are found in particular among Dutch, Western and

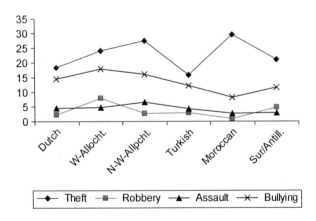

Figure 6.3   Last year prevalence of victimization by ethnicity

non-Western migrants but only rarely among Turkish, Moroccan and Surinamese kids. In this respect it should be remembered that all ethnic groups, with the exception of Western migrants, tend to live in poorer neighborhoods than most of the Dutch juveniles, and that they attend lower stream schools, many of which are plagued by problems of misbehavior, vandalism and fights.

The way young people spend their leisure time is related to both delinquency and their risk of victimization. To the extent that they often spend free evenings with a large peer group on the street there is an increase in their opportunity to commit offenses, but so does the risk of becoming a victim of a property offense or assault. This is also the case in our study as demonstrated in table 6.3 below ($r = .13$). It is clear that juveniles who commit serious offenses are most frequently victims of two different offenses. But even young people who commit only non-serious offenses are more often victimized than youngsters who commit no offenses.

We also examined the relationship between offending and victimization according to the nature of the offense committed. Thus, the committal of property offenses – the most frequently committed offenses – is hardly related to the degree young people are victimized ($r = .08$, $p < .01$). On the other hand, the committal of non-serious violent offenses is positively related to victimization ($r = .17$, $p < .01$) and so is the committal of serious violent offenses ($r = .12$, $p < .01$). We may conclude that the relationship between delinquency and victimization is to a large degree dependent on the nature of the delinquent behavior. Young people who only commit property offenses run less of a risk of being victimized as compared to juveniles who (also) commit violent offenses. The latter run a high risk of becoming a victim of theft, robbery or assault. This may be related to the group character of much youth violence such as vandalism and group fights, although a role may also be played by the environment and the type of peer group with which some young people commit serious offenses such as robbery, threats with violence and assault. In that respect our findings confirm what has

Table 6.3 Relationship between delinquency and degree of victimization

Delinquency	No offense	Non-serious offense	Serious offense	Combination
Victimization	N = 1612	N = 410	N = 49	N = 171
Not victimized	79.2	70.7	65.3	60.8
Of 1 off. type	18.9	24.4	32.7	31.7
Of 2 off. types	1.9	3.9	2.0	6.4
Of 3 off. types	0.1	1.0	0.0	1.8

Note: $p < .001$.

been found in the longitudinal Denver study (Huizinga et al., 2003, p. 61) as best predictors of victimization: (1) delinquent behavior of the victim's peers; (2) delinquent behavior of the victim himself, in particular violent offending; (3) being male; and (4) frequent substance use.

Ethnic minorities and criminal justice

Although the Dutch constitution expresses the principle of equality before the law of all its residents (Art. 1 of the constitution), in practice, Art. 1 only refers to those who have Dutch nationality, including most of the Surinamese and Antilleans. The status of those who do not have Dutch nationality is dealt with under the provisions of the Aliens Act, which stipulates that some foreigners are not allowed residence in the country. Three types of foreigners can be expelled from the country: residents with no legal status, asylum seekers who are not admitted to the country and those who lose their legal right to residence because of a criminal conviction. All three groups are detained in police cells or in jail until they are expelled. Expulsion in the case of a criminal conviction is not an automatic process. It depends on a number of factors, such as the seriousness of the crime, the length of the prison sentence, the length of legal residence, the level of integration in Dutch society, whether they belong to the first or second generation, and the risk of recidivism.

Interactions between the police and ethnic minorities are often strained and police officers tend to be rude to them. Many members of ethnic minority groups complain because the police stop them repeatedly to ask for their papers or to carry out stop and search procedures. It is true that many police officers are prejudiced against minorities or misinterpret their speech or behavior (Vrij et al., 1991). However, the question is not whether the police cannot interpret the behavior or speech of minorities or are prejudiced against them. The question is whether official police reports are a reflection of committed offenses or of police prejudice or preconceptions.

Earlier studies (for example, Willemse and Meyboom, 1978) found that, although the police were less respectful and polite to minority suspects, arrests were based on concrete offending behavior or attempts and not on ethnicity or appearance. A large-scale study in 13 cities on internal immigration control by the police confirmed these outcomes (Aalberts, 1990). Despite complaints by minorities about these controls, most police officers exercise their controlling and supervising role in an even-handed manner when they suspect that a crime has been committed by a member of a minority group. In fact, there is no evidence that police decisions when suspecting the commission of a crime are influenced by the suspects' ethnicity. Junger (1990) has found that police officers on duty are confronted with powerful constraints derived from the police organization, the particular local situation in which they find themselves and the prevailing values and norms, all of which oppose racial discrimination. Moreover, the police are well aware that, if they present unfounded cases to the public prosecutor, the latter will reject these and admonish them about that practice.

The public prosecutor has to make three essential decisions: whether to hold the suspect in custody; whether the case should be taken to court; and what sentence to demand in court.

Controlling for the nature of the offense foreigners are remanded in custody more often than Dutch citizens. This is also the case for foreigners with a permanent address, although those with no fixed abode are even more likely to be remanded in custody. This is often attributed to the fear that foreigners with no fixed address will abscond. There may be two reasons why foreigners are more often sent for pre-trial detention: either foreigners commit more serious offenses than the population of Dutch origin, or nationality influences decisions in relation to detention policy. Differences between ethnic minorities and nationals in seriousness of delinquency are not great, although minorities tend to commit more drug offenses and violence. However, it is in non-serious cases that the prosecutor decides more frequently on pre-trial detention for foreigners than for Dutch citizens. The more serious the crime, the less the disparity in decisions relating to pre-trial detention: the higher the maximum possible sanction, the less the disproportion (Berghuis and Tigges, 1981). However, in this respect there are large policy differences between courts, variations that may be related to the number of migrants in the respective court districts: in a city such as Amsterdam pre-trial detention is imposed on more suspects than in a rural district.

Within the court system, the prosecutor occupies a powerful position. S/he plays a key role in penal proceedings since s/he demands the penalty in court and the judge will generally be guided by that demand when determining the level of sentence. In 80 percent of cases, the nature of the sentence is as proposed by the prosecutor (Slotboom et al., 1992), although in general the prison sentence is somewhat shorter in terms of length. Analysis shows that the nature of the sentence is explained most by whether or not there was a pre-trial detention. Eliminating process variables, the majority of the variance was explained by nationality and unemployment. The explanation given for the higher number of prison sentences imposed on migrants is that a higher proportion of foreigners do not appear at their trial. This is also the explanation for the higher number of foreigners remanded in custody. An additional reason is the fact that – Moslem suspects in particular – are not prepared to plead guilty even when proof is overwhelming, a circumstance related to cultural attitudes about dignity and shame. This variable has an effect on the way cases are dealt with by prosecutor and judge, a situation also observed in the United Kingdom (Hood, 1992).

Among juveniles, controlling for the seriousness of the offense, minorities are more likely than Dutch young people to be sentenced to detention within a judicial institution, and they are less likely to be placed in a Youth

Protection Home. They are also less likely to be sentenced to a community sanction (Van der Laan, 1988; Maas and Stuyling de Lange, 1989).

Once they are in detention, detainees have a number of fundamental rights that are guaranteed by the Dutch constitution as well as by the European Court of Human Rights in Strasbourg. These rights are elaborated in penitentiary legislation and regulations. One difficulty in ensuring these rights to imprisoned ethnic minorities is related to the fact that the detention situation is characterized by a certain degree of favoritism, creating dependency and some arbitrariness. This is felt more acutely by ethnic minorities than by native inmates because they suffer the consequences of stereotyping, and communication problems.

The following problems were identified in a study of three penitentiary institutions (Post, 2005). All detainees, when entering the prison, are entitled to receive information about their rights and duties and it is up to the governor of the institution to make sure that this information is both available and comprehensible. While the detention situation does not provide for sufficient clarity the information does not always reach minority prisoners. Similarly, the right to medical care is assured for all inmates; however, contacts between the prison general practitioner (GP) and minorities are frequently complicated by language and communication problems. In addition, minorities sometimes have wrong expectations with respect to the GPs' reticence in prescribing lots of medication or to refer patients to a specialist, both being in accordance with national basic principles on good-quality medical care. Finally, in terms of the freedom of religion and belief, the Islamic denomination is the second-largest, but whereas representatives of the three regular denominations (Catholicism, Protestantism and Humanism) are working regularly in all penal institutions, imams are there for only a few hours a week, because of problems in appointing them.

Post (2005) concludes that there is no difference in the formal legal position between natives and minorities in detention. In practice, however, a number of problems arise from the actual impediments in achieving the minorities' rights: minorities simply have more limited possibilities to make sure their rights are respected. However, both detainees and staff members attach much importance to a respectful approach to minorities and try to realize equality in the exercise of their fundamental rights.

Self-report data, and evidence from the International Self-reported Delinquency Study

As is well known, police statistics have a number of drawbacks. They are, first and foremost, a reflection of police activities and these are heavily influenced by policy measures of national and local authorities and the chiefs of police departments. For example, in 1999, the state ordered the police to prioritize the fight against juvenile crime,[6] setting annual targets for the numbers of police arrests. This led to an increase in the instances of tracking down and prosecuting young people, and a greater risk for them of being caught. The consequence was a huge increase in police statistics on juvenile crime, an increase that one does not find in the bi-annual self-report studies among the Dutch population aged 12–18 that are conducted by the Research Centre of the Ministry of Justice. The percentage of juveniles that admitted to have committed one or more delinquent acts in the year before the survey took place was 36.5 percent in 2005, while between 1990 and 2005 this ranged between 37 percent and 39 percent, showing a high degree of stability.

One additional problem with respect to ethnic minorities is that the police registration of ethnicity is relatively imprecise. Migrants who have Dutch nationality – such as those from former colonies – are not recorded according to their country of origin, giving an incomplete view of the total presence of minorities in the population. Self-report surveys do provide additional information and are particularly useful in ethnicity research. This is all the more so since these surveys – contrary to police data – allow us to analyze important background variables, leading to possible explanations for the young people's behavior.

A third problem might be that the police may be focused on arresting more minorities as suspects than Dutch people, leading to an over-representation of minorities in police statistics. However, studies by Junger (1990), Aalberts and Kamminga (1983) and Vrij et al. (1991) conclude that there are no indications that the Dutch police registration is based on selective arrest policies disadvantaging ethnic minorities.

In general, self-report surveys are considered to be a welcome addition to research methodology and a reasonably valid and reliable method (Elliott et al., 1980; Hindelang et al., 1981; Van der Heijden, 1995; Farrington et al., 1996; Junger-Tas and Haen Marshall, 1999). The question is, however, whether this method is as valid when applied to young migrants. In a study comparing police figures with self-report data of different ethnic minority groups, Junger (1990) found that Turkish and Moroccan boys were more reluctant to self-report (registered) offenses than Dutch and Surinamese boys. Among Dutch and Surinamese boys 13 percent did not report any offense that had been registered as a police contact, while among Turkish and Moroccan boys the levels were 37 percent and 44 percent, respectively. Now Junger found that the length of stay in the host country was negatively related to under-reporting offenses and at the time of her study only 14 percent of minorities was born in the host country. At this moment – 20 years later – more than 60 percent of minorities has been born in the Netherlands, so one might expect more valid delinquency self-reports.

Taking into account all of the considerations, however, one major conclusion drawn from these studies is that, while the total volume of crime is probably more accurately measured by victimization studies than by self-reporting, the self-report method remains a viable and valuable way to test

Table 6.4 'Last year' prevalence of delinquent behavior by ethnic background – 2006 (in %)

Offenses	Netherl.	Western Migrants	Non-W. Migrants	Turkey	Morocco	Surinam/ Antilles
N	1454	149	209	140	115	172
Vandalism	7.3	14.2	10.1	7.9	6.9	10.1
Shoplifting	6.9	7.3	8.0	4.3	7.8	11.6
Burglary	0.9	2.7	1.9	2.2	2.7	0.6
Bicycle theft	3.4	5.3	6.6	5.1	5.1	5.8
Car theft	0.3	0.0	0.0	0.7	1.0	1.8
Theft out of car***	0.5	2.6	1.4	2.9	5.1	1.2
Hacking	5.2	3.3	5.2	5.9	3.5	4.1
Robbery	2.1	0.0	3.9	1.5	2.7	1.8
Carrying weapon**	8.6	17.1	9.5	9.3	6.9	14.0
Threats w. violence***	1.5	2.7	2.9	3.6	2.7	3.0
Group fights***	12.9	17.2	16.5	25.7	16.5	20.5
Assault*	2.5	5.3	2.4	6.4	1.7	2.9
Deal. drugs	3.4	4.6	4.3	2.9	6.0	3.5

Notes: $^*p < .05$, $^{**}p < .01$, $^{***}p < .001$.

theory, and to identify correlates of individual differences in delinquent participation (Junger-Tas and Haen Marshall, 1999).

The chapter will therefore continue with considering the results of Table 6.4, which gives an overview of the last year prevalence of 13 delinquent acts and, surprisingly, differences with Dutch respondents are not that extreme. Five of thirteen offenses, of which four are acts of aggression, show clear differences: theft from cars; carrying a weapon (usually a knife); threatening with violence; and group fights and assault. Group differences of two offenses, vandalism and car theft, are almost significant ($p < .06$). Western migrants, of which a large proportion come from the new EU member states and the former Yugoslavia, score high on vandalism, carrying a weapon and assault. This preference for weapons and aggression might be the result of the prevalent culture and traditions in the country of origin. Non-western migrants tend to concentrate only on vandalism, bicycle theft and robbery, which might be explained by the number of illegal (undocumented) newcomers. Robbery in particular is a very simple and easy offense, and one often committed by illegal migrants (De Haan, 1993).

Rates of delinquency are highest among those who have lived in the host country for a substantial period of time, most of whom were born there. There is a striking difference in delinquency between Turkish and Moroccan juveniles. Turkish boys commit very few offenses, but when they do these tend to be violent: not only do they fight, but they also commit (serious)

Table 6.5 Seriousness of offenses by ethnicity (%)

Offenses	Netherl.	Western Minorities	Non-W- Minorities	Turkish	Moroccan	Surin/ Antil.
N	1490	153	215	140	117	174
Non-serious	25.3	33.3	27.3	29.8	24.8	34.5
Serious*	9.3	14.4	12.0	11.3	11.1	10.9

Note: $*p < .05$.

assaults and threaten with violence. By contrast, Moroccan boys are not really violent, but they tend to commit serious property offenses, such as thefts of cars, thefts from cars, robberies and drug dealing. The latter is especially surprising in light of the fact that young Moslems hardly ever use drugs or alcohol.

The Surinam/Antillean group commits property offenses such as shoplifting and car theft, but they also fight a lot and threaten others – although less so than in the case of Turkish boys. It should be observed that the percentage of missing answers is rather high for car theft (4.8 percent) and robbery (6.8 percent). Taking into account the high number of police contacts with specific ethnic groups, this might suggest some under-reporting of these – serious – offenses. On the other hand, the three major ethnic groups in the Netherlands –Turkish, Moroccan and Surinamese/Antillean – report the greatest number of offenses, which is in accord with official police data.

We also looked at the relationship of ethnicity with seriousness of reported offenses. Surprisingly the data showed no significant difference with respect to non-serious offenses[7] ($p < .38$), but they did so regarding serious offenses[8] as shown in table 6.5 (top of page) ($p < .05$).

In particular both Western and Non-Western juveniles as well as the Surinamese/Antillean group score very high.

Some explanations of delinquent behavior by ethnic minorities

Family and delinquency

A considerable number of studies have been devoted to the broken family and its impact on delinquency, and most of the research indicated the existence of such relationship (Hirschi, 1969; Nye, 1958; Wilkinson, 1980; Johnson, 1986; Morash and Rucker, 1989; Wells and Rankin, 1991; Rutenfrans and Terlouw, 1994; Junger-Tas et al., 2003a; Haas et al., 2004). However, meta-analysis showed only a weak relation of 13 percent to 15 percent (Wells and Rankin, 1991). One Dutch study did not find a significant difference in delinquency according to complete or broken family. Moreover, they found that the strength of the relation differed according to ethnic

Table 6.6 Parental bonding by ethnicity***

	Low bonding	Medium bonding	High bonding
Netherlands	0.7	28.2	71.1
Western minorities	2.0	36.2	61.8
Non-Western minorities	0.5	44.4	55.1
Turkish	0.0	23.4	76.6
Morocco	1.7	34.2	64.1
Surinamese/Antillean	3.4	39.1	57.5

Note: ***$p < .001$.

group (Blom et al., 2005). This was confirmed by our own study, although there remained a significant result over the total sample ($p < .001$).

However, it is clear that family quality is much more important than family structure. That is why there were questions about the relationship between the young people and their parents, whether or not they took evening meals with their parents and whether or not their parents spent leisure time with their children. On the basis of mean scores of the answers a bonding scale was constructed ranging from negative to positive ($\alpha = .52$).

Table 6.6 shows that non-Western and Surinamese/Antillean juveniles have fewer interactions with their parents (in many cases only the mother) and have less positive bonds with them than the other groups, while Dutch juveniles as well as Turkish ones reported to have very positive bonds with their parents ($p < .001$).

Minority parents generally exercise little control on their children's behavior – with the exception of Turkish parents – and they often have no knowledge of the identity of their children's friends. Interestingly, in all ethnic groups parents differentiate in terms of the degree of control by gender. Dutch parents exercise the greatest degree of control over their daughters, more so than Western (the new EU member states included) and non-Western minorities. As is made clear in Figure 6.4 (below) control that is exercised 'most of the time' is highest on Dutch females and is lowest in relation to non-Western males. At the same time control 'sometimes' and 'seldom' is increasing from Dutch girls to non-Western male migrants.

The school

A number of international replications of Hirschi's Social Control theory (Hirschi, 1969; Junger, 1990; Tanioka and Glaser, 1991; LeBlanc, 1994; Junger-Tas et al., 2003a) show that bonds and commitment to school correlate negatively with delinquent behavior. The school environment provides opportunities and encourages young people to establish friendship ties with conventional others and to strive for conventional goals. Other

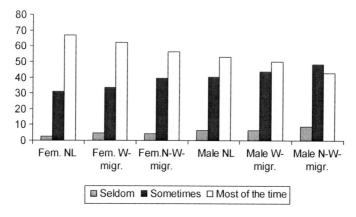

Figure 6.4 Parental control by ethnic groups (%)

research has demonstrated that risk factors at the level of the school, such as a lack of school bonding, school failure and truancy present adolescents with risks for delinquent behavior (Maguin and Loeber, 1996; Gottfredson, 2001). Adherents of Opportunity theory (Felson, 1998) see the school as a place that may promote delinquency, if only because it brings together many youngsters who are at the criminally most active age, in a situation where there may be only minimum supervision. How well do young migrants at school do if one considers truancy and repeating classes – two signs of a failing school career?

Truancy does not differentiate significantly among students, which is no surprise since at age 12–15 attending school is still compulsory ($p < .06$).

It is clear from Figure 6.5 that Dutch students and young migrants from West and East Europe differ little in respect of either truancy or repeating

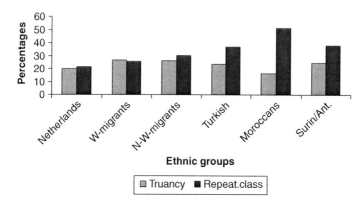

Figure 6.5 School functioning by ethnicity (%)

Table 6.7   Last year prevalence of delinquency by school failure (%)

	Truancy***			Repeating classes***		
	Never	once	2–3 times	Never	Once	Twice or >
N	1783	357	130	1673	561	37
Non-serious offense	15.9	28.8	29.2	18.5	17.6	21.6
Non-ser. + serious off.	5.2	15.1	21.5	5.6	12.8	27

Note: ***$p < .000$.

classes (20–25 percent). However, 30 percent of non-Western migrants had to repeat a class at least once and this percentage rises to more than 50 percent for Moroccan students and about 37 percent in the case of Turkish, Surinamese and Antillean students.

One further question is to what extent these variables are related to delinquent behavior. This is shown in Table 6.7 where we found that both variables are strongly related to delinquency, and in particular to the combination of non-serious and serious offending.

The neighborhood

Every neighborhood has specific characteristics which may either curb or encourage antisocial behavior. The neighborhood is important for at least two reasons. First, because most young people find their friends there; and secondly, because much crime and troublesome behavior takes place in one's own neighborhood.[9]

It is unsurprising that unemployment is related to specific neighborhoods ($p < .001$). But the fact that neighborhood was also found to be related with family bonding and parental control ($p < .001$) as well as with the school performance of juveniles ($p < .001$) did strike us as noteworthy. These findings tend to confirm those of Sampson and Laub (1993) and Sampson et al. (1993), who stated that macro-sociological variables such as unemployment and neighborhood are not related directly to delinquency, but instead are mediated by the educative skills of parents, which are in turn strongly affected by unemployment, poverty and living in a deprived neighborhood. Moreover, the fact that many criminal activities take place in disorganized neighborhoods creates good conditions for juveniles to become involved in a deviant youth culture (Felson, 1998).

Young people's bonds with the neighborhood they live in is measured by a scale developed by Olweus (1979) and Sampson et al. (1999) and consisting of 13 items.[10] Scores range from very negative (1) to very positive (4). The scale measures neighborhood quality and has an α of .81.

Most young people have an attachment to their neighborhood and would miss it if they had to move away. Dutch children are the most positive, seeing the fewest problems in their neighborhood. One striking fact is that Turkish juveniles have the same scores as Dutch juveniles, which could be related to the strong social cohesion of that ethnic group and the effective informal controls that parents and the Turkish community exercise on their children (Junger-Tas et al., 2003b). Non-Western migrants, the Surinamese/Antillean group and juveniles of Moroccan origin are the most negative about their neighborhood.

But independently of young people's appraisal of the quality of their neighborhood, concentrations of migrant populations are found principally in neighborhoods characterized by high-rise apartments and cramped accommodation. These circumstances force young people to spend much of their leisure time on the streets and this offers many opportunities for troublesome behavior and the committssion of offenses. However, most juveniles spend time with a permanent (smaller or larger) peer group and in that respect at least all ethnic groups are alike.

However, as Table 6.8 shows, Dutch juveniles do not frequently spend leisure time in public places such as a mall, a square or their own neighborhood, which might explain why they do not harass people 'for fun' as often as non-Western and Moroccan youngsters. It is also noteworthy that Surinamese and Turkish juveniles do not participate in this sort of low-level antisocial activity.

Youth gangs

As mentioned above, most of the youngsters in the study – about 70 percent and independent of ethnicity and gender – have a permanent group of friends with whom they spend time and undertake activities. In that respect we wanted to know to what extent such a group could be considered to be a youth gang. An international research group – the Eurogang group (Decker and Weerman, 2005) – developed six characteristics on which a juvenile

Table 6.8 Some neighborhood variables by ethnicity (%)

	Netherlands	Western migrants	Non-W- migrants	Turkish	Moroccan	Surin/ Ant.
Deprived neighborhood***	6.7	12.6	16.3	7.9	18.1	21.5
Leisure time spent						
In public places***	58.8	69.6	79.2	80.2	85.9	78.8
Harassing people***	1.8	3.4	4.4	2.1	4.3	1.8

Note: ***$p < .000$.

must score positively in order to be defined as a gang member ($\alpha = .80$). The six items are as follows: (1) being a member of a permanent youth group, (2) that group should be in existence for at least 3 months, (3) its members must meet each other in public places, (4) illegal activities are normatively accepted, (5) the group undertakes also illegal activities together and (6) the juvenile in question considers the group as a gang.

Taking 70 percent as a basis, Table 6.9 shows that juveniles underwrite in a decreasing order the following characteristics. About two-third of migrant groups report that their group of friends has been in existence for 3 months or longer and about half of them, compared with 40 percent of Dutch juveniles, declare that the group is street oriented. However, considerably fewer youngsters – on average between 20 and 25 percent – report that the group accepts normatively illegal behavior and even fewer state that their group is committing offenses. Finally, only 6 percent of Dutch and Surinamese young people consider their group to be a youth gang, although 14.5 percent of non-Western, 10 percent of Moroccan and 18.5 percent of Turkish youth do so. It is to be observed that as far as the latter two groups are concerned the same percentages are recorded both for declaring that the group of friends commits offenses and that their group constitutes a youth gang.

At the same time it does not seem a coincidence that the lowest percentage of youth gang membership is to be found among Dutch, Western and Surinamese children. These are all groups who do not meet too many obstacles in life and are being relatively successful in society. The other groups, in

Table 6.9   Membership of youth gangs by ethnicity (%)

	Netherl.	W-Migr.	N-W-Migr.	Turkish	Morocco	Surin/Antill.	Sign.
N	1490	153	215	140	117	174	
1) Perman. peer group	69	74	70	76.5	66.5	64	n.s
2) Exists > 3 months*	63.5	69.5	65.5	73	64	65.5	$p < .04$
3) Street-oriented***	40.5	51	54.5	63	57.5	47	$p < .000$
4) Accept illegal behavior**	23.5	34.5	26.5	22	20.5	18	$p < .01$
5) Group com. illeg. Acts***	19.5	29	26	18.5	10.5	18	$p < .001$
6) Cons. it youth gang***	6	8	14.5	18.5	10.5	6.5	$p < .000$

Notes: *$p < .05$, **$p < .01$, ***$p < .001$.

particular Turkish and Moroccan young people, record considerable higher percentages.

In this connection one may wonder to what extent – self-reported – youth gang members deviate from those young people who do not belong to a youth gang. Controlling for delinquency we found that, compared with the other youths, juveniles who state they are members of youth gangs live disproportionately in deprived neighborhoods with high levels of crime. They are also less subject to control by parents, attend schools with problems of vandalism and theft, display higher levels of risk behaviors such as truancy and drinking alcohol, have less self-control and score higher on aggression. In other words, these juveniles differ significantly from other delinquents on a number of crucial variables with respect to background, family, school career, personality and delinquency.

Multivariate analysis

If one wished to say something about possible explanations for the higher delinquency involvement of minorities as compared to Dutch juveniles, one of the first questions to consider would be whether that explanation was to be found in their ethnic origin or in their weak socio-economic situation. Blom et al. (2005) have examined the question of to what extent the risk of being suspected of having committed an offense is related to demographic and socio-economic background factors by way of a logistic regression. They entered age (12–17), sex, family structure, the percentage of non-Western migrants living in the neighborhood, the parents' dependency on social benefits and family income in the analysis. All minority groups run a higher risk of being recorded as suspects than Dutch juveniles, but that risk is highest in the case of first-generation Antilleans (odds ratio 2,0) and Moroccans (odds ratio 3,3). However, the analysis showed that the differential delinquency involvement of Dutch and ethnic minority juveniles is explained to a great extent by differences in age and sex composition. When socio-economic characteristics are also taken into account, differences in delinquency involvement are reduced still further.

In our own study we carried out a multiple regression analysis shown in table 6.10 (next page) and if one looks at the variables in the model (explained variance is $R^2 = .43$), one finds a number of predictors which are also mentioned in the research literature. For example, a variable which has often been considered as less important by social control theory (Hirschi, 1969), but is increasingly judged as one of the most important explanative factors (Warr, 2002; Huizinga et al., 2003; Thornberry et al., 2003; Decker and Weerman, 2005), is the peer group with risky behavior. This variable provides the highest contribution in our study ($\beta = .31$).

There is also a strong relationship between substance use and delinquency ($\beta = .21$) as is the case for a positive attitude to violence ($\beta = .12$). Subsequently, sex, living in a disorganized neighborhood and frequently going

Table 6.10 Stepwise multiple regression – dependent variable is delinquency involvement

Model	Unstandardized coefficients		Standardiz. coefficients			Correlations	
	B	Std. Error	Beta	T	Sig.	R	R²
11 (Constant)	−,148	,058		−2550	,011		
Risky behavior of peers	,005	,000	,312	14,222	,000	.545	.297
Positive attitude to violence	,003	,000	,118	5224	,000	.590	.348
Substance use	,103	,010	,216	9982	,000	.623	.388
Sex	,116	,016	,128	7134	,000	.634	.402
Disorganized neighborhood	,001	,000	,066	3298	,001	.640	.409
Going out at night	,016	,004	,074	3816	,000	.644	415
Truancy	,061	,015	,077	4032	,000	.648	.419
Age	−,043	,009	−,093	−4776	,000	.651	.424
Repeating classes	,065	,017	,069	3700	,000	.655	.429
Self-control	−,002	,001	−,068	−2932	,003	.657	,431
Ethnicity	,019	,010	,038	2016	,044	.658	.433

Notes: $R = .66$, $R^2 = .43$.

out at night – variables related to the antisocial peer group behavior – contribute to the prediction of delinquent behavior. School failure and its consequences, such as repeating classes and frequent truancy, are also clear predictors of delinquency.

Finally, ethnicity hardly predicts delinquent behavior ($\beta = .04$, sign. $= .04$), demonstrating that stereotypes about ethnic minorities are unfounded and short-sighted.

Concluding discussion

Differences in the socio-economic situation between the population of origin and ethnic minority migrants could clearly be established in both studies (Bijl et al., 2006; Blom et al., 2005; Junger-Tas et al., 2008). For example, the lowest percentage of unemployed parents are to be found among Dutch and West-European parents and the highest among migrants from Africa, Morocco and the Antilles. Moreover, the latter groups live in deprived neighborhoods with the worst houses and high levels of crime.

Compared with Dutch juveniles, young people in these neighborhoods do not get along so well with their parents and are not as effectively controlled by them. In addition, our study shows that both parents' unemployment and living in a disorganized neighborhood are related to school failure and frequent truancy from school. These factors are strong predictors of delinquent behavior. They confirm Sampson and Laub's finding that social structural variables are related indirectly to delinquency. Turkish juveniles offer a remarkable exception to this finding in that they have both strong bonds with their parents and are also well controlled by them. This situation might explain why the rates of delinquency among Turkish young people – both boys and girls – are relatively low.

With respect to spending leisure time the peer group is extremely important, in particular because juveniles living in cramped conditions in disorganized neighborhoods spend most of their time on the streets with friends they have been raised with and which they know best. They also go out at night with a large peer group and one of their preferred leisure time occupations is the harassment of other people 'just for fun'. These factors are also predictors of delinquency and it is no surprise that many of these juveniles are members of a youth gang. The unstimulating school environment, the street-oriented peer group and the negative characteristics of the neighborhood combine to present juveniles with many opportunities to commit offenses. Because of their school failures and frequent truancy, such young people have little hope for a successful social and economic future (see also Felson, 1998). Of course, personality factors also play a role in the prediction of delinquency. For example, most delinquents have low levels of self-control and a relatively positive attitude to violence (see also Gottfredson and Hirschi, 1990). In this respect Turkish juveniles are again an exception in that they tend to resort to violence even more frequently than the other youths: when they commit an offense this tends to be violent in nature.

In summarizing our findings, the following conclusions may be drawn. First, the socio-economic situation of ethnic minority groups is found to be an important factor. It has both a direct and an indirect relationship with delinquent behavior, since the low position on the social ladder determines the neighborhood in which a child will be raised. Both low social position and the disorganized neighborhood have a negative impact on a juvenile's upbringing, his school career, his peer group and his leisure occupations. All these factors may influence his behavior: the more his chances of social and economic success are diminished, the less he has to lose in breaking the law and the greater the risk of becoming a career criminal.

Second, cultural influences on second-generation migrants also play a – limited – role. These are, in particular, expressed in the raising of of their children, where boys receive considerable freedom, while most girls are strictly controlled. The consequences of such upbringing increase the risk of boys harassing people and committing offenses, while at the same time Moslem girls have more successful school careers and tend to commit few delinquent acts. The favorable attitude toward violence among Turkish boys may also be linked to the culture of their home regions of Turkey .

However, these influences should not be overstated. They are likely to disappear slowly to the extent that these ethnic groups participate more successfully in Dutch society and achieve higher levels of prosperity.

Notes

1. And 1.4 million migrants from Western countries.
2. The Social Cultural Planning Office presents bi-annual Minority reports.
3. There exist three levels in the Dutch Secondary education system: the lowest level consists of 3 years of vocational training, the second level consists of 4 years of general or professional education and the third level leads to higher education and takes 6 years.
4. According to Dutch Juvenile Penal Law, the age of criminal responsibility is age 12 (under that age children are dealt with by the Youth Protection system). The age of Criminal majority is 18, although in exceptional cases youths aged 16–18 may be judged under adult penal law. Police data often cover juveniles as well as young adults.
5. The study is the Dutch part of the *International Self-report Delinquency Study* (ISRD-2), in which 30 countries collaborate: EU member states, including the ten new member states, Armenia, Russia, Bosnia-Herzegovina, the USA, Canada, Venezuela, Surinam and the Antilles.
6. Policy planning document Dutch police 1999.
7. Non-serious offenses are: vandalism, shoplifting, 'hacking', group fighting and carrying a weapon (knife).
8. Serious offenses are: bicycle theft, car theft, theft from a car, burglary, assault, threatening with violence, robbery and drug dealing.
9. In addition, much crime takes place in the city center and in areas of the city where there are large numbers of shops, bars, and clubs (Hesseling, 1994).
10. Negative remarks include, for example, 'there is a lot of fighting in my neighborhood' or 'there is a lot of crime/drugs dealing in my neighborhood'; positive items are 'people in my neighborhood help each other' or 'I like my neighborhood'.

References

Aalberts, M.M.J. (1990), *Politie tussen Discretie en Discriminatie: Operationeel Vreemdelingentoezicht in Nederland*, Antwerpen: Kluwer.

Aalberts, M.M.J. and E.M. Kamminga (1983), *Politie en Allochtonen*, Den Haag: Staatsuitgeverij.

Berghuis, A.C. and L.C.M. Tigges (1981), 'Voorlopige Hechtenis bij Buitenlanders', *Delikt en Delinkwent*, 11(4): 24–30.

Blom, M., J. Oudhof, R.V. Bijl and B.F.M. Bakker (eds) (2005), *Verdacht van Criminaliteit-Allochtonen en Autochtonen nader bekeken*, Den Haag: CBS/WODC.

Blokland, A. (2005), *Crime over the Life Span – Trajectories of Criminal Behavior in Dutch Offenders*, Dissertatie Universiteit: Leiden.

Bottoms, A. and J. Dignan (2004), 'Youth Justice in Great Britain', in M. Tonry and A.N. Doob, *Youth Crime and Youth Justice*, Chicago: University of Chicago Press, pp. 21–185.

Bovenkerk, F. and J. Junger-Tas (2000), *De Oorzaken van Criminaliteit onder Etnische Minderheden: Twee Invalshoeken (Causes of Crime among Ethnic Minorities: Two Perspectives)*, The Hague: National Science Organisation.

Bovenkerk, F., D. Siegel and D. Zaitch (2003), 'Organized Crime and Ethnic Reputation Manipulation', *Crime, Law and Social Change*, 39(1): 23–7.

Bijl, R.V., A.Zorlu, A.S. van Rijn, R.P.W. Jennissen and M. Blom (2005), *Integratiekaart 2005- Trend- en Cohortanalyses*, The Hague: CBS/WODC.

Bijl, R.V., M. Blom, J. Oudhof and B.M.F. Bakker (2006), 'Criminaliteit, Etniciteit en Demografische Ontwikkeling', in *Justitiële Verkenningen- Demografische Ontwikkelingen*, jrg. 32 (3): 55–75.

Centraal Bureau voor de Statistiek (2004), *Allochtonen in Nederland*, Voorburg/ Heerlen: CBS.

Central Bureau of Statistics, Statline (2006), *Allochtonen in Nederland*, Voorburg/Heerlen: CBS.

Decker, Scott H. and Frank M. Weerman (eds) (2005), *European Street Gangs and Troublesome Youth Groups*, New York: Altamira Press.

De Haan, W. (1993), *Beroving van Voorbijgangers: Rapport van een Onderzoeknaar Straatroof in 1991 in Amsterdam en Utrecht Report of Street (Robbery in Amsterdam and Utrecht in 1991)*, The Hague: Ministry of Internal Affairs.

De Haan, W. (1997), 'Minorities, Crime, and Criminal Justice in the Netherlands', in I. Haen Marshall (ed.), *Minorities, Migrants and Crime*, Sage, pp. 198–224. Los Ageles, London.

De Kort, M. and D-J. Korf (1990), 'The Development of Drug Trade and Drug Control in the Netherlands: A Historical Perspective', in *Crime, Law and Social Change*, 17(1): 123–44.

Elliott, D.S. and S.S. Ageton (1980), 'Reconciling Race and Class Differences in Self-reported and Official Estimates of Delinquency', *American Sociological Review*, 45: 95–110.

Engbersen, G., J. van der Leun and J. de Boom (2007), 'The Fragmentation of Migration and Crime in the Netherlands', in M. Tonry and C. Bijleveld (eds), *Crime and Justice in The Netherlands*, 35, 389–453.

Etman, O., P. Mutsaers and H. Werdmölder (1993), 'Onveiligheid en Allochtonen', in *Integrale Veiligheidsrapportage* (Report to the Minister of Internal Affairs), The Hague: Ministry of Internal Affairs.

Farrington, D.P., R. Loeber, M. Stouthamer-Loeber, W. van Kammen and L. Schmidt (1996), 'Self-reported Delinquency and a Combined Delinquency Seriousness Scale based on Boys, Mothers and Teachers: Concurrent and Predictive Validity for African Americans and Caucasians', *Criminology*, 34: 493–517.

Felson, M. (1998), *Crime in Everyday Life – Insight and Implications for Society*, 2nd edn, Thousand Oaks/London: Pine Forge Press.

Gottfredson, D.C. (2001), *Schools and Delinquency*, Cambridge: Cambridge University Press.

Gottfredson, M.R. and T. Hirschi (1990), *A General Theory of Crime*, Stanford, California: Stanford University Press.

Gijsberts, M. (2003), 'Minderheden in het Basisonderwijs en in het Voortgezet Onderwijs', in *Rapportage Minderheden 2003*, Den Haag: Sociaal Cultureel Planbureau, pp. 63–143.

Gijsberts, M. (2004), 'Minderheden en Integratie', in *Sociaal en Cultureel Rapport 2004 – In het Zicht van de Toekomst*, Den Haag: SCP, pp. 131–77.

Haas, H., D.P. Farrington, M. Killias and G. Sattar (2004), 'The Impact of Different Family Configurations on Delinquency', *British Journal of Criminology*, 44(4): 520–32.

Hesseling, R.B.P. (1994), *Stoppen of Verplaatsen? Een Literatuuronderzoek over elegenheidsbeperkende Preventie en Verplaatsing van Criminaliteit*, The Hague, Ministry of Justice: WODC.

Hindelang, M.J., T. Hirschi and J.G. Weis (1981), *Measuring Delinquency*, Beverly Hills: Sage.

Hirschi, T. (1969), *Causes of Delinquency*, Berkeley, Los Angeles: University of California Press.

Hood, R. (1992), *Race and Sentencing: A Study in the Crown Court*, Oxford: Clarendon Press.

Huizinga, D., A. Wylie Weiher, Rachele Espiritu et al. (2003), 'Delinquency and Crime: Some Highlights from the Denver Youth Survey', in T.P. Thornberry and M.D. Krohn (eds), *Taking Stock of Delinquency – an Overview of Findings from Contemporary Longitudinal Studies*, New York, US: Kluwer Academic/Plenum Publishers, pp. 47–93.

Huls, F.W.M. (1995), *Minderheden in Nederland, 1987–1993 (Minorities in The Netherlands, 1987–1993)*, The Hague, NL: Central Bureau of Statistics.

Johnson, R.E. (1986), 'Mother's versus Father's Role in Causing Delinquency', *Adolescence*, 22(86): 305–15.

Junger, M (1990), *Delinquency and Ethnicity-an Investigation on social Factors Relating to Delinquency among Moroccan, Turkish, Surinamese and Dutch Boys*, Deventer/Boston: Kluwer Law and Taxation.

Junger-Tas, J. and I. Haen Marshall (1999), 'The Self-Report Methodology in Crime Research', in *Crime and Justice: A Review of Research*, 25: 291–368.

Junger-Tas, J., I. Haen Marshall and D. Ribeaud (2003a), *Delinquency in an International Perspective*, Monsey, NY: Criminal Justice Press.

Junger-Tas, J., M.J.L.F. Cruyff, P.M.v. de Looij-Jansen and F. Reelick (2003b), *Etnische minderheden en het Belang van Binding: een onderzoek naar antisociaal gedrag van jongeren*, The Hague, NL: SDU/Vermande.

Junger-Tas, J., M. Steketee and M. Moll (2008), *Achtergronden van Jeugddelinquentie en Middelengebruik*, Utrecht: Verwey-Jonker Instituut.

LeBlanc, M. (1994), 'Family, School, Delinquency and Criminality, the Predictive Power of an elaborate Social Control Theory of Males', *Criminal Behavior and Mental Health*, 4: 101–17.

Maas, C.J. and J. Stuyling de Lange (1989), 'Selectiviteit in de Rechtsgangvan Buitenlandse Verdachtenen Verdachten behorende tot Etnische Groepen', *Tijdschrift voor Criminologie*, 1, 1–14.

Maguin, E. and R. Loeber (1996), 'Academic Performance and Delinquency', *Crime and Justice – A Review of Research*, 20, 145–227.

Morash, M. and L. Rucker (1989), 'An Exploratory Study of the Connection of Mother's Age at Childbearing to Het Children's Delinquency in Four Data Sets', *Crime and Delinquency*, 35(1): 45–93.

Nye, I. (1958), *Family Relationships and Delinquent Behaviour*, New York: Wiley.

Olweus, D. (1979), 'Stability of Aggressive Reaction Patterns in Males: A Review', *Psychological Bulletin*, 86(4): 852–75.

Post, M. (2005), *Detentie en Culturele Diversiteit*, Utrecht: Boom Juridische Uitgeverij, Pompe Reeks.

Rutenfrans, C.J.C and G.J. Terlouw (1994), *Delinquentie, sociale controle en 'Life events'*, Arnhem: Gouda Quint/WODC.

Rutter, M., H. Giller and A. Hagell (1998), *Antisocial Behavior by Young People*, Cambridge: Cambridge University Press.

Sampson, R.J. and J. Laub (1993), *Crime in the Making – Pathways and Turning Points through Life*, Cambridge, MA: Harvard University Press.

Sampson, R.J., Raudenbusch, S.W. and Felton Earls (1993), 'Neighborhood and Violent Crime: A Multilevel Study of Collective Efficacy for Children', *Science*, 277, 914–18.

Sampson, R.J., S.W. Raudenbusch and Felton Earls (1997), 'Neighborhoods and Violent Crime: A Multilevel Study of Collective Efficacy', *Science*, 277: 914–18.

Sampson, R.J., Morenoff, J.D. and Felton Earls (1999), 'Beyond Social Capital: Spatial Dynamics of Collective Efficacy for Children', *American Sociological Review*, 64: 633–60.

Slotboom, A., H. Koppe, I. Passchier, L. de Jonge, and R. Meijer (1992), 'De Relatie tussen Eis en Vonnis:Strafvordering en Straftoemeting in vier arrondissementen', *Justitiële Verkenningen*, 8: 59–72.

Sociaal Cultureel Planbureau (2003), *Rapportage Minderheden 2003*, Den Haag: SCP.

Tanioka, I. and D. Glaser (1991), 'School Uniforms, Routine Activities, and Social Control of Delinquency in Japan', *Youth and Society*, 23: 50–75.

Thornberry T.P, A.J. Lizotte, M.D. Krohn, C.A. Smith and P.K. Porter (2003), 'Causes and Consequences of Delinquency-Findings from the Rochester Development Study', in T.P. Thornberry and M.D. Krohn (2003), *Taking Stock of Delinquency – An Overview of Findings from Contemporary Longitudinal Studies*, New York, US: Kluwer Academic/Plenum Publishers, pp. 11–47.

Van der Heijden, P.G.M., K. Sijtsma and H.'t Hart (1995), 'Self-report Schalen zijn nog steeds Betrouwbaar', *Tijdschrift voor Criminologie*, 37: 71–7.

Van der Laan, P.H. (1988), 'Innovations in the Dutch Juvenile Justice System', in J. Junger-Tas and Richard L. Block (eds), *Juvenile Delinquency in the Netherlands*, Amsterdam: Kugler Publishers.

Van Dijk, J.J.M. and P. Mayhew (1992), *Criminal Victimization in the Industrialized World: Key-Findings of the 1989 and 1992 International Crime Surveys*, The Hague: Ministry of Justice.

Van Dijk, J.J.M. and D. Van Soomeren (1993), 'Slachtofferenquête allochtonen,' in *Integrale Veiligheidsrapportage*, Report to the Minister of Internal Affairs, The Hague: Ministry of Internal Affairs.

Vrij, A.F., W. Winkel and L. Koppelaar (1991), 'Interactie tussen Politiefunctionarissen en Allochtone Burgers', *Nederlands Tijdschrift voor de Psychologie*, 46(1): 8–19.

Warr, M. (2002), *Companions in Crime – The Social Aspects of Criminal Conduct*, Cambridge, UK: Cambridge University Press.

Wells, L.E. and J.H. Rankin (1991), 'Families and Delinquency: A Meta-analysis of the Impact of Broken Homes', *Social problems*, 38, 1, 71–93.

Wilkinson, K. (1980), 'The Broken Home and Delinquent Behavior: An Alternative Interpretation of Contradictory Findings', in Tr. Hirschi and M. Gottfredson (eds), *Understanding Crime: Current Theory and Research*, Beverly Hills: Sage Publications.

Willemse, H.M. and M.L. Meyboom (1978), 'Personal Characteristics of Suspects and Treatment by the Police: A Street Experiment', *Abstracts on Police Science*, 6: 275–301.

Yinger, J.M. (1994), *Ethnicity*, New York: State University of New York Press.

7
Race, Crime and Criminal Justice in Portugal

Manuela Ivone Cunha
University of Minho, CRIA-UM, Portugal

Introduction: On ethnic foreigners, immigrants and state statistics

Any focus on the issue of ethnicity, crime and criminal justice in Portugal has to take into account two specificities which have comparative implications – not to mention the fact that comparability may be hindered from the start at the more general level of the statistical data infrastructure itself.[1] First, Portuguese official statistics register only nationalities, not ethnicity or phenotype. Direct or indirect registration by the state of data allowing for the identification of such information is prevented by law in order not to reinforce stereotyping (see Cabecinhas 2007) or the racialization of society.[2] The existence of ethnic/racial minorities is therefore not formally acknowledged by the state, which recognizes only individual citizens. Portuguese citizens thus include, without any ethnic specification, ex-immigrants who have acquired the Portuguese citizenship.[3]

Second, state crime statistics only use the generic category of foreigners, making no distinction between residents – whether documented or undocumented – and visitors. Official statistics do not single out immigrants. 'Foreigners' cannot, however, be used as a proxy category for immigrants as it is wider, including both residents and non-residents. As an example, between a quarter and an eighth of the convicted foreigners in the period 1997–2003 were resident abroad prior to their conviction (Seabra and Santos 2005: 96).

The numbers of foreigners residing legally in Portugal rose from a mere 0.3 percent (29,579) of the total resident population in 1960 to 3.9 percent (414,717) in 2005, although undocumented residents may currently be between 50,000 and 100,000 (Guia 2008: 39, 53). For a long time Portugal has been a country with consistent emigration trends. However, since the 1970s, it has also become an immigration country: first following the end of the Portuguese colonial empire and the independence of former colonies that took place after the 1974 democratic revolution; and, later on, in the 1980s and 1990s, with the economic boom and the country's entrance into the European Union in 1986. The end of the former Soviet Union also contributed to shape the landscape of immigration in more recent times (for an overview of the evolution of immigration patterns in Portugal, see Baganha, Marques and Fonseca 2000; Baganha and Marques 2001; Pena Pires 2003).

Initially, the country received mostly Africans from the Portuguese-speaking African countries[4] (especially Angola, Guinea-Bissau, Cape Verde and Mozambique). From the 1990s onward, the range of nationalities in Portugal was transformed again by a sharp increase of arrivals from Brazil and, a decade later, from Eastern Europe, mostly from Ukraine and Russia. In 2004, 41 percent of the legal foreign residents came from Europe, 34 percent from African countries (mostly from lusophone countries) and 19 percent from Latin American countries (especially Brazil) (Guia 2008: 48–50). This overall distribution of nationalities has not changed significantly since that time.

Immigrants account for 8 percent of the total working population in Portugal (Almeida 2003). For the most part, they tend to work in the construction sector and in the bottom tier of the service economy, whether formal or informal (Baganha 1996; Baganha, Ferrão and Malheiros 2002; Fonseca 2005). Considering the compared structure of the national and foreign resident populations, the latter has a proportionally higher presence in the labour market (only 20 percent of foreigners in the country don't work, compared to 39 percent of nationals). With the exception of Cape-Verdeans, foreigners are, however, more concentrated in low-paid jobs than nationals, despite their higher level of education (Seabra and Santos 2005: 35). In addition to this economic integration into the lower ranks of the country's workforce, they also face harsher living conditions in terms of housing and work (Seabra and Santos 2005: 60). I will return to these social characteristics at a later point.

The chapter first examines disparities in offending rates and simultaneously presents explanations for the variations. Subsequently, it presents a case study that draws upon data from the author's fieldwork in a female prison to illustrate the intersections of ethnicity and class in offending, the law enforcement response to offending and the negotiation of identity both within and outside the prison setting.

Offending rates: A comparison

For the time being, it is important to keep in mind some of the above-mentioned inequalities in order to interpret compared offending rates.[5] A raw comparison between national and foreign residents seems to suggest a higher involvement of the latter in criminal behavior (7 percent and

11 percent, respectively), and thus could reinforce perceptions, popularized by the media, that associate immigration with criminality (Carvalheira 2008; see Vale de Almeida 2007 for discourses on difference). However, these numbers can be misleading and their meaning cannot be taken at face value, as they hide the distorting effect of different demographic structures. According to data from the more recent Census,[6] foreign residents present an overall demographic structure which differs considerably from nationals'. Children and the elderly are under-represented among immigrants, whereas there is an over-representation of single young men. Once gender, age and job status are accounted for equally in the comparison between the two populations, offending rates are similar for national and non-national residents: 11 percent (Seabra and Santos 2005: 118).

From court to prison

Foreigners are, however, over-represented behind bars (3 percent compared with 1 percent of nationals) as well as in the preceding stages of the crime control system.[7] It is nevertheless worth mentioning that this tendency appears to be modest when compared with the experiences of other countries of the European Union (EU-25): Portugal stands fourth among those which present the lower over-representation of foreigners in the prison system (an over-representation measured by relation to the respective weight of foreigners within each country's resident population). Of the share of 18.5 percent of foreigners incarcerated in 2005[8] (which is double the figure observed a decade earlier) in Portuguese prison facilities,[9] those of African nationalities, especially from lusophone countries (particularly Cape Verde and Angola), are still substantially in the majority (54.6 percent), even if their relative weight has declined in recent years in favor of an increase in the proportion of Europeans (25.8 percent) and Latin Americans (17.2 percent).

Sixty-six percent of the imprisoned foreigners had been resident in Portugal at the time of their arrest (Seabra and Santos 2006; Guia 2008), and the majority of those who did not had been convicted of drug trafficking (many of them drug couriers arrested at the airport). They were predominantly male, 33 years of age on average and they served prison sentences of slightly longer than 6 years (70 percent served prison sentences of between 3 and 9 years). For reasons related to the circumstantial unavailability of alternative detention facilities (transit airport zones or specific shelters), a significant proportion (14 percent) of imprisoned foreigners waited behind bars, along with common criminals, an administrative decision that would expel them from the country, even though the undocumented/illegal presence within the borders is not criminalized by law.

Finally, those studies which have tried to estimate the proportion of the Portuguese gypsy ethnic minority behind bars have suggested an average of between 5 percent and 6 percent of the inmate population (Moreira 1998, 1999). In the last two decades, the main criminal activities perpetrated by members of this community have shifted from property offenses (smuggling, petty thefts) to drug offenses, especially drug trafficking.[10]

The discrepancy between foreigners and nationals in the Portuguese criminal justice system has become especially salient since 1998, when there began to be a fall in both the total prison population of Portugal and also the number of Portuguese defendants. Over the same period in the case of foreigners, and particularly in relation to foreign women, the trend has been in the opposite direction. According to a study by Seabra and Santos (2005) that focused on the period between 1997 and 2003, the number of foreign defendants increased 118 percent, and the rise in the conviction rate has been proportionally much higher for foreigners (257 percent) than for nationals (50 percent) (Seabra and Santos 2005: 92). Also, the former were overall more likely to be convicted than the latter (81 percent of convictions in the case of foreign defendants, against 66 percent for Portuguese nationals). Other recent studies focus specifically on two more narrow periods of rapid increase: a rise of 67.4 percent between 1994 and 1996, and another of 50.8 percent between 2001 and 2005. The latter was strongly characterized by the rise in the numbers of Eastern European prisoners, especially Ukrainians, Moldavians and Russians (Moreira 2005; Guia 2008).

As far as imprisonment is concerned, it is worth noting three facts in order to understand the disproportionate number of foreigners held behind bars. First, they are more likely to await trial in prison than Portuguese (in 2003, 9 percent of foreigners but only 2 percent of Portuguese were remanded in custody). The fact that the proportion of foreigners in this situation who are acquitted is twice as high as the proportion of Portuguese nationals acquitted reinforces the supposition that their remand custody was all the more unjustified in the first place (Seabra and Santos 2005: 80, 85). Second, foreigners in general are more likely to face a prison sentence than Portuguese and they have less access to alternative measures such as electronic surveillance. Third, foreigners are given longer prison sentences than national citizens. Whereas in the period 1997–2003 national citizens amount to a proportion of less than 50 percent among the defendants sentenced to more than 3 years of firm (unsuspended) imprisonment, the proportion of foreigners receiving the same sentence stood at between 65 percent and 70 percent (Seabra and Santos 2005: 107).

As studies have pointed out in relation to other countries (for example, Tonry 1997), neutral legal reasons may contribute to these discrepancies. For example, among other reasons, remand custody is applied on the basis of the assessed risk of escape and/or the seriousness of the offense. In Portugal, in general it applies to an offense punishable by more than 3 years of imprisonment. But following specific procedural norms (*Código do Processo*

Penal), judges deem the risk of escape to be higher in the case of foreigners, regardless of the seriousness of the offense. Furthermore, on the one hand, it is true that like their Portuguese counterparts foreigners face trial mostly for road crimes (driving under the influence of drink or drugs, driving without a license), drug offenses and property offenses (assault, theft, larceny and dub cheques) (Seabra and Santos 2005, 2006). On the other hand, however, foreigners are proportionately more concentrated than Portuguese precisely in the types of offenses which lead to higher conviction rates and harsher sentences – namely drug offenses. This pattern is even more salient in the case of foreign women. Among the foreign men sentenced in the same year to a firm prison sentence, 48.9 percent were convicted for drug offenses, compared to 27 percent in the case of nationals. With regard to their female counterparts, there were 61.1 percent of nationals against 85.6 percent of foreigners (Miranda Pereira 2005).

Even so, for the same offence – such as a drug offense – and everything else being equal, the probability of a foreigner being given a prison sentence is significantly higher than for a national (in 2003, 86 percent against 65 percent, Seabra and Santos 2005: 110).

Therefore, the over-representation of foreigners in the prison population seems to stem both from their greater involvement in crimes that are subject to more severe punishment (see also Pallida 1996; Tonry 1997) and from a tendency of the criminal justice system to punish foreign citizens more harshly (see also Tournier and Philippe 1991; Wacquant 1999b, 2005), even though the Portuguese Penal Code stresses the imperative of equal treatment for foreign and national prisoners.

Deportation: A double punishment?

But even if equal treatment were indeed applied to sentencing practices, there is nevertheless a sentencing measure which is aimed exclusively at foreigners, regardless of their resident status. This is the deportation sentence, whereby the convicted person may be compelled by a judicial decision to return to his/her country of origin – usually for a period of 10 years. In the case of prisoners, this happens after they have served their prison sentence or immediately upon their release on parole (*liberdade condicional*). According to the *Serviço de Estrangeiros e Fronteiras*, which enforces the legislation regarding foreigners, the crimes that motivate the most a deportation decision attached to a prison sentence are drug offenses, extortion, theft and robbery (see http://www.sef.pt). Where non-residents are concerned, this deportation may be sought by the prisoners themselves even before the sentence of imprisonment is completed, insofar as they may prefer to serve their sentence closer to relatives and friends, and, in general, closer to their usual social environment. The two countries involved are then supposed to make the necessary arrangements to meet the prisoners' request in this matter. But when the object of this same measure is a long-time resident, it can have dramatic consequences for him/her and his/her family, as it implies a separation. Immigrants are thus subjected to what becomes a true exile, as the ties with the country of origin may have faded long ago.

But the deportation sentence has an additional collateral effect. Most of the time it impacts on the way in which foreign prisoners serve their sentence and may or may not benefit from the periodical leaves to which every prisoner is entitled to apply. Foreigners are often denied these leaves. They are refused to non-resident foreigners on the grounds that they would be useless insofar as they would not fulfil their reintegration purpose (Cunha 1994). From the first non-residents are presumed to lack social bonds in Portugal or a social world to which their reintegration should be fostered or secured. Residents, on the other hand, are denied such leaves not so much on the grounds of the risk of escape from prison *per se*, but because this risk is deemed to be higher when they are due to be deported upon their release (Cunha 2002).

Imprisonment in a foreign land

The absence of visitors or the scarcity of visits may also render the experience of imprisonment harsher for non-resident foreign prisoners. In an attempt to alleviate this problem, the Portuguese Prison Administration tends to facilitate the transfer of some of these prisoners (especially Latin American) to Funchal prison, on the island of Madeira, where they can be more easily visited by relatives, as travel is supposed to be less expensive and time consuming (Cunha 1994; Abrunhosa Gonçalves 2007). Otherwise, in general – continental Portuguese prisons included – regulations concerning visit days and visit schedules are applied in more flexible ways in the case of foreign visitors (Cunha 1994). Job access within prison can also be made easier to foreigners when they are deprived of the family support that would allow for the acquisition of in-prison consumer goods.

In the absence of family or NGO support, the assistance provided by embassies and consulates may take the form of essential goods and some financial support, in addition to other types of assistance such as the provision of legal representation and contacts with family members. In spite of the law (*Código do Processo Penal*, no. 2 art. 92) that establishes the obligation of providing foreigners with an interpreter in court, lawyers have reported difficulties in rendering trials understandable to foreigners who do not speak Portuguese (in *Público* 2009). As far as the experience of confinement is concerned, until recently language differences have not, however, hindered severely daily communication or caused major difficulties as the majority of foreign prisoners have come from Portuguese-speaking countries. The present wider diversification of nationalities, especially following the arrival of North/East European prisoners, may have increased these problems, although English has also become a *lingua franca* used by more people, including nationals.

Dynamics of class and ethnicity: A case study

This section will draw on fieldwork that I conducted in the main women's Portuguese prison (Estabelecimento Prisional de Tires, EPT) on two different periods[11] – to show the way ethnicity is framed and shapes sociality among prison inmates, a scenario illustrative of the negotiation of ethnicity beyond the narrow contours of the prison setting. It will focus on two aspects. First, the relative weakness of 'race' and ethnicity as categories of identity and discourse, a weakness which partakes in a general dynamics of blurring boundaries between prisoners. Second, these categories are examined in the light of their interplay with class, mediated by conditions such as the neighborhood and the economy of retail drug markets. Such contextual meanings are all the more important to underline, insofar as: (i) categories of 'race'/ethnicity are highly variable; (ii) a *white/black* dichotomy is not an analytical construct with universal contours, but a culturally specific one, and as such is not necessarily the best suited for post-colonial contexts such as Iberian ones (Pina Cabral 1998);[12] (iii) when categories of race/ethnicity travel from one cultural context to another in scholarly discourse, they may arrive charged with an excessive voltage that short-circuits or obscures local dimensions of class (see in this light Cunha 2002 about Fikes 1998); and (iv) social identity and difference can be established without ethnic referents and class is not always subsumed in 'race' in the same way as – say, for example – in the USA.[13] This is why it may be useful to specify these dimensions separately in order to be able to grasp their contextual interplay.

By the end of the 1990s, the overwhelming majority of inmates were being incarcerated for drug offenses – thereby reducing the diversity of offences that prevailed a decade earlier.[14] In addition to this criminal homogeneity, there was also a social levelling at the bottom, which was apparent in a blatant impoverishment in respect of economic, social and educational capital (Cunha 2002). Moreover, prisoners now came systematically from the same poor neighborhoods. Most of them were already known to each other before imprisonment, and they were connected by ties of friendship, neighborhood or kinship.[15] Therefore, when behind bars, they reproduced former relational circles.[16] The reasons for this phenomenon lie in the law enforcement agencies' selective targeting of specific socio-spatial categories, and in the structure of the Portuguese retail drug markets.

The neighborhood under surveillance

Retail drug trafficking came to induce specific patterns of repression in the penal system. It favored a proactive style of law enforcement, which increased exponentially the potential for selectivity and bias. Police interventions were increasingly aimed at specific poor urban neighborhoods, which have become collective targets of surveillance and of routine indiscriminate sweeps. Under such intense police attention, the probability of arrest is higher in these territories. As in several other countries where drugs repression has reinforced similar styles of crime control (see, for example, Dorn et al. 1992; Duprez and Kokoreff 2000), these stigmatized areas are now massive suppliers of prisoners.

Authors have reported that the arrest rates of members of ethnic/racial minorities are lower in the case of crimes in which investigation is triggered by a complaint from victims unaware of the perpetrator's ethnicity, than for those in which intervention rests mainly on police initiative (Wilbanks 1987; Smith 1997) – precisely the case of drug offenses. Other authors noticed that while the gaps between white and non-white arrest rates have narrowed over time, the notorious exception remained with the arrests related to drugs, regardless of the evolution of offending patterns (see, for example, Sampson and Lauritsen 1997 for the USA; see also a similar observation by Roberts and Doob 1997 for Canada). Be it as it may, bias tends to be more salient at the frontline of the criminal justice system, more precisely in relation to proactive law enforcement. However, race/ethnicity *per se* may not be as decisive as it appears in determining police targets and they may operate indirectly, either through other factors or in interaction with them. Studies indicate that police action tends to be triggered less by suspects' characteristics than by the social status of residential areas considered as a whole. Even when the concentration of minorities is higher in poor urban areas, once inside these areas' visible ethnicity ceases to be a predictor of police behavior (Smith 1986; Jefferson 1993).

Ethnicity, class and the retail drug economy in the neighborhood

In reference to the USA, Sampson and Lauritsen (1997: 400) stated that 'By the nineties, "race", class and drugs became intertwined. It is difficult, if not impossible, to disentangle the various elements of the problem'. Portuguese urban neighborhoods are areas characterized by a specific interplay between categories of 'race'/ethnicity and class. They are socially and economically homogenous and ethnically diverse. While in Portugal minorities (mainly Gypsies and immigrants from lusophone African countries) *are* disadvantaged, they share this disadvantage – more than is the case in other countries – with large segments of the white Portuguese population, for instance in the labor and the residential market (1992).[17] Moreover, as the general socio-economic gap has widened, these same social segments of both minorities and non-minorities have found themselves further removed from the more affluent segments of the population. To draw a brief comparison with other geographies, US inner-city neighborhoods tend to be racially/ethnically more uniform than European ones, where poverty tends to congregate more diverse populations in deprived urban areas (Wacquant 1995; Sampson and Lauritsen 1997). But the Portuguese case presents additional specificities in relation to other destitute urban settings in Europe, where the poor are stratified along ethnic lines. An example of such infra-hierarchies, or stratifications among the poor, is previous blue-collar residents who resent deprived immigrant neighbors, perceiving their proximity as a sign of social demotion, or as an obstacle to social mobility (see, for example, Althabe, 1993 and Sélim 1993 for France). In Portuguese low-income neighborhoods and in the few remaining shanty towns, poverty is more severe and survival is a priority for both minority and non-minority groups. Such urban settings are not usually the scene of similar symbolic struggles around upward or downward social trajectories.[18]

The retail drug economy's inscription in poor urban neighborhoods reflects this same specific interplay between categories of 'race'/ethnicity and class. Neighbors from different ethnicities take part side by side in the illegal – as well as the legal – economy. Race/ethnicity – anymore than gender (see Cunha 2005a) – do not determine or restrict involvement in the local retail drug industry, which provides a relatively open illegal structure of opportunities. Unlike similar drug markets elsewhere in Europe and the USA, which are ethnically stratified and where the lower, riskier and less rewarding segments of activity are left to a variety of minorities (Ruggiero and South 1995, 1996; Maher 1997), the Portuguese retail drug economy is indistinctly occupied by both minorities and non-minorities. At the bottom of the market, drug dealing has become one of the vectors of ethnic social leveling.

One of the reasons for this lies in the structure of the drug market. During the 1990s, a mutation in the structure of retail drug markets occurred not only in the USA but also in European contexts. Such markets had by that time adopted a business profile which (according to the typology proposed by Johnson, Hamid and Sanabria 1992) consists of vertically integrated organizations with a rigid centralized structure and involving crews of employees with almost no autonomy. Ruggiero and South (1995: 195) characterized similar structures in Europe as 'crime in organization'. Up until that decade the prevailing model was a different, more fluid, one. With little hierarchical interdependency or permanent wage relationships, a weak functional division of labor, it rested mostly on individual entrepreneurs. It was thus characterized as 'free-lance' (Johnson, Hamid, and Sanabria 1992), or 'crime in association' (Ruggiero and South 1995: 195). Even if free-lance markets shared the same gender ideologies and ethnic cleavages that filter access of potential participants to the drug economy in its more structured 'business' format, ethnic and gender barriers were rendered much more permeable and inefficient by the very organizational fluidity of these markets. It is precisely the free-lance market structure that prevails in the Portuguese retail drug economy, where the evolution has even been opposite to the one I have so far described for European and US contexts. That is, the business model evolved in the 1990s toward a free-lance one (Chaves 1999; Cunha 2007).

Ethnic categorization behind bars

This interplay between ethnicity and class mediated by local conditions such as the neighborhood and the economy of illegal drug markets helps to shed some light on the fact that, in prison, 'race' and ethnicity do not act as critical categories of identity or have a potential to organize social relations. Ethnic/racial referents are present in the prison vocabulary under the terms 'white', 'black', African, Cape-Verdean, Angolan, Gypsy and *corrilha* (non-Gypsy). However, in daily life these discursive categories have almost no salience. This was not the case in the 1980s, during my first fieldwork, when these categories were activated constantly. At that time, the stake was the collective denigration of some prisoners and two terms in particular were mobilized in this process: Gypsies and Cape-Verdeans. Elsewhere I have dealt with the first case (Cunha 2005b), which is too complex to analyze here. I will stick to the latter in this chapter. The category of Cape-Verdean had a particularly flexible and contextual definition in the discursive practices of non-African prisoners, for whom the facts of nationality, origins or place of birth seem to be largely irrelevant. Skin color sufficed as a criterion, and thus the majority of inmates of African origin were included in that category. Why subsume skin color in cape-verdeanity instead of the other way round, which would be more predictable an encompassment? That is, that Angolans, Guineans, Mozambicans... – *and* Cape-Verdeans – would be classified for example as 'blacks'? Because, I propose, the notion of Cape-Verdean was at the time well suited to stigmatize, or at least better suited to this effect than those tied to phenotype. The attribution which endowed the Cape-Verdean category with such a gravitational force was not alien to hegemonic perceptions that in the 1980s isolated the Cape-Verdean community as a 'problem' and identified it with a propensity to violence, delinquency and deviance (see for example, Saint-Maurice 1997: xii; Rodrigues 1990: 63). Given the overall in-prison stigmatizing dynamics that prevailed in carceral sociality at the time (see below), the term 'Cape-Verdeans' was appropriate to reinforce local strategies of demarcation and was readily integrated within them, as it carried in itself a disqualifying element.

This resonates with criminalization processes analyzed in the UK by Michael Keith (1993) as racializing discourses. In these processes, the category of *black* does not apply invariably and exclusively to a given parcel of the population which would thus be an object of racism. It would be, above all, a fluctuating subject created by the discourse of criminalization. The racial forms which result from such processes would be considerably mutable and contextual, and they would coexist and interact with those pertaining to other discursive fields. In that, Keith distances himself from standard labeling theories (see Becker 1963; Goffman 1975):

> [I]t is important to differentiate between the notion of criminalization advanced here and standard labelling theory. A demographic fraction

of society is not picked out and victimized. It is not so straightforward. A construction of criminality which draws on the glossary of racial difference is applied to define the varying subject positions of black communities at particular times and places.

(Keith 1993: 196)

In the same manner that Cape-Verdeans emerged, inside and outside prison, as a conspicuous discursive subject during the 1980s, so would they dissolve as such a decade afterward. They were then replaced by other discursive 'dangerous classes' (Chevalier 1984), that is, from now onward, a categorization that amalgamated several ingredients: 'blacks' (among which, Cape-Verdeans), Gypsies, drugs and neighborhood-ghetto. In the 1990s, a small minority of middle-class white prisoners employed ethnic/racial labels in line with these new categorizations. For most prisoners, however, these notions did not impact in any way on daily sociality. An ethnic category did not generate, for example, preferential associations except those derived out of kinship; in addition, ritual kinship (godparents) is often inter-ethnic. More importantly, ethnic categories became merely descriptive and ceased to be instrumental in identity struggles. Even this relatively neutral descriptive use occurred mostly on occasions in which I took part as an interlocutor (as interviewer rather than observer) and for my benefit. Speaking of a friend or co-prisoner, an inmate could offer that 'She's white like you'. Given that the majority of the imprisoned population was nevertheless white, although poor and from the same stigmatized urban neighborhoods as their non-white co-inmates, this was also a way to underline my social exteriority to this mixed universe.

It is important, however, to note that if in the 1980s 'race' and ethnicity were relevant categories of identity and discourse in prison, they were so mostly in the same manner as other categories. In other words, they were among many other materials available for drawing boundaries, from someone's sexual orientation (homosexual relationships were stigmatized) to the crime which had led to their imprisonment (for example, whereas one's own crime is always presented as a justifiable or an accidental single event, that of a co-prisoner is usually identified as being an expression of an unredeemable delinquent nature). Like in a mirror game of mutual oppositions, each inmate tried to conjure away her sensed stigmatized status (signified by the imprisonment itself) by disqualifying her co-inmates. 'Race' and ethnicity did not therefore generate the social dynamics of mutual distancing. They merely took part in a dynamics that was already there.

A decade later, in the 1990s, these identity struggles had almost disappeared. Moreover, for the first time this absence of cleavages was voiced by the inmates themselves, who often took pride in stating that 'we're all in the same boat, we're all equals – blacks, gypsies, everybody'. There was now a sense of shared identity that was not alien to the new structural/class proximity – which was also a very tangible one, comprising pre-prison networks of neighborhood and kinship relations.[19] It was as if integration within exclusion had occurred. Furthermore, the stigma which had been attached to prison in the 1980s was from now on instituted prior to imprisonment, by the very fact of belonging to ill-reputed neighborhoods. And prison had already become a reality embodied in daily life in the neighborhood. Everybody had a friend, a neighbor or a relative who either was in prison or had been imprisoned at some time in the recent past. The symbolic boundary that the prison used to signify had also somehow eroded.

Conclusion: Crime, criminal justice and categories of difference

How is 'difference', then, reflected in crime and the criminal justice system in Portugal? In the end, this seems indeed to be the adequate phrasing of the question addressed by this chapter. The kind of answers obtained depends on which local notions we can translate 'difference' into: 'race', 'ethnicity', 'foreigners', 'immigrants', 'minorities'. This, in turn, depends also on whether we focus on statistics, rates or, from another angle, experiences of crime and of the criminal justice system. Quantitative and qualitative data highlight different, but complementary aspects of the same landscape.

Portuguese official statistics allow for grasping the 'difference' mentioned above only in terms of the pair: foreigners/citizens, regardless of race or ethnicity. As far as offending rates are concerned, raw numbers indicate a discrepancy between national and foreign residents. These numbers neglect, however, the respective demographic structures, and, in particular, the over-representation of single young men among immigrants. The discrepancy disappears once gender, age and job status are accounted for equally in the comparison between the two populations. Notwithstanding this, the discrepancy reappears in every stage of the crime control system, and foreigners end up over-represented behind bars. This stems both from a tendency of the criminal justice system to punish foreigners more harshly and from the fact that the latter are proportionately more concentrated than Portuguese on the offenses which motivate higher conviction rates and harsher sentences – namely, drug offenses. This pattern becomes even clearer when foreigners are women.

This overall discrepancy has widened since the second half of the 1990s. In that same period, I conducted an ethnographic study in a women's prison where drug offenses stood out as a major cause of imprisonment. This study allowed for the highlighting of the way categories of difference which are excluded from the official statistics – that is, race and ethnicity, regardless of national/foreigner citizenship status – may be at play in crime, law enforcement and the experience of imprisonment. In all three domains class and the nature of residential areas emerge as important conditions for the relevance of race and ethnicity. This relevance is also determined, at another level, by the open structure of local drug markets, which provides 'equal opportunities' to different ethnicities. The Portuguese retail drug economy is indistinctly occupied by both minorities and non-minorities. Furthermore, the Portuguese urban neighborhoods in which the retail drug economy takes hold present a specific interplay between categories of race/ethnicity and class. Poverty congregates ethnically diverse populations in a uniform position. Given a socio-economic gap that had widened over the course of the preceding decade, segments of both minorities and non-minorities have found themselves further removed from more affluent segments of the population.

It is this changing intersection between ethnicity and class, mediated by conditions such as the neighborhood and the workings of the drug economy, that now helps to prevent, in prison, strong expressions of race and ethnicity as categories of identity and social organization. Categories of difference have changed between the 1980s and 1990s, as has the definition of 'dangerous classes' by criminalization discourses that draw on the glossary of 'difference'.

Notes

1. Contrary to criminal statistics of other European countries, until very recently Portugal did not have an integrated system of data registration. Each law enforcement department or State bureau had its own data base for internal purposes, without an overall coordination which would establish uniform categories, criteria, and methods. It did not allow either for studying the way a given criminal event is dealt with by the criminal justice system from the moment it is reported until it is tried. The current attribution of a single number to each criminal event (Número Único de Identificação de Processo Crime) is intended to address this issue. Furthermore, in addition to the obstacles surrounding the analysis of officially reported delinquency, it is difficult to circumvent the problem of the dark figures of unreported crime, as victimization and/or self-reported delinquency surveys are still scarce or incipient (Crucho de Almeida 1995, 1998; Gersão and Lisboa 1994). For this same reason, the importance of specific types of criminal victimization such as hate crime is also even harder to assess.
2. See the 1994 Decreto-Lei 28/94.
3. In this text I use the words Portuguese/national/Portuguese national to designate those who have Portuguese citizenship, regardless of phenotype, ethnicity (whites, blacks, Gypsies…) or country of birth (Africans who have acquired Portuguese citizenship, for example). 'Foreigners' apply to those who do not have Portuguese citizenship, even if they reside in Portugal.
4. African countries where the official language is Portuguese are known under the acronym PALOP (Países Africanos de Língua Oficial Portuguesa). Besides the countries mentioned above, they include also S. Tomé e Príncipe.
5. Several studies have contributed to contextualize this issue in Portugal: e.g. (Baganha 1996; Ferreira 1998; Lourenço and Lisboa 1998; Barra da Costa 1999; Pereira 1999; Baganha et al. 2000; Cunha 2002; Machado 2002; Rocha 2001, 2005; Seabra and Santos 2005).

6. XIV Recenseamento Geral da População, Instituto Nacional de Estatística (2001).
7. For the statistical analysis of the imprisonment of foreigners in Portugal see (Esteves and Malheiros 2001; Rocha 2001, 2005; Seabra and Santos 2005, 2006; Guia 2008).
8. In the same year foreigners amount to 2,386 in a universe of 12,889 prisoners.
9. I use here the general term 'prison' for the 54 carceral institutions existing in Portugal, whether small local facilities, bigger central prisons or special prison facilities (prison-hospitals, carceral institutions for juveniles and for women). Apart from the level of security, the distinction between detainee and convict is but one of the criteria for distributing inmates within the Portuguese prison system. But although there are no convicts serving long sentences in the closest Portuguese equivalent to *jail* (holding detainees or mostly those convicts sentenced to serve up to a year), people awaiting trial can be confined in prisons, especially when they are accused of serious crimes. The allocation of prisoners is initially based on the place where the offense was perpetrated and in which court it was tried. But after the sentence is issued, prisoners can request to be transferred to a prison closer to their family in order to make visits easier. Depending on the rate of occupation and the capacity of the requested prison, this is usually granted (see Cunha 1994; Abrunhosa Gonçalves 2007).
10. For a compared characterization of the prison experiences of gypsies and non-gypsies, see Cunha (1994, 2002).
11. I returned in 1997 to the Estabelecimento Prisional de Tires for a year-long fieldwork, a decade after a sojourn of 2 years in the same institution.
12. See in this light the debate in *Theory, Culture and Society* between Bourdieu and Wacquant (1999), and e.g. Friedman (2000), Hanchard (2003).
13. Focusing on the semantic organization of these categories in what she calls American cultural discourse, Shirley Ortner points out that '[T]here is no class in America that is not always already racialized and ethnicized, or, to turn the point around, racial and ethnic categories are already class categories' (1998: 10).
14. In January 1997, there were 820 prisoners in the main women's penitentiary of the country, mostly (69 percent) serving sentences of more than 5 years. Seventy six percent were imprisoned for drug trafficking and sixty three percent of those accused/convicted for property offenses were drug users.
15. Between one half to two-thirds of the inmates shared Tires with family members (a conservative estimate based on data registered in social-educational files), and many more with neighbors or acquaintances: the prisoners originating from the two main metropolitan areas (78 percent) came from the same neighborhoods (89 and 86 percent, respectively), and similar patterns of concentration occurred within the remaining urban provenances.
16. For the analytical implications of such clusters for prison studies, see Cunha (2008).
17. Analyzing census data, Machado concludes that:

> In comparison with countries such as France, United Kingdom, Germany or Italy, in Portugal the social contrasts between 'third world' immigrant minorities and the national population are narrower, not so much because of a homogeneity in the class composition of minorities, a homogeneity which does not exist in their country of origin, but mainly because in Portugal *the weight of ethnic minorities is lighter within the set of underprivileged social categories.*
> (1992: 128. My translation, emphasis in the original)

18. This state of affairs is specific to this kind of urban settings and the peculiar conjunction of race/ethnicity and class as stated above. In other Portuguese contexts such struggles can be strong, not to mention the existence of racism, xenophobia and anti-immigrant hostility. I am not implying, therefore, that, at the national scale, race/ethnicity do not generate social discrimination.
19. Not incidentally, this discursive playing down of racial/ethnic categories was also reported for poor ethnically mixed neighborhoods (Rodrigues 1990; Saint-Maurice 1997). For a more detailed analysis see Cunha (2002).

References

Abrunhosa Gonçalves, R. (2007), 'Portugal', in A. M. Van Kalmthaut, F. B. A. M. Hofstee-van der Meulen and F. Dünkel (eds), *Foreigners in European Prisoners*, vol. 2, The Netherlands: Wolf Legal Publishers, pp. 691–709.

Almeida, A. C. (2003), *Impacto da Imigração em Portugal nas Contas do Estado*, Lisbon: Alto Comissariado para a Imigração e Minorias Étnicas.

Althabe, G. (1993), 'La Résidence Comme Enjeu', in G. Althabe et al. (eds), *Urbanisation et Enjeux Quotidiens. Terrains Ethnologiques dans la France Actuelle*, Paris: L'Harmattan, pp. 11–69.

Baganha, M. I. (1996), *Migrants Insertion in the Informal Economy: The Portuguese Case*, First Report. Coimbra: CES – Universidade de Coimbra.

Baganha, M. I., Marques, J. C. and Fonseca, Graça F. (2000), *Is an Ethniclass Emerging in Europe? The Portuguese Case*. Lisboa: Fundação Luso Americana.

Baganha, M. I. and Marques, J. C. (2001), 'A Cada Sul o seu Norte. Dinâmicas Migratórias em Portugal', in B. Sousa Santos (ed.), *Globalização. Fatalidade ou Utopia?* Porto: Afrontamento, pp. 135–59.

Baganha, M. I., Ferrão, J. and Malheiros, M. (eds) (2002), *Os Movimentos Migratórios Externos e a Sua Incidência no Mercado de Trabalho em Portugal*, Colecção 'Estudos e Análises', 14, Lisbon: Observatório do Emprego e Formação Profissional.

Barra da Costa, J. M. (1999), *Práticas Delinquentes, De Uma Criminologia Do Anormal A Uma Antropologia Da Marginalidade*, Lisboa: Edições Colibri.

Becker, H. (1963), *Outsiders*, New York: Free Press.

Bourdieu, P. and Wacquant, L. (1999), 'On the Cunning of Imperialist Reason', *Theory, Culture and Society*, 16(1): 41–58.

Código de Processo Penal Português, Decreto-Lei n. 78/87, de 17 de Fevereiro.

Cabecinhas, R. (2007), *Preto e Branco. A Naturalização da Discriminação Racial*, Porto: Campo das Letras.

Carvalheira, J. R. (2008), *Do Bidonville ao Arrastão. Media, Minorias e Etnicização*, Oeiras: Celta.

Chaves, M. (1999), *Casal Ventoso: Da Gandaia ao Narcotráfico*, Lisboa: Imprensa de Ciências Sociais.

Chevalier, L. (1984) [1978], *Classes Laborieuses et Classes Dangereuses à Paris, Pendant la Première Moitié du XIX Siècle*, Paris: Hachette.

Crucho de Almeida, M. R. (1995), *Inquérito à Vitimação 1994*. Lisboa: Gabinete de Estudos e Planeamento do Ministério da Justiça.

Crucho de Almeida, M. R. (1998), *Vitimação e insegurança no Concelho de Lisboa*. Lisboa: Gabinete de Estudos e Planeamento, Ministério da Justiça.

Cunha, M. P. da (1994), *Malhas que a Reclusão Tece. Questões de Identidade numa Prisão Feminina*, Lisboa: Cadernos do Centro de Estudos Judiciários.

_____ (2002), *Entre o Bairro e a Prisão: Tráfico e Trajectos*. Lisbon: Fim de Século.

_____ (2005a), 'From Neighborhood to Prison. Women and the War on Drugs in Portugal', in Julia Sudbury (ed.) *Global Lockdown: Race, Gender, and Prison-Industrial Complex*. New York: Routledge, pp. 155–65.

Cunha, M. P. da (2005b), 'Les gitans, la prison et le quartier: d'une relation spécifique devenue le modèle ordinaire', *Études Tsiganes*, 21: 34–47.

Cunha, M. P. da (2007) 'Les liens du trafic: parenté, voisinage et genre dans des narco-marchés', in M. Kokoreff, M. Péraldi and M. Weinberger (eds), *Économies criminelles et mondes urbains*, Paris: PUF: pp. 109–119.

Cunha, M. P. da (2008), 'Closed Circuits: Kinship, Neighborhood and Imprisonment in Urban Portugal', *Ethnography*, 9(3): 325–350.

Dorn, N., Murji, K. and South, N. (1992), *Traffickers: Drug Markets and Law Enforcement*, London: Routledge.

Duprez, D. and Kokoreff, M. (2000), *Les mondes de la Drogue*, Paris: Odile Jacob.

Esteves, A. and Malheiros, J. M. (2001), 'Os Cidadãos Estrangeiros nas Prisões Portuguesas', in Magda Pinheiro, Luís V. Baptista and Maria João Vaz (eds), *Cidades e Metrópole. Centralidades e Marginalidades*, Oeiras: Celta.

Ferreira, E. V. (1998), *Crime e insegurança em Portugal, padrões e tendências, 1985–1996*, Oeiras: Celta.

Fikes, K. (1998), 'Domesticity in Black and White: Assessing Badia Cape Verdean Challenges to Portuguese Ideals of Black Womanhood', *Transforming Anthropology*, 7(2): 5–19.

Fonseca, L. (2005) *Migrações e Território*, Lisbon: Centro de Estudos Geográficos, Universidade de Lisboa.

Friedman, J. (2000), 'Americans Again, or the New Age of Imperial Reason?', *Theory, Culture and Society*, 17(1): 139–146.

Gersão, E. and Lisboa, M. (1994), 'The Self Report Delinquency Study in Portugal', in J. Junger-Tas, Gert-Jan Terlouw and Malcom W. Klein (eds), *Delinquent Behaviour Among Young People in the Western World: First Results of the International Self-Report Delinquency Study, Studies on Crime and Justice*, The Dutch Research and Documentation Centre: RDC – Ministry of Justice, pp. 212–37.

Goffman, E. (1975) [1963], *Stigmate. Les Usages Sociaux des Handicaps*, Paris: Minuit.

Guia, M. J. (2008), *Imigração e Criminalidade: Caleidoscópio de Imigrantes Reclusos*, Coimbra: Almedina.

Hanchard, M. (2003), 'Acts of Misrecognition: Transnational Black Politics, Amti-Imperialism and the Ethnocentrisms of Pierre Bourdieu and Loïc Wacquant', *Theory, Culture and Society*, 20(4): 5–29.

Instituto Nacional de Estatística (2001), XIV *Recenseamento Geral da População*, INE.

Jefferson, T. (1993), 'The Racism of Criminalization: Policing and the Reproduction of the Criminal Other', in L. Gelsthorpe and W. McWilliam (eds), *Minority Ethnic Groups and the Criminal Justice System*, Cambridge: University of Cambridge Institute of Criminology.

Johnson, B., Hamid, A. and Sanabria, H. (1992), 'Emerging Models of Crack Distribution', in T. Mieczkowski (ed.), *Drugs, Crime, and Social Policy: Research, Issues, and Concerns*, Boston: Allyn and Bacon, pp. 56–78.

Keith, M. (1993), 'From Punishment to Discipline? Racism, Racialization and the Policing of Social Control', in M. Cross and M. Keith (eds), *Racism, the City and the State*, London: Routledge, pp. 193–225.

Lourenço, N. and Lisboa, M. (1998), *Dez Anos de Crime em Portugal. Análise Longitudinal da Criminalidade Participada às Polícias (1984–1993)*. Caxias: Gabinete de Estudos Jurídico-Sociais do Centro de Estudos Judiciários.

Machado, F. L. (1992), 'Etnicidade em Portugal. Contrastes e Politização', *Sociologia. Problemas e Práticas*, 12: 123–36.

Machado, F. L. (2002), *Contrastes e Continuidades. Migração, Etnicidade e Integração dos Guineenses em Portugal*, Oeiras: Celta.

Maher, L. (1997), *Sexed Work: Gender, Race and Resistance in a Brooklyn Drug Market*, Oxford: Clarendon Press.

Miranda Pereira (2005), 'Workshop', in H. M. Seabra and T. Santos, *A Criminalidade de Estrangeiros em Portugal. Um Inquérito Científico*, Lisbon: Alto Comissariado para a Imigração e Minorias Étnicas: 207–226.

Moreira, J. J. S. (1998), 'Ciganos na Prisão. Um Universo Diferente?', *Temas Penitenciários*, II Série, 2: 5–18.

Moreira, J. J. S. (1999), 'Ciganos em Privação de Liberdade', *Revista do Ministério Público*, 77: 59–88.

Moreira, J. J. S. (2005), *Estatísticas Prisionais – 2005. Apresentação e Análise*. Lisbon: Direcção Geral dos Serviços Prisionais.

Ortner, S. (1998), 'Identities: The Hidden Life of Class', *Journal of Anthropological Research*, 54(1): 1–17.

Pallida, S. (ed.) (1996), *Délit d'Immigration/Immigrant Delinqueny*, Brussels: European Commission.

Pena Pires, R. (2003), *Migrações e Integração*, Oeiras: Celta.

Pereira, Á. P. (1999), 'Prisões: decidir ou conhecer', in Helena Carreiras, Fátima Freitas and Isabel Valente (eds), *Profissão Sociólogo*, Oeiras: Celta Editora.

Pina Cabral, J. (1998), 'Racismo ou Etnocentrismo?', in H. Gomes de Araújo et al. (eds), *Nós e os Outros. A Exclusão em Portugal e na Europa*, Porto: Sociedade Portuguesa de Antropologia e Etnologia, pp. 19–26.

Público (Jornal) (2009), 'Estrangeiros têm mais dificuldade em defender-se', *Terça-feira*, February 24, p. 6.

Roberts, J. and Doob, A. (1997), 'Race, Ethnicity and Criminal Justice in Canada', in M. Tonry (ed.), *Ethnicity, Crime and Immigration*, Chicago: University of Chicago Press: pp. 469–522.

Rocha, J. L. M. (2001), *Reclusos Estrangeiros. Um Estudo Exploratório*, Coimbra: Almedina.

Rocha, J. L. M. (ed.) (2005), *Entre a Reclusão e a Liberdade. Estudos Penitenciários*, Coimbra: Almedina.

Rodrigues, W. (1990), 'Minorité Cap-Verdienne: Espaces, Identités et Processus de Marginalisation', *Sociedade e Território*, Setembro, Special number: 63–7.

Ruggiero, V. and South, N. (1995), *Eurodrugs: Drug Use, Markets and Trafficking in Europe*, London: UCL Press.

Ruggiero, V. and South, N. (1996), 'La Ville de la Fin de l'Ère Moderne en Tant que Bazar: Marchés de Stupéfiants, Entreprise Illégale et les Barricades', *Déviance et Société*, 20(4): 315–33.

Saint-Maurice, A. de (1997), *Identidades Reconstruídas. Cabo-Verdianos em Portugal*, Oeiras: Celta.

Sampson, R. J. and Lauritsen, J. L. (1997), 'Racial and Ethnic Disparities in Crime and Criminal Justice in the United States', in M. Tonry (ed.), *Ethnicity, Crime and Immigration – Comparative and Cross-national Perspectives*, Chicago and London: The University of Chicago Press: pp. 311–76.

Seabra, H. M. and Santos, T. (2005), *A Criminalidade de Estrangeiros em Portugal. Um Inquérito Científico*, Lisbon: Alto Comissariado para a Imigração e Minorias Étnicas.

Seabra, H. M. and Santos, T. (2006), *Reclusos Estrangeiros em Portugal. Esteios de uma Problematização*, Lisbon: Alto Comissariado para a Imigração e Minorias Étnicas.

Sélim, M. (1993), 'Une Cohabitation Pluri-Ethnique', in G. Althabe et al. (eds), *Urbanisation et Enjeux Quotidiens. Terrains Ethnologiques dans la France Actuelle*, Paris: L'Harmattan: pp. 71–111.

Smith, D. (1997), 'Ethnic Origins, Crime and Criminal Justice', in M. Maguire, R. Morgan and R. Reiner (eds), *The Oxford Handbook of Criminology*, Oxford: Clarendon Press, pp. 703–759.

Smith, D. (1986), 'The Neighborhood Context of Police Behavior', in A. Reiss and M. Tonry (eds), *Communities and Crime*, Chicago: University of Chicago Press.

Tonry, M. (1997), 'Ethnicity, Crime and Immigration', in M. Tonry (ed.), *Ethnicity, Crime and Immigration – Comparative and Cross-national Perspectives*, Chicago and London: The University of Chicago Press: pp. 1–29.

Tournier, P. and Philippe, R. (1991), *Etrangers et Délinquances, Les Chiffres du Débat*, Logiques Sociales, Paris: L'Harmattan.

Vale de Almeida, M. (2007), 'On Difference and Inequality: The Lessons of Ethnographic Experience', in António Pinto Ribeiro (ed.), *The Urgency of Theory*, Manchester: Carcanet & Fundação Calouste Gulbenkian, pp. 44–78.

Wacquant, L. (1995), 'The Comparative Structure and Experience of Urban Exclusion: Race, Class and Space in Paris and Chicago', in K. McFate et al. (eds), *Poverty, Inequality, and the Future of Social Policy: Western States in the New World Order*, New York: Russell Sage Foundation, pp. 542–70.

Wacquant, L. (1999a), *Les Prisons de la Misère*. Paris: Raisons d'Agir Éditions.

Wacquant, L. (1999b), 'Suitable Enemies. Foreigners and Immigrants in the Prisons of Europe', *Punishment and Society*, 10(2): 215–22.

Wacquant, L. (2005), ' "Enemies of the Wholesome Part of the Nation". Postcolonial Migrants in the Prisons of Europe', *Sociologie*, I: 31–51.

Wilbanks, W. (1987), *The Myth of a Racist Criminal Justice System*, Monterey, CA: Brooks/Cole.

8
Race, Crime and Criminal Justice in Spain

Joshua Goode
Claremont Graduate University, USA

Introduction

Any discussion of the intersections of race and crime remains a relatively new topic for contemporary scholars of Spanish society. The reason the topic is new remains rooted in two interrelated problems, both relating to Spanish history – or at least a general interpretation of Spanish history. The first problem is a historical unwillingness to acknowledge the role that racial identity, or ethnic difference, has played in forging Spanish notions of national identity. This view is generally buttressed by the claim that Spain remained relatively isolated and inward-looking during a period when the rest of Europe became dominated by racial definitions of 'national identity'. For one, Spain stood apart as the rest of Europe spread outward in imperialist adventures which brought notions of race and social Darwinist explanations of difference back to the metropole. How can there be racism if there is no deep sense of racial hierarchy?

The second impediment to analyzing race and crime is an ironic outgrowth of this isolation. For much of the 20th century, Spaniards have subscribed to the notion that they are generally less racist, and that they live in a more tolerant and open society than most other European countries. This claim is often followed by the assertion of Spanish homogeneity throughout the last two centuries, over even the last five centuries. According to this argument, racial thought never developed in the country and, as a result, no racial animus ever took hold in Spain. How could one study racial otherness if there were no racial others? Times are changing, of course, and today Spain, like many other European countries, is experiencing challenges to its notions of race, ethnicity, nationalism and citizenship in the midst of increased immigration levels and a more globally interconnected economy. This chapter examines how Spain has greeted such changing contemporary circumstances with historical notions of an otherwise homogeneous ethnic nation, one of shared culture and shared appearance. This focus remains one of the most interesting and least studied elements informing contemporary

Spanish attitudes toward race and crime, including even the absence or non-use of the term 'race' or 'ethnicity' in crime discourse, and the general relegation of crime data that details race or ethnic factors to the non-public or internal domain of official agencies.

In the last two decades, political, economic and social realities have strained the argument that Spain remains free of racism. Spain's transition to democracy after the death of Francisco Franco, and the economic expansion that followed in the 1980s, have transformed Spain into one of the fastest-growing recipients of immigrants among European countries. But sporadic and increasingly violent attacks on immigrant populations have materialized alongside the rising influx of immigrants. Invariably, the public response to these attacks has been primarily one of surprise. How could a nation free of racial animus, open to difference, historically at the crossroads of Europe and Africa, engage in racial attacks? As one sociologist put it, the first racist attacks in Spain forced a national introspection akin to Narcissus looking in a mirror only to find a very dirty reflection looking back (Calvo Buezas et al, 2000: 15).

Most responses to the public debate about immigration have made the rather commonsensical assumption that this racism is born of economic competition, poverty and xenophobia. Some have noted that these racial tensions are an entirely new phenomenon in Spain, the product of standard universally shared conundrum of globalized markets and cultural exchange and information sharing mixed with older and more entrenched nationalist, ethnic identities (Calvo Buezas et al, 2000: 17). According to this reading of contemporary circumstances, racist attitudes are certainly fresh arrivals – and unwelcome guests – on the Peninsula. Ironically, racism becomes an unintended symbol of Spain's modernity, an illness contracted while fraternizing for the first time in the modern, globalized world (*The Economist*, 24 July 1999). The writer Eduardo Haro Tecglen once asserted that Spaniards are like

> all who orbit today between nationalism and internationalism. They are affected by the little ruptures brought on by the centripetal force of celebrating supranationalism and the desire to conserve our particularities, between the fear of shipwreck in which we imagine ourselves as a dark ocean of lost individualisms sinking into some unknown new collective.
>
> (Haro Tecglen, 1993: 15)

Haro Tecglen, in common with many other Spanish commentators, views this racism as a new import, the product of an international tension born of globalization and the particularities of national identity.

However, confronting difference and associating this difference with criminality and abnormality is not a new phenomenon, nor are they informed solely by shared ideas about race and the challenges of a newly globalized labor force. In fact, how the past informs policy, how historic sensibilities and national identities condition the actual responses to new social phenomenon are subjects that have received scant attention in contemporary Spain, or, for that matter, in Europe more broadly. A new wave of scholarship about Spain examines these changes not just as reflections of a globalized condition shared in many European countries dealing with immigration but also as products of the particular historical and social circumstances found in individual European nations. These studies tend to contemplate more broadly the gulf between national self-perception and the actual content of racial ideas. In particular, a growing historical awareness of the role of difference and ethnicity in shaping the Spanish past has begun to allow historians to ponder the role that racial thought has played in forming Spanish conceptions of nationalism, ethnic identity and difference (Calavita, 2005; Goode, 2009). Much of this recent work is informed by the now almost facile observation that race is a social construction, created by and reflective of social, historical or political tensions, rather than the product of any meaningful physical difference. As a social construction, racial thought relies upon the creation, not the reality, of physical, cultural and behavioral differences. The differences in racial formations, as Howard Winant and Michael Omi have put it, exist far away from the obvious physical differences in appearance (Omi and Winant, 1994). Long-term, inheritable and immutable characteristics are manufactured, not revealed.

Yet this process of racial formation is also historical and remains reflective of local context and variation. The way in which differences are racialized does have a historical component. Sociologists and urban ethnographers tend to perform a synchronic analysis about how race is formulated at any one moment. This study is usually a universalizing one but does not show how historical patterns underline the process of racial formation. This process unfolds across different national, urban and social settings. A more diachronic approach, usually the purview of historians, considers how racial others are created over time in one or more contexts. The process that historians might study will be the same, but the definition of the racial 'others' changes according to the historical context. Through an exploration of this more diachronic approach, this chapter will demonstrate that the process of making 'others' in Spain is not necessarily new, just that the objects of this process are. One example of this process of racialization, the criminalization of behavior or the association of identity with illegality, will be shown to have had a long lineage in Spain. Spaniards, like most other Europeans, have engaged in the process of defining different political attitudes, social behaviors and differences in culture, within the Spanish population as something deeper and more inherent than would be produced by mere circumstance and social context. The objects of this effort have changed over time but the process has not.

One way to understand the historical association of race and criminality in Spain is to examine first how racial thought influenced the formation of criminology, specifically criminal anthropology, of the late 19th century, when racial theories had their greatest influence on developments in European thought. Working with a shifting definition of race that reflected the malleability of racial ideas and their social application, Spanish criminologists were able to ascribe criminal proclivities to a wide variety of groups that were defined not by their ostensible political ideas or social behaviors but rather by a supposed biological compulsion. The early twenty-first century shares a similar tendency to conflate criminality with different social groups and particular behaviors that are widely defined as anti-social or anti-nationalist. While obvious differences in physical appearance might exist today, Spanish criminal anthropologists of the late 19th century created physical differences from groups that were seen as ill-fitting in the national body. Social comportment and a willingness to assimilate or participate in the national state became important markers of a profound, if not readily identifiable difference. What defined the Spanish approach to crime in the late nineteenth and early twentieth centuries was an effort to align biological notions of the causes of crime with more politically and socially derived identification of criminals. Spanish anthropologists and criminologists suggested that criminals may have been born that way but it was social context that unleashed their criminality.

Crime and race in the late 19th and early 20th centuries[1]

As a discrete field of scientific inquiry, criminology in Spain had the same origins as in the rest of Europe (Bierne, 1993: 233–8). Physicians initially began the study of the supposed organic causes of criminal behavior in Spain in the early 19th century. Phrenologists gave way to psychiatrists who attempted – throughout the first half of the 19th century – to seek the roots of criminal behavior in different physical formations, either in cranial shape or in unseen biological lesions hidden deep inside the brain. In Spain, the first successful attempts by physicians and psychiatrists to effect changes in the criminal code appeared in the new Penal Code of 1870. Article 8 of this Code stipulated that insanity and 'uncontrollable urges' would be possible mitigating factors in the assessment of criminal responsibility and grounds upon which to sentence criminals to asylums for treatment rather than to prisons or execution (in capital cases) (Silvela, 1870).[2] By the end of the century, conflicts that were prevalent throughout European jurisprudence began to form between physicians and lawyers in Spain. Medical doctors argued for the use of psychiatric information in criminal defenses. Lawyers demanded firm categories of guilt and innocence to adjudicate crime (Kaplan, 1969). Anthropology helped to fill the breach between these conflicting parties.

Criminology informed by the anthropological study of human difference came to dominate debates about criminal law. As in other European countries, the transformation in Spain was deeply influenced by Lombroso and the publication of his work, *L'Uomo Delinquente* in 1876.

Oddly, Spain benefited from developing a scientific field of criminology later than its European counterparts. While Lombroso's initial association of criminality with atavism, the idea that criminals represented a decay in the evolution of a national body, was accepted in Spain at an early stage, the 1887 translation of his *Delinquent Man*, replete with revisions inspired by a student, Enrico Ferri, had the greatest impact (Gibson, 1998: 105). Ferri had forced Lombroso to modify his purely biological determinism. By the time of the 1887 French translation, which was the edition familiar to most Spanish criminologists, Lombroso had begun to suggest that the 'born criminal' might also be the product of a particular social milieu and individual temperament rather than just an atavism in a nation's evolution. Ferri further claimed that born criminals represented only the most recalcitrant and irremediable of criminals while most others combined a particular racial propensity for crime with environmental and social factors, like poverty, that compelled criminal behavior.

Devised along anthropological lines that promoted rather than rejected the idea of racial mixture, Spanish criminal anthropology did not view the criminal as the product of decayed, retrogressive or atavistic racial components (see Gibson, 1998; Pick, 1989; Nye, 1984) Instead, Spanish criminal anthropologists came to see criminal behavior as being the product of missteps, breaks or derailments in the process of proper racial fusion that had characterized the rest of the non-criminal Spanish population. Thus, criminals were missing an element or had a corrosive ingredient in their particular racial composition that led them to commit criminal acts. Like their colleagues in anthropology, however, Spanish criminal anthropologists saw the process of racial fusion not solely as the product of immutable, inexorable biological identity, but also as a process affected by environmental conditions. Thus, when Spanish criminologists spoke of racial roots, they were not necessarily limiting themselves to physical lineage. Spanish criminal anthropologists saw race – and indeed racial fusion – as being either promoted or inhibited by the social or cultural make-up of the groups that composed them. They saw the physical environment in which both individuals and large groups of people developed also as playing formative roles in their racial make-up. The question for Spanish criminal anthropologists was to diagnose what corrupted aspect of the various elements of Spain's racial fusion was causing criminality.

In the creation of Spanish criminal context, history and environment functioned as some of the key driving forces. In 1898, one of Spain's most important criminal anthropologists, Rafael Salillas y Panzano, published the first book-length study of the unique national characteristics of the Spanish criminal, *Hampa: El Delincuente Español*. For Salillas, the mixing of races was seen as the mechanism that brought about the creation of the Spanish criminal. He began his study by noting that the kinds of crime prevalent in Spain showed that criminal populations were among the most retrograde in development among Europeans. The prevalence of murder and political violence indicated that, at least among criminals, some racial element was creating a lag in the development of Spanish civilization. In *El Delincuente Español*, Rafael Salillas argued that this racial element was the direct result of an historic infusion of gypsy populations into the Spanish race (Salillas, 1898b: 14).

This racial component combined with the inhospitable environment of southern Spain to create what Salillas has labeled nomadic instincts within Spanish criminals. These nomadic instincts led Spaniards to feel, despite the realities of their surroundings, a certain desperation for always needing to find sustenance and shelter. According to this analysis, criminal behaviors, both violent and non-violent, emerged from this desperation. Thus, the mixture of nomadic populations into the Spanish racial stock had left a unique mark on Spaniards, a mark observable in 'sociological, psychological and even anatomic characteristics' (Salillas, 1898b: xii). Salillas added:

> ...in order to make precise the affinities between our people and theirs, we must recognize that these affinities have come to be constituted by virtue of certain national habits and types, a fused personality. This fusion has resulted in the coupling of picaresque and gypsy, that is, of the blood relations of gypsy and criminal. This affinity can only be explained through the intermingling of characteristics between one people and another. Such a strong intermingling, of course, would indicate a similar nature in the constitutive groups, a similarity rooted in one clearly shared trait, nomadism.
>
> (1898b: xviii)

If the criminal underworld in Spain emerged from gypsy populations and as a result of the effects of the rugged environment in the South, Spain's law-abiding population was the product of continued fusion with other more advanced populations and the dispersion of these populations to other more hospitable areas of Spain. Like his anthropological colleagues, Salillas suggested that the advanced fusion of the law-abiding citizens emerged not only in physical make-up but also in cultural and political behaviors. Unlike the work of Olóriz, Salillas argued that this fusionary process was not a mere evolutionary inevitability, free from the influence of human action. Rather, Salillas argued that evolution was mutable. In fact, the racial fusion could be artificially skewed to rework the combination of ingredients and the environments in which they mixed to create a more desirable human product. For Salillas, one could not directly weed out the racial mixture of the past in a physical sense (Maristany, 1973: 38). What humans could alter were the environmental conditions that fostered and reinforced the psychological traits associated with nomadism (Salillas, 1898b: 517–18).

If nomadic instincts and the desperate sense of survival they engendered were the product of fusion with nomadic populations and interactions with an inhospitable environment, Salillas argued political and social reforms, the will of the state, could be enlisted to overcome some of the most lasting and corrosive effects. Securing more access to property ownership and providing sustenance via education in cultivating the land, for example, would all be effective measures to weed out the lasting negative effects of mixture with nomadic populations. Gypsies were unredeemable by state intervention because they preferred separation from larger populations, resisting the beneficial aspects of racial mixing. Yet their effects on the Spanish racial mix, though physically indelible, could be altered socially and culturally. Gypsies were a block in an otherwise successful racial fusion. Gypsies, in fact, suffered too from their own, albeit self-imposed, lack of intermixture:

> the present population of Spain does not have a complete homogeneity, and in fact, offers quite a diversity of types, costumes, customs, of related peoples and origins. The work of national unity centered on fusing all of these diverse elements into a politico-religious configuration to which even many Jews and Moors, who were not expelled, submitted. But the gypsy, who does not have a political personality, who doesn't have nor even want a *patria*, who will fight against no institution, does not represent political or social dangers, who loves nothings else but his independence and wandering life, do not fuse, but rather hold on their customs and way of life…the representatives of that people who remain in Spain do not constitute a true community, a nation, but rather an aggregate of all the influences acting on it, the product, it must be said, of some of the vicious indifference of Spanish society.
>
> (Salillas, 1898b: 10)

Salillas' approach left an indelible mark on the subsequent development of criminology. The goal was not the removal of born criminals from society, but rather the reform of the social conditions that produced them. Unlike the Italian positivists, many of whom were Socialists like Lombroso, Salillas and the growing Spanish school of criminology did not assume that the removal of criminals would eliminate the disease from society and consequently produce an equal, just, democratic, socialist or communal society of good, healthy citizens (Pick, 1989). Salillas summed up this position writing a eulogy for a Spanish Carmelite nun, Concepción Arenal, whose *Letters to Delinquents* (1865) and *Estudios Penitenciarios* (1877) had helped draw attention to the deplorable conditions and inhumane treatment of criminals in Spanish prisons that had activated the first efforts in prison reform in the

1870s. Arenal did not favor new medical treatment of prisoners; their criminality was the result of moral degeneration due to poor living conditions or improper religious training. As a result, she long supported religious education in the prisons rather than medical or psychiatric treatment. Salillas considered her the founder of modern criminology because her writing was marked by the same kind of two-sided approach that later came to dominate Spanish criminology. She focused on the need to save the soul by improving the conditions in which the body lived. Criminal anthropologists replaced the soul with environment and psychology and saw the body in terms of its racial history. The lessons of criminal anthropology in Spain, he wrote, were that in the treatment of crime, saving the soul included understanding the body of the criminal (Salillas, 1898a: 98–101).

One of Salillas' most important students was Constancio Bernaldo de Quirós, who worked under Salillas in the Ministry of Grace and Justice. Quirós offered one new element to the internal dynamic of crime and biological difference. Quirós presented the city as the first, obvious proving ground of racial amalgation. Modernity really forged the bond between race and crime. In 1898, Quirós wrote the first textbook of criminal anthropology in Spain, entitled *Modern Theories of Criminality*. The work was designed to be an introduction to the field for both the student and for the general public. The work was translated into English by the American Institute of Criminal Law and Criminology in 1912. The committee, composed primarily of the new representatives of Legal Sociology Roscoe Pound and Ernst Freund at the University of Chicago, chose Quirós' work precisely because of its synthetic quality:

> [Quirós' work] reveals in all the shades of thought which have marked the development of the science and constitutes a compendium that no student of the subject can ignore without disadvantage.
>
> (Quirós, 1912: xvi)

Quirós had already established this international reputation with a study published in 1901 about the urban roots of crime entitled 'The Low Life of Madrid.' Later translated into German and Italian, with an introduction by Lombroso, Quirós' book presented a view of the criminal in Madrid as the mixed product of the various racial influences on the Spanish population. The urban context of Madrid fostered the creation of criminals. The city's unhygienic living conditions for the poor and the ingathering of criminal elements from throughout Spain, who were able to avoid the scrutiny of the police amid the large population, exacerbated the nomadic, parasitic tendencies of those few who already had the 'protoplasm of criminal life' in their racial mix (Quirós, 1912: 108). The argument had already been introduced in the craniological studies of a Dr. Porpeta and a military doctor, Carlos Slocker, among them the most famous *Capacidad Craneana en Madrid*.

After measuring the crania of both living and dead Madrileños, these doctors concluded that the process of racial fusion took place in cities at a much faster rate. They added, however, that certain racial elements were more robust than others and better resisted this fusion.[3] Criminality was one of these elements. Despite this evolutionary view of criminality in Madrid, Quirós' idea also relied on the Haeckelian approach of Salillas, suggesting that even during the life of a criminal, certain stages of development were linchpins in the creation of different criminal behaviors:

> Thus it happens that, adopting as a definite occupation one of the said modes of life and practicing it habitually, [criminals] become identified with delinquency, prostitution, or criminality, producing the delinquents, the prostitutes, or the beggars.
>
> (Quirós, 1912: 108)

Quirós' theory relied on a hodge-podge of scientific views of evolutionary development. He adopted Haeckl's stage theory of development, yet added the neo-Lamarckian perspective that criminals acquired characteristics over the course of their lives that were then passed on to successive generations of criminals.

Quirós was presenting the argument that criminal development could potentially be curtailed through the appropriate treatment, or some form of medical, psychological or social intervention. If certain aspects of criminality were acquired, then perhaps intervention in peoples' lives prior to their acquisition would thwart criminal development. What differentiated Quirós' view from other environmental arguments was his belief that people who exhibited criminal traits, either behavioral or physical, had indeed followed not only a different social path, but had entered that path already predisposed to criminality because of their racial lineage. Criminals were, in fact, either a distinct species born to criminal life or a people once altered by circumstances, who developed criminal dispositions:

> A product of vagabond temperament, of early neglect and social decadence, the outlaw lives as a parasite of the social organism, devoting himself to theft, prostitution and beggary. We find in him the aptitude and, at times, even the practice of these three phases of life... when [criminals] become settled in any of these differentiated states, they experience also a series of changes and transformations related to the adaptation to the new mode of life... the differentiation [between criminals] is never so complete as to atrophy altogether the primary aptitudes for every kind of parasitism... biological species abandon or hide the characteristics for which they are persecuted and imitate others in order to mask themselves.
>
> (Quirós, 1912: 108–9)

In the volume on modern theories of criminality, Quirós discussed over a dozen books and articles on Spanish criminals published after Salillas' *El Delincuente Español*. The portrait that emerged from these studies, he wrote, was of a Spain still dominated by violent or 'blood' crimes and 'assaults and insults against authority and public functionaries' (Quirós, 1912: 104). Spanish criminals, given their retrogressive fusion with gypsy populations and the inhospitability of the environment that nurtured them, were lower down in this evolutionary scale. Yet, using a statistical analysis of Spanish crime, Quirós noted that the intensity of violent crime varied throughout the nation. He concluded that this variation provided further evidence of incomplete racial fusion and the possibility of localizing and thus isolating the particular, corrosive influences within Spain's regions. The variation of intensity within the Peninsula indicated that racial fusion was not uniform throughout Spain. Even more, these variations were brought about by the Peninsula's distinct environments. He wrote, for example, that the uneven intensity of violence in Spain was

> generally due to racial distribution. In the Northwestern provinces of Lugo and Oviedo, where they brachycephalic (eurasian) type prevails, there is a minimum intensity of crimes of blood; while in the regions mainly inhabited by dolichocephalics (eurafricans), including the upper plateau of Castile, the lower Ebro, the eastern slope and the elevation of Andalucia, there is a maximum intensity, especially in the second and last places.
>
> (Quirós, 1912: 105–6)

This mapping of the racial distributions in Spain duplicated other ethnological studies of Spain, especially from Spain's key anthropologists (Goode, 2009). Yet Quirós came to slightly different conclusions about the effects of racial mixture than did his anthropological colleagues. In fact, it is interesting to note the different inflections that Quirós gave, for example, to the effects of the infusion of African peoples in the Peninsula than did his colleague, Manuel Antón y Ferrándiz, who held the Chair of Anthropology at the Central University in Madrid. Antón had argued that the influence of African races brought a fiery sense of independence, a character that served Spain well in foreign wars and in the conquest of the Americas, but had aroused regional aspirations within the country (Antón, 1903: 5). Quirós placed more emphasis on the negative effects of this mixture, connecting the infusion of African races with an increase in violent crime, and the proliferation of retrograde behaviors. Yet, the method for dealing with the effects of this mixture was not simply extracting this fused element from the Spanish race. Such an unbinding of the racial mix could also be detrimental to Spanish racial health. Quirós, like Antón, found certain qualities inherent in the African race. Since crime could be understood as rooted in physical differences, Quirós argued that other influences, more controllable and mutable elements of crime would be the criminologists' focus. Following Salillas' argument, Quirós wrote that these other factors also helped fashion Spain's criminal element:

> the influence of culture and of the density of population is sufficiently noticeable in the distribution of criminality; but what determines it better are the natural forces, like temperature and humidity.
>
> (Quirós, 1912: 106)

Quirós displayed a distinct inability to follow any one particular school of thought, preferring instead to blend different approaches. For example, when data appeared to contradict his arguments about environment's role in creating crime, he used race, now defined in terms of permanent biological inheritance, to explain such contradictions. He observed, for example, that the province of Logroño, which had normal humidity, a climate usually associated with less criminal activity, also had a very high level of violent crime. The explanation for this apparent anomaly lay in the fact that Logroño existed in a 'zone ... which preserves in sufficient purity the ancient, impulsive and violent Iberian race' (Quirós, 1912: 106). The Basque race which lived in proximity to the region surrounding Logroño was the ostensible culprit in this improper racial fusion.

In these late 19th- and early 20th-century efforts to define race and crime, Spanish criminologists emerged as flexible interpreters of anthropology and behavior. The causes of criminal behavior were written indelibly into people's basic identities. Race, defined as a fusion of different peoples, required careful analysis of these component parts. Crime was a bad stitch in the racial fabric. Rather than simply arguing that race did not exist, Spanish criminologists argued that race and criminality were intricately interwoven within Spain's existing internal populations and urban contexts. What made Spanish criminologists interesting was their assumption that despite obvious physical differences or lineages, different groups could intermix successfully into the Spanish racial mix, as long as careful attention was paid to how they were intermixed. Values, attitudes and carefully controlled state intervention all emerged as the tools to ensure proper racial intermixture.

Race and crime discourse in contemporary Spain

This process of optimistic assimilation has lingered in more contemporary discussions of race and crime. The city in particular remains the central locus of associating race and crime. Yet, one new factor, immigration into Spain, differentiates the present discourse on race and crime from that of a century ago. Surprisingly, the manner in which race and crime are associated together remains similar. The recent phenomenon of immigration into Spain and the historical sensibility that Spanish history is marked by tolerance and anti-racism both play important roles in shaping how Spaniards view crime and in defining who criminals are. The two groups in Spain largely and automatically identified with criminality, immigrants and Spain's Roma/Gitano, or Gypsy, population reflect these separate tendencies, one new and one very old (ECRI, 2003).[4] These groups and their treatment are beginning to challenge long-held notions of Spanish openness.

One success in overturning the dismissive notion of Spain's freedom from racism and racial thought has been the recent scholarship that applies new definitions of racial thought, informed by critical race theory, to contemporary understanding of racial difference and crime. Kitty Calavita, in particular, shows how race and criminality have been bound together in contemporary Spain in response to recent immigration (Calavita, 2005). Other scholars are beginning to show how historically based anti-racist discourses shape this association of race and criminality. Critical race theory, in particular the idea of cultural racism, has proven effective in showing how policies toward immigrants and racial others rooted in a historically defended celebration of Spanish anti-racism still serve to isolate and mistreat populations based not on their actions but on presuppositions about their behavior. The two factors work together dialectically to foster a view that celebrates open acceptance of immigrants but also essentializes ethnic differences in such a way as to view newly arrived immigrants as permanent racial others and, then, racial others as potential criminals (Calavita, 2005: 148–9).

This process is also a dynamic one, changing over time in a way that confounds continuing nostrums about Spanish difference and the freedom from racism. Two common attitudes served to distinguish Spain from European neighbors in the period following the death of Franco and Spain's economic expansion in the 1980s and 1990s. The first was the sense that the immigration posed an ethnic challenge to Spain's historical homogeneity. Missteps in the integration of immigrants and racist violence were partially the products of discomfort and newness. Ironically, a US newspaper columnist voiced this position most clearly in an article about the rise of anti-immigrant attacks in Spain in the early 1990s. The US columnist, Eugene Robinson, was surprised by a fatal shooting of immigrants from the Dominican Republic in a Madrid suburb in 1992 because, for one, the violence belied a Spanish historical freedom from such racist attacks. 'Immigration,' he wrote, 'has not been a major issue in Spain since the Jews and the Moors were violently expelled in the late 1400s' (Robinson, 1992: 27). Robinson was not wrong to note that immigration was a relatively new phenomenon of the past 200 years. But, more interesting is his association of new immigrants, mostly from Africa and South America, with the supposedly 'foreign immigrants' of Spain's past, Jews and Muslims. Were Spanish Jews and Muslims, living in the Iberian Peninsula for centuries prior to their expulsion, 'immigrants' in the same way arrivals of the early 1990s were? There is a clear presumption of a separate Spanish identity that remains uncluttered from mixture with other populations.

Interestingly, this confused assumption of a historical Spanish homogeneity collided in the same article with the other historical celebration of Spanish openness and a tolerance for difference. Quoting the then Spanish Foreign Minister and diplomat, Javier Solana, Robinson presented the other image of Spain, not racist and exclusionary, but rather open and welcoming. Spain remains relatively free of racial hatreds, because of a long history of multiculturalism, because Spain had always existed at the crossroad between Europe and Africa. Littoral life abjures automatic hatreds; xenophobia ironically cannot take root in well-trodden soil. Solana said, 'It is unfortunate that in our country anything could happen that has to do with outbreaks of racism...Spain is a country where others have always been taken in with great generosity and solidarity' (Robinson, 1992: 27). Spain is seen therefore as a country that has jealously defended its homogeneity while at the same time welcoming and being generous toward foreigners. One might wonder what the impact of this historical confusion and accommodating of the contradiction between openness and homogeneity has on contemporary policies toward immigrants and racialized populations.

The legal responses to Spain's changing demographics provide clear testimony of the dual impact that supposed ethnic openness has amid a historical sensitivity to the plight of minorities. Spain has enjoyed a reputation for being open and tolerant of newly arriving populations. It has one of the largest foreign-born populations of any European Union nation, accounting for roughly 11 percent of the country's 46 million people. Spain has also been energetic in legalizing illegal immigrants, engaging in six legalizations since 1986. The result is a legal population of about 600,000 immigrants of a total immigrant population today of roughly 4 million. Spain has received plaudits for the treatment of immigrants and minorities once in the country, either when they were welcomed in or, even now, when they are encouraged to leave. One immigrant-rights organization leader, critical of recent policies, has celebrated the Socialist government's efforts to grant legal immigrants the right to vote: 'we can see,' he recently said, 'that the government has a strategy for integration' (Abend and Mimigliano, 2008: 4).

Yet, such openness is fragile. Unemployment and the general economic decline that has engulfed Europe in 2008 and 2009 have led to a slight shift in this openness. Spain started encouraging immigrants to leave in late 2008, with the government even offering financial incentives to do so (DeParle, 2008: 1). In general, this shift is blamed on changes in the economic fortunes of Spain in recent years. Immigrants who helped fuel Spain's post-Franco economic expansion are now viewed as competition and weakening agents in Spanish society (Matlack and Tarzian, 2007: 50).

Yet, many who study Spanish racial attitudes do not see the shift in policies as reflective of a particular welcoming spirit or open attitude toward different ethnic groups. Here, the tension between Spanish anti-racist attitudes and the practice of racial attitudes is clearest. Especially after 2004, the criminal law pertaining to ethnic and racial difference and status acknowledged the presence of new populations. The Spanish constitution recognizes racist motivations as a special aggravating circumstance in crimes. Ethnic origin cannot be taken into account in employment decisions, education, housing, social protection among other civil matters. However, many NGOs complain about the sporadic and woefully incomplete implementation of these laws (ECRI, 2005: 9–10). This kind of discrepancy between the law as it is written down and its actual application, especially regarding the protection of minorities, has received particular criticism. There are no special units within the police that deal with racially motivated crimes. According to 2005 statistics, non-citizens of Spain account for 30 percent of the total number of arrests but only 10 percent of the convictions (ECRI, 2005: 8–11). The foreign-born and Roma also seem to receive longer sentences for similar crimes than those handed down to Spanish defendants (ECRI, 2005: 10–11). Spain's main immigrant groups and ethnic minorities, including Moroccans, South Americans, sub-Saharan Africans and Roma/Gitanos, are often the victims of ethnic or racial profiling, though the Spanish police statistics on profiling, though recorded, are generally not made public (ECRI, 2005: 11; Wagman, 2006: 4–5).

Yet, one should not also discount the role of history, both real and imagined, that also shapes contemporary attitudes alongside the lived experience, or the actual arrival, of new populations into Spain. In a recent work on anti-Semitism in Spain, historian Gonzalo Álvarez Chillida notes a telling statistic that after Moroccans and Muslims, Spaniards polled in a survey cited Jews as the third gravest immigrant threat in Spain (Álvarez Chillida, 2002). With Jewish immigration rates into Spain measured in smaller than single digits, one might assert that this concern with Jewish immigration reflects other tensions, memories or attitudes rooted in historical sensibilities rather than purely a reaction to conditions on the ground (Jacobson, 2003). Clearly, attitudes toward difference and reactions to immigration in Spain are conditioned by historical factors and historical memories. Kitty Calavita also cites this poll in her own work on attitudes toward immigrants in Spain but argues that it is 'curiously enough' an interesting sidelight at best (Calavita, 2005: 127).

One might instead argue that history infuses notions of difference and conditions how people respond to these differences, both at the level of public and social policy and also in lived, everyday, interpersonal experience. How different groups are defined and treated, criminalized or assimilated toward race and to illicit or improper social behavior, national feeling and so on are clearly inflected with historical sensibilities about how the nation handled difference in the past and what composes the 'proper' ethnic state. Other recent work has unpacked this seemingly contradictory assertion of ethnic homogeneity and also the Spanish openness and welcoming of different peoples. Not surprisingly, a recent Council of Europe report on Spain noted that Spain's particular issue relating to the incorporation and treatment of minorities in its population is the 'lack of awareness' and recognition of racial discrimination and racism in Spanish society (ECRI, 2005: 30).

Policy and practice response to immigration: Implications for criminalization

Certainly, historical sensibilities play the role of mediator between different social codes of racial difference, criminality and assimilation. Spain has been particularly energetic in crafting legal and social methods of integrating Spain's immigrant populations. A 1994 'Plan for Social Integration,' formed at the moment that immigration into Spain began to build, offered a commitment to include immigrants into regional, local and national immigration-policy making. Throughout both socialist party leadership (*PSOE*) and conservative party leadership (the *Partido Popular*) in the 1990s and 2000s, respectively, financial outlays for health care, education, reception centers and housing for immigrants continuously increased (Calavita, 2005: 93–4). Yet, even the efforts to curtail the energetic and positive means of incorporating immigrant populations collide against other attitudes and policies that simultaneously produce criminalized views of immigrant behavior. Kitty Calavita has recently shown how legal regimes in southern Europe that preach tolerance, openness and integration have actually worked to foster the racial othering of populations, in modes that lead to and help justify violence and attacks on populations as criminal attacks on the national body. She notes the fundamental irony in modern Spain, like most contemporary states, that immigrant labor, especially illegal labor, is both welcomed and desired precisely because it is illegal. Its illegality helps justify low wages, poor working conditions. Yet the process is dialectical. Immigrants, welcomed throughout the 1990s, who found plentiful work in Spain, were also viewed as a suspect, dangerous, illegal population. Immigrants are placed in an inescapable political–economic matrix, or more simply, a Catch-22:

> The advantage of immigrants for these economies resides precisely in their Otherness. At the same time, that Othernesss is the pivot on which backlashes against immigrants turn. For, if marginalized immigrant workers are useful in part *because* they are marked by illegality, poverty and exclusion, this very marking, this highlighting of their difference, contributes to their distinction as a suspect population... Immigration law then must simultaneously preserve immigrant Otherness, and combat the political, social and fiscal fallout of that Otherness. In concrete terms,

it both constructs and reconstructs illegality and difference, and spends millions on doomed projects of integration.

(Calavita, 2005: 11–12)

Accordingly, the very reasons for the immigrant's presence furthered the notion of them as suspect and dangerous.

The Spanish news media reinforces this Catch-22. Media coverage has generally crystallized the association of immigrants with criminality through constant focus on immigrant efforts to sneak into Spain. The language used to describe immigrants has both a historical resonance, when they become 'boat people,' or an air of dangerous natural, uncontrollable threat, as when they arrive in floods, waves, avalanches or storms (Calativa, 2005: 138). Their illegality is inscribed in the use of the derogatory term 'wetback' to describe those who enter Spain from the Mediterranean (*El País*, 12 January 1997). One recent article in the Spanish newspaper *El País* melds both the historical and natural discourses of threat. Discussing the successful interception of a group of illegal immigrants attempting to enter Spain from the Strait of Gibraltar, the writer celebrated 'the recent stretch of good weather that followed the strong winds has still brought a new avalanche of clandestine expeditions of African immigrants. A total of 90 "wetbacks" were captured by Guardia Civil patrols...' (Romaguera, 1998). Other reports that detail the appearance of immigrant mafia groups within Spain and the strange cultural practices of immigrant communities help further a sense that the very culture of immigrants exudes criminality. Statistics testify to the effects: the proportion of Spain's prison population that is foreign-born is 25 times higher than the proportion of immigrants in the general population (Calavita, 2005: 139).

Yet, in the present day, as in the late nineteenth and early twentieth centuries, the idea of ingrained, immutable cultural difference plays a far deeper role in providing a sense of ingrained, permanent difference between immigrant and non-immigrant, as some scholars have recently shown (Calavita, 2005). This phenomenon, known as cultural racism, describes the tendency to assume fundamental, racial distinctions between people based on non-biological or non-physical criteria. Despite the apparent fungibility of behaviors, cultural racism presumes fixity of group identities; that different groups act and behave in certain unshakeable ways that years of coexistence with other peoples do not seem to alter. This idea helps clarify the confusion between the two views of the Spanish past and its present-day attitudes toward immigrants.

The idea that culture serves a more dominant exclusionary role between people than purely somatic or physical differences has led Etienne Balibar to coin a new locution, 'neo-racism' or 'racism without race' (Calavita, 2005: 148). Physical differences in appearance are not the only codes through which racial hierarchies are created. Rather, if race is a social construction, a figment of the imagination, then quite often the modes of casting indelible, essentialist differences are made in cultural rather than physical terms. Skin color fades as the marker of difference and instead reappears only as a sign of a deeper behavioral and cultural difference. Racial thought only presumes some kind of difference that is inherited, timeless and transmitted. Cultural characteristics are seen to adhere to certain groups indelibly and are then turned into 'problematic differences,' conflicting with Spanish culture and values (Calavita, 2005: 154). Hence, arguing that groups should return 'home' after decades of living away speak to the cultural characteristics imbued with racist group ordering and hierarchies. As Laura Otis put it, when one begins to assume hereditary bonds between people, racial thought follows closely behind (Otis, 1994). Different people are presumed to behave differently, to view the world differently. Some scholars have, as a result, expanded the meanings of racial thought to argue that cultural racism exists in a manner that assumes clear, overwhelming differences and hierarchies of value in how people behave, act, think. It is not the appearance that conditions the difference; behavior does. Skin color merely is the marker of the differences that 'lurk beneath' (Calavita, 2005: 146).

Ironically, the appropriation of US anti-racist discourse in Spain has fostered the development of cultural racism. The general sense that expressing animus toward groups defined by their physical appearance has grown so unpalatable and objectionable that other modes of defining groups emerge (Calavita, 2005: 148). The idea that people still possess historical, mutually exclusive and static identities expressed in reified cultural practices indicates that cultural racism is as operative in Spain as elsewhere. Cultural racism only perpetuates the criminalization of immigrant groups. Cultural practices speak the inherent criminality of the groups. Destitution, for example, becomes a marker of permanent difference, and then criminality is an attendant component of this difference. As one housing official in the Spanish city of Almeria put it,

> [immigrants] live in very bad conditions. In the field, without water or electricity or bathrooms...It's all very bad and must be changed...but... they are accustomed to it because they come from countries where it is much worse.
>
> (Calavita, 2005: 150)

Thus, social policies, especially those designed to ameliorate the condition of immigrant workers, have inadvertently promoted the kinds of racist cultural assumptions that Spaniards have long argued are absent from their society. The writer Daniel Wagman has pointed out that state plans to build workers' communities in Spain have had the unintended consequence of creating immigrant neighborhoods and ghettoes. Sequestering populations in cities has produced neighborhoods marked by danger and criminality.

Urban space also then gets coded as safe versus dangerous, criminal versus secure, not based on actual crime rates or lived experiences with crime, but rather as the product of immigrant groups increasingly concentrated in new communities that are constructed in and for their isolation. The irony of course is that actual crime rates are no higher and are in fact lower in these neighborhoods (Wagman, 2004).

In addition to social isolation, the creation of neighborhoods with high concentrations of immigrant populations works more insidiously to further mark immigrant populations as different in habits, in living conditions, associating different kinds of cultural life with ethnic difference and skin color rather than with more structural forces that actually produce these neighborhoods. Cultural racism develops around the mistaken visual cue of certain immigrant populations living together and apart from the rest of the Spanish population. Separate neighborhoods or immigrant districts have a visual impact on the larger population, what the French sociologist Tahar Ben Jelloun has called the creation of an 'aesthetics of immigration,' that symbolically shows that immigrants 'do not fit into wider community' (Calavita, 2005: 154–5). The result of such identification leads to the belief that immigrants, isolated, staying with their own kind, are also in turn victimizing the Spanish population, mostly by drawing too much on the public resources of the state, in schools, public health services, security concerns (Goytisolo and Naïr, 2000: 150–1; Wagman, 2006: v). In its Third Report on Spain published in 2005, the European Commission against Racism and Intolerance cited polls that show overall 60 percent of the Spanish population identifying immigration with crime and 'hostile attitudes toward immigrants' ballooning from 8 percent in 1997 to 32 percent (ECRI, 2005).

But the association of criminality with ethnic minorities is directed not just at the newly arrived immigrants into Spain. The confluence of historical sensibilities and attitudes toward Others comes together in attitudes toward Spain's Roma population, or gypsies. Spain's Roma/Gitana make up a little more than 1 percent of the Spanish population, with official estimates ranging between 500,000–600,000 Roma, and non-governmental estimates coming in as high as 800,000 (ECRI, 2003; and Calvo Buezas, 1992: 328). As noted in the historical discussion of late 19th- and early 20th-century association of crime with Roma, Spain's gypsy population is dealt with as an internal enemy either too recalcitrant to participate in society or as dangerously taking too much from Spain's social welfare system. They are both cheats and abusers or too unwilling to avail themselves of the services offered. In either reading, they exist outside the bounds of normal society. One European commission described the condition of the Roma population in Spain as 'coexistence without togetherness' (ECRI, 2003: 21). Similar patterns of criminalization and racial differentiation are applied to Spain's Roma population. Media framing, for example, of Spain's Roma is strikingly similar to how immigrants appear in press coverage of Spain's minorities. While immigrants are usually referred to as arriving in avalanches, waves, storms, Spain's Roma are still often referred to as members of the 'Gypsy race' or as 'clans,' and 'tribes' in the press (Calvo Buezas, 1992: 14; EU Monitoring and Advocacy Program (EUMAP), 2002: 290; ECRI, 2003: 21). Accounts of crimes often describe the 'Gitano-like' characters suspected of committing crimes. Discussion of the Roma/Gitana population in general frames them as an outsider group, naturally different, at best incompletely assimilating into the larger population.

The tacit othering of the Roma/Gitano population also appears in a general governmental ambivalence toward this internal population. The unintended consequences of policies that seek amelioration of the condition of Roma housing have created social isolation, and the perpetuation of cultural and social stigmatization. As in the efforts to provide discrete areas of immigrant housing, the creation of transitional housing programs for Spain's Roma populations has perpetuated a ghettoization of certain urban Romani populations (EUMAP, 2002: 284). Poverty rates, the absence of access to education and the unequal treatment of Romani children in Spanish schools all leave Roman populations at or near the bottom of Spain's social ladder. The lack of governmental statistics on Romani populations only bespeaks the ambivalence about the success or failure of social programs (EUMAP, 2002: 283). The irony of this failure to monitor Spain's Roma is how strenuously the state has worked historically to keep an eye on this population. Tomás Calvo Buezas notes, for example, the 1942 Civil Guard Orders to keep 'scrupulous vigilance' over the Gitanos, annulled only in 1978, when the Romani population received Spanish citizenship, after 550 years in the Iberian Peninsula (Calvo Buezas, 1990).

The results of these structural problems play out in the cultural attitudes toward Roma and the way in which their populations, as racial others, are associated with crime and criminality. The cultural racist assumptions associated with immigrants of having a discrete cultural identity that denies the possibility of assimilation are also attributed to Roma. Their 'ugly habits' are ancient and make 'coexistence impossible,' an attitude expressed long after Spain's Roma received citizenship rights (EUMAP, 2002: 287–8). Troubling statistics support the idea that culturalist assumptions of fundamental differences reinforce racial attitudes. Near majorities in polls of Spaniards have rejected the idea of marrying a Roma. In surveys 70 percent expressed disgust at the thought of their children marrying a Gitano/a, while 43 percent believed that Roma are responsible for their own poverty and marginalization (EUMAP, 2002: 288). These attitudes also seem to spur a generalized criminalization of the Spanish Roma population. The Baraní Project in Spain has recently asserted that Romani women make up upward of 30 percent of Spain's women's prison population, roughly 20 times greater than the population of Roma women in Spain's overall population of about 44 million people (Equipo Baraní, 2001: 7). These statistics allied with data on racial profiling of the Spanish national and municipal police forces confirm that Spain's Roma population receives disproportionate attention from Spain's security forces, even though profiling is not officially sanctioned (Wagman, 2006: 19–21).

Yet one possible way in which the perception of Roma differs from that of immigrants in Spain is the effect that the Roma's historical presence on the Peninsula has on how they are treated – or not treated – in the Spanish discourse. One recent NGO report noted that because racism is framed in Spain solely in terms of xenophobia, racism is only perceived to exist in relation to immigrants. 'In the process [of protecting the immigrant], the problems of Roma/Gitano citizens have been forgotten,' the NGO concluded (EUMAP, 2002: 291). Hence, improvements in the treatment of immigrants, in programs designed to foster their integration into Spanish society, even if they might in the end produce their own failures, generally ignore or forget about historical minorities, like the Roma, who are long established within the Spanish population. Added to this circumstance is the fact that most Roma in Spain are Spanish citizens. As a result, state policies meant to ameliorate the plight of ethnic minorities, or immigrants, do not extend to Roma, and, in fact, create a Catch-22 particular to the Roma. Their amelioration requires special treatment, special policies, both under the law and in practice. Under the law, special treatment for Roma would appear to run afoul of laws relating to equal protection. In practice, discrimination among people actually leads to differential and unequal treatment. Combining this negative legal position and the statistics that consistently reflect negative attitudes toward the Roma, at levels similar to those directed against Arab and Muslim immigrants, who are perceived to pose the greatest threat to Spain, the attitudes toward and treatment of the Roma/Gitana population in Spain represent the definition of cultural racism (Calavita, 2005: 127; EUMAP, 2002: 288). The Roma experience social isolation, are perceived to have an inescapable identity, broadly defined, that predetermines their access to social life and prescribes how they will be treated by state agencies, all of which combine to leave them as 'objects without autonomy or liberty' (Wagman, 2006: 68).

Perhaps the key to any difference between the treatment of Roma and immigrants rests in the fact that Roma are, in reality, long-time residents of Spain. Yet, in general discussions, their presence has not necessarily engendered their general acceptance. The Spanish Roma/Gitano remains an internal other. What role does historical memory of the Roma, the fact that they have been in Spain for so long, affect attitudes toward them? In the late 19th century, criminal anthropologists attempted to understand the failure of Roma to assimilate in terms of natural predispositions that could potentially, at least in the case of Rafael Salillas, be overcome with more aggressive state interventions. Now, in the age of cultural racism, one wonders how much the contemporary animus directed toward Spain's Roma is the product of a particularly timeless hatred, taught over centuries, rather than a product of newfound state responses. Here, perhaps, policies toward immigrants to Spain, the desire to integrate, the sense that Spain itself was once a nation of immigrants, show how close the late 19th century was to the present-day. What is today called cultural racism was then better thought of as open racial understanding. Salillas' call to improve the lot of the Gitanos in order to wean them of their criminality is repeated today in calls to assimilate them into the population. Yet, the role of historical prejudice and assumptions about their basic, essential difference still complicate the process. It is a subject that bears further study.

Conclusion

The real issue at the heart of racial thought and criminalization of different groups remains how Spaniards define their own nationalism, their own sense of self and ethnic identity. Race emerged in Europe tethered to the idea of the modern state, and embedded in various definitions of modern nationalism. Spaniards must assess how much their own sense of Spanishness is derived from a historical sensibility of timeless, deeply inscribed, cultural practices and physical appearances. For even as Tomás Calvo Buezas, who has long deserved credit as one of the first post-Franco scholars to draw attention to the definition and plight of ethnic minorities in Spain, once confirmed that, like Jews, Spain's Roma/Gitana have long been an internal other, the enemy within. But, more importantly, he has assumed an old 'Spanish' ethnic identity against which to define Spain's minorities:

> Spain has been a homogeneous society since the expulsion of Jews and Arabs. The only ethnic minority has been the gypsy, and we have not learned how to live in peace and tolerance with them in 500 hundred years.
>
> (Calvo Buezas, 1992: 329)

When a supposed homogeneity is no longer seen as the victim of what immigrants and other minority populations have done to complicate Spanish collective identity, when 'we' do not have to learn how to live with 'them,' race and crime can be untethered.

Notes

1. Some sections of this historical discussion have been published in *European History Quarterly*, April 2005, vol. 35, no. 2.
2. The impact of these changes was much more ambiguous. Over the next two decades, doctors complained ceaselessly about the failure of their expert testimony to sway judges or juries to acquit on the grounds of mental illness and sentence prisoners to asylums for treatment. For examples of these complaints, see Luís de Hoyos Sainz, 'La Medicina en el Derecho', *España Moderna*, 64 (April 1894): 178–81;

El Dr. [José María] Esquerdo, *Locos Que no lo Parecen* (Madrid: Ateneo de Internos 1880), p. 4.
3. The author has not been able to locate the original studies by Dr. Porpeta and Carlos Slocker, *Estudio de topografía craneocerebral* or *Capacidad Craneana en Madrid* (Madrid: n.p., n.d.), but they were discussed widely in the anthropological and military press in the period. See for example, Luis de Hoyos Sainz and Telésforo de Aranzadi, *Unidades y Constantes en la Crania Hispanica*, Presented to the Asociación Española para el Progreso de la Ciencias, Congreso de Granada, 1911 (Madrid: Eduardo Arias, 1913), pp. 31–2.
4. The European Commission against Racism and Intolerance used the term 'Roma/Gitana' to describe Spain's Roma population, to capture both the popular terms used to identify this population and its more accurate ethnic designation.

References

Abend, L. and Momigliano, A. (2008) 'Spain, Italy: Two Tactics for Tackling Illegal Immigration', *The Christian Science Monitor*, 7 August, p. 4.

Álvarez Chillida, G. (2002) *El Antisemitismo en España: La imagen del judío (1812–2002)*. Madrid: Marcial Pons.

Antón y Ferrándiz, M. (1903) *Razas y Tribus de Marruecos*. Madrid: Sucesores de Rivadeneyra.

Bernaldo de Quirós, C. (1912) *Modern Theories of Criminality*, trans. Alfonso de Salvio. Boston: Little, Brown, and Company.

Bierne, P. (1993) *Inventing Criminology: Essays on the Rise of Homo Criminalis*. Albany: State University of New York Press.

Calavita, K. (2005) *Immigrants at the Margins: Law, Race and Exclusion in Southern Europe*. Cambridge: Cambridge University Press.

Calvo Buezas, T. (1990) *¿España Racista? Voces Payas sobre los gitanos*. Madrid: Anthropos.

Calvo Buezas, T. (1992) 'Otras identidades en España: el caso de Extremadura y de las minorías étnicas', in R. Avila Palafox and T. Calvo Buezas (eds), *Identidades, Nacionalismos, y Regiones*. Madrid: Universidad Complutense.

Calvo Buezas, T. et al. (2000) *Inmigración y racismo: asi sienten los jóvenes del siglo XXI*. Madrid: Cause Editorial.

DeParle, J. (2008) 'Spain Grappling with Illegal Immigrants, Tries Forgiveness', *New York Times,* 10 June, p. A1.

Equipo Barañí (2001) *Mujeres Gitanas y Sistema Penal*. Madrid: Ediciones Metyel.

European Commission against Racism and Intolerance [ECRI] (2003) *Second Report on Spain*. Strasbourg: Council of Europe.

European Commission against Racism and Intolerance (ECRI) (2005) *Third Report on Spain*. Strasbourg: Council of Europe.

EUMAP (EU Monitoring and Advocacy Program) (2002) *Monitoring the EU Accession Process: Minority Protection: The Situation of Roma in Spain*. Madrid: Open Society Institute.

Gibson, M. (1998) 'Biology or Environment? Race and Southern "Deviancy" in the Writings of Italian Criminologists', in J. Schneider (ed.), *Italy's 'Southern' Question: Orientalism in One Country*. Oxford and New York: Berg.

Goode, J. (2009) *Impurity of Blood: Defining Race in Spain, 1870–1930*. Baton Rouge: Louisiana State University Press.

Goytisolo, J. and Naïr, S. (2000) *El Peaje de la Vida: Integración o rechaoz de la emigración en España*. Madrid: Aguilar.

Haro Tecglen, E. (1993) 'Racismo, xenofobia y comunicación', in I. Arias et al. (eds), *Racismo y Xenofobia*. Madrid: Fundación Rich.

Jacobson, S. (2003) 'A Mixture of Spaniards', *The Times Literary Supplement*, 5244, 3 October, p. 28.

Kaplan, T. (1969) *Luís Simarro and the Development of Science and Politics in Spain, 1868–1917*, Ph.D. Dissertation, Harvard University.

Maristany, L. (1973) *El Gabinete del Dr. Lombroso: Delincuencia y Fin de Siglo España*. Barcelona: Editoriales Anagrama.

Matlack, Carol and Joan Tarzian (2007). 'Immigrants Welcome', *Business Week*, 21 May, p. 50.

Nye, R. (1984) *Crime Politics and Madness in Modern France: the Medical Concept of National Decline*. Princeton, NJ: Princeton University Press.

Omi, M. and Winant, H. (1994) *Racial Formation in the United States: From the 1960s to 1990s*. New York: Routledge.

Otis, L. (1994) *Organic Memory: History and the Body in the Late Nineteenth & Early Twentieth Centuries*. Lincoln: University of Nebraska Press.

Pick, D. (1989) *Faces of Degeneration: A European Disorder*. Cambridge: Cambridge University Press.

Robinson, E. (1992) 'Immigrants Gunned Down, Raising the Specter of Racsim in Spain', *The Washington Post*, 18 November, p. A27.

Romaguera, C. (1998) 'Capturados 90 imigrants 'ilegales'en seis operaciones en Algeciras y Tarifa', *El País*, 8 May.

Salillas, R. (1898a) 'El Alma y la Cabeza del Cuerpo', *Revista de Prisiones y de Policia* VI (11), 16 March, pp. 98–101.

Salillas, R. (1898b) *Hampa: El Delincuente Español o La Antropología Picaresca*. Madrid: Librería de Victoriano Suarez.

Silvela, Luis. (1870) 'Sección Legislativa',. *Revista General de Legislación y Jurisprudencia* 70: 339–372.

Wagman, D. (2004) 'Areas of ill-repute. Immigrants, the city and security', Valladolid: Universidad de Valladolid, http://www.ciudad-derechos.org/english/pdf/aaf.pdf. Accessed 21 January 2009.

Wagman, D. (2006) *El Perfil Racial en España: Investigaciones y recomendaciones*. New York: Open Society Institute. Accessed 21 January 2009.

Part III

Beyond Europe: Is There Race in Crime and Criminal Justice?

9
Race, Crime and Criminal Justice in Australia and New Zealand

Greg Newbold
University of Canterbury, New Zealand

Samantha Jeffries
Queensland University of Technology, Australia

Introduction

Although they are only 2,000 kilometres apart and were briefly governed as a single entity (1840–1842), Australia and New Zealand have now been politically independent for over 160 years. To outsiders the speech patterns, sporting interests and cultural values of Australians and New Zealanders make them appear quite similar but closer examination reveals considerable differences. This is reflected not only in their disparate histories, but also in their modern political systems, their population sizes and make-up and their treatment of native peoples. Crime profiles of both minority and majority ethnic groups are manifested in these differences as well as in the criminal justice systems of the two countries.

Both nations have significant numbers of non-Anglophone immigrants as well as an aboriginal population. However, it is not the intention of the current chapter to discuss crime and justice in relation to this diaspora of ethnic and racial groups. Rather, our intention is to restrict analysis to the Indigenous populations of the two countries. Therefore, we will analyse, compare and contrast the crime and criminal justice profiles of 'Indigenous' or 'Aboriginal' Australians and New Zealand Maori. For the sake of clarity in the comparative analyses, this chapter will first consider the situations in each of the two countries in turn; subsequently, they will be assessed comparatively in order to draw out similarities and differences between the two countries. The chapter starts with a discussion of the Australian perspective, providing historical and contemporary background information for understanding the current relationships between the Indigenous population, crime and criminal justice in Australia. Following this, a similar structure of discussions is applied to New Zealand. This is followed by a comparative discussion of perspectives from the two countries.

Australian perspective

Australia is an antipodean subcontinent, approximately half of which lies north of the Tropic of Capricorn. Its native population, consisting of both Aborigines from the mainland and Torres Strait Islanders (collectively referred to as either 'Indigenous' or 'Aboriginal' Australians), are the descendants of migrants who arrived from Southeast Asia at least 40,000 years ago (Stobbs, 1986: 18). Before the beginning of European colonisation in 1788, Indigenous peoples, numbering between 300,000 and 1,000,000 at the time of contact (Elder, 2003: 256), lived primarily as palaeolithic hunters and gatherers on Australia's verdant tropical and sub-tropical coasts. The arrival of Europeans in the 18th century proved catastrophic for the native populace. Tribal groups were pushed off their lands and decimated by disease and often by systematic or semi-systematic extermination programs (Elder, 2003).

According to Cunneen (2001: 51), when the British arrived in Australia, they had established legal principles relating to the acquisition of territories. Colonies could be acquired by way of peaceful settlement of unoccupied land, or by way of conquest or cession of occupied territory. In the case of Australia, because Aboriginals were primarily nomadic hunters who often moved from place to place, much of the subcontinent was deemed to be 'unoccupied' (*terra nullius*), and thus available for settlement. Unlike the New Zealand Maori, discussed below, Australia was therefore colonised under the assumption that the land belonged to no-one and was thus free for the taking (Cunneen, 2001: 238). The notion that Australia was unoccupied resulted in the disavowal of Indigenous rights, meaning that the inhabitants were 'dispersed' from land on which they had subsisted for thousands of years. Whilst Aboriginal Australians offered pockets of resistance against this colonial land-grabbing, "dispersal became the euphemism for armed conflict and some 20,000 Aboriginal people were killed during the 'peaceful settlement' of an 'uninhabited' land" (Cunneen, 2001: 53). Influenced by the social Darwinism that was popular in the early 19th century, many Europeans in fact believed that in the natural course of events, the atavistic natives would soon die out (Haebich, 2000: 70).

In the mean time, however, the growth of Christian humanitarianism led to attempts to alleviate the plight of Aboriginal peoples through the establishment of a series of reserves to which many of the survivors were taken by force and confined. Strict rules controlled Indigenous activities within the reserve. For example, inhabitants had to seek permission to leave. If such permission was granted, strict limits were placed on their movements. There were also severe restrictions placed on the amount of time parents could spend with their children, the speaking of their native language was forbidden and all wages earned were 'held in trust' by the state, only being accessible via an application process that was usually unsuccessful (Jeffries and Dillon, 2009: 146–147). Those who broke the rules or attempted to escape could be charged by the police and ran the risk of being removed to another, more punitive, reserve (Cunneen, 2001: 66; Jeffries and Dillon, 2009: 146–147). Thus denied the rights of full citizenship, it was not until 1967 that Indigenous Australians were even given the vote. Since then, while their political status has improved, their social and economic situation as we shall see remains largely basal.

At present, the population of Australia is approximately 21 million. Indigenous people, who declined dramatically in the early years of colonisation, have since recovered from their low point of 60,000 in the 1920s to a current size of 517,000, or 2.5 percent of the total population (Australian Bureau of Statistics, 2001a: 134, 2006a: 5). Other principal ethnic groups are Middle Eastern (1.9 percent), and Asian (1.3 percent). White or Anglo-Australians constitute roughly 88 percent of the population (Australian Bureau of Statistics, 2001b: 16).

Unlike the Maori, Indigenous Australians are a more rural people – only 31 percent live in major cities, compared with 68 percent of all Australians. Aboriginal levels of urbanisation vary – for example, in the Northern Territory 81 percent of all Indigenous peoples live in remote communities (Australian Bureau of Statistics, 2007a: 6, 2008a: 1). Approximately 25 percent of Indigenous people continue to subsist on the sites of the old colonial reserves (now called 'communities') or in other rural or remote areas where traditional law, spirituality, custom and language remain integral (Blagg, 2008: 178). In the Northern Territory, for instance, around 65 percent of Aboriginal people report speaking their traditional language at home and that English is a second language (Australian Bureau of Statistics, 2007a: 5, 2006a: 146).

Recent figures show that 13 percent of the Indigenous population (compared with only 4 percent of the general population) is described as being unemployed, but available for work. In reality, the level of 'unemployment' is far higher, since many Indigenous people live in communities where work and opportunities are limited (Australian Bureau of Statistics, 2008b: 6). Once employed, Aboriginals are found predominantly in lower-paid occupations. The main occupation group for Indigenous people is labouring and related work (25 percent) while for the non-Indigenous population it is professional (19 percent) (Australian Bureau of Statistics, 2004: 123). As a result, the average gross median individual wage for Indigenous persons is AU$14,456 per year – around half that of non-Indigenous[1] Australians (Australian Bureau of Statistics, 2006b: 103).

The marginal socio-economic status of Aboriginal Australians is also clearly reflected in health statistics. Many rural and remote Indigenous communities lack basic health services, housing, sanitary facilities and regular supplies of nutritious, affordable food. These factors are related to poor health and a life expectancy that is 17 years lower than the national average.

In addition, Indigenous adults (46 percent) are more than twice as likely as non-Indigenous adults to be cigarette smokers (Commonwealth of Australia, 2007: 3.4, 8.9). Although reported rates of long-term risky alcohol consumption are similar for Indigenous and non-Indigenous persons, alcohol abuse in more remote communities is widely recognised as a problem, which is often absent from the data in nationwide surveys. Moreover, drug survey figures show that Aboriginal peoples are disproportionately high users of illicit drugs, particularly marijuana (Commonwealth of Australia, 2007: 8.27–8.29; Clough et al., 2004). Youthful petrol sniffing is also a major problem in remote areas (Commonwealth of Australia, 2007: 8.29).

The above scenario of Indigenous marginalisation is extended to the political arena. Australia is a democratic republic which, since 1901, has been practically (although not constitutionally) independent of Britain. Operating under a federal system, Australian political power is divided between the central Commonwealth government and the six states of New South Wales, Queensland, South Australia, Tasmania, Victoria and Western Australia, plus two territories – the Australian Capital Territory and the Northern Territory. The Commonwealth Parliament is responsible for making and enforcing laws that affect the whole of Australia (e.g. taxation, immigration and social security), while state and territory governments administer their own criminal law and criminal justice systems. In these areas of government Indigenous peoples, who have only been allowed to vote for the a little over four decades, lack full political representation. Currently there are no dedicated Indigenous seats in Parliament, nor any special measures to promote the election of Indigenous candidates to Commonwealth, state or territory parliaments. As a result there has been little Indigenous representation in the Parliament.

Offending and victimisation

It is difficult to get an accurate picture of the frequency and types of offending in Australia, particularly in relation to the treatment of Indigenous peoples. Nationwide self-report surveys are limited to illicit drug offending and victimisation surveys provide little information about Indigenous status. Police data can be used as an approximate measure of Indigenous crime. However, Australia-wide police data are only available for cases of homicide due to the dedication of the National Homicide Monitoring Program which was established in 1990 to collate data on numerous variables relating to homicide incidents coming to the attention of the police (Mouzos, 2001).

Jurisdictional police data by Indigenous status are produced sporadically at best, with Western Australia being the only exception to this rule. Since 1991, the Western Australian Crime Research Centre has been publishing police data by Indigenous status on an annual basis. The Australian Bureau of Statistics presents national-level victimisation statistics on a selected range of offences recorded by the police but 'breakdowns' by Indigenous status were not provided until 2006. Even then only three jurisdictions – New South Wales, Queensland and the Australian Capital Territory – provided data of sufficient quality for national reporting (Australian Bureau of Statistics, 2007b: 2). This is due partially to the fact that Indigenous status is only being reliably self-identified and in these three jurisdictions.

Despite these problems, the general pattern is one of Indigenous over-representation in offending and victimisation. For example, Indigenous Queenslanders comprise approximately 4 percent of the state's population, but represent 23 percent of all police-reported offences (Queensland Police Service, 2007: 76–7). In Western Australia, the imbalance is similar, albeit slightly worse (Ferrante et al. 2005: 42). The most important points of contrast between Indigenous and non-Indigenous Australians are in the areas of illegal drug use, violence and crimes of disorder – the latter two often alcohol-related.

Drug household surveys show that 24 percent of Indigenous people aged 14 and over report having used illegal drugs in the last 12 months, compared with only 15 per cent of non-Indigenous people. Marijuana is the most common regularly used drug, with Indigenous people (14 percent) twice as likely as non-Indigenous persons (7 percent) to report its use in the preceding 12 months. The second most commonly used drug are amphetamines, with 7 percent of Indigenous people reporting recent usage (Commonwealth of Australia, 2007: 8.27–8.29). One weakness of the preceding data is that the survey was only carried out among urban populations. In remote populations, the levels of Indigenous drug use are even higher. For example, in Clough et al.'s (2004: 381) study of remote Northern Territory Aboriginal communities 67 percent of men and 22 percent of women self-reported current marijuana use.

Patterns of violence, particularly serious and lethal violence, are emphasised within Indigenous communities. The Indigenous homicide rate rests at around 20 per 100,000, with victimisation at 14 per 100,000. In stark contrast, non-Indigenous homicide offending and victimisation have never exceeded 2 per 100,000. A higher proportion of Indigenous homicides appear to be intra-racial: they occur within the family (often being the outcome of a domestic altercation), in rural locations, where alcohol is often a factor (Mouzos, 2001: 1). Indigenous females are twice as likely as non-Indigenous females to commit a homicide (20 percent of all homicides compared with 10 percent); and Indigenous females are more likely to be homicide victims than non-Indigenous females (41 percent of all victims compared with 32 percent) (Mouzos, 2001: 2–4).

The offending and victimisation patterns exhibited in homicide are reproduced in the area of non-lethal violent crime. In self-report surveys Indigenous people are more likely to report having been a victim of physical violence (Johnson, 2005: 18). For example, results from the Australian component of the International Crime Victimisation Survey show that being Indigenous significantly increases the risk of assault (or being threatened with assault) (Johnson, 2005: 18). New South Wales police data show that Indigenous people are around three times more likely than non-Indigenous people to come to the attention of the police as victims of assault, sexual assault and childhood sexual assault, four times more likely to be the victim of a serious assault (occasioning grievous bodily harm) and five times more likely to be a domestic violence victim (Australian Bureau of Statistics, 2007b: 2; Fitzgerald and Weatherburn, 2001: 1). Indigenous victims in this jurisdiction are significantly more likely to be victimised by another Indigenous person. Offenders are Indigenous in 80 percent of assaults, 73 percent of sexual assaults, 72 percent of child sexual assaults, 86 percent of assaults occasioning grievous bodily harm and 85 percent of domestic violence-related assaults (Fitzgerald and Weatherburn, 2001: 2).

Police data show that Indigenous people are particularly over-represented in figures for offences against good order, including offensive behaviour (five times as likely), resisting or obstructing police (11 times) and indecent language (15 times) (White, 2002: 29). In all areas of Aboriginal violence, alcohol emerges as a contributing factor, with Indigenous people self-reporting that they have assaulted someone while under the influence of alcohol four times more often than non-Indigenous persons; Indigenous people are significantly more likely than non-Indigenous to self-report having created a disturbance while drunk (Commonwealth of Australia, 1994: 40).

Policy and practice in criminal justice

Before considering criminal justice issues as they relate to Indigenous and non-Indigenous populations, this section initially introduces the reader to a brief overview of the structure of the Australian criminal justice system. Australia has a federal- and state-based system of policing and courts. The six states have their own individual police forces, as does the Northern Territory. The Australian Federal Police is a national organisation which applies federal criminal laws and also provides local conventional policing to the Australian Capital Territory. Police misconduct and corruption is an ongoing problem in Australia. Often brought to public attention through Commissions of Inquiry, the result has been the creation of independent 'watchdog' bodies for police (Prenzler and Sarre, 2002: 59–64).

Each Australian jurisdiction has its own court system including lower, higher and, in some jurisdictions, intermediate courts where breaches of state/territory criminal law and sometimes federal law are adjudicated. Courts of criminal appeal operate in each of the states and territories. The federal court system has jurisdiction over offences against Commonwealth law. The High Court of Australia serves as the ultimate court of appeal at the federal, state and territory level (Urbas and Bronitt, 2002: 73–80).

Correctional systems, including prisons, are the responsibility of state and territory governments (Dawes and Grant, 2002: 93). Offenders sentenced to prison under state, territory and commonwealth law serve their time in state or territory prisons. Latest information available from the Australian Institute of Criminology (2008) lists 77 prisons for sentenced offenders, seven of which are private facilities. There are currently 27,200 prisoners in Australian jails with an imprisonment rate of 169 prisoners per 100,000 adult population (Australian Bureau of Statistics, 2007c).

As a result of higher offending rates, combined with racially skewed policing practices, Indigenous people are more likely than their non-Indigenous counterparts to come into contact with the police and be arrested. Evidence suggests that the police are more likely to intervene in criminal situations – or what are perceived to be potentially criminal situations – involving Indigenous rather than non-Indigenous peoples. Moreover, police tend to focus on areas where large numbers of Indigenous people are concentrated (Cunneen, 2001: 30–1; Jeffries and Dillon, 2009: 150). In addition to increasing the detection of crime, over-policing of this type may incite criminal reactions from Indigenous citizens, often resulting in arrest and a further inflation of 'crime' statistics (Cunneen, 2001: 96–7; Jeffries and Dillon, 2009: 150).

Among the judiciary, however, recent research suggests a measure of tolerance towards Aboriginal offenders, who are less likely to be sent to prison than non-Aboriginals, even when offences and other key circumstances are held constant. The explanation for the leniency appears to lie in the courts' recognition of Indigenous people's socially disadvantaged backgrounds and the special circumstances (e.g. historical legacy of colonisation) of Indigenous offenders (Jeffries and Bond, 2009; Bond and Jeffries, 2009). At times, however, this approach has also allowed defence lawyers to argue that 'tribal law' mitigates domestic violence and child sexual abuse based on distorted understandings of traditional Indigenous society, affording special status and entitlements to adult males. In some cases, judges have accepted such pleas, resulting in the passing of less severe sentences (Blagg, 2008: 173). Policing attitudes in the area of Indigenous family violence also tend towards leniency. It is reported that police fail to take female Indigenous complaints of partner assault seriously by responding too slowly or failing to respond at all (Cunneen, 2001: 164).

A corollary of the higher arrest rates of Indigenous persons is their over-representation in prisons. This issue surfaced in the late 1980s following concern about the high numbers of deaths among Indigenous people in custody. In 1991, a final report of the Royal Commission into Aboriginal Deaths in Custody (RCIADIC) was tabled, concluding that the deaths were a result of extraordinarily high levels of Indigenous contact with the criminal justice system. The RCIADIC (1991) made 339 recommendations for reform and a number of different policies and programs have subsequently been introduced to reduce the levels of Indigenous over-representation in imprisonment. These initiatives align with theoretical understandings of Indigenous offending from the perspectives of social disorganisation, anomie, social learning and/or conflict criminological notions of criminal justice system inequity. Subsequent policy and program developments have sought to reform Indigenous people/communities, and/or the criminal justice system often with the assistance of direct Indigenous involvement (Webb, 2004).

Emerging from social disorganisation, strain/anomie and social learning perspectives, some governmental responses to Indigenous offending have sought to reduce it through measures aimed at changing community social environments. Many such measures have involved interventions aimed at reorganising these communities, increasing social control and reducing substance abuse (associated with violent offending) (Webb, 2004: 228). Initiatives have included alcohol and pornography bans; cultural and employment programs; community 'clean up' programs; the deployment of Indigenous community police; and increased Elder involvement with offenders through police, court and correctional programs (Webb, 2004: 172–230).

Criminal justice reform has also occurred. First, there have been developments at police and court levels to divert Indigenous offenders away from further contact with the system in order to reduce the disproportionate criminalisation of Indigenous people (Webb, 2004: 172–230). Diversionary programs grew from recognition of the socially disadvantaged position of Indigenous Australians and an understanding that contact with the criminal justice system may exacerbate this situation. Nonetheless, well-intentioned policies do not always result in improved practices. Police diversionary programs are a case in point. Most frequently targeted at youth, these initiatives involve the diversion of young people by police from the formal youth court process (usually to a restorative justice conference) (Mazerolle, Marchetti and Lindsay, 2003: 69–90; Jeffries and Dillon, 2009: 154). However, research shows that there is not yet a consistent attempt to divert Indigenous young people from the formal court process, with diversion being less likely for Indigenous youth (Cunneen et al., 2005: 46). On the other hand, court diversion appears slightly more successful. As discussed previously, Indigeneity appears to be mitigating sentences and judicial discretion is being used to divert Indigenous people from imprisonment (Jeffries and Bond, 2009; Bond and Jeffries, 2009).

There have also been changes to criminal justice policy that attempt to involve Indigenous people more fully in the criminal justice process. Examples include Indigenous community policing programs and Indigenous sentencing courts. These programs are marketed under the auspice of self-determination because Indigenous people are present in both program development and implementation. By actively involving Aboriginal and Torres Strait Islanders in the process of policing and sentencing their own community, social control is potentially improved (reducing social disorganisation and anomie) as is the quality and equity of justice delivery (Webb, 2004: 172–230).

Nonetheless, critics argue that these initiatives may at best pay 'lip service' to notions of Indigenous self-determination and thus empowerment (Blagg, 2008; Webb, 2004: 172–230). Perhaps this is why results have been somewhat disappointing at least in terms of reducing Indigenous over-representation in prison. Imprisonment rates have actually risen since the RCIADC, with Aboriginal people now even more strongly over-represented than before. Thus, in 1992, Indigenous persons were only 14 percent of the prison population; today, they are 24 percent – almost 13 times what would be expected on the basis of population (Australian Bureau of Statistics, 2007c: 6; Australian Institute of Criminology, 2007: 88). Indigenous incarceration rates and levels of over-representation have increased in all jurisdictions but significant jurisdictional variance exists. For example, over-representation is highest in Western Australia where Aboriginals are 21 times more likely to be imprisoned, and lowest in Tasmania at only four times greater (Australian Bureau of Statistics, 2007c).

New Zealand perspective

Consisting of two main islands in the South Western Pacific Ocean, New Zealand was discovered and populated by Eastern Polynesian voyagers in around 900AD. The people who became known as the New Zealand Maori lived as neolithic fishers, bird hunters and horticulturalists for their first 900 years. As the population grew and the pressure on resources intensified, warfare between various tribal groups became endemic. By the time the English navigator James Cook arrived in 1769 the Maori were living in or around large, fortified redoubts with a full-fledged warrior culture, defined tribal lands and a well-defined and steeply stratified social matrix (Davidson, 1992).

The first permanent European settlement of New Zealand dates from about the time of the arrival of English missionaries in 1814. Dedicated to converting the Maori to Christianity and stopping endemic cannibalism, the philanthropic missionaries were responsible for protecting Maori from the degree of exploitation and destruction that their Australian neighbours were suffering (Moon, 2008). Nonetheless, between about 1815 and about 1845, the introduction of modern weaponry led to bloody warfare among Maori tribes which resulted in perhaps as many as 10,000 deaths (Crosby, 2001). In 1840, a number of Maori chiefs signed a treaty known as the Treaty of Waitangi, by which New Zealand became a British possession and subject to English law. Under the Treaty's Article Two, Maori were also guaranteed "the full and exclusive possession of their Lands and Estates Forests Fisheries and other properties that they may individually or collectively possess...". Broken treaty promises and general dissatisfaction led to more warfare – this time between certain Maori tribes and the government – in the 1860s, during the course of which the tribes were ultimately defeated. As the European population of the country grew – reaching 1 million by 1908 – the Maori population, decimated by warfare and introduced diseases, declined from its original estimation of 200,000 to a nadir of 42,000 (5.6 percent of the total population) in 1896. From here the people recovered, however, and Maori currently constitute 14 percent of the population. However, for the purposes of crime statistics, it is noteworthy that Maori comprise only 12.5 percent of those over the age of 14 (Statistics New Zealand, 2006).

Presently, the population of New Zealand is approximately 4.2 million, with around 565,000 (14 percent) identifying as Maori or part-Maori. Other principal ethnic groups are Pacific Island Polynesian (3.2 percent), and Asian (2 percent). White New Zealand Europeans (known as Pakeha) constitute roughly 83 percent of the population. As far as the native people are concerned, extensive interbreeding between Maori and non-Maori[2] over the last 200 years makes it impossible to identify Maori by way of genetic differential. Rather, Maori are usually defined in terms of self-identification in census and electoral returns (Statistics New Zealand, 2006). That said, Maori can still be seen as a distinctive ethnic and social group in New Zealand society. Although virtually all Maori speak English as a first language, an increasing number (24 percent) also claim conversational proficiency in their native tongue, which since 1987 has been recognised as an official language. Today the New Zealand Maori are overwhelmingly urban, with 84 percent living in towns and boroughs, and 87 percent located in the more populous North Island (Statistics New Zealand, 2006).

In spite of relatively complete social integration within New Zealand society and a virtual absence of racial conflict, Maori still constitute a distinct underclass. Relative to the non-Maori population, for example, Maori unemployment rates have been high for many years, ranging between 11 percent and 16 percent over the past decade (more than three times that the rate found among the working-age non-Maori). Maori in work tend to be employed in manual occupations, with about one-third of employed Maori working as labourers or drivers (more than double the national average), and earning a median wage of around NZ$20,000 per year. This is approximately half the gross median income among the general population (Statistics New Zealand, 2006, 2007).

Maori have a life expectancy that is approximately 10 years less than non-Maori, largely as a result of greater susceptibility to lifestyle diseases like diabetes, cancer and heart disease. These illnesses are partially a result of Maori being more than twice as likely as non-Maori to smoke cigarettes,

1.5 times as likely to be heavy drinkers and more than twice as likely to be regular marijuana smokers. Due largely to their unhealthy eating and drinking habits, Maori children are twice as likely to be obese as non-Maori, and Maori adults are 1.5 times as likely to be so (Statistics New Zealand, 2006, 2008). As will be discussed, these factors have ramifications for Maori levels of criminality.

Politically, Maori have always had the same voting rights as Pakeha, although Maori have a choice of voting on either the General roll or the Maori roll. New Zealand has a national parliamentary system similar to what it inherited from England in 1840. Seven of the 69 seats in Parliament are reserved for Maori roll representatives. A number of Maori also hold General seats.

Offending and victimisation

In New Zealand, comprehensive and current crime figures are published on the Web by Statistics New Zealand (2008). This department's figures, drawn largely from police data, show Maori to be over-represented in apprehensions for all major areas of recorded crime. The only exception is serious fraud. Maori constitute 42 percent of all apprehensions, meaning they are more than three times as likely to be arrested as expected. They are three to four times as likely to be arrested for violence, drugs or dishonesty, and 2.5 times as likely to be convicted of sexual violation.

According to the statistics, Maori over the age of 14 are 3.4 times as likely as the population as a whole to be apprehended for a violent crime and more than three times as likely to be convicted. Nearly half of all violence convictions involve Maori offenders (Ministry of Justice, 2008: 157). If we break violence figures down, we find that the more serious the violence, the more likely Maori are to be involved. Thus, Maori over 14 are 5.2 times as likely to be arrested for a criminal homicide, 4.7 times as likely to be arrested for a robbery and 3.9 times as likely to be arrested for a grievous assault, but only 2.9 times as likely to be arrested for a minor assault. They are 2.2 times as likely to be arrested for a sexual attack, and 2.5 times as likely to be apprehended for the more serious crime of sexual violation.

Although there are few data, anecdotal evidence suggests that much Maori crime, particularly violent crime, is intra-racial: committed in gang conflicts, in pubs, in neighbourhood situations and of course, within families. In relation to offending within the domestic context, a wealth of evidence supports the intra-racial victimisation thesis, with violence being prominent in many Maori homes. A national victimisation survey in 2001 (Ministry of Justice, 2003: 143) found that Maori women reported having been assaulted by a partner more than twice as often as non-Maori, and they were almost three times as likely to have been threatened or assaulted with a weapon. Maori women were apparently less violent, with Maori men reporting female violence towards them only about a third more often than non-Maori. However, Maori men said that their female partners had used or threatened to use a weapon against them 3.6 times more often than non-Maori men.

In agreement with the above, Maori men are 3.8 times as likely as the total population to be convicted of assaulting a female. Violence towards children is a special problem. Maori infants are nearly five times as likely as non-Maori to be hospitalised during their first year of life as a result of an assault. Maori children are also 3.4 times as likely to be notified to welfare authorities for neglect or abuse (Newbold, 2000: 123–5). Nearly all of the reported cases involving the murder or manslaughter of children under the age of 12 are Maori children. Abuse and neglect during childhood are major factors in adult maladjustment (Newbold, 2000: 126).

Maori are also over-represented in other crime statistics. In relation to the population aged over 14, Maori are 3.8 times as likely to be arrested for dishonesty. Once more, their predominance is more visible in crimes at the upper end of the scale. Thus, they are 4.4 times as likely to be arrested for burglary or car conversion, 3.5 times as likely to be arrested for theft and only 2.5 times as likely to be arrested for fraud. There is a slightly different pattern for drugs. Maori over 14 are more than three times as likely to be arrested for drug offending, although 94 percent of these arrests involve cannabis, and 98 percent of all drug arrests are for use or possession. In the small number of cases involving the marketing of drugs, Maori are twice as likely to be arrested as the national average (Statistics New Zealand, 2008).

One feature of New Zealand society which causes considerable social concern is the growth of gang culture. Street and motorcycle gangs have been known in New Zealand since the 1950s, but it was not until the mid-1960s, coinciding with a period of urban drift, that Maori began to feature prominently in them. Today three major types of gang can be identified in New Zealand: ethnic gangs such as the Mongrel Mob and Black Power, which are almost exclusively Maori; motorcycle gangs such as the Head Hunters, the Hell's Angels and Highway 61, most of which are multi-racial; and amorphous youth street gangs such as the Bloods and the Crips, which model themselves roughly on their Los Angeles counterparts. These youth street gangs have predominantly Maori and Pacific Island membership. Although accurate statistics are impossible to obtain, by far the largest gangs are the Mongrel Mob and Black Power, which constitute at least half of all gang membership in New Zealand. Other gangs also have a strong Maori presence, so it can be said that Maori predominate in this area. New Zealand gangs are associated with a considerable amount of high-profile violence, and are a major factor in the organised marketing of cannabis and methamphetamine (Dennehy and Newbold, 2001; Newbold 2000, 2004).

Policy and practice in criminal justice

New Zealand has a four-tiered criminal court system consisting of the District and High Courts, which operate as trial courts, and the Court of Appeal and the Supreme Court, which function as appeal authorities. The highest court in the land is the Supreme Court. There is a single police force, the New Zealand Police, which is politically independent, maintains a high standard of service, and, unlike many countries, is virtually free of systemic corruption. Like the police, the corrections system too is centralised, with all prisons, probation offices and community correctional services coming under the authority of the Department of Corrections. New Zealand currently has 20 different prisons, all state-run, and in comparison to first world nations apart from the USA, a relatively high prison population of 8,000 (190 per 100,000).

In New Zealand, the numbers of Maori in prison remained below their national representation until the mid-1930s, but rose thereafter to a fairly stable rate of around 18 percent until the mid-1950s. Since then, largely as a result of post-war urban drift, the representation of Maori has increased steadily, reaching 50 percent in 1984 and remaining at around that proportion ever since. Thus we can say that Maori (over 14 years of age) are over-represented in New Zealand prisons by a factor of four (Newbold, 2007: 55). Within the New Zealand Police, where 11.3 percent of police are themselves Maori, and where responsiveness to Maori is identified in the 2007 Annual Report of the New Zealand Police as a 'Key Intervention' (*Appendices to the Journals of the House of Representatives, G.6*, 2007: 26–7), there is no hard evidence of racial discrimination *per se*, although intervening factors such as poverty, high alcohol intake and gang membership contribute to high Maori arrest rates. Likewise, there is no evidence of negative bias from the courts.

The principal reason for the large numbers of Maori in prison is that they predominate in crime figures, especially in the area of serious violence. New Zealand law mandates imprisonment for most crimes of violence. Crimes of violence also tend to attract the longest sentences, with the result that about 60 percent of all New Zealand prisoners are doing time principally for crimes of violence. Most of these are Maori. Like Indigenous Australians, theoretical explanations of social disorganisation, anomie and deviant social learning can be applied to Maori patterens of offending. Although their situation is less extreme than that encountered in Australia, Maori may be seen to have been dislocated from their native culture by the experience of colonisation, to have been denied full participation within the replacement culture through a process of social alienation and to have developed, in consequence, a deviant subculture with values favourable to criminality. In time, anomic responses have become institutionalised, leading to transmission of deviant values from one generation to the next.

The New Zealand Department of Corrections is well aware of the inter-generational (social learning) nature of Maori violence and makes strenuous efforts to address Maori offending by spending large amounts of money on culturally appropriate policing and treatment initiatives. A system of de facto native policing in the form of unsworn but uniformed Maori Wardens has existed since 1945, and a large number of social programs exist to promote Maori pride in their native language and culture. In 1975, the Treaty of Waitangi was legally ratified and since then has become a domi-nant feature of ethnic politics. From the early 1990s, hundreds of millions of dollars have been paid to Maori tribes in compensation for losses in fishing rights and land ownership that were guaranteed under the Treaty. Thus the government has taken significant steps to counter the processes of cultural dislocation and economic deprivation that were consequences of 19th-century colonisation.

In prisons, this process continues, with the restoration of Maori cultural pride a dominant concern of correctional policy. Maori are targeted in cor-rectional recruitment campaigns (thus constituting 22 percent of staff), the use of Maori language by all employees is encouraged, Maori art is hung on prison walls, a large number of Maori cultural programs are offered, there are several Maori Focus Units spread around the country and all offi-cial ceremonies are dominated by Maori language and procedural protocols (Newbold, 2007: 113–15). On current figures, it is difficult to perceive any impact from these efforts to counter the effects of cultural dislocation and anomie. Maori incarceration rates remain as high as ever and recidivism rates among Maori – 90.7 percent within 5 years – are higher than for any other ethnic group (Spier, 2002: 4). It appears that the solutions to high levels of crime and incarceration are more complex than current policies are able to provide.

Comparative discussion of Australian and New Zealand perspectives

It can be seen that the Indigenous populations of Australia and New Zealand are quite different: the former palaeolithic hunter-gatherers, the lat-ter neolithic 'slash and burn' farmers with a pronounced social hierarchy and endemic warfare. The two peoples also experienced very different treatment from the early colonists, with the relatively defenceless natives of Australia subject to harsh treatment and, at times, genocide. Whereas Indigenous Australian sovereignty and land tenure was denied completely, a large num-ber of Maori warrior chiefs voluntarily ceded governance by signing a treaty that promised equal rights and the protection of land and resource own-ership. Although today both groups rightfully claim they were cheated and exploited, the colonising experience of the Maori was benign by comparison with their hapless neighbours on the other side of the Tasman Sea.

The current status of Australian Indigenous people and Maori is an extension of their respective traditional cultures combined with their experiences at the hands of early European settlers. The leap from their old stone age technology to an industrial one has been far greater for the Indigenous Australians than for the neolithic Maori, and the Maori's more developed farming economy and material culture allowed them to adapt more easily to the lifestyle of the colonists. The Maori are highly urbanised and the amount of racial intermarriage that has taken place often makes it difficult to make racial distinctions between Maori and Pakeha. Unlike the Indigenous Australians, Maori are also well represented in business, the professions and in government. Australia and New Zealand operate as constitutional parliamentary democracies, however we see a marked distinction in the political positions of their indigenous citizens. Unlike the native peoples of Australia, who were not granted electoral franchise until 1967, there have never been any rules prohibiting Maori from voting and arguably they enjoy a degree of political power unknown to Aboriginal Australians.

Nonetheless, like the Indigenous Australians, albeit to a lesser extent, Maori can still be identified as economically underprivileged, with higher rates of unemployment, lower average incomes and associated lower health status and higher levels of smoking and alcohol abuse. In contrast to Maori, Indigenous Australians experience a higher degree of societal marginalisation and, to a large extent, are culturally separate from mainstream (that is, white) Australian society. Nevertheless, Indigenous Australians and Maori both display higher rates of crime and victimisation in comparison to the European majority. In either nation, such rates are manifested in violent crime, domestic crime, child abuse and petty drug offending. These are for the most part the disorganised offences of a deprived underclass, and it must be said that Indigenous Australians, whose social position is far worse than the Maori, also feature much more prominently in crimes of this type. The point of difference where the Maori are concerned is their deeper involvement in the more organised offending and associated gang membership. This possibly reflects a higher degree of urbanisation and level of 'social integration'.

The main explanations posited for high rates of Indigenous Australian and Maori offending and victimisation can be broadly categorised within the theoretical traditions of community disorganisation, strain/anomie and social learning (Webb, 2004). With reference to Indigenous Australians, their communities have been described as relatively disorganised and disintegrated, lacking in clear norms, values and, as such, lacking in social cohesion (see, for example, State of Queensland, 1999: xxxiv; Webb, 2004: 172–230). It is proposed that this relative lack of solidarity, cohesion or integration of communities is critical to explaining higher rates of Aboriginal crime (especially violent offending) and related substance abuse (see, for example, Northern Territory Government, 2007: 12, 18, 57, 226; Webb, 2004).

Historical colonisation is, in turn, suggested as being the driving force behind Indigenous social disorganisation and strain/anomie (see, for example, State of Queensland, 1999: xxi, 29 and 47; Snowball and Weatherburn, 2007: Webb, 2004: 97–171). The same is partially true for the Maori, where we see an urbanised, integrated culture which at its lower levels lacks the checks and balances on things like alcohol consumption and functional family operation that are visible in the higher strata.

In both cases, 19th-century colonisation brought rapid social change, fracturing established communities along with their systems of norms, roles and values. During this process, traditional senses of meaning, status and role became uncertain, supervening tribal regulatory power and causing breakdowns in social control mechanisms including customary law, spirituality, family processes and traditional authority structures (Snowball and Weatherburn, 2007). The resulting cultural vacuum, it is said, could only have been avoided by full acceptance into, and integration within, the replacement colonial order. Unfortunately, this was not to be. From the outset, social and economic marginalisation among Indigenous peoples created an anomic situation, with the attendant economic and social deprivation producing a sense of helpless frustration. Loss of traditional culture, combined with a perception of being locked out of mainstream society, encouraged the adoption of anomic norms, manifested in substance and alcohol abuse, gang membership (in the case of Maori), violence and other crime (see, for example, Northern Territory Government, 2007: 12, 193; Webb, 2004: 97–171).

A social learning approach is also commonly used to explain the incidence of violence in Indigenous Australian and Maori communities (Webb, 2004: 97–171). It is postulated that criminal behaviour, especially violence, is learned through interaction with intimate personal groups. As postulated by the social disorganisation/anomie perspective, Indigenous peoples live in contexts that are considered far from ideal, being afflicted by disorganisation, anomie and subsequent substance abuse and crime. By logical extension, Indigenous Australian and Maori children are surrounded by a preponderance of definitions favourable to offending and highly susceptible to being socialised into crime (see, for example, New South Wales Attorney General's Department, 2006: 60; Northern Territory Government, 2007: 199; State of Queensland, 1999: xv; Webb, 2004: 97–171).

In contrast to the above perspectives, discourses based on conflict theory are also used to illuminate over-representation in crime in the cases of both the Indigenous Australians and the Maori. From this perspective, European control and repression are viewed as the problems needing attention. The process of criminalisation now becomes the central concern and, by extension, the focus shifts to the 'problem' of Indigenous peoples' treatment to within the inequitable 'white' justice system (see, for example, The Royal Commission into Aboriginal Deaths in

Custody, 1991; Blagg, 2008; Cunneen, 2001; Webb, 2004: 97–171). As already discussed, the over-representation of Indigenous Australians and Maori in crime is consistent with their respective predominance in criminal justice statistics and prison populations. And once more, the skewed representation of Indigenous Australians is higher than for the New Zealand Maori.

In Australia and New Zealand – although perhaps more robustly in New Zealand – attempts have been made to address this problem through the application of social and cultural programs. The fact that such initiatives have so far failed suggests that the solutions are deeper and more complex than superficial cultural measures can achieve. In both countries it has been mooted that the solution may lie in establishing an indigenous justice system (Blagg, 2008; Jackson, 1987–88). This is perhaps feasible in some Indigenous Australian communities because, as argued by Blagg (2008: 202), "Aboriginal people continue to assert an identity that differentiates them from others: they are not simply a disadvantaged ethnic minority within society, but a distinctive, subordinated society with its own values, beliefs and law". The development of a separate Maori justice system may be less realistic given that Maori and Pakeha coexist in a geographically and socially integrated sense, and that there are no separate Maori communities. For example, Maori possess political power and their culture is integral to New Zealand society. Although Maori disadvantage remains, self-determination already exists at a level fantastical to Indigenous Australians whose subsequent marginalisation is considered by many to be a national disgrace.

Conclusion

Comparing and contrasting the offending and criminal justice profiles of the Indigenous Australians and the New Zealand Maori offer an interesting lesson in the effects of two quite distinct historical processes. The colonisation of Australia can perhaps best be described as one of genocide against a predominately non-violent hunter-gatherer society, the outcome of which has been high levels of Indigenous marginalisation. By contrast, the Maori, protected by a belligerent and sophisticated warrior tradition, fared much better and secured political equality from the commencement of British annexation through the Treaty of Waitangi.

The consequences of these historical differences are visible today. The Maori, although still socio-economically distinct, enjoy a far higher level of equality and 'integration' than is the case for their trans-Tasman neighbours. These differences are mirrored in the crime figures. Although both groups exhibit rates of disorganised and violent offending that are higher than their 'parent' populations, among the Indigenous Australians the differential is far more pronounced. Moreover, the higher social standing of the Maori gives them the potential for more organised forms of offending through gang membership and occasionally through positions of influence and power within the structure of conventional society. Thus we can see that the similarities and differences between offending patterns of the Indigenous Australians and the New Zealand Maori are largely a result of the different statuses that the two groups occupy within their respective communities, a situation which itself has been deeply affected by historical circumstance.

Notes

1. It is worth noting that the criminal justice data and self-report data we report lumps other Australians and other New Zealanders who are not Indigenous (or Aboriginal) and Maori together in the non-Indigenous (or non-Aboriginal) and non-Maori categories, respectively. This means that the non-Indigenous and non-Maori data we report include all other non-Indigenous ethnic groups (including whites) in Australia and New Zealand, respectively.
2. See note 1.

References

Australian Bureau of Statistics (2001a), *Year Book Australia*, Canberra: Australian Bureau of Statistics.

Australian Bureau of Statistics (2001b), *Australian Ancestries*, Canberra: Australian Bureau of Statistics.

Australian Bureau of Statistics (2004), *Australian Social Trends*, Canberra: Australian Bureau of Statistics.

Australian Bureau of Statistics (2006a), *Year Book Australia*, Canberra: Australian Bureau of Statistics.

Australian Bureau of Statistics (2006b), *Population Characteristics, Aboriginal and Torres Strait Islander Australians*, Canberra: Australian Bureau of Statistics.

Australian Bureau of Statistics (2007a), *Population Distribution, Aboriginal and Torres Strait Islander Australians*, Canberra: Australian Bureau of Statistics.

Australian Bureau of Statistics (2007b), *Recorded Crime Victims Australia*, Canberra: Australian Bureau of Statistics.

Australian Bureau of Statistics (2007c), *Prisoners in Australia*, Canberra: Australian Bureau of Statistics.

Australian Bureau of Statistics (2008a), *Australian Social Trends*, Canberra: Australian Bureau of Statistics.

Australian Bureau of Statistics (2008b), *Labour Force Characteristics of Aboriginal and Torres Strait Islander Australians*, Canberra: Australian Bureau of Statistics.

Australian Institute of Criminology (2007), *Australian Crime: Facts and Figures, 2006*, Canberra: Australian Institute of Criminology.

Australian Institute of Criminology (2008), *Australian Correctional Facilities*, available on www.aic.gov.au. Accessed on July 2008.

Blagg, H. (2008), *Crime, Aboriginality and the Decolonisation of Justice*, Sydney: Hawkins Press.

Bond, C. and Jeffries, S. (2009), Sentencing Indigenous and Non-Indigenous Women in Western Australia's Higher Courts. *Psychiatry, Psychology and Law*, 9999:1.

Clough, A.R., D'Abbs, C. S., Gray, D., Maruff, P., Parker, R. and O'Reilly, B. (2004), 'Emerging Patterns of Cannabis and other Substance use in Aboriginal Communities in Arnhem Land, Northern Territory: A Study of Two Communities', *Drug and Alcohol Review*, 23(4): 381–90.

Commonwealth of Australia (1994), *National Drug Strategy Household Survey: Urban Aboriginal and Torres Strait Islander Supplement*, Canberra: Commonwealth of Australia.

Commonwealth of Australia (2007), *Overcoming Indigenous Disadvantage: Key Indicators 2005*, Canberra: Commonwealth of Australia.

Crosby, R. (2001), *The Musket Wars: A History of Inter-Iwi Conflict 1806–45*. Auckland: Reed.

Cunneen, C. (2001), *Conflict, Politics and Crime: Aboriginal Communities and the Police*, Crows Nest: Allen and Unwin.

Cunneen, C., Collings, N. and Ralph, N. (2005), *Evaluation of the Queensland Aboriginal and Torres Strait Islander Justice Agreement*, Sydney: University of Sydney.

Davidson, J. (1992), 'The Polynesian Foundation', in G. Rice (ed.), *The Oxford History of New Zealand*, Auckland: Oxford University Press.

Dawes, J. and Grant, A. (2002), 'Corrections', in A. Graycar and P. Grabosky (eds), *The Cambridge Handbook of Criminology*, Melbourne: Cambridge University Press.

Dennehy, G. and Newbold, G. (2001), *The Girls in the Gang*, Auckland: Reed.

Elder, B. (2003), *Blood on the Wattle: Massacres and Maltreatment of Aboriginal Australians since 1788*, 3rd edn, New Holland: Sydney.

Ferrante, A.M., Loh, N.S.N., Maller, M.G., Valuri, G.M. and Fernandez, J.A. (2005), *Crime and Justice Statistics for Western Australia, 2004*, Perth: The University of Western Australia.

Fitzgerald, J. and Weatherburn, D. (2001), *Aboriginal Victimisation and Offending: The Picture from Police Records*, Sydney: New South Wales Bureau of Crime Statistics and Research.

Haebich, A. (2000), *Broken Circles: Fragmenting Indigenous Families 1800–2000*, Fremantle: Fremantle Arts Centre Press.

Jackson, M. (1987–88), *Justice and the Maori: A New Perspective*, Wellington: Department of Justice.

Jeffries, S. and Bond, C. (2009). 'Does Indigeneity Matter?: Sentencing Indigenous Offenders in South Australia's Higher Courts', *Australian and New Zealand Journal of Criminology* 42, 1, pp. 47–71.

Jeffries, S. and Dillon, C. (2009), 'Policing Indigenous Peoples,' in R. Broadhurst and S.E. Davies (eds.). *Policing in Context*. Melbourne: Oxford University Press.

Johnson, H. (2005), 'Crime Victimisation in Australia: Key Results of the 2004 International Crime Victimisation Survey', *Australian Institute of Criminology, Research and Public Policy Series, 64*, Canberra: Australian Institute of Criminology.

Mazerolle, L., Marchetti, E. and Lindsay, A. (2003), Policing the Plight of Indigenous Australians Past Conflicts and Present Challenges. *Police and Society*, 7, pp. 77–104.

Ministry of Justice (2003), *New Zealand National Survey of Crime Victims 2001*, Wellington: Ministry of Justice.

Ministry of Justice (2008), *Conviction and Sentencing of Offenders in New Zealand: 1997–2006*, Wellington: Ministry of Justice.

Moon, P. (2008), *This Horrid Practice: The Myth and Reality of Traditional Maori Cannibalism*, Auckland: Penguin.

Mouzos, J. (2001), 'Indigenous and Non-Indigenous Homicides in Australia: A Comparative Analysis', *Trends and Issues in Crime and Criminal Justice*, 210, Canberra: Australian Institute of Criminology.

New South Wales Attorney General's Department (2006), *Breaking the Silence, Creating the Future: Addressing Child Sexual Assault in Aboriginal communities in NSW/NSW Aboriginal Child Sexual Assault Taskforce*, Sydney: New South Wales Attorney General's Department.

Newbold, G. (2000), *Crime in New Zealand*, Palmerston North: Dunmore.

Newbold, G. (2004), 'The Control of Drugs in New Zealand', in R. Hill and G. Tait (eds), *Hard Lessons: Reflections on Governance and Crime in Late Modernity*, Hants: Ashgate.

Newbold, G. (2007), *The Problem of Prisons: Corrections Reform in New* Zealand, Wellington: Dunmore.

Northern Territory Government (2007), *Ampe Akelyernemane Meke Mekarle 'Little Children are Sacred': Report of the Northern Territory Board of Inquiry into the Protection of Aboriginal Children from Sexual Abuse*, Darwin: Northern Territory Government.

Prenzler, T. and Sarre, R. (2002), 'The Policing Complex', in A. Graycar and P. Grabosky (eds), *The Cambridge Handbook of Criminology*, Melbourne: Cambridge University Press.

Queensland Police Service (2007), *Annual Statistical Review*, Brisbane: Queensland Police Service.

Snowball, L. and Weatherburn, D. (2007), *Theories of Indigenous Violence: A Preliminary Assessment*, Australian Social Policy Conference Proceedings, 11–13 July, University of New South Wales: Sydney.

Spier, P. (2002), *Reconviction and Reimprisonment Rates for Released Prisoners*, Wellington: Ministry of Justice.

State of Queensland (1999), *The Aboriginal and Torres Strait Islander Women's Task Force on Violence Report*, Brisbane: State of Queensland.

Statistics New Zealand (2006), *New Zealand Official Yearbook*, Wellington: David Bateman.

Statistics New Zealand (2007), *QuickStats About Maori*, www.stats.govt.nz/2006-census-data. Accessed on July 2008.

Statistics New Zealand (2008) *Table Builder: Criminal Conviction and Sentencing Statistics; Recorded Crime Statistics*, www.statistics.govt.nz. Accessed on July 2008.

Stobbs, N. (1986), 'Aboriginal Societies and the Experience of Contact', in Law Reform Commission (ed.), *The Recognition of Aboriginal Customary Law*, Sydney: Law Reform Commission.

The Royal Commission into Aboriginal Deaths in Custody (1991), *National Report*, Canberra: Federal Government.

Urbas, G. and Bronitt, S. (2002), 'Courts, Criminal Law, and Procedure', in A. Graycar and P. Grabosky (eds), *The Cambridge Handbook of Criminology*, Melbourne: Cambridge University Press.

Webb, R. (2004), *Maori Crime: Possibilities and Limits of an Indigenous Criminology*, Thesis submitted for the degree of Doctor of Philosophy in Sociology, Auckland: University of Auckland.

White, R. (2002), 'Indigenous Young Australians, Criminal Justice and Offensive Language', *Journal of Youth Studies*, 5(1): 21–34.

10
Race, Crime and Criminal Justice in Brazil

Ignacio Cano
State University of Rio de Janeiro, Brazil

Ludmila Ribeiro
Candido Mendes University, Brazil

Elisabet Meireles
State University of Rio de Janeiro, Brazil

Introduction

In the last few decades, Brazilian society has had to deal with the issues of racial discrimination and the role that race plays in the development of social relations. For a long time, the old myth that Brazil was a 'racial democracy' (Freyre, 1933) avoided the need for any deeper debate or closer scrutiny. Over time, this myth was eroded, among other things, by empirical research that revealed the existence of bias against the black population in various domains. For instance, several studies showed that blacks earn less than whites for comparable jobs – even when educational level and other variables are controlled for – and that their chances of social mobility are lower (Hasenbalg, 1979; Silva, 1985; Ribeiro, 2006).

From a methodological point of view, one of the main problems with this type of research is how to differentiate the effect of race from that of social class, given that there is a strong correlation between the two in Brazilian society. Blacks and mulattos are far worse off than whites in socio-economic terms, so there is always the question of whether the more negative treatment accorded to the former is triggered by their social origin or by their membership of a specific ethnic group. Hence, the challenge for any research in this area is to isolate the impact of race from that of class.

In broad terms, any research that intends to test the hypothesis of racial bias needs to demonstrate that members of racial minorities receive, *under the same conditions*, worse treatment than members of the ethnic majority. The difficulty is precisely how to place both groups under the same conditions from an analytical perspective, i.e. how to implement the *ceteris paribus* clause. An experimental design, that is typically suited to control for the effect of extraneous variables, is often impossible in this area.

Another common methodological problem that arises in this line of research is the definition of 'race' itself. In some cases, as in the racial composition of the general population obtained through the census, race is defined by the self-attribution of the subject, who chooses from among the options on offer: white, brown, black, yellow or indigenous. Yet several pieces of research have shown that self-attributed race is not necessarily a fixed attribute. In other words, at different times in their lives individuals may define themselves in different racial terms (Wood, 1991) and they may even do this in response to different contextual demands. Indeed, several studies have pointed out that coincidence between self-attributed race and race as determined by an external observer is only partial and is subject to the influence of social and contextual factors (Harris, 1964; Telles and Lim, 1998). In other cases, however, race is defined by the civil servants who produce the documents without necessarily consulting the subject. This is what happens, for instance, in the case of legal documents. There is some logic in this approach since these documents are often used for internal communication within government departments. Yet there is no guarantee that different officials will classify race in a similar manner. Indeed, recent research has shown that people tend to racially classify others in the same group that they classify themselves (Cano and Schweiger-Gallo, 2008). As a result of these considerations, any research on bias should, in principle, measure race in the same way and in moments not too far apart.

The criminal justice system is an environment that might be considered favourable for the expression of any prejudice. First, it deals primarily with citizens from the lowest strata of society, where there is typically an over-representation of non-whites. Second, law-enforcement agencies are authorized to use force in the course of their duties and are indeed often accused of excessive use of force (Chevigny, 1991; Human Rights Watch, 1997; Cano, 1998; Alston, 2007) and of maintaining inhumane conditions in the prisons, so this would be an opportunity for any prejudice to be vented against certain social targets. Indeed, there is a traditional stereotype in Brazil that associates black minorities with danger and crime. For some time now, a number of authors have defended the thesis that the criminal justice system as a whole tends to be harsher against black people in Brazil (Paixão, 1983; Silva, 1998).

Racial bias might occur at any stage of the interaction between citizens and the criminal justice system, starting from police stop and search patterns all the way to sentencing and prison conditions. In principle, racial bias would be most likely in interactions that are: (a) the least recorded; (b) the least subjected to legal norms; and (c) the least subjected to scrutiny by other state agents. This is the case of police stop and search practices, that are not even recorded, let alone scrutinized by other agencies or even by superior officers.

In other words, police agents are allowed ample discretion in the performance of their duties with a minimal degree of internal or external oversight. By contrast, bias is less likely to occur in sentencing, since judges have to adhere to a strict legal procedure and their decisions are often appealed to a higher court. However, this does not mean that there is no possibility of racial bias in judicial decisions, since judges do not simply apply the law but have to interpret it and must take into account very many circumstances.

Victimization rates are not uniform across racial groups in Brazil. For example, homicide rates are traditionally much higher among non-whites (Cruz and Batittuci, 2007). However, recent data suggest that, overall, crime rates may be higher against whites, principally because of crimes against property. Thus, data from the 'Americas Barometer', a survey carried out by the American Public Opinion Project in 2006, estimated that in 2005, 12 percent of blacks, 14 percent of mulattos and 18 percent of whites had been a victim of a crime in Brazil. Another victimization survey carried out by the Public Security Institute[1] in Rio de Janeiro in 2007 revealed that 47 percent of blacks, 49 percent of mulattos and 53 percent of whites claimed to have been a victim of a crime in the previous 5 years.

On the other hand, non-whites are traditionally over-represented in Brazilian prisons. National figures recently released by the Ministry of Justice (Ministério da Justiça/DEPEN, INFOPEN, 2008) show that almost 56 percent of all prison inmates in Brazil are black or mulatto, compared to 40 percent of whites. The corresponding figures for the overall population, extracted from the 2000 Population Census, are 54 percent of whites and 45 percent of blacks/mulattos. A study that identified prison populations from the data of the 2000 Census itself (Neri, 2006) found out that in the state of São Paulo 36 percent of the inmates were either blacks or mulattos (compared to 26 percent in the population), whereas in the state of Rio de Janeiro 67 percent of inmates were blacks/mulattos (compared to 40 percent in the population). This racial discrepancy in the prison system is a first indication of the possibility of racial bias, though there are many other alternative hypotheses that could explain this fact.

Although bias in sentencing is a popular research topic in a number of countries, traditionally it has received little attention in Brazil. However, a number of studies have in fact tried to address this issue. Costa Ribeiro (1995) analysed a sample of sentences related to 'blood crimes' – that is, homicides and attempted homicides – that were tried by the First Jury Court in the city of Rio de Janeiro between 1900 and 1930. His main conclusion was that blacks were more likely to be convicted than mulattos[2] and, particularly, than whites. Furthermore, defendants accused of attacking white victims also showed a higher probability of being found guilty than those who allegedly attacked mulatto or black victims. According to the author, these results were to be expected at that time, given the prevalence of negative racial stereotypes. As a matter of fact, some scholars at the time claimed

openly that blacks were more prone to crime due to certain innate tendencies (Cunha, 1936; Rodrigues, 1994) or to 'cultural backwardness' (Hungria,
1959). Fausto (2001) analysed a sample of homicide cases that were tried
between 1890 and 1924. These results also revealed that blacks were more
likely than whites to receive a conviction. Adorno (1995a, 1995b) analysed
more recent data and studied a sample of 'qualified robberies' allegedly committed by more than one person in the city of São Paulo in 1990. He found
that blacks and mulattos had private attorneys and presented defence witnesses less often than whites. Indeed, the likelihood of being found guilty
was 9 percent higher for blacks and mulattos than for whites. Hence, he
concluded that there was racial bias in the judiciary. Kahn (1999) reviewed
sentences for the crimes of homicide, robbery and theft in the state of São
Paulo, controlling only for the number of crimes allegedly committed by
the defendant. He did not find significant differences among the sentences
for various racial groups. Vargas (2004) studied judicial enquiries and sentences related to crimes of rape committed between 1993 and 1994. She
concluded that blacks were more likely to be sentenced to prison than whites
and that the judicial process took significantly less time when the defendant
was black.

In sum, most existing research points to the existence of racial bias in
Brazilian criminal sentences. However, it is important to assert that there are
methodological limitations in several of these studies. In fact, many of the
factors that influence the sentences were not taken into consideration, thus
applying an implicit assumption that all racial groups were equal on all
these other variables. In addition, some of the samples were fairly small and
therefore had small statistical power.

This chapter is an addition to the relatively limited studies on race and
sentencing in Brazil. It draws upon findings from our research,[3] which was
conducted in São Paulo and Rio de Janeiro in 2000/2001. The research
objective was to test the possibility of racial bias in criminal sentences for
homicide, robbery and drug-related crimes. In a broader sense, this may also
be considered a test of the wider hypothesis according to which the criminal
justice system may discriminate against black people.

Criminal sentencing: The research

Two methodological issues were central to the research design: (a) the sample size had to be large enough to detect effects of moderate magnitude. The
authors had carried out previous exploratory research on the same topic, but
the sample size was too small to obtain reliable results; and (b) information
had to be gathered, as far as possible, on victims, offenders and the circumstances of the crime, taking into account, in particular, any aggravating or
mitigating circumstances. This information was meant to be used as controlling variables so that racial bias could be tested over and above the influence

of these factors that had an important bearing on the final sentence. Past studies included relevant dimensions, such as whether the defendant had access to a private attorney or not. However, we are not aware of any research that incorporated aggravating or mitigating circumstances into the model. As argued before, racial bias should be tested on people from different ethnic groups that are, otherwise, subjected to the same conditions. As a result, the more information we have in relation to all of the the factors that influence the sentence, the more valid and reliable the test will be.

As a result of the above considerations, several crucial decisions related to research design were taken. First, the collection of data was focused on the Penal Execution Courts (*Varas de Execução Penal*[4]) since they were the only courts that could grant access to a sizeable number of convictions. Fieldwork was carried out in two Penal Execution Courts: one in the city of Rio de Janeiro and the other in the city of São Paulo. Ordinary courts only have the cases they try themselves and, after a certain period of time, files are transferred to an archive. Access to these archives and case selection within them were considered far more difficult than in the Penal Execution Courts. On the other hand, this decision implied some restrictions, particularly since in so doing we would not have access to acquittals. In fact, only disposals that result in penalties (prison or otherwise) are sent to the Penal Execution Court. As a result, our dependent variable had to be the length of the prison sentence rather than the probability of a conviction, in contrast to several previous studies. Length of sentence is a ratio-level variable, compared to conviction which is a dichotomous variable (convicted vs acquitted), which lends itself in theory to more powerful statistical tests that may be relevant to the detection of moderate effects. Still, it would have been interesting to analyse whether the impact of race on the probability of conviction is the same as its impact on sentence length.

In principle, bias can be revealed through several different comparisons. The first and most straightforward one is to compare the raw average sentence of defendants of different racial groups convicted of the same crime: robbery, homicide or drug trafficking. Obviously, the risk here is that the characteristics related to the crimes and to the legal cases (whether the defendant was caught in the act or not, whether her or she had access to a private attorney and so on) might not be exactly the same for all racial groups. In other words, some racial groups might be more involved in certain types of crimes than in others. As a result, one might argue that differences in the average length of sentences do not prove any bias on the part of the judges since crimes and legal cases attributed to various ethnic categories might be different in nature and might, therefore, merit different sentences. Hence, any inference of bias from these average sentences would depend upon the assumption that the characteristics of crimes, enquiries and judicial proceedings are, on average, the same for all racial groups. Most importantly, the assumption would mean that the seriousness of the average crime is the same across all ethnic groups. This would justify the expectation of the same average sentence for all races, allowing for the existence of random error. The above mentioned assumption might be considered a reasonable one, but there is no evidence either to confirm or refute it.

A second approach to testing bias would be to compare average sentence length while controlling for the effect of characteristics of the crime and of the legal cases that might affect the sentence, for example through a multiple statistical regression. Hence, bias would be reduced and unexplained variance would be diminished, increasing the chance of finding significant results. This seems to be a sounder methodological strategy, but it depends on whether or not relevant variables are available to be collected. In any case, there will always be doubts as to whether all relevant independent variables have been included in the model, since the availability of information in official records is typically limited.

A third analytical strategy entails a comparison of the average sentences for defendants of various racial groups that were accused of the same crime by the prosecutor. The assumption here is that the prosecutor will identify the relevant circumstances of the crime, so that any difference in sentences could be attributed to bias on the part of the judge. For instance, if black defendants that are accused of the same crime by the prosecutors (with the same qualifying circumstances) receive a longer sentence than whites in the same situation, this could be attributed to bias in the sentencing process. Obviously, this strategy cannot test whether prosecutors themselves acted with some kind of racial bias since the decisions of the prosecutors are the criterion against which judicial bias is tested. Yet judges could always argue that there might be some relevant crime characteristics that had not been identified by the prosecutors and that would justify different sentences. The fact that the charges pressed by the prosecutors only refer to the qualifications of the crime but do not include aggravating or mitigating circumstances, in contrast to the final sentence, is a limitation of this methodological strategy, since judges could sustain that it might be precisely these aggravating or mitigating circumstances that justify different sentences.

The fourth analytical strategy is the comparison between average sentences of defendants of different ethnic groups that were convicted of the same type of crime, with exactly the same crime characteristics. This would be operationalized though sentences that contemplated exactly the same aggravating and mitigating circumstances. As such, this would be the most blatant – and therefore probably the least likely – kind of bias. It would imply that judges would sentence members of some groups to harsher penalties, even when the crime and the circumstances considered in the sentence were the same. If such a thing happened, it would be much more difficult for any member of the judiciary to justify. Indeed, the differential use of aggravating or mitigating circumstances would seem to be a much more subtle way to exercise racial discrimination. This possibility of a differential use of aggravating or mitigating circumstances could not be tested under this approach, which compares sentences which contain exactly the same circumstances as the criterion against which to test bias. This methodological strategy could be complemented by the use of other independent variables as controls, such as the use of private lawyers, and whether or not the defendant was caught in the act. This approach could be applied through two different statistical tests. The first is the classical use of multiple regression, which would incorporate all aggravating and mitigating circumstances as independent variables. This option has the advantage of taking all cases into account. On the other hand, there are some disadvantages: (a) it uses up a high number of degrees of freedom through the incorporation of a high number of aggravating/mitigating circumstances; (b) there may be just a few cases under each combination of all these independent variables (type of crime, aggravating/mitigating circumstances and others) which might lead to unstable estimates; and (c) the possibility of interactive effects among the various aggravating/mitigating circumstances would be difficult to test and to interpret.

The second option for this fourth analytical approach would be to match sentences that refer to the same crime and exactly the same aggravating/mitigating circumstances. These sentences with identical circumstances would comprise a group (including black and white defendants) and we could then compare the average sentences for people of different racial origins within the group. Groups with just a few cases would be discarded so that a minimum number of cases would be required for the group to be considered. A joint analysis of all these groups would be carried out through multiple regression or multiple analysis of variance (MANOVA), using group membership as an independent variable. This matching technique has some strong advantages: (a) optimization of the control on all relevant independent variables (exactly the same aggravating/mitigating circumstances); (b) reasonable sample size for every configuration of independent variables, which should turn into reliable estimates; (c) ability to ignore complicated interaction terms. The main disadvantage is the fact that part of the total sample is lost, i.e. those configurations of aggravating/mitigating circumstances with just a few cases.

Whatever the statistical option used for this fourth approach, if results show significantly longer sentences for blacks, this would be a strong indication of racial bias on the part of the judge, since ethnic groups would have been given different treatment even when cases are classified in legal terms in the same manner. The conclusion would then be more solid since the level of control over all relevant circumstances would have been as high as possible. However, if results of these tests do not yield significant differences between racial groups, this does not mean that there is no bias, since bias can manifest itself in other ways, as argued above. For instance, the differential use of aggravating and mitigating circumstances is not analysed under this approach.

In short, there are various analytical possibilities. None of them is perfect: each of them starts from different assumptions and deals with different types of biases.

Data gathering

Our aim was to gather a sample of a minimum of 1000 convictions in each state (São Paulo and Rio de Janeiro) in order to achieve a reliable sample size.

The main selection criterion was as follows: legal cases where there was an accusation (by the prosecutor) related to a single count of one of the following three types of crime: robbery (art. 157 of the Penal Code), homicide (art. 121 of the Penal Code) or drug-related crimes (Special Law 6368/76). In order for cases to be included in the sample, crimes had to be committed in 1995 or later. Attempted crimes were disregarded.

Even though cases with accusations involving more than one count of the relevant crime or several types of crimes simultaneously were not accepted, we did decide to examine cases with accessory crimes related to the main one (robbery, homicide or drugs). Had we decided to exclude cases with accessory crimes, we would have been left with a much smaller (and probably unrepresentative) sample, since accessory crimes are indeed very common. The list of the crimes that were accepted as accessories crimes is summarized in Table 10.1.

Table 10.1   List of accessory crimes considered

Crime	Law
Gun possession	Article 10 – Law 9437/97
	Article 19 – Law of Misdemeanours
Gun export	Article 18 – Law of Misdemeanours
Corruption of minors	Article 1 – Law 2252/54
Gang formation	Article 288 – Penal Code
Resistance to prison	Article 329 – Penal Code
False identity	Article 307 – Penal Code
Corruption – offering bribes	Article 333 – Penal Code
Unintentional bodily harm	Article 129 § 6° – Penal Code
Reception of stolen goods	Article 180 – Penal Code
Destruction, subtraction or concealment of corpses	Article 211 – Penal Code
Use of false public documents	Article 299 – Penal Code
Kidnapping	Article 148 caput – Penal Code
Driving a vehicle without a license	Article 309 – 9503/05
Illegal constraints	Article 146 – Penal Code
Disrespect of public officers	Article 331 – Penal Code

It has to be emphasized that the selection criterion depends upon the accusation presented by the prosecutor rather than on the sentence itself. This is relevant since the defendant could be accused of one crime and convicted of a different one by the judge.

Each legal case contained at least one sentence. Cases where there had been an appeal and the appeal had already been tried had two sentences: the first from the First Court and the second by an Appeal Court. As explained before, the Penal Execution Court (PEC) contains only convictions and not acquittals, since the court is in charge of the application of penalties. As such, defendants who had been cleared in the first sentence but convicted on appeal are also included in the court and in the sample. Conversely, defendants that were convicted on the first sentence but acquitted on appeal are not kept in the PEC files and, as a result, are not part of our sample. Hence, the last disposition was the ultimate criterion: if the defendant was convicted in the last sentence, be it a first sentence or an appeal sentence, he or she is contemplated in the study.

A team of two researchers worked in each state for approximately 8 months (October 2000 to May 2001 in São Paulo and February to August 2001 in Rio) to collect the data. Case selection followed a random procedure. In the Penal Execution Court of São Paulo, cases were collected at random and read through by the research team, one by one, to decide whether they met the selection criteria. In the archives of the Penal Execution Court of Rio de Janeiro, cases are filed according to the procedural situation of the defendant: prison, parole, conditional suspension (suspended sentence) or non-prison penalties (community service, etc.[5]). Case selection in Rio also followed a random procedure, but stratified by procedural situation, i.e. we tried to sample from each of these different procedural groups (prison, parole, etc.) so that the weight of each of them in our final sample would match – as far as possible – the weight this group had on the total number of cases in the Court. Indeed, the next table presents the procedural profile of cases in the Court and in the sample (Table 10.2).

Table 10.2   Comparison of the procedural situation of cases in the Penal Execution Court and in the sample: Rio de Janeiro

Procedural situation of the convict	Number of cases in the Court	%	Number of cases in the sample	%
Parole	13,546	15.7	200	15.6
Non-prison penalties	13,860	16.1	199	15.5
Conditional suspension	9187	10.7	147	11.5
Prison	49,556	57.5	736	57.4
Total	86,149	100	1282	100

The size of the final sample is as follows: 1055 cases from São Paulo and 1282 cases from Rio de Janeiro, making a total of 2337 cases.

In both Rio de Janeiro and São Paulo the proportion of cases in each of the three crimes – homicide, robbery and drugs – was not pre-determined. Cases that met the selection criteria were admitted regardless of which of the three crimes they belonged to. As a result of this random procedure, the weight of each crime in the sample must reflect the relative frequency of that crime among the convictions in that state. In fact, crime composition varies: in São Paulo the most common crime is robbery, whereas in Rio de Janeiro the most frequent crimes are drug offences (Table 10.3).

The researchers read all the documents related to each legal case and filled in a form with the relevant information. The types of documents most commonly found were the following: Formal Sentence, Individual Bulletin, Criminal History, Prison Warrant, 'Flagrante',[6] etc. Despite the existence of various documents, information about the personal characteristics of the defendant and the victim and also about the crime was not always available. This produced a relatively high degree of missing cases in some variables. Forms were coded and processed to generate the database used in this research.

Variables used in the analysis

Our main independent variable is race of the defendant. In Brazilian criminal proceedings, this information is inserted by the civil servant without necessarily asking the defendant him- or herself. Often, several documents of the same case contained information on race. In some cases, the racial classification of the various documents was not identical. Thus, the defendant might have been described as 'black' in one document and as 'mulatto' in another. The types of documents that had, most often, information on race were the following: Prison Warrant (57 percent of the cases); Formal Sentence (43 percent); Individual Bulletin/Criminal Identification (36 percent); Calculation of Penalty (27 percent); Police Record (22 percent); and Interrogation Term (22 percent).

Table 10.3　Number of cases by type of crime

Type of crime	Rio de Janeiro		São Paulo	
	Total	%	Total	%
Robbery	451	35.2	744	70.5
Homicide	84	6.6	26	2.5
Drugs	747	58.3	285	27
Total	1282	100	1055	100

Table 10.4 Race of defendant[7]

Race	Number of cases	Percentage	Valid percentage
White	811	34.7	36.3
Mulatto	650	27.8	29.1
Black	369	15.8	16.5
White/Mulatto	256	11.0	11.5
Mulatto/Black	123	5.3	5.5
White/Mulatto/Black	10	0.4	0.4
White/Black	16	0.7	0.7
Total of valid cases	2235	95.6	100
Missing/without information	102	4.4	
Total	2337	100.0	

Race categories often followed the official options (black, mulatto, white and Asian), but some other terms, such as 'negro' and 'moreno', also appeared occasionally. Excluding 'negro' (which was used for 7 percent of the defendants), all other terms corresponded to less than 1 percent of the cases and were ignored. 'Negro' was interpreted to mean 'black'[8] and was therefore integrated into this category. In addition, there were eight cases of Asians ('yellow') that were considered as 'white'. The racial composition of the sample is summarized above (Table 10.4).

Around 82 percent of all defendants were racially classified consistently, whereas the remaining 18 percent were categorized in different ways. Most of the discrepancies occur between adjacent categories – white and mulatto; mulatto and black. However, there were a few improbable inconsistencies, such as defendants being described as black in some documents and white in others.

Originally, we planned to use these racial inconsistencies to test whether bias followed some kind of colour intensity. Thus, for instance, we hypothesized that, if there was indeed bias, it would be strongest against the blacks and less intense against 'mulattos'. Furthermore, we planned to test the possibility of treating these inconsistent categorizations as intermediate racial categories. For instance, bias against those identified as white/mulattos should be stronger than against whites but weaker than against mulattos. If results confirmed this hypothesis, the evidence for racial bias would be reinforced. Nevertheless, it turned out that racially inconsistent cases tended to receive longer prison sentences. A deeper analysis revealed that: (a) cases that received harsher penalties tended to contain more documents;[9] and (b) a higher number of documents was associated, as could be expected, to a higher likelihood of finding at least one inconsistent racial category among these documents. The result of these two facts was a spurious correlation between inconsistency and severity. Hence, this methodological artefact (i.e. the overestimation of sentence length for racially inconsistent cases) prevented the possibility of testing the above-mentioned hypothesis about inconsistent racial categories.

In order to proceed with the analysis, a final race variable was created which adopted, for each individual, the race category most frequently attributed to him or her by the different documents. In a few cases, the person was associated with two different race labels on the same number of occasions. These cases were lost from the analysis since no predominant racial category could be attributed. As explained before, highly inconsistent cases tended to have a different profile and longer sentences. In any case, the proportion of missing cases for this final race variable was not very high, i.e. under 8 percent (Table 10.5, below).

As described above, many pieces of research on racial bias face the caveat that race is measured in different ways by different sources. For example, rates are often calculated in which the numerator depends on racial classification carried out by civil servants and the denominator results from racial self-categorization obtained in the Census. In our study, this is not a particularly serious problem, since all racial categorizations are carried out by the same source, i.e. the criminal justice system. Indeed, the focus in our research is placed on race as perceived by state agents, who might act accordingly in a biased way, and not as perceived by the subject him- or herself.

The main dependent variable in this study is length of the prison sentence, measured in months. Sentences which apply community service or fines had a value of 0 in this variable. The value depended only on the original sentence and not on the convict's later status, bearing in mind that s/he may enjoy legal benefits that shortened their actual stay in prison. For instance, individuals who obtained suspended sentences or paroles at a later stage did not have any alteration in their value in this variable (number of months in prison in the original sentence). Only when the judge applied a different punishment in substitution of the prison penalty in the sentence itself did we consider the number of months to be zero.

As explained above, each case has a first sentence and some of them, where there was an appeal and the appeal had already been tried, also had a second

Table 10.5 Race of defendant: final variable

Race	Frequency	Percentage	Valid percentage
White	927	39.7	43.0
Black	802	34.3	37.2
Mulattos	427	18.3	19.8
Total of valid cases	2156	92.3	100.0
Missing/without information	181	7.7	
Total	2337	100.0	

sentence. From these two sentences, two other dependent variables were created.

One is the length of the *final sentence* (also measured in months). A final sentence exists when the first sentence was not appealed or when there was an appeal and the appeal had already been tried. In this sense 'final' means that it could not be altered (except for the very few cases where there might be a further appeal to the Supreme Court). When there was an appeal but it had not yet been tried, the case had a missing value in this variable. As a result, not all cases have final sentences. The other variable is length of the *valid sentence* (also measured in months). This corresponds to the last sentence that was issued for the case, whether or not it was final. For example, if the appeal had been tried, then the valid sentence was the second sentence. But if there was an appeal which was still untried then the valid sentence was the first sentence.[10] If there was no appeal, the valid sentence was obviously the first sentence. As such, this is the variable with the highest number of valid cases since, by definition, all cases have a valid sentence regardless of whether it is the first or the second sentence. This advantage is counterbalanced by the fact that the variable contains decisions taken by courts at different levels, which may undermine their comparability.

Average sentences for each of the four dependent variables are summarized in Table 10.6, below. The average sentences imposed by second-level courts are 6 months longer than those imposed by first-level courts. Although this might appear to indicate that appeal courts are harsher than ordinary courts, a closer analysis reveals that the real explanation lies elsewhere: appeals by prosecutors and defence attorneys are more likely when penalties are more severe. As a result, a subset of the harsher sentences is more often appealed and that is why their final average is higher than that of the first sentences. Indeed, when we regard only cases with appeals, we observe that the real inclination of the appeal courts is to reduce the severity of the penalty (4 months on average) (Table 10.6).

Average *final* sentences are considerably shorter than both first and second sentences, since they are made up of non-appealed cases (which tend to receive shorter penalties) and second-level sentences (which tend to be more lenient than their respective first-level dispositions). Average valid sentences

Table 10.6 Length of prison sentence (in months) by type

Type of sentence	Number of cases	Mean	Standard deviation
First-level court sentence	2312	57.2	51.2
Second-level (Appeal) court sentence	1041	63.8	55.1
Final sentence	1922	53.1	49.5
Valid sentence	2337	55.4	48.6

are, in turn, also lower than first- and second-level sentences, but not as low as final sentences, since they also include appeals that have not been tried yet (and therefore have not had their severity reduced).

In order to determine length of prison sentence, the judge considers, in addition to the nature of the crime, a number of circumstances related to the crime and the defendant. There are three types of circumstances that can affect the disposition:

(a) aggravating circumstances that are part of the penal type of the crime (for example, art. 157 second paragraph, section I of the Penal Code, which prescribes that the penalty will be augmented by a third if the robbery is committed with a gun);

(b) aggravating or mitigating circumstances specified by the Penal Code, that can be applied to all kinds of crime (for example, articles 61, 62 and 63 of the Penal Code enumerate general aggravating circumstances); and

(c) aggravating or mitigating circumstances that do not appear explicitly in the law but which the judge can use in his or her sentence (indeed, article 59 of the Penal Code determines that the judge can take into consideration the history of the defendant, his or her social behaviour, his or her motivation, etc.).

All three types of circumstances present in the sentence were recorded by the research team.

Typically, the judge would start the calculation of the penalty with the general guidelines determined by the article in the Penal Code, which offers a range of penalties from a minimum to a maximum. Second, the judge would consider aggravating circumstances and, finally, mitigating circumstances. If the judge decides to impose the minimum penalty, there is no need to justify the decision, but if the penalty is higher than the minimum contemplated in the guidelines, then s/he has to specify the circumstances which led to the decision. Often, the wording of the sentence mentioned aggravating circumstances that were already considered in the specific article chosen by the judge. Since an element cannot be used twice to aggravate the penalty, we decided to elaborate a general list of aggravating and mitigating circumstances and code, for each case, the absence or presence of each of them regardless of where they appeared (in the article of the Penal Code devoted to that crime, in a general article of the Penal Code or in the personal considerations of the judge). This allowed us to register all aggravating or mitigating circumstances in a non-redundant way.

Criminal sentencing: Research results

For the sake of simplicity, of the four possible dependent variables (first sentence, second sentence, final sentence and valid sentence) we opted to present only the results of the last one – that is, the valid sentence. This is the variable with the highest number of valid cases (i.e. with the smallest number of missing cases), as explained above. In any case, results from all four dependent variables were quite consistent so that a full presentation of all four of them would be for the most part redundant.

Average length of prison sentence, according to crime and race of the defendant,[11] is shown in Table 10.7. For robbery, the mean sentence for white defendants is longer than for black and mulatto defendants, but this difference is not statistically significant[12] ($F = 2.49$; $d.f. = 2$ and 1135; $p = 0.083$). For homicide, the mean length of prison sentence for blacks is shorter than for the other two groups, but the differences are again non-significant ($F = 1.018$; $d.f. = 2$ and 98; $p = 0.365$). In relation to drug-related crimes, punishment for blacks is slightly harsher, but this effect does not reach statistical significance ($F = 0.793$; $d.f. = 2$ and 914; $p = 0.453$). The number of homicide cases is, in fact, very small to allow reliable estimates, but the sample of robbery and drug crimes should be large enough to be sensitive to moderate differences. In short, there is no indication of racial bias on the average sentence for the three types of crime. Nevertheless, this is only a first and generic comparison, which does not take into account many relevant factors. Furthermore, it would be conceivable that the various ethnic groups get involved in crimes of different average seriousness, yet are sentenced to the same penalties. Under such circumstances,

Table 10.7 Length of prison sentence according to crime and race of defendant

CRIME Race	Valid sentence	
	N	Mean
Robbery		
White	500	73.9
Mulatto	427	68.5
Black	211	66.1
Total	1138	70.4
Homicide		
White	59	113.8
Mulatto	30	118.3
Black	12	82.3
Total	101	111.4
Drugs		
White	368	32.0
Mulatto	345	32.9
Black	204	34.6
Total	917	32.9

the similarity of the dispositions would be a manifestation of bias in its own right.

The *second analytical strategy* defined above would be to take into consideration other relevant variables, i.e. those that may have an impact on sentence length, through multiple regression. The first step will be testing whether or not individual variables that are available are correlated with sentence length. Those that are will be included in the multivariate model, which should diminish unexplained variance and help isolate the effect of race. Whether or not the defendant was caught in the act is of primary concern in Brazilian penal law, since police and judicial proceedings are different in both cases. If the defendant was caught in the act, in principle police do not have to conduct a lengthy investigation to identify the criminal and proof of guilt is supposed to be much stronger. For all other cases, police investigations, which include the identification of the suspect, tend to be longer and the proof of guilt weaker. Previous research has shown that this variable can affect the disposition, particularly the probability of conviction. Even though probability of conviction and length of sentence are two separate dimensions, they might be related.

In our data (see Table 10.8 below), those who are caught in the act receive longer sentences in the case of homicides, but the difference does not reach statistical significance ($F = 4.658$; $d.f. = 1$ and 108; $p = 0.033$). As for robberies and drug-related crimes, the result is the opposite: those caught in the act are sentenced to significantly less severe penalties (robberies: $F = 118.502$; $d.f. = 1$ and 1193; $p < 0.001$. drug crimes: $F = 13.275$; $d.f. = 1$ and 1030; $p = < 0.001$).

Table 10.8 Average prison sentence (in months) according to whether the defendant was caught in the act

Was the defendant caught in the act?	Valid sentence	
	N	Mean
Robbery		
No	154	107.6
Yes	1041	64.6
Total	1195	70.1
Homicide		
No	66	100.4
Yes	44	139.8
Total	110	116.1
Drugs		
No	28	47.6
Yes	1004	31.5
Total	1032	31.9

One possible interpretation in the case of robberies and drug-related crimes is that, given the high number of reported crimes, police have to concentrate their investigative resources on the more serious crimes, cases which would lead to longer sentences if police were to be successful in their investigation. On the other hand, cases where the defendant was caught in the act would not need significant levels of police investigation, since the identity of the criminal and the proof of guilt would be much more straight-forward, and as a result would not result in any selectivity associated with seriousness.

Of course, this interpretation would not explain why the results are different in the case of homicides. It would be fair to assume that homicide, being the most serious offence, would have to be investigated in all cases and thus would not lead to any process of selectivity. In fact, more than 90 percent of cases of robberies and drug crimes but only 50 percent of homicides involved defendants who were caught in the act. Yet this does not fully account for the fact that being caught in the act does not even seem to show an effect in the same direction for the crime of homicide compared to other crimes. In any case, the high number of defendants sentenced for robberies and drug crimes caught in the act – over 90 percent – reveals the poor performance of the investigative phase of the criminal justice system in Brazil, which bases their convictions mainly on cases in which defendant identification and existence of witnesses are established at the start of the legal proceedings.

One other element that was pointed out in the literature as an important determinant of final disposition is access to a private attorney (Adorno, 1995a, 1995b). In principle, private attorneys tend to give more attention to their client and, therefore, reduce the probability of a conviction or a lengthy prison sentence. It is relatively rare to find any mention of a private attorney in the documents analysed in this research. Hence, we decided to operationalize this variable as follows. We coded it in a dichotomous way, with a 'yes' if there was any mention to a private lawyer in the case, regardless of whether it was in the first trial, in the second trial or in any petition of prison benefits at a later stage. All other cases were coded with a 'no'. We assume then that this lack of reference to a private attorney means that the defendant was assisted by a public lawyer or by an attorney paid by the state[13].

Contrary to expectations, there were no significant differences for the average sentences for robbery and homicide between those defendants who had access to a private lawyer and those who did not (Table 10.9). The only significant difference occurred for drug-related crimes and in a direction opposite to the hypothesis: defendants convicted of drug crimes were subjected to significantly longer sentences when they were assisted by private attorneys ($F = 16.433$; $d.f. = 1$ and 1030; $p < 0.001$). One could speculate that drug dealers at the highest levels of the crime structure will probably receive

Table 10.9   Average prison sentence (in months) by type of attorney

Did the defendant have the assistance of a private attorney?	Valid sentence	
	N	Mean
Robbery		
No	811	70.7
Yes	384	69.0
Total	1195	70.1
Homicide		
No	80	117.5
Yes	30	112.4
Total	110	116.1
Drug crimes		
No	773	30.3
Yes	259	36.9
Total	1032	31.9

longer sentences and will always be able to afford private attorneys. Nevertheless the fact remains that access to a private lawyer did not function as predicted for any of the three crimes studied.

Another set of variables that might affect prison length is related to the profile of the defendant. However, the documents consulted offered little information on many of the variables that we would have liked to test. Two variables that did not have a high proportion of missing values and that could therefore be examined were schooling and marital status. Schooling was coded according to educational level: (1) for primary education; (2) for secondary education; and (3) for university. More than 90 percent of the total number of cases corresponded to defendants who had only received primary education (whether they had completed it or not). In any case, an analysis of variance revealed that length of sentence did not vary significantly according to educational level for any of the three crimes.[14]

Marital status was coded as single or non-single (a category that included married, divorced and widowed). Around 83 percent of all cases corresponded to single defendants. Average disposition did not appear to correlate with the defendant's marital status.[15] Thus, we did not find any of the defendant's documented individual characteristics to be associated with sentence length.

Another set of variables that could be potentially correlated with the harshness of the penalty was related to the profile of the victim. Indeed, only crimes of robberies and homicides have a victim, since drugs are the typical example of a victimless crime. Among the dimensions that were contemplated in the study and included in the form were gender, schooling and race. In fact, prison sentence did not significantly depend on victim's gender.[16] Schooling was coded in the same way as for the defendant, according to educational level. Homicide had very few cases valid for the analysis and had to be discarded. As for robbery, victim's educational level was not significantly associated with sentence length.[17] Information on victim's race was also scarce. Homicide had to be excluded from this analysis for this reason so that only robbery could be submitted to it. Since most of the victims of robbery were white, the variable was coded as white and non-white. In fact, victim's race did not appear to be correlated with the disposition.[18]

The second step within this second analytical strategy was the use of a multivariate regression model that tests the effect of defendant's race on sentence length while controlling for all the above-mentioned variables that have an impact on it. Hence, rather than a bivariate analysis of each independent variable as shown before, the purpose here is to integrate them all into a multivariate model. We carried out a different model for each type of crime, given that, as we have seen, independent variables do not always work in the same way for all crimes. Homicides had to be excluded, once again, because of the small number of cases.

The model for robberies had the following independent variables: (a) race of defendant (white, mulatto and black); and (b) caught in the act ('yes' or 'no'). Race was coded into two dummy variables: one for mulattos and one for blacks. Thus, the implicit category (i.e. the one with which the others were compared) was 'white'. The result of the analysis (Table 10.10) shows that defendants who were caught in the act were sentenced to a significantly shorter sentence, much as we had seen in the bivariate analysis. However, race of the defendant did not seem to play a role in the severity of the sentence.

The model for drug-crimes (Table 10.11) had the following independent variables: (a) race of defendant (white, mulatto and black), coded as above; (b) caught in the act (yes or no); and (c) access to a private attorney (yes or no).

Table 10.10 Regression on sentence length: robberies[19]

Variables in the model	Unstandardized coefficients		Standardized coefficients		
	B	Std. Error	Beta	t	Sig.
(Constant)	112.961	4.07		27.755	0.000
Caught in the act	−45.02	4.054	−0.313	−11.105	0.000
Race of defendant: Mulattos	−5.363	3.013	−0.054	−1.78	0.075
Race of defendant: Blacks	−6.958	3.755	−0.056	−1.853	0.064

Table 10.11   Regression on sentence length: drug crimes[20]

Variables in the model	Unstandardized coefficients		Standardized coefficients		
	B	Std. Error	Beta	t	Sig.
(Constant)	45.171	4.806		9.4	0.00
Caught in the act	−15.8	4.74	−0.109	−3.334	0.001
Access to private lawyer	6.341	1.75	0.12	3.624	0.00
Race of defendant: mulattos	1.606	1.716	0.034	0.936	0.349
Race of defendant: blacks	3.987	2.015	0.072	1.978	0.048

Results confirmed that the length of prison sentence is larger when the defendant has a private attorney and smaller when the defendant was caught in the act. Once again, race of defendant did not seem to have a significant impact on the sentence. Yet the results of blacks, who receive longer sentences, are close to statistical significance. In short, a multivariate regression basically confirms the results of bivariate analyses and fails to find significant differences between the dispositions of the various ethnic groups. However, there are many other factors that could influence these results and that could be incorporated into the model.

The *third analytical approach* involves a comparison between the sentences issued by the courts against individuals of different races for legal cases in which the charges pressed by the prosecutors were exactly the same. The assumption here is that the prosecutors took into consideration all relevant elements of the case and, as such, any difference in the penalty is the result of a bias on the part of the judge. The prosecutor's formal accusation includes only the qualifying circumstances of the crime[21] that appear on the Penal Code for that type of crime, but do not contemplate a wide array of aggravating and mitigating circumstances that appear commonly in the sentences issued by the judges.

Hence, we identified cases which were identical according to the crime and the qualifications in the accusation pressed by the prosecutor. We discarded crime types that had only a few cases. A minimum of 40 cases (with the same crime and qualifications) was required for them to be included into the analysis. Cases which were identical but included accessory crimes were also discarded. Homicides, given their small sample size, had to be excluded altogether. In the end, this process of selection yielded six types of robbery and four types of drug crimes, which comprised more than 85 percent of the total number of cases, i.e. there was a loss of under 15 per cent of the sample. Below is the average sentence length for each of the following ten types of crimes[21b] (Table 10.12).

We tested a model for robberies (the first six categories in the table above) and another one for drug crimes (the last four categories), given that the two types of crimes do not always yield identical results. The dependent variable was, again, the length of prison sentence in months (valid sentence). Independent variables in the model were: (a) a dichotomous variable ('dummy

Table 10.12 Average sentence length (in months) according to the accusation pressed by the prosecutors

Type of crime with qualifications	White		Mulatto		Black	
	N	Mean	N	Mean	N	Mean
Robbery committed with weapons, violence or threat	49	55.2	30	56	13	48.3
Robbery committed by two or more individuals	58	55.6	60	55.8	37	54.8
Robbery committed when the victim was transporting valuables and the defendant knew about it	255	66.8	238	64.8	117	64.5
Robbery committed with weapons, violence or threat, when the victim was transporting valuables and the defendant knew about it, and the victim was being held hostage while the crime was being committed	45	71.6	23	74.4	7	68.6
Robbery committed in conjunction with homicide or grievous bodily harm	23	249.2	13	262.1	3	292
Simple robbery	28	43.6	30	45.3	16	38
Drug trafficking	205	35	185	35.6	111	34.1
Drug trafficking committed by two or more individuals	34	50.2	32	49.4	14	52.6
Drug use	64	4.5	56	6	32	11
Drug trafficking committed by two or more individuals, at least one of them under 18 years old	24	37.5	40	45.5	21	47.5
Total	785	55	707	52.7	371	48.6

variable') for the presence or absence of each type of crime (with its qualifications). Thus, the model for robbery had five dummy variables (the omitted variable is the reference category) and the drug model had three. This procedure guarantees that we are testing the impact of race on crimes that are identical; (b) whether the defendant was caught in the act or not; (c) whether the defendant had access to a private attorney; and (d) race of defendant was decomposed into two dummy variables, one for mulattos and one for blacks, as indicated in the previous model. This means that both of these groups are in practice compared to whites, the omitted category.

Table 10.13 displays the results of the model for robberies, which does not reveal a statistically significant difference between blacks or mulattos in comparison to whites. Dummy variables, as expected, are clearly significant, since the qualifications imply longer or shorter sentences. Being caught in the act is associated with shorter sentences, as in previous models, whereas access to a private attorney is non-significant. The high value of the Adjusted R square in this model means that most of the variance is accounted for in this model, so tests of racial bias should be more powerful.

The model for drug crimes presents similar results (Table 10.14). Only the dummy variables are significant, whereas race does not seem to have an impact on the disposition.

In sum, there is no apparent racial bias in the length of prison sentence issued by the judges in cases of robbery and drug crimes when controlling for type of crime and its qualifications as interpreted by the prosecutors. Obviously, that does not imply that bias cannot exist in other moments of the legal procedure or even by the prosecutors themselves.

The *fourth analytical strategy* consisted in comparing dispositions for defendants of different racial groups that were sentenced for crimes committed under the same aggravating and mitigating circumstances. On the one hand, as explained above, this is the methodological option that allows for the strongest control on the impact of the characteristics of the crime and, as a result, it is the clearest evidence of bias if bias were to be found. On the other hand, this is a measure of only the most blatant type of bias, that which would result in different penalties for different racial groups despite the fact that the judges considered the same aggravating and mitigating circumstances for the crime. Bias that would translate in the differential use of aggravating and mitigating circumstances for the various ethnic groups, for example, is altogether ignored in this strategy.

In order to proceed with this analysis, new dummy variables were created for every crime characteristic that could have an impact on the sentence, whether they appeared as crime qualifications or as general aggravating or mitigating circumstances. Since it was not uncommon that the same characteristic might appear in the qualification of the crime and also as an aggravating circumstance mentioned in the considerations of the judge, this served the purpose of avoiding redundancy so that a single element did

Table 10.13 Length of prison sentence (in months) regressed on types of robbery and other relevant variables[22]

Variables in the model	Non-standardized coefficients		Standardized coefficients		
	B	S.E.	Beta	t	Sig.
Constant	54.643	3.547		15.406	0.000
Robbery committed with weapons, violence or threat	10.749	3.602	0.069	2.984	0.003
Drug trafficking committed by two or more individuals	28.028	3.803	0.164	7.37	0.000
Robbery committed when the victim was transporting valuables and the defendant knew about it	12.049	3.252	0.097	3.704	0.000
Robbery committed with weapons, violence or threat, when the victim was transporting valuables and the defendant knew about it, and the victim was being held hostage while the crime was being committed	21.633	2.842	0.241	7.613	0.000
Robbery committed in conjunction with homicide or grievous bodily harm	207.744	4.692	0.891	44.275	0.000
Simple robbery (reference category)					
Caught in the act (yes or no)	−11.772	2.243	−0.088	−5.249	0.000
Access to private attorney (yes or no)	0.125	1.556	0.001	0.08	0.936
Race of defendant: mulattos	**−0.299**	**1.593**	**−0.003**	**−0.188**	**0.851**
Race of defendant: blacks	**−1.424**	**2.008**	**−0.012**	**−0.709**	**0.478**
White (reference category)					

not enter twice in the model, which might create problems for analysis and interpretation.

There were two options for this type of analysis. The first one was to apply a multivariate regression model that uses a dummy variable for every crime characteristic (aggravating or mitigating) and also incorporates race and other relevant independent variables. The advantage of this option is that it considers all cases. The disadvantages can be summarized as

Table 10.14   Length of prison sentence (in months) regressed on types of drug crime and other relevant variables[23]

Variables in the model	Non-standardized coefficients		Standardized coefficients		
	B	S.E.	Beta	t	Sig.
(Constant)	21.957	5.574		3.939	0.000
Drug trafficking committed by two or more individuals	27.879	1.736	0.6	16.063	0.000
Drug use	43.1	2.557	0.566	16.859	0.000
Drug trafficking committed by two or more individuals, at least one of them under 18 years old	36.992	2.494	0.499	14.831	0.000
Drug trafficking (reference category)					
Caught in the act	−16.897	5.362	−0.09	−3.151	0.002
Presence of private attorney	2.105	1.525	0.041	1.38	0.168
Race of defendant: mulattos	**1.565**	**1.461**	**0.034**	**1.072**	**0.284**
Race of defendant: blacks	**2.404**	**1.737**	**0.044**	**1.384**	**0.167**
White (reference category)					

follows: (a) the number of aggravating and mitigating circumstances is very large, which implies the loss of many degrees of freedom; (b) many aggravating and mitigating circumstances are applied to very few cases, which may result in unreliable estimates; (c) the linear regression model implies that all these aggravating and mitigating circumstances have a linear and additive effect on the dependent variable. However, the way the penalty is calculated does not exactly fit this additive model. For instance, legal codes determine a minimum and a maximum sentence so that even when there are many aggravating and mitigating circumstances the final sentence cannot go beyond or below a certain limit. Therefore a cumulative effect is not always possible. As a result, this translates into an interactive effect among all these circumstances; and (d) the possibility of introducing these interactive effects into the model would imply very complicated interaction terms which would be very hard to interpret.

The second analytical option is the use of matching, i.e. grouping cases that have exactly the same crime characteristics, including the same aggravating and mitigating circumstances used by the judge. A dummy variable would be created for every one of these groups, so that the effect of race could be tested using crimes that share exactly the same characteristics. Only crimes with a minimum number of cases would be considered. This option guarantees maximum control on these crime characteristics, but has the drawback that a part of the sample, that is, cases belonging to groups that do not reach a minimum frequency, is lost from the analysis. Both options were carried out and their results were compared. The regression on robbery using every crime characteristic (aggravating or mitigating circumstances) as a dummy variable yields the following results (Table 10.15).

As expected, many of the aggravating and mitigating circumstances had a significant impact. However, being caught in the act and having access to a private attorney did not. Most importantly, race of defendant did not

Table 10.15 Length of prison sentence (in months) for robbery regressed on crime characteristics (aggravating and mitigating circumstances) and other relevant independent variables[24]

	Non-standardized coefficients		Standardized coefficients		
	B	S.E.	Beta	t	Sig.
Constant	62.346	2.707		23.035	0.000
Aggravating circumstances					
Use of weapon	2.999	1.417	0.028	2.116	0.035
Physical violence	0.865	4.47	0.002	0.194	0.847
Previous criminal record	5.519	3.248	0.019	1.699	0.090
Crime that does not offer any possibility of resistance by the victim/Crime with betrayal of trust	8.5	3.322	0.029	2.559	0.011
Serious crime	2.479	12.352	0.002	0.201	0.841
High social risk	16.331	8.587	0.027	1.902	0.057
Futile motivation	−3.799	8.764	−0.005	−0.433	0.665
Premeditation	108.255	17.619	0.067	6.144	0.000
Distorted personality of the defendant: antisocial, hostile, violent	−19.436	12.375	−0.017	−1.571	0.117
Intense motivation to commit the crime	4.023	10.818	0.005	0.372	0.710
Crime against infant, older or pregnant woman	7.496	13.111	0.008	0.572	0.568
Death of the victim	−0.252	8.83	0	−0.029	0.977
Coercion of co-offender to participate in the crime	191.038	3.118	0.836	61.267	0.000
Grave threat	5.294	17.47	0.003	0.303	0.762

Table 10.15 (Continued)

	Non-standardized coefficients		Standardized coefficients		
	B	**S.E.**	**Beta**	**t**	**Sig.**
Inappropriate social behaviour	−1.733	2.918	−0.006	−0.594	0.553
Participation of minors	−4.123	24.014	−0.003	−0.172	0.864
Crime committed by two or more individuals	22.082	17.737	0.014	1.245	0.213
Crime against foreigners	20.75	3.372	0.07	6.154	0.000
Robbery against poor people	17.985	12.469	0.016	1.442	0.149
Economic damage for the victim	−11.57	17.868	−0.007	−0.647	0.517
Victim held hostage while the crime was being committed	−2.547	17.688	−0.002	−0.144	0.886
More than one crime committed in the same course of events	4.804	2.106	0.026	2.281	0.023
Continued crime – the crime starts in one moment and lasts for some time	−7.846	18.228	−0.005	−0.43	0.667
High number of victims	31.867	10.702	0.034	2.978	0.003
Gunshots	7.376	17.958	0.005	0.411	0.681
More than one crime committed through several actions	6.344	1.768	0.054	3.588	0.000
Use of fake weapons	−2.595	10.083	−0.003	−0.257	0.797
Cruelty	42.767	17.429	0.026	2.454	0.014
Potential harm	75.366	21.784	0.046	3.46	0.001
Crime committed to avoid being prosecuted for another crime	−3.876	5.039	−0.009	−0.769	0.442
Robbery of valuables	7.501	12.357	0.008	0.607	0.544
Simple robbery	−8.512	2.702	−0.048	−3.151	0.002
Presence of accessory crimes according to law 8072/90	108.211	17.606	0.067	6.146	0.000
'Active corruption' – offer of money to bribe someone	14.085	17.544	0.009	0.803	0.422
Simple theft	−47.431	6.896	−0.077	−6.878	0.000
Theft committed by two or more individuals	−43.542	5.977	−0.084	−7.285	0.000
Simple grievous bodily harm	−9.221	17.598	−0.006	−0.524	0.600
Reception of stolen goods	−34.86	10.262	−0.037	−3.397	0.001
Use of false public documents	37.438	17.491	0.023	2.14	0.033

Mitigating circumstances					
Lack of previous convictions in the last 5 years	−1.596	1.215	−0.016	−1.313	0.189
Lack of previous criminal record	9.173	8.19	0.013	1.12	0.263
'Spontaneous confession'	−3.973	2.361	−0.019	−1.683	
Ancillary participation in crime	−18.342	12.331	−0.016	−1.488	0.093
Under the influence of drugs	−26.69	17.479	−0.016	−1.527	0.137
Defendant suffered a gun shot	20.693	19.747	0.013	1.048	0.127
Appropriate social behaviour	−8.865	13.138	−0.008	−0.675	0.295
Attempted crime	−30.928	1.627	−0.216	−19.008	0.500
Repentance	12.695	17.413	0.008	0.729	0.777
Defendant is under 21 (but older than 18)	−3.648	12.89	−0.003	−0.283	0.896
Crime was committed without violence	0.192	1.461	0.001	0.131	0.796
Appropriate social behaviour	−3.233	12.505	−0.003	−0.259	0.701
Crime committed without a weapon	−0.527	1.37	−0.005	−0.385	0.725
Other variables					
Caught in the act (yes or no)	−3.579	10.178	−0.004	−0.352	0.005
Access to private attorney (yes or no)	−4.647	1.67	−0.032	−2.783	0.233
Race of defendant: mulattos	**1.375**	**1.152**	**0.013**	**1.194**	**0.682**
Race of defendant: blacks	**0.484**	**1.179**	**0.005**	**0.41**	**0.295**

show a significant impact on sentence length. The high value of the Adjusted R Square confirms that most of the variance has been accounted for and the test of the impact of race should be much more powerful than in other models. Table 10.16 shows the same model, using crime characteristics as dummy variables, for drug crimes.

Once again, being caught in the act, having access to private attorneys and, most importantly, race of defendant did not appear to be correlated with sentence length for drug crimes. Next, we present the results of the matching strategy, whereby cases with exactly the same crime characteristics (including aggravating and mitigating circumstances) were grouped and a dummy variable was used for each of these groups. For this analysis, in

Table 10.16 Length of prison sentence (in months) for drug crimes regressed on crime characteristics (aggravating and mitigating circumstances) and other relevant independent variables[25]

	Non-standardized coefficients		Standardized coefficients		
	B	S.E.	Beta	t	Sig.
Constant	18.223	6.082		2.996	0.003
Aggravating circumstances					
Use of weapon	−2.024	8.554	−0.006	−0.237	0.813
Previous criminal record	4.435	2.454	0.039	1.807	0.071
Previous convictions	7.118	2.37	0.063	3.003	0.003
Distorted personality of the defendant: antisocial, hostile, violent	−2.001	11.421	−0.005	−0.175	0.861
Grave threat	30.735	18.808	0.044	1.634	0.103
Inappropriate social behaviour	3.936	14.452	0.006	0.272	0.785
Unintentional negative consequences	29.353	8.686	0.073	3.379	0.001
Significant quantity of drugs	12.759	16.38	−0.018	−0.779	0.436
Participation of minors	24.452	4.274	0.134	5.722	0.000
Diversity of drug substances	8.964	1.49	0.131	6.017	0.000
Disobedience to the court	−6.656	15.02	−0.01	−0.443	0.658
Drug user	1.346	10.372	0.003	0.13	0.897
Inter-state drug trafficking	10.195	6.072	−0.194	−1.679	0.094
Crime committed by two or more individuals	32.669	14.988	0.047	2.18	0.030
Non-appearance at court hearings	30.099	2.708	0.257	11.117	0.000
Crime committed inside the prison	−0.436	14.504	−0.001	−0.03	0.976
International drug trafficking	14.845	3.902	0.082	3.805	0.000
Simple drug trafficking	23.642	5.987	0.454	3.949	0.000
Defendant is a civil servant	32.322	8.456	−0.08	−3.822	0.000
Gun Possession (Penal Law – new legislation)	3.781	5.121	0.015	0.738	0.460
Gun possession (Law of Misdemeanours – old legislation)	5.91	8.37	0.015	0.706	0.480
Formation of a criminal organization	65.589	23.26	0.094	2.82	0.005
Hideous crime	35.964	14.874	−0.073	−2.418	0.016
'Active corruption' – offer of money to bribe someone	33.084	8.318	0.082	3.977	0.000

Mitigating circumstances

Lack of previous convictions in the last 5 years	−1.138	1.136	−0.023	−1.001	0.317
Lack of previous criminal record	3.32	4.438	0.016	0.748	0.455
'Spontaneous confession'	3.469	2.253	0.036	1.54	0.124
Ancillary participation in crime	−9.382	10.239	−0.019	−0.916	0.360
Defendant was in danger	−0.286	14.465	0	−0.02	0.984
Under the influence of drugs	−0.482	7.807	−0.002	−0.062	0.951
Drugs had small value	−1.794	5.155	−0.007	−0.348	0.728
Cooperation with the police investigation	25.241	14.378	−0.036	−1.755	0.080
Necessity (partially driven to commit the crime by the circumstances)	14.378	14.35	−0.021	−1.002	0.317
Defendant practiced the crime because he/she was in a dire economic situation	−3.707	14.592	−0.005	−0.254	0.800
Defendant is under 21 (but older than 18)	−1.656	1.945	−0.018	−0.851	0.395
Appropriate social behaviour	−1.704	1.497	−0.026	−1.138	0.255
Other variables					
Caught in the act	−3.486	3.29	−0.024	−1.06	0.290
Access to private attorney	0.501	1.159	0.009	0.432	0.666
Race of defendant: mulattos	**−0.437**	**1.108**	**−0.009**	**−0.394**	**0.694**
Race of defendant: blacks	**1.332**	**1.295**	**0.024**	**1.028**	**0.304**

contrast to all the previous ones, we chose the first sentence (before any appeal), rather than the valid sentence at that time, as dependent variable. This was due to the fact that it proved easier to find identical cases for the first sentence than for other possible dependent variables. Only groups with a minimum of 20 cases were considered in the analysis in order to avoid unstable estimates. By establishing this criterion we lose approximately 46 percent of the sample, but, as explained above, we maximize our level of control over independent variables. Groups included in the analysis correspond to the following crimes and crime characteristics (Table 10.17).

A dummy variable was created for each of these groups and these variables were introduced into the model together with race of the defendant and other relevant independent variables. The regression model for robbery presents the following results (Table 10.18).

Table 10.17 Matching groups in terms of crime and crime characteristics, by frequency

Type of crime	Frequency	Percentage	Valid Percentage
Robbery committed with weapons, violence or threat	22	1.1	2
Robbery committed by two or more individuals	32	1.6	2.9
1. Lack of previous criminal record and previous convictions	23	1.1	2.1
Robbery committed when the victim was transporting valuables and the defendant knew about it	165	8.2	15.1
1. Lack of previous convictions in the last 5 years	65	3.2	6
2. Defendant is under 21 (but older than 18)	31	1.5	2.8
3. Appropriate social behaviour	21	1	1.9
4. Lack of previous convictions in the last 5 years and appropriate social behaviour	83	4.1	7.6
5. Lack of previous convictions in the last 5 years and appropriate social behaviour, and under 21	20	1	1.8
Drug trafficking	233	11.6	21.4
1. Previous convictions	22	1.1	2
2. Lack of previous convictions	76	3.8	7
3. Lack of previous criminal record	23	1.1	2.1
4. Lack of previous criminal records and lack of convictions	61	3	5.6
Drug use	102	5.1	9.3
1. Lack of previous convictions	56	2.8	5.1
Drug trafficking committed by two or more individuals, at least one of them under 18 years old	56	2.8	5.1
Sub-total	1091	54.1	100
Missing cases	924	45.9	
Total	2015	100	

Unlike in previous models, variables representing crime characteristics are non-significant and Adjusted R Square is very low. This means that average sentences for the types of crimes selected are very similar to each other. Further, it is apparent that there is no significant difference between dispositions

Table 10.18   Length of prison sentence (in months) for the crime of robbery regressed on *matched groups* according to crime characteristics and other relevant independent variables[26]

	Non-standardized coefficients		Standardized coefficients		
	B	S.E.	Beta	t	Sig.
Constant	69.08	3.277		21.082	0.000
Robbery practiced with weapons, violence or threat	1.966	3.892	0.027	−0.505	0.614
Robbery practiced by two or more individuals	3.001	4.569	0.034	−0.657	0.512
1. Lack of previous criminal record and previous convictions	3.846	4.814	−0.04	−0.799	0.425
Robbery committed when the victim was transporting valuables and the defendant knew about it					
1) Lack of previous convictions in the last 5 years	0.004	3.106	0	−0.001	0.999
2) Defendant is under 21 (but older than 18)	3.497	2.556	0.088	1.368	0.172
3) Appropriate social behaviour	6.58	3.993	0.087	1.648	0.100
4) Lack of previous convictions in the last 5 years and appropriate social behaviour	2.737	4.938	0.028	−0.554	0.580
5) Lack of previous convictions in the last 5 years and appropriate social behaviour, and under 21	5.169	4.734	0.056	−1.092	0.275
Caught in the act	0.161	2.63	0.003	0.061	0.951
Access to private attorney	.229	1.878	0.031	−0.654	0.513
Race of defendant: mulattos	−.425	1.988	0.062	−1.22	0.223
Race of defendant: blacks	2.868	2.544	0.057	−1.127	0.260

issued for white, black and mulatto defendants convicted of robbery, while controlling for all existing aggravating and mitigating circumstances. The model for drug crimes yields the following results (Table 10.19).

Once again, race of defendant did not present a statistically significant impact on the final disposition. In short, neither multivariate regression

Table 10.19 Length of prison sentence (in months) for drug crimes regressed on *matched groups* according to crime characteristics and other relevant independent variables[27]

	Non-standardized coefficients		Standardized coefficients		
	B	S.E.	Beta	t	Sig.
Constant	42.034	2.815		14.934	0.000
Drug trafficking					
1. Previous convictions	−1.427	1.274	−0.024	−1.12	0.263
2. Lack of previous convictions	15.634	1.379	0.244	11.34	0.000
3. Lack of previous criminal record	−35.782	1.198	−0.667	−29.863	0.000
4. Lack of previous convictions and previous criminal records	−35.71	1.481	−0.513	−24.107	0.000
Drug use					
1. Lack of previous convictions	−1.806	1.368	−0.028	−1.32	0.187
Drug trafficking committed by two or more individuals, at least one of them under 18 years old	12.498	2.099	0.123	5.955	0.000
Caught in the act	−3.125	2.754	−0.023	−1.135	0.257
Access to private attorney	−0.557	0.914	−0.013	−0.609	0.543
Race of defendant: mulattos	−0.35	0.876	−0.009	−0.399	0.690
Race of defendant: blacks	0.834	1.033	0.018	0.807	0.420

with all the aggravating and mitigating circumstances as independent variables nor the analysis of groups matched on crime circumstances reveal indications of racial bias on sentence length.

Conclusions

The first result of this study is that the raw average of sentence length, measured in months, for the crimes of robbery, homicide and drug crimes does not differ significantly according to the race of defendant. Furthermore, when we estimate a multivariate model that takes into account other independent variables that may also impact sentence severity, such as whether the defendant was caught in the act and whether he or she had access to a private attorney, the harshness of the penalty does not seem to correlate with race either.

A third analytical strategy compared cases where accusations by the prosecutors were identical (including crime type and its qualifying circumstances) to see whether the sentences issued by the judges for members of the various racial groups were significantly different, using the prosecutors' position as a benchmark. Results again yielded no significant impact of race. The fourth analytical strategy was to compare sentences for crimes that contemplated exactly the same aggravating and mitigating circumstances. This was carried out in two different ways: including all crime characteristics as independent variables through the use of dummy variables in a multivariate regression; and comparing groups matched in all of these crime characteristics. Both of these analyses failed to show a significant role of defendant's race on sentence length.

Hence, this study failed to find evidence of racial bias in sentencing in Brazil. We may interpret that the decisions of the judges are strongly guided by legal procedures and are probably taken by the judges upon reading legal documents before even meeting the defendant, all of which reduces the space for any possible bias to manifest itself. Nevertheless, bias in the criminal justice system is more likely to have occurred at the previous stages, such as contact with the police, where institutional constraints are far weaker and there is more intense contact with the suspect.

Notes

1. This is an official body which integrates the Secretary of Public Security, Government of the state of Rio de Janeiro.
2. The official racial categories of the Brazilian Census actually refer to 'color': whites ('brancos'), blacks ('pretos'), mulattos or browns ('pardos'), Asians or yellows ('amarelos') and indigenous ('indígenas'). Even though significant sectors of society consider that these terms do not adequately represent ethnicity and further demand the use of the term 'negro' to stand for both black and mulatto, we will have to stick to official categories since this research is based on official documents.
3. Besides the authors, the research team was composed also of Rose Carvalho, Eduardo Ribeiro, Ariel Alves and Cristina Jakimiak. This study was supported by the Ford Foundation.
4. Penal Execution Courts monitor the application of penalties on convicts. As such, they control all legal aspects of life in prison, including releases, benefits and punishments.
5. There was one more section in the files devoted to prisoners that had been released but we did not have access to that section.
6. 'Flagrante' is a legal procedure that is started when the person is caught in the act. In Brazilian penal and procedural law, legal proceedings in this situation are different from those that are carried out when the person is arrested at a later moment.
7. Mixed categories, such as 'white/mulatto', indicate that the defendant was categorized in different ways by different documents.
8. Data analysis supported this choice since individuals who were classified as 'negro' were much more likely to be identified as 'black' than as 'mulatto' in the remaining documents.
9. This was particularly the case for homicides and drug-related crimes.

10. When documents mentioned the appeal but did not contain any additional information about the decision, we assumed that it had not been tried yet.
11. Racial composition is different for each crime – more white defendants for homicide and less for drug crimes – so an overall analysis that would not separate the type of crime would yield misleading results.
12. The level of significance (alpha) used in these tests will be 0.01.
13. In some Brazilian states, such as Rio de Janeiro, there is a state institution called 'Public Attorney's Office' that grants juridical assistance to all those accused who cannot afford a private lawyer. In the states that do not have this institution, such as Sao Paulo, the state hires a private attorney to assist those accused who do not have access to a private lawyer.
14. Robbery: $F = 0.636$, $d.f. = 2$ and 1024, $p = 0.529$; Homicide: $F = 0.026$, $d.f. = 2$ and 65, $p = 0.975$; Drug crimes: $F = 0.006$, $d.f. = 2$ and 792, $p = 0.994$.
15. Robbery: $F = 0.423$, $d.f. = 1$ and 1154, $p = 0.516$; Homicide: $F = 0.153$, $d.f. = 1$ and 105, $p = 0.696$; Drug crimes: $F = 4.77$, $d.f. = 1$ and 1012, $p = 0.029$.
16. Robbery: $F = 2.895$, $d.f. = 1$ and 781, $p = 0.089$; Homicide: $F = 0.153$, $d.f. = 1$ and 86, $p = 0.697$.
17. Robbery: $F = 0.126$, $d.f. = 2$ and 371, $p = 0.882$.
18. Robbery: $F = 0.769$, $d.f. = 1$ and 360, $p = 0.381$.
19. ADJUSTED R SQUARE: 0.100.
20. ADJUSTED R SQUARE: 0.026.
21. These circumstances that are included in the article that defines the crime in question in the Penal Code are known as 'majorantes' in Portuguese and are different from the far more numerous aggravating and mitigating circumstances that the judge can invoke in a sentence. For example, article 157 of the Penal Code distinguishes a simple robbery from a qualified robbery. According to the law, the latter implies a higher minimum sentence than the former.
21b. Missing values for race meant that one of the crime groups fell slightly below the 40 cases limit.
22. ADJUSTED R SQUARE: 0.729.
23. ADJUSTED R SQUARE: 0.345.
24. ADJUSTED R SQUARE: 0.871.
25. ADJUSTED R SQUARE: 0.617.
26. ADJUSTED R SQUARE: 0.003.
27. ADJUSTED R SQUARE: 0.761.

References

Adorno, S. (1995a) 'Discriminação Racial e Justiça Criminal em São Paulo' *Novos Estudos. CEBRAP* 43: 26–44.
Adorno, S. (1995b). 'Racismo, criminalidade violenta e justiça penal: réus brancos e negros em perspectiva comparativa', *Estudos Históricos* 18 (9), 283–300.
Alston, P. (2007) *Report of the Special Rapporteur on Extrajudicial, Summary or Arbitrary Executions.* Addendum. MISSION TO BRAZIL. Office of the United Nations High Comissioner for Human Rights. Document number A/HRC/11/2/Add.2 future. Obtained from: http://www2.ohchr.org/english/issues/executions/docs/A_HRC_11_2_Add_2_English.pdf on May, 31, 2009.
Cano, I. (1998) *The Use of Lethal Force by Police in Rio de Janeiro.* Rio de Janeiro: ISER.
Cano, I. and Schweiger-Gallo, I. (2008) '*El impacto de la información estereotípica y de la autocategorización sobre la categorización racial em Brasil*' *Revista de Psicologia Social.* Fundación Infância y Aprendizaje. Madrid. 23 (3), 329–346.

Chevigny, P. (1991) 'Police Deadly Force as Social Control: Jamaica, Brazil and Argentina', *Série Dossiê NEV*, 2. São Paulo: Núcleo de Estudos da Violência, USP.

Cruz, M. V. G. and Batittuci, E. C. (orgs) (2007) *Homicídios no Brasil*. Rio de Janeiro: Fundação Getúlio Vargas.

Cunha, E. da (1936) *Os sertões, Campanha de Canudos*. Rio de Janeiro: Livraria Francisco Alves.

Fausto, B. (2001). *Crime e cotidiano: A criminalidade em São Paulo (1880–1924)*. São Paulo: Brasiliense.

Freyre, G. (1933) *Casa Grande e Senzala*. Rio de Janeiro: Maia & Schmidt.

Harris, M. (1964) *Pattern of Race in the Americas*. New York: Walker.

Hasenbalg, C. (1979) *Discriminação e desigualdades raciais no Brasil*. Rio de Janeiro: Graal.

Human Rights Watch (1997) *Police Brutality in Urban Brazil*. New York: Human Rights Watch/Americas.

Hungria, N. (1959) 'A criminalidade dos homens de cor no Brasil', *Comentários ao Código Penal*, vol. III. Rio de Janeiro: Revista Forense.

Kahn, T. (1999) 'Justiça e Discriminação Racial' Boletim Informativo do Grupo de Pesquisa da Discriminação da USP, 1 (5). São Paulo: USP.

Ministério da Justiça/DEPEN, INFOPEN, (2008). http://www.mj.gov.br/data/Pages/MJD574E9CEITEMIDC37B2AE94C6840068B1624D28407509CPTBRNN.htm. Accessed in February, 2009.

Neri, M. (2006) *Retratos do Cárcere*. Centro de Políticas Sociais. EPGE. Rio de Janeiro: Fundação Getúlio Vargas.

Paixão, A. L. (1983) 'Crime e criminosos em Belo Horizonte. 1932–1978', in Pinheiro, P. S. (ed.), *Crime, Violência e Poder*. São Paulo: Brasiliense.

Ribeiro, C. A. C. (1995) *Cor e Criminalidade. Estudo e Análise da Justiça no Rio de Janeiro (1900–1930)*. Rio de Janeiro: Editora UFRJ.

Ribeiro, C. A. C. (2006) 'Raça, classe e mobilidade social no Brasil', *Dados – Revista de Ciências Sociais* 49 (4): 833–73.

Rodrigues, N. (1994) *As raças humanas e a responsabilidade penal no Brasil*. Rio de Janeiro: Guanabara.

Silva, J. da (1998) *Violência e Racismo no Rio de Janeiro*. Rio de Janeiro: EDUFF.

Silva, N. d. V. (1985) 'Updating the Cost of Not Being White in Brazil', in Fontaine, P. M. (ed.), *Race, Class and Power in Brazil*, Los Angeles: UCLA Center for Afro-American Studies.

Telles, E. E. and Lim, N. (1998) 'Does It Matter Who Answers the Race Question? Racial Classification and Income Inequality in Brazil', *Demography* 35 (4): 465–74.

Vargas, J. (2004). *Estupro: que justiça?*. Tese de doutorado em sociologia. Rio de Janeiro: IUPERJ.

Wood, C. (1991) 'Categorias Censitárias e Classificações Subjetivas de Raça no Brasil', in Lovell, Peggy A. (ed.), *Desigualdade Racial no Brasil Contemporâneo*. Belo Horizonte: Universidade Federal de Minas Gerais: Centro de Desenvolvimento e Planejamento Regional, pp. 93–113.

11
Race, Crime and Criminal Justice in Canada

Clayton J. Mosher
Washington State University, Vancouver, WA

Taj Mahon-Haft
Washington State University, Vancouver, WA

Introduction

Certain racial/ethnic minority groups are greatly over-represented in Canada's criminal justice system. While scholars examining this over-representation have pointed to issues of bias in the system, historically there has been a decided tendency on the part of several criminal justice system officials, legislators, some academics and media commentators to deny that such bias exists. Unfortunately, it is difficult to disentangle the causes of this over-representation, due to an informal ban on the release of race-based crime statistics in Canada. As Hagan (1998: xii) comments with respect to this issue,

> The reluctance to enumerate crime in racial terms is an unexpected product of an odd coalition of forces that, for a variety of dubious reasons, bans the necessary data collection. An unfortunate and little-recognized result of this ostrich-like behavior is complacent support for a posture of denial that pervades our justice system.

An additional feature of the discourse on race and crime issues in Canada has been the tendency on the part of the media, both historically and in the current context, to engage in the racialization of crime, 'part of a broader process that inferiorizes or excludes groups in the population' (Tator and Henry, 2006: 8) – a topic to which we devote considerable attention in subsequent sections of this chapter.

In order to contextualize the issue of race, crime and criminal justice in Canada, we begin with a brief description of trends and geographical variation in crime and incarceration rates in which we incorporate a discussion of the over-representation of Aboriginals[1] in the Canadian criminal justice system. Particular attention is given to Aboriginal relations with the criminal justice system principally because of Aboriginals' historical and contemporary experiences of colonialism. We recognize the importance of these experiences as we discuss the historical and contemporary antecedents of Aboriginal over-representation in the criminal justice system, especially in relation to the colonial policies of the Canadian federal government, and current issues of social structural factors and bias in the criminal justice system. Aboriginals continue to experience significant social–structural disadvantages in Canada and these, combined with bias on the part of criminal justice system officials, contribute to disturbingly high rates of incarceration of Aboriginal peoples, particularly in the prairie provinces of Manitoba and Saskatchewan.

Following the discussion of the Aboriginal situation, this chapter explores the experiences of Black people in relation to crime, victimization and criminal justice. As noted above, race-based crime statistics are not collected systematically in Canada. However, both historical (Mosher, 1998) and more recent (Tanovich, 2006; Tator and Henry, 2006; Wortley and Tanner, 2003) research indicate that, in certain areas of the country, Blacks are over-represented in the criminal justice system. This over-representation has sparked interesting debates and considerable controversy surrounding the issue of racial profiling on the part of law enforcement, which we document below. In addition, we discuss recent government reports (McMurtry and Curling, 2008) which have focused on the impact of social–structural disadvantages that contribute to African–Canadian youth's involvement in crime.

We then address issues related to other minority groups and crime, including East Asians, South Asians and West Asians (Muslims/Arabs). While the extant data do not indicate the over-representation of members of such groups in the criminal justice system, historical studies have indicated the targeting of Chinese in the enactment and enforcement of Canada's first drug and other 'public morals' legislation (Mosher, 1998). In the current context, there has been frequent reference in official government and media sources to East Asians' involvement in gangs and organized crime, constituting an additional example of the racialization of crime. And, similar to the situation in the United States following the September 11, 2001, terrorist attacks, there is evidence to suggest that Muslims/Arabs in Canada have been targeted by immigration and law enforcement officials (Tanovich, 2006).

The final section of this chapter examines hate crimes in Canada, beginning with a brief history of the government's treatment of the issue, followed by discussion of the prevalence of hate crimes and their effects on different subgroups. A historical lack of attention to hate crimes by Canadian officials and researchers prior to the 1990s was then supplanted by sentencing enhancement provisions and numerous federal studies after national and international media attention highlighted the social costs (Janhevich, 2001). From those studies, it is now clear that hate crimes continue to occur, most of them are racially motivated (Walsh and Dauvergne, 2009), and they impact Aboriginals, Blacks and Asians to varying degrees.

Given the absence of official data on racial differences in crime rates, and given the relative paucity of scholarly attention to these issues in Canada, in the discussion below we rely extensively on a variety of government reports and media sources. Media descriptions of the race-crime issue are especially important to consider, as many Whites rely almost exclusively on the media for their information about minority groups.

Crime, incarceration rates and aboriginals

Canada's crime rate trends over the past 20 years have been very similar to those observed in the United States – after rising to peaks in 1991, both have declined since (Gannon, 2004). Although rates for most crimes are significantly higher in the United States, rates for breaking and entering and motor vehicle theft have been higher in Canada for several years (Gannon, 2006). In 2007, Canada's overall crime rate declined for the third consecutive year (MacQueen, 2009). Homicides fell for the second year in a row, from 606 in 2006 to 594 in 2007[2] (which translates to a rate of 1.8/100,000 population). While one-fifth of those murders were committed in Toronto, Canada's largest city, its per capita murder rate was lower than that observed in several other Canadian cities and virtually every major US city.

National crime statistics, of course, tend to mask variations between provinces and cities, which appear connected to issues about race and crime. Notably, cities with proportionally greater Aboriginal populations often have crime rates above the national average. For instance, in 2007, the prairie region included the three (large) cities with the highest Aboriginal populations (10 percent) that also topped the crime rankings. These were led by Saskatoon, Saskatchewan (163 percent above the national average) and followed closely by Winnipeg (153 percent) and Regina (136 percent). Crime rates were even higher in the smaller northern cities with high Aboriginal populations. For example, in 2007 the rate of aggravated assault was 350 percent above the national average in Yellowknife and 1300 percent higher in Iqaluit, where the sexual assault rate was also 1270 percent higher (MacDonald, 2009). It is also notable that, in 2008 and early 2009, the Greater Vancouver region, where there is a large Asian population, witnessed a significant increase in gun-related violence, with 58 murders in 2008 and 45 shootings (17 fatal) between January 1 and March 28, 2009 (Hainsworth, 2009). Law enforcement officials in Vancouver attributed these increases largely to organized crime groups and drug trafficking.

With respect to incarceration rates, under Canadian federal law, adult offenders sentenced to custodial terms of 2 years or more are the responsibility of the federal penitentiary system, while those given sentences of less than 2 years fall under provincial jurisdiction (Beattie, 2006).

In 2007/2008, an average of 36,330 adults and 2018 youths (aged 12 to 17 years) were in custody on any given day, a rate of 117/100,000 (Statistics Canada, 2008a). This rate is considerably higher than several Western European countries, but significantly lower than in the United States (762/100,000). However, as with crime rates, there was considerable variation in incarceration rates across provinces and territories in Canada, ranging from a low of 42/100,000 in Nova Scotia to 160/100,000 in the Northwest Territories.

The incarceration data presented above conceal tremendous over-representation of Aboriginals throughout Canada's criminal justice system. In 2006, Aboriginals comprised approximately 4 percent of the Canadian population, but represented 24 percent of admissions to provincial institutions, and 18 percent of admissions to federal prisons. For women, 46 percent of all federally sentenced females classified as maximum security are Aboriginal (Prison Justice Day Committee, 2008).

Aboriginal incarceration rates are even more disproportionate in some provinces. In Manitoba, for instance, Aboriginals constitute 11 percent of the population but 71 percent of the prisoner population; in British Columbia, they are 4 percent of the population but 20 percent of those incarcerated. Aboriginal over-representation is greatest in Saskatchewan and has been growing more exaggerated. Aboriginals there represent 15 percent of the population, and constituted 60 percent of prisoners in 1981 (Johnson, 2005), a percentage that increased to 79 percent by 2006 (Prison Justice Day Committee, 2008). In addition, the over-representation of Natives in the criminal justice system can be seen in the case of particular cities. For example, in the Northern Ontario community of Kenora in the 1980s, Aboriginals comprised approximately 30 percent of the population, but 75 percent of males and 94 percent of females admitted to jail (Morris, 1985). Notably, this was largely due to incarcerating Natives for public intoxication offenses.

A 1998 Task Force on Aboriginal peoples in the federal correctional system found that Aboriginal prisoners were less likely to receive temporary absences or parole, served more time before parole was granted and were more likely to have their parole revoked (Prison Justice Day Committee, 2008). Recidivism rates among Aboriginals are also high compared to non-Aboriginals. A study of convicted adult offenders in Saskatchewan found that 57 percent of Aboriginal people returned to the correctional system within 4 years, compared to 28 percent of non-Aboriginals (Johnson, 2005).

The over-representation of Aboriginals is also evident in Canada's juvenile justice system. A one-day 'snapshot' of youth incarcerated in 2003 revealed that the incarceration rate of Aboriginal youth was 64.5/10,000 while the rate for non-Aboriginal youth was 8.2/10,000. While Aboriginal youth comprise 5 percent of the Canadian population, 33 percent of youth in custody were Aboriginal (Latimer and Casey-Foss, 2004). In the province of

Saskatchewan, Aboriginal youth represent 75 to 90 percent of all youth in open and closed custody (MacQueen and Treble, 2008). Referring to these high rates of Aboriginal youth incarceration, the Canadian Supreme Court stated, 'Placed in an historical context, the prison has become for many young Native people the contemporary equivalent of what the Indian residential school represented for their parents' (*R. v. Gladue*, 1999). And given that young people under the age of 19 comprise half of the Aboriginal population, compared to approximately one-third of the non-Aboriginal population, in the coming years there will be an increasingly large proportion of Aboriginal people in the age cohorts that are at risk of committing offences (Johnson, 2005).

In addition to the over-representation in Canada's correctional system, Aboriginals also have much higher rates of violent offending. Between 1997 and 2000, the average homicide rate for Aboriginals[3] was 8.8/100,000, almost seven times the rate among non-Aboriginals (1.3/100,000) (Brozowski et al., 2006). This pattern also held among juveniles, as Aboriginals were responsible for 30 percent of the homicides committed by juveniles from 1961 to 1983 (Meloff and Silverman, 1992).

As most violent crime is intra-racial, the over-representation of Aboriginals is also apparent in victimization rates. According to data from the 2004 Canadian General Social Survey, Aboriginal people were three times more likely than non-Aboriginals to experience violent victimization (319 vs 101 incidents per 1000 population) and three and a half times as likely (21 percent vs 6 percent) to report having experienced physical or sexual violence by a spouse in the 5 years preceding the survey.

Historical and contemporary roots of aboriginal over-representation

The seeds of these high rates of Aboriginal offending, victimization and incarceration were planted at the time of Canadian Confederation in 1867. As former head of the Assembly of First Nations, Ovide Mecredi (2000: 4) noted

> The original societies and cultures of the First Peoples have been diminished by more than a century of colonization and virtual dislocation of Indigenous traditions, cultures, and institutions.... [Canada] is most certainly directly responsible, by its past and present laws and policies (that removed Indigenous peoples from their lands and territories) for the breakdown of the Aboriginal economies and institutions of self-sufficiency and self-governance.

In this context, it is worth considering some of the official descriptions of Native peoples in Canada produced by government officials and in media sources from the late 1800s and 1900s, which were used to justify a variety of colonial policies and undoubtedly influenced the wider Canadian public's perception of Natives. Scott (1900), writing in *Canadian Magazine*, quoted John Smith of the United Presbyterian Mission (1874) as stating:

> A more degraded set of human beings, I am sure, did not exist on earth. The mind of a man could not conceive that human beings could be so low on the scale of humanity as they were; and I am sure, if they had been left to the instincts of their own wild savage nature, they could never have been so low down as they were.... their women taught to believe that lewdness was a commendable practice, even a virtue.
>
> (p. 210)

Similarly, in a 1932 book, Diamond Jenness, a pioneer of Canadian anthropology, wrote: 'The Indians had no conception of hygiene, they seldom washed, unless for ceremonial reasons, and their homes were squalid and filthy. Rotting meat and fish strewed the floors and ground outside; dogs, mice, and parasites of every kind shared the interior with human inmates' (p. 99). As late as 1959, Schmidt expressed these opinions in the popular magazine *Saturday Night*:

> [The Indian] is a dull, slow, untidy person and careless workman.... When the urge comes upon them they up and leave their homes.... The Indian has a built-in sense of irresponsibility... Reserves are conducive to inbreeding and subsequent lowering of intelligence.... The Indian has been given a chance. But it seems that he can't or won't pull himself into an improved status in today's Canada. The fault is no one's but his own.
>
> (Schmidt, 1959)

Several such views were apparently held by Canadian government officials, and were thus manifested in formal legislation. Under Canada's first Indian Act (enacted in 1876), the federal government was granted exclusive authority to legislate in relation to Indians and lands reserved for Indians. Under the act, Indians were allowed to hunt and fish for a living, and were to be provided with government-funded education and health care. However, the act deprived Indians of the right to govern themselves, denied them citizenship (eventually granted in 1960), and prevented them from voting in federal or provincial elections.[4] The Act also placed restrictions on their ability to conduct commerce and prohibited them from leaving their reserves without permission from government-appointed Indian agents. In addition, Native women were dispossessed under conditions of the act, which provided that any Native woman who married a non-Native forfeited her rights to Native status and band property. This law was not changed until 1984 (Hale, 1990).

Later amendments to the Indian Act prohibited Indians from consuming alcohol[5] due to a belief on the part of government officials and others that alcohol had particularly deleterious effects on Natives. For example, in the 1890 Department of Indian Affairs report, it was noted that 'The use of liquor by an Indian appears to arouse in him his savage nature afresh, and to lead him to the commission of the most fiendish crimes' (Canada, 1890: xx). In a later report, Clifford Sifton, Superintendent of Indian Affairs, commented

> Undoubtedly, there is no one vice so dangerous to Indians as that of indulgence in strong drink, for not only are they peculiarly predisposed by temperament to such indulgence, but they lack the stamina of constitution which enables white men longer to resist its deleterious action, and when under its immediate influence they more completely lose control of themselves in all directions.
>
> (Canada, 1898: xxiv)

Although Whites in Canada had long been fascinated by a number of Native traditions, in 1884, the federal government began to pass criminal laws preventing, among other things, the ceremonial dances of Aboriginals and potlatches. Included among the justification for such legislation were claims that the dancing caused physical deterioration and mental instability among those who engaged in it (Backhouse, 1999). In the Report of the Department of Indian Affairs in 1885, it was noted

> The legislation ... with a view to the abolition of the wasteful, and in other respects, pernicious Indian feast known as the "potlatch" which is so much in vogue in this province, and for the suppression of the heathenish dance called the "tamanawas," the celebration of which is attended with much that is disgusting and degrading to the Indians indulging in or witnessing it, takes effect from this date.
>
> (Canada, 1885: lv)

It is estimated that between 1900 and 1904, at least 50 Aboriginal people were arrested and 20 were convicted for involvement in such ceremonies (Backhouse, 1999). It was not until 1951 that the Indian Act was amended to allow such ceremonies.

Essential to an understanding of Natives' over-representation in the criminal justice system, both historically and in the current context, is a discussion of residential schools, which Haig-Brown (1991) has referred to as manifestations of cultural genocide. Although the traditional education of Native children took place through their total involvement in community life and through interactions with elders (Miller, 1996), in the 1880–1881 Report of the Department of Indian Affairs, the Superintendent (and Canadian Prime Minister John A. MacDonald) set the stage for these residential schools, commenting

> The Indian youth, to enable him to cope successfully with his brother of white origin, must be dissociated from the prejudicial influences by which he is surrounded on the reserve of his band. And the necessity for the establishment of institutions, whereat Indian children, besides being instructed in the usual branches of education, will be lodged, fed, clothed, kept separate from home influences, taught trades and instructed in agriculture, is becoming every year more apparent.
>
> (Canada, 1880–1881: 8)

In these schools (the last of which was not closed until 1996), Native children were subjected to widespread physical and sexual abuse, were told their language 'belonged to the devil,' had their heads shaved, were forced to eat their own vomit, had their faces rubbed in underwear in which they had defecated and, in cases in which they had wet their bed, were forced to parade through the school with the damp sheet over their head (Miller, 1996). Interviews by the Cariboo (British Columbia) Tribal Council of 187 Natives who attended residential schools found that 89 had experienced sexual abuse, while 60 refused to comment (cited in Miller, 1996). It is also estimated that as many as half of the Aboriginal children attending early residential schools died of tuberculosis, despite repeated warnings to federal government officials that overcrowding, poor sanitation and substandard medical care were creating conditions conducive to the rapid spread of the disease (Curry and Howlett, 2007).

As a result of attendance at residential schools and never having been nurtured by their own parents, many of today's First Nations' peoples did not learn parenting skills themselves (Ball, 2008) – numerous studies have emphasized the criminogenic effects of poor parenting.

In 2005, the Canadian federal government offered the roughly 80,000 survivors of residential schools a $10,000 lump sum payment, in addition to $3000 for every year they had spent in such institutions (Gordon, 2005). And while, in 2008, the Canadian federal government issued an official apology for residential schools and the general assimilation policies directed towards Natives (Diebel, 2008), financial payments and official apologies cannot compensate for the enduring negative effects of these policies on Native peoples.

As already noted, First Nations peoples are highly over-represented in Canada's criminal and juvenile justice system. In explaining this over-representation, it is important to consider Aboriginals' current social structural situation alongside the historical antecedents of and experiences in the criminal justice system. A host of social, economic and health data underline the extremely disadvantaged position of Aboriginals in

Canadian society. In 2001, 48 percent of the Aboriginal population aged 15 or older had not completed high school (compared to 31 percent of non-Aboriginals), and only 4 percent of Aboriginals had completed a university degree (compared to 16 percent of non-Aboriginals). In 2001, the unemployment rate for Aboriginals was 19 percent and for non-Aboriginals 7 percent. The median income from all sources in the same year was $13,500 for Aboriginals and $22,400 for non-Aboriginals (Brozowski et al., 2006). In 2006, Aboriginal people were almost four times as likely as non-Aboriginal people to live in a crowded dwelling (defined as more than one person per room) and three times as likely to live in houses requiring major repair (Statistics Canada, 2008b).

Substance abuse is a major problem for First Nations' peoples and is manifested in data showing that the rate for alcohol-related deaths is 43.7/100,000 in the Aboriginal population, almost twice the rate found in the general population (23.6/100,000). Similarly, the rate of death due to illicit drugs for Aboriginals is almost three times the rate found among the general population (Chansonneuve, 2007). Substance abuse and historical disadvantages have led to related health problems. First Nations' people suffer diabetes at a rate three to five times the rate of the general Canadian population (Assembly of First Nations, 2006) and as of 2000, life expectancy for Aboriginal males was 7.4 years lower than for males in the general population; at the same time, life expectancy for Aboriginal females was 5.2 years lower than for females in the general Canadian population (Statistics Canada, 2002).

The homes of Native youths demonstrate their structural disadvantages. Aboriginal youth are 1.5 times as likely to die before their first birthday, have significantly higher rates of apprehension by child welfare services and also a greater likelihood of living in a series of foster homes (Ball, 2008). In fact, as of 2007, it was estimated that 10 percent of Aboriginal children were in foster care, compared to only 1 in 200 non-Aboriginal children. Among Aboriginal children residing in urban areas, more than 50 percent live in single-parent homes (Ball, 2008). Interestingly, approximately 27,000 Aboriginal children younger than 17 years of age were in government care, and it has been estimated that this number is three times the number enrolled in residential schools at the peak of their operations (Ball, 2008). In addition to adjustment issues and greater criminal involvement, being placed in foster care can also lead to problems in the development of their own parenting skills.

Aboriginal youth also have high rates of substance abuse and suicide. A 2001 *New York Times* article documented the high rates of suicide and gas sniffing in the Labrador villages of Sheshatshiu and Davis Inlet, where more than half of the children between the ages of 5 and 14 were chronic gas sniffers (Rogan, 2001). Among incarcerated Aboriginal youths, one in six were either suspected of or confirmed of having fetal alcohol spectrum disorder and more than 80 percent were suspected of or confirmed of having a problem of substance abuse (Latimer and Casey-Foss, 2004). More generally, in 2000, the Canadian Institute of Child Health estimated that First Nations' males between the ages of 15 and 24 had suicide rates of 126/100,000, compared to a level of 24/100,000 among the Canadian population as a whole (Wadden, 2006). In 2003, the suicide rate among Inuit males between the ages of 15 and 24 was approximately 40 times the national average (Harding, 2007).

Despite the strong indicators of social disadvantage for First Nations' peoples, some commentators in the Canadian media have adopted a 'blame the victim' approach in discussing Aboriginals' plight. For example, reporter Ben Sillas noted 'The Department of Indian Affairs and Northern Development now spends $7.8 billion a year on Canada's status Indians and Inuit, yet half of reserve residents are unemployed and the rates of alcoholism, suicide, and crime among Natives are nearly three times the Canadian averages' (Sillas, 1997). Link Byfield (2001), a columnist for *Alberta Report*, similarly criticized federal government spending on Natives, commenting

> There have been cases of chiefs paying themselves salaries amounting to hundreds of thousands annually, while people on their reserves live two and three families to a shack. Drunkenness abounds as the substance abuse counselors take Caribbean cruises.... From the 1960s through the 1990s, it was fashionable to imagine Indians as unspoiled children of nature, and to see their beads and buckskin culture as morally superior to the one which supplanted it. The historical reality, of course, was that the Indian culture was in a great many respects backward, disorganized, insular, self-indulgent, and improvident.

Numerous provincially and federally sponsored inquiries have referred to biases in the criminal justice system in explaining Aboriginals' over-representation. These include the Canadian Corrections Association report, *Indians and the Law* (Monture, 1967); *The Royal Commission on the Donald Marshall Prosecution* (Nova Scotia, 1988); *The Report of the Aboriginal Justice Inquiry of Manitoba* (Manitoba, 1991); *The Task Force of the Criminal Justice System and Its Impact on the Indian and Metis People of Alberta* (Alberta, 1991); *The Report on the Task Force on Federally Sentenced Women* (Correctional Service of Canada, 1991); *Report on Aboriginal Peoples and Canadian Justice* (Law Reform Commission of Canada, 1991); the *Reports of the Saskatchewan Indian and Metis Justice Review Committee* (Indian Justice Review Committee, 1992); and the *Royal Commission on Aboriginal Peoples* (Canada, 1996). The underlying theme of all these reports is that Aboriginal people who encounter the Canadian criminal justice system are confronted with both overt and systemic discrimination.

Academic studies have examined the impact of these structural disadvantages and culturally discriminatory practices, finding that they both contribute significantly to Aboriginal over-representation in prisons. Examining the characteristics of the neighborhoods were inmates previously resided, Fitzgerald and Carrington (2008) found that structural disadvantages explained much of the Aboriginal over-representation in prisons. Utilizing interviews with prisoners, guards and social workers, Grekul and LaBoucane-Benson (2008) also found that structural disadvantages were referenced in explaining over-representation. In addition, prisoners and criminal justice officials alike referenced cultural discrimination and discriminatory effects from labeling as contributing factors.

While it is not necessarily widespread, one of the more disturbing manifestations of this bias is a practice engaged in by members of police forces in Canada variously known as 'starlight tours' and 'midnight rides,' whereby police officers apprehend Aboriginals, before driving them to remote areas and releasing them. In Saskatchewan, several Native peoples have died as a result of this practice. One such case was that of Neil Stonechild in Saskatoon, whose death eventually led to a public inquiry, headed by Justice David Wright. Wright's (2004) report concluded that the incident that resulted in the death of Stonechild was a manifestation of structural and individual racism in the police institutional culture, and that anti-Native racism exists in the police system. However, reflecting ongoing denial of systemic racism in Canada by police, a spokesman for the Saskatoon Police Association commented about the Stonechild casse, 'People freeze to death in Saskatchewan. It happens, we have harsh winters here. The conditions where people freeze to death, it could have easily happened without any explanation. It just happens in Saskatchewan' (quoted in Perraux, 2001). As Tanovich (2006) notes, incidents like the Stonechild case do not appear to be aberrations – police in Vancouver and Victoria (Cernetig, 2007) have also engaged in such practices, and in its 2001 report, Amnesty International noted that the practice of police abandoning Aboriginals was a significant human rights concern for Canada.

There have been recent sentencing amendments and developments in the criminal justice system relating to Native incarceration. In 1996, the Canadian Criminal Code was amended, and under section 718.2, judges were encouraged to consider alternatives to incarceration, with particular attention to the circumstances of (but not exclusive to) Aboriginal offenders[6] (Welsh and Ogloff, 2008). In the *R. v. Gladue* (1999) decision, the Supreme Court concluded:

> The drastic overrepresentation of aboriginal peoples within both the Canadian prison population and the criminal justice system reveals a sad and pressing social problem. It is reasonable to assume that Parliament, in singling out aboriginal offenders for distinct sentencing treatment

in s. 718.2(e) intended to attempt to redress this social problem to some degree.

The court recognized that many Aboriginal offenders come into contact with the criminal justice system as a result of systemic discrimination, while identifying background factors relevant to sentencing, including economic deprivation, high unemployment, substance abuse and the fragmentation of Aboriginal communities. As Roberts and Melchers (2003) note, however, the court made it clear that for the most serious crimes, there should not be a difference in sentencing. This principle was confirmed in the case of *R. v. Wells*, in which the court stated 'the more violent and serious the offense, the more likely as a practical matter that the appropriate sentence will not differ as between Aboriginal and non-Aboriginal offenders' (cited in Roberts and Melchers, 2003).

While in principle this modification to Canada's Criminal Code represents a positive change, it is not likely to provide a 'silver bullet' to cure the over-representation of Aboriginal people in Canadian prisons. Roberts and Melchers' (2003) analysis of trends in Aboriginal incarceration rates from 1978 to 2001 revealed that, although the volume of Aboriginal admissions to custody had declined since 1993–1994, non-Aboriginal rates declined even more, suggesting little progress at the aggregate level. It is also notable that certain segments of the Canadian media have not reacted favorably to this change in sentencing policy. For example, after a judge in the province of Alberta sentenced a Native offender to 1 year's imprisonment for stabbing a person to death, reflecting the fact that 'the accused is an Aboriginal and past injustice have contributed to his commission of this offense,' an editorial in the *Edmonton Sun* noted 'A truly colour-blind justice system sentences people despite their race, not because of it. Getting a lighter sentence because you're an Aboriginal, even a poor, dependent one, is not a treaty right' (January 16, 1999).

While significant reductions in the disproportionate incarceration of Aboriginals will require substantial improvements in their social and economic situations[7] and the elimination of any racial bias in Canada's criminal justice system, there is room for optimism when considering recent changes. For example, as a result of the Supreme Court decision, the city of Toronto has established 'Gladue Court,' available to all Aboriginal persons, which is distinguished by the fact that 'those working in it will have a particular understanding and expertise of the range of programs and services available to Aboriginal people in Toronto' (Gladue Court, 2001). Federally, the Aboriginal Justice Strategy provides funding for community-based justice programs 'that aim to reduce rates of crime and incarceration among Aboriginal people and assists them in assuming greater responsibility and accountability for the local administration of justice within their communities' (Department of Justice Canada, 2008). Several prisons in Canada have also established

Aboriginal healing lodges within the institutions (Nielsen, 2003). In 2009, the juvenile justice system opened the first secure custody facility for Aboriginal youth in Fort Frances, Ontario. The facility offers traditional teachings, Aboriginal history and cultural ceremonies, as well as education, anger management and life skills programs to help Aboriginal youth in conflict with the law (Meadows, 2009).

Blacks, crime and criminal justice

While Blacks comprise approximately 2 percent of Canada's population, in 1997 they constituted over 6 percent of the federal prison population, and the Black incarceration rate of 146/100,000 is several times higher than the rates for either Whites (42/100,000) or Asians (16/100,000). In Ontario, the Commission on Systemic Racism in the Criminal Justice System (Ontario, 1995) noted that the 1992/93 provincial incarceration rate for Black adult males was five times the rate for white adult males. More recently, it has been found that this over-representation of Blacks has been increasing. In 2002, they still constituted 2 percent of Canada's total population, but now made up 6 percent of the incarcerated population and 7 percent of those serving community supervision sentences (Trevethan and Rastin, 2004). While much of the research has indicated that this is a relatively recent phenomenon, Mosher (1998) found that, in 1911, Blacks were incarcerated in Canadian federal prisons at a rate almost 18 times higher than Whites. Additionally, from 1908 to 1960, Blacks convicted of violent offenses received significantly harsher sentences than Whites, particularly when they victimized Whites (Mosher, 1998).

As noted in the introduction, Canadian law enforcement agencies do not systematically collect information on the race of offenders, making it difficult to determine the extent of Blacks' over-representation in criminal offending. However, a number of recent studies in local jurisdictions have documented relatively high levels of arrests and victimization for Blacks. In addition, survey research has revealed that Blacks are much more likely to be apprehended by police. Collectively, these studies have led to concerns, and often heated debate, regarding the existence of racial profiling in particular Canadian jurisdictions. Several members of the media, some legislators and criminal justice system officials have denied the existence of racial profiling. At the same time, they engaged in the racialization of crime, attributing Blacks' disproportionate incarceration rates to alleged cultural deficiencies. But as the National Anti-Racism Council of Canada (2007) noted, 'The troubled relationships between African-Canadians and the criminal justice system, and the police in particular, must be understood in the socio-historical context of enslavement, segregation, exclusion, and legally sanctioned discrimination.'

A 1989 Ontario Task Force on Race Relations and Policing concluded that visible minorities did not believe they were policed fairly (Ontario Human Rights Commission, 2003). Three years later, the Report to the Premier on Racism in Ontario presented by Stephen Lewis (former leader of the Federal New Democratic Party) similarly concluded that visible minorities, particularly African-Canadians, experienced discrimination in policing and the criminal justice system. The more extensive Report of the Commission on Systemic Racism in the Criminal Justice System (Ontario, 1995) presented evidence of extensive racism at virtually all levels of the province's criminal justice system. A study in the Commission's reports compared the processing of 821 black and 832 white adult male offenders charged with various crimes, finding that Blacks were less likely to be released by police before trial, and were more likely to be refused bail, even when other legally relevant factors were taken into consideration. In the same sample, 49 percent of Blacks convicted of the possession of drugs were incarcerated, compared with 18 percent of white drug offenders. In addition, the Commission found evidence of mistreatment of Blacks in Ontario's prison system, including racial segregation within institutions, and differential use of punishment powers by custodial officials against black prisoners.

In response to the Commission's findings, several in the media and criminal justice system denied the existence of racial bias. For example, an editorial in the *Globe and Mail* (January 18, 1996) asserted that the Commission's research was not objective, and implied that the entire effort was a waste of time:

> Racism is about looking at the world through a distorting lens, the better to see what you want to see, the better to avoid a confrontation with unpleasant surprises. This self-reinforcing and parochial world view is unfortunately shared by investigations of racism. So it is with Stephen Lewis' 30-day inquiry into the 1992 Yonge Street "riot" and so it is with the task force he recommended, and its $5 million, two years in the making report.

This denial was also expressed by a general divisional court judge in Ontario, who commented,

> I anticipate that the Commission, driven by the force of political correctness, will find that racism is rampant in the justice system ... a conclusion that will not be based on hard evidence but ... on anecdote and unsubstantiated complaint. Failing all else, the Commission will find invisible racism, visible only to the commissioners.
>
> (Ontario, 1995)

Debates surrounding the existence of racial profiling and bias in the Ontario criminal justice system continued in the late 1990s and intensified following a series of articles published in the *Toronto Star* in October, 2002. The *Star* analyzed approximately 800,000 criminal charges issued by the Toronto Police Service from 1996 to 2002, finding that Blacks were over-represented in certain categories, including drug charges. The analysis also revealed that Blacks were treated more severely after arrest, were less likely to be released at the scene of the encounter and were more likely to be held in custody for bail hearings (Wortley and Tanner, 2003).

In response to the *Star's* allegation of racial profiling, the Toronto Police Union initiated a $2.7 billion class lawsuit (eventually dismissed) on behalf of its 7200 members (Tyler, 2002). Reflective of the theme of denial, law enforcement and other officials dismissed the findings. Toronto Police Chief Julian Fantino commented 'We do not deal with people on the basis of their ethnicity, their race, or any other factor' (Fantino, 2002). The head of the Toronto Police Association, Craig Bromell, similarly asserted 'No racial profiling has ever been conducted by the Toronto Police Service and we question the Star's interpretation of its statistical information' (as quoted in Porter, 2003). The chair of the Toronto Police Services Board, Norm Gardner, described the *Star's* findings as 'reckless' (*Toronto Star*, 2002). Even Toronto's mayor Mel Lastman weighed in, commenting 'I don't believe the Toronto police engage in racial profiling' (ibid.).

An additional response to the *Star's* allegations involved what Tator and Henry (2006: 125) refer to as the 'discourse of competing experts.' Toronto police chief Fantino enlisted two 'experts' on racial profiling to dispute the *Star's* findings. Professor Edward Harvey of the University of Toronto analyzed the same data used in the *Star* series, and claimed that he could find no evidence of racial profiling. Fantino's second 'expert,' the prominent Toronto lawyer Alan Gold, referred to the *Star* articles as 'junk science' (as quoted in Wortley and Tanner, 2003: 374). However, Wortley and Tanner (2003) reviewed Harvey's report and concluded that his claim that racial profiling was not occurring was not valid because his 're-analysis of the data base is plagued with both methodological issues and problems of interpretation' (p. 384).

Additional evidence of racial bias on the part of law enforcement officials in Toronto was provided by Wortley and Tanner's 1994 survey of approximately 1200 residents. The survey revealed that 44 percent of black males reported that they had been stopped by police at least once in the previous 2 years; one-third of the respondents claimed they had been stopped on two or more occasions, compared to 12 percent of white males and 7 percent of Asian males (cited in Wortley and Tanner, 2003). Wortley and Tanner also surveyed over 3400 Toronto high school students in 2002, finding that over half of black students reported being stopped and questioned by police on two or more occasions in the previous 2 years, compared to 23 percent of Whites, 11 percent of Asians, and 8 percent of South Asians (cited in Wortley and Tanner, 2003). Later, when their analysis was questioned and they were accused of making 'baseless' and 'inflammatory' accusations (Gabor, 2004), Wortley and Tanner (2005) reanalyzed their survey data, finding that the evidence of racial profiling still existed even when controlling for involvement in criminal activity, gang membership, drug/alcohol use and participation in public leisure activities. In fact, they found that for those who reported no criminal activity, the likelihood of having been stopped and questioned by the police more than once was many times higher for Blacks than for Whites.

Further, in response to allegations that police in Kingston, Ontario were targeting racial minorities, the Kingston Police Department became the first department in Canada to collect their own data on the racial characteristics of those in which they came into contact. This study found that Blacks were several times more likely than Whites to be stopped (Rankin and Powell, 2008). In response to the findings of the Kingston study, *Globe and Mail* columnist Margaret Wente (2005) continued the theme of denial, saying

[The Kingston study] found that Blacks (who make up only 1% of Kingston's population) are stopped nearly three times as often, per capita, as Whites. Therefore, it concluded, the police are racially biased. But if that's true, the police are also ageist and sexist. Only 7 percent of the people stopped by the police were 55 or older, while 35 percent were between 15 and 24. And roughly three times as many men were stopped than women.

While law enforcement officials and certain members of the media have denied that racial profiling occurs, courts and other official bodies in Canada have acknowledged its existence. For example, in 2003, the Ontario Court of Appeal overturned the drunk-driving conviction of Toronto Raptors basketball player Dee Brown because there was evidence to suggest that the Toronto police had engaged in racial profiling when they stopped him (Tanovich, 2006). Similarly, in 2004, Ontario Superior Court Justice Anne Molloy dismissed drug trafficking charges against black real estate developer Kevin Khan, who, she argued, 'was targeted for [this stop] because of racial profiling. He was a black man with an expensive car' (quoted in Tanovich, 2006). In 2007, an Ontario Human Rights Tribunal decision indicated that there was mounting proof that racial profiling was a 'systemic' practice in police forces. In this case, a black woman from Mississauga, Ontario, was subjected to a 'more intensive, suspicious, and prolonged investigation' due to her skin color (Ontario Human Rights Commission, 2008).

While most of the evidence about the racial profiling of Blacks has come from the province of Ontario, studies have also revealed its existence in Quebec. A 1994 report on the Montreal Urban Community Police Force commissioned by the Quebec government found that the force was poorly supervised, insufficiently trained, inadequately equipped and characterized by a 'totally unacceptable' level of racism (Farnsworth, 1995). And in 2008, the Quebec Human Rights Commission found in favor of four Montreal teenagers who claimed they were victims of racial profiling by the Montreal police (*Toronto Star*, 2008).

In addition to denials of racial profiling, several Canadian reporters have actively engaged in the racialization of crime (or, more specifically, as Tator and Henry (2006: 142) note in the context of Toronto, the 'Jamaicanization' of crime), promoting the notion that Black crime is the result of cultural deficiencies in the black community. After a civil disturbance in Toronto in 1992 following the verdict in the Rodney King case in Los Angeles and the acquittal of two Peel Region police officers in the killing of a black male, *Maclean's* columnist Barbara Amiel (1992) attributed the event to 'a fatally flawed liberal perspective on racism that for the past 30 years has sold Blacks in North America on the notion that nothing in life is their fault, that they are entitled to vent their unhappiness by stealing or destroying what belongs to others.' In early 2006, responding to a number of homicides committed by Blacks in Toronto, *Globe and Mail* columnist Margaret Wente noted 'the gun murder rate in Jamaica is among the highest in the world. But nobody mentioned that. In fact, the word "Jamaica" can't be found in any of these penetrating analyses, even though the police will tell you off the record that 80 percent or more of the city's gun crime is Jamaican related' (cited in Fromm, 2006).

Similarly, in a 2006 column, John McFarlane, editor of *Toronto Life* magazine, noted 'Nobody wants to talk about it, but the increase in gun-related homicides in Toronto has a cultural component. Many of the young men involved – shooters and victims alike – are of Caribbean descent and many are from fatherless homes' (cited in Fromm, 2006). Fromm (2006) further commented 'A cycle of welfare mamas, baby mothers breeding children by serial gangster fathers and doing it all in taxpayer subsidized housing just doesn't cut it.' Furthermore, consistent with the popular argument of Herrnstein and Murray's (1994) *The Bell Curve* that Blacks are less intelligent, Fromm (2006) added 'According to psychologist Richard Lynn, Jamaican IQs average 72 (North American Negroes score 85, Whites 100). Then add in indifferent parenting and superior motor skills and you've got real trouble.'

While it is important to consider racial profiling and the racialization of crime, it is also clear that Blacks, particularly youths, have higher rates of offending and victimization in some Canadian jurisdictions. For instance, an analysis of 113 homicides in the Greater Toronto Area (GTA) in 2007 found that, while African–Canadians represent only 7 percent of the GTA population, they comprised close to 40 percent of the city's homicide victims (McMurtry and Curling, 2008). In response to a fatal shooting of a 9th grade black male in a Toronto high school, the Ontario government created the Commission on the Review of Youth Violence, headed by Alvin Curling, the first black cabinet minister in the province of Ontario, and former Ontario Supreme Court Justice Roy McMurtry. The report concluded that high levels of social inequality in the black community contributed to these high rates of crime, but also noted 'we were taken aback by the extent to which racism is alive and well and wreaking its deeply harmful effect on Ontarians and the very fabric of this province' (ibid.: 35). The report also noted that the Ontario government's 2001 Safe Schools Act, which allowed for suspension or expulsion of students for involvement in certain behaviors was having a disproportionate (negative) impact on racialized students. But in a familiar theme, several media sources criticized the report. *National Post* columnist Craig Offman (2008) referred to it as 'an apocalyptic opinion piece,' and argued that 'as harsh as the judgement ... seemed, there is little hard data in the desk-thumping tone to support it. Do all these anecdotes and indirect data add up to the rampant reawakening of bigotry?'

Asians, other minority groups, crime and criminal justice

As noted above, Asians in Canada have much lower rates of incarceration than both other minority groups and Whites. While they make up 8 percent of the population, they represent only 2 percent of those incarcerated federally and 4 percent of those incarcerated in the community (Trevethan and Rastin, 2004). This under-representation is likely the result of the fact that those of Asian descent do not experience the structural disadvantages of Blacks and Aboriginals. Those of East Asian, South Asian and West Asian (Muslim/Arab) descent have slightly higher poverty rates than Whites, but they are much lower than those found among other minority groups, and they have much higher rates of educational attainment than all other groups, even Whites (Chui et al., 2005; Lindsay, 2001).

However, while perhaps not to the same extent as for Blacks, the Canadian media along with some law enforcement officials have stereotyped Asians as being involved in drug crime and as gang members, both historically and today. That bias is reflected in recent data showing that in 2002, despite making up only 8 percent of Canada's population, 25 percent of those imprisoned and 58 percent of those under community supervision for drug offenses at the federal level were of Asian descent (Trevethan and Rastin, 2004).

Backhouse (1999) has documented the long history of legislation at both the federal and provincial levels in Canada that discriminated against Asian people with respect to immigration, taxation, suffrage and employment. Opposition to Asians and the array of restrictive legislation directed towards them were predicated on the basis of the economic threat they posed to white Canadian workers and their supposed moral inferiority (Mosher, 1998). Between 1878 and 1899, more than 20 statutes with the aim of preventing or restricting the settlement of Asians were passed in the province of British Columbia, where large numbers of Asian males had immigrated in the 1850s to work in the gold mines and later on the construction of the

Canadian Pacific Railroad. The preface to a proposed provincial immigration law in that province starkly illustrated the racist sentiments of British Columbia legislators:

> Whereas [they] are not disposed to be governed by our laws; are dissimilar in habits and occupation from other people; evade the payment of taxes...are governed by pestilential habits; are useless in instances of emergency; habitually desecrate graveyards by the removal of bodies therefrom; and generally the laws governing the whites are found to be inapplicable to Chinese, and such Chinese are inclined to habits subversive to the comfort and well-being of the community.
>
> (quoted in Kobayashi, 1990: 451–2)

In 1875, the Canadian federal government imposed a $50 head tax on Chinese brought into the country by employers, a charge that was increased to $100 in 1899.[8] However, as the result of continued Asian immigration to Canada, and the attendant rise in anti-Asian feelings, in 1923 the Canadian government passed legislation refusing the entry of all Chinese to Canada, which was not repealed until 1947 (Mosher, 1998).

Mosher and Hagan (1994) also note how Canada's first narcotics legislation, the Opium Act of 1908, was passed in response to concerns about Asians' use of opium. In enforcing this law, police across the country focused on Asians, who were also sentenced more severely, particularly in connection with drug trafficking offenses. This discrimination continued during World War II, when more than 21,000 Canadian-born people of Japanese origin were interned in camps and had their property seized. Close to 4000 Japanese–Canadians were deported to Japan after the war, one-third of whom were Canadian citizens (Tanovich, 2006).

More recently, there has been a tendency to stereotype members of Asian groups as being disproportionately involved in organized crime. A 1997 Royal Canadian Mounted Police (RCMP) report noted 'One spin-off of the large Asian organized crime groups is the growing number of Asian youth street gangs. These loosely organized and well armed groups are associated with drug use and drug trafficking, prostitution, and violent crimes such as home invasions and drive-by shootings' (RCMP, 1997). Similarly, a report prepared for the Federal Research Division of the United States Library of Congress warned 'Faced with the likely spread of Asian organized crime groups and given border porosity and immigration laws, for the foreseeable future Canada will continue to serve as an ideal transit point for crime groups to gain a foothold in the United States' (Library of Congress, 2003: 4). This report made reference to the 'Big Circle Boys Gang,' who are 'extensively involved in the South Asian heroin trade and are responsible for a high percentage of the counterfeit credit cards in North America,' and 'Vietnamese organized crime groups,' who are 'expanding rapidly in high-technology crimes and are believed to be involved in the trafficking of women' (p. 4). These stereotypical depictions have also been a prominent feature of local news media reports, particularly in the province of British Columbia, which has a relatively high proportion of Asian immigrants. For example, a Victoria, BC newspaper noted 'At the local level, Asian gangs are involved in a long list of criminal activities, credit card fraud, luxury car theft, prostitution, home invasions, staged vehicle accidents, contract killings, assaults, welfare and employment insurance fraud, drug trafficking, software piracy, loan sharking, and illegal gaming' (Delaney, 2006).

There is also considerable evidence of racial profiling of Asians in Canada. In a 2006 case, the Ontario Supreme Court stayed charges against Van Trong Nguyen, a Vietnamese immigrant who had been charged with operating a marijuana-growing facility. In his investigation, an Ontario Provincial Police officer identified Nguyen and other members of the Canadian Vietnamese community through a land title search, focusing on them because of previous incidents of Vietnamese Canadians being involved in the growing of marijuana. In staying the charges, Mr. Justice Kruzick commented 'It is a stereotypical assumption that because some grow operations have been run by East Asians, that anyone purchasing a new home who is Vietnamese must be conducting a grow operation' (quoted in *Toronto Star*, 2006). Profiling of Filipino youth by law enforcement has also been alleged. Carlo Sayo, Chairman of the Filipino-Canadian Youth Alliance, claimed that young Filipino men in British Columbia are 'routinely stopped by police and asked for their identification based on a "negative stigma" that unfairly associates them with gang activity and the illegal drug trade' (quoted in Hansen, 2009).

After the events of September 11, 2001, there was emerging evidence of profiling of Muslims and Arabs in Canada, facilitated by the passage of Bill C-36, the Anti-Terrorism Act.[9] As Tanovich (2006) notes, after 9/11, the Royal Canadian Mounted Police essentially warned law enforcement and security officials that any young, educated, well-dressed Arab or Muslim male living in Canada could be a terrorist, and therefore had to be investigated. One of the most prominent cases was that of Monia Mazigh and her husband Maher Arar, who were labeled 'Islamic extremists' by the RCMP and the Canadian Security Intelligence Service. Arar was wrongly arrested by American authorities, interrogated and eventually sent to Syria where he was tortured. Subsequently, a Canadian federal government inquiry cleared him and paid him $10 million in compensation (Black, 2007).

Victimization: Hate crimes

Since 1990, there have been rapid increases in Canada's visible minority population (Statistics Canada, 2003), during which time surveys have found many Canadians to be 'less comfortable' with visible minorities (Berry and

Kalin, 1995). Known broadly to involve greater physical and psychological harm for victims (Herek and Berrill, 1992; Levin and McDevitt, 1993) and their communities (OSCE, 2005), hate crimes are uniquely serious. Therefore, any discussion of the experiences with hate crimes of Blacks, Aboriginals and Asians in Canada first requires an understanding of their historical context as a socio-legal issue.

Until recently, Canadian officials and researchers paid minimal attention to hate crimes, first acknowledging them as a social concern in the Cohen Report (Canada, 1966), though it still concluded that they were only isolated incidents. This led to the Hate Propaganda provisions of the Criminal Code in 1970, the first hate crime to be deemed a punishable offense. Then, during the 1970s, 'advocating genocide' was also added, in response to high-profile cases involving Holocaust deniers (Janhevich, 2001). In the early 1990s, increased media and qualitative research attention to hate-related violence and racial profiling in Toronto finally led to meaningful government attention. The first quantitative study of hate crimes found over 1000 such cases reported by only three major police forces, projecting this to estimate that 60,000 such incidents occurred in 1994 alone (Roberts, 1995). Thereafter, hate/bias police units were established and, in 1996, the Sentencing Reform Bill (C-41) legislated stronger punishments for crimes when there was 'evidence that the offence was motivated by bias, prejudice or hate based on race, national or ethnic origin, ... or any other similar factor.' Additionally, this inspired more extensive collection of data on hate crimes, via police reports and victimization surveys.

The prevalence of hate crimes varies by data source, with official police reports suggesting these constitute only 0.04 percent (785 hate crimes, or 2.7/100,000 population) of official crimes (Walsh and Dauvergne, 2009). However, victimization surveys suggest a much greater prevalence, ranging from 3 percent to 9 percent of crimes (Dauvergne et al., 2007; Silver et al., 2004). This discrepancy results from interpretations during police classification (Gannon and Mihorean, 2005) and under-reporting, as less than 40 percent of hate crimes are reported to the police (Walsh and Dauvergne, 2009). Based on limited data, the prevalence appears fairly consistent across time in both victimization surveys (Dauvergne et al., 2007) and police data (Walsh and Dauvergne, 2009). Across all studies, race has consistently been found to be the most common motivation, constituting 60 percent or more of hate crimes (Walsh and Dauvergne, 2009).

Of the racially focused hate crimes, there are distinct differences in victimization between subgroups, though such distinctions rely entirely on official police data. Surprisingly, and perhaps due to data collection practices, Aboriginals experience the fewest hate crimes. Anti-Aboriginal crimes represented only 1 percent of race-based hate crimes in 2001/2002 (Silver et al., 2004), rising slightly to about 3 percent in 2006 and 2007 (Walsh and Dauvergne, 2009).

Blacks, on the other hand, are clearly the most victimized group, as the greatest portion of race-related hate crimes has consistently been anti-Black (Roberts, 1995; Walsh and Dauvergne, 2009). In 2006 and 2007, Toronto, home of the largest Black population and recently publicized racial tensions, reported the greatest number of hate crimes (Walsh and Dauvergne, 2009). Not surprisingly, 15 percent of Blacks reported being worried or very worried about hate crimes, also the most of any group (Silver et al., 2004). However, anti-Black crimes did drop significantly from 2006 (48 percent of race-based crimes) to 2007 (32.8 percent) (Walsh and Dauvergne, 2009).

Other subgroups have hate crime victimization levels that lie between those of Aboriginals and Blacks. East Asians were the second most victimized group in 2007, representing 11.7 percent of race-based hate crimes – an alarming increase from 5.0 percent in 2006. Though still high, crimes targeting South Asians declined steadily – from 18.2 percent in 2001/2002 to 11.3 percent in 2007. Likewise, those against Arabs/West Asians dropped from 13.6 percent in 2001/2002 to 6.2 percent in 2007 (Walsh and Dauvergne, 2009). Continuous victimization has taken a particular toll on South Asians, 13 percent of whom report serious fears about hate crimes. This compares with 10 percent of East Asians, and only 6 percent of Arabs/West Asians (Silver et al., 2004).

Despite limited data, racially motivated hate crimes are an ongoing social problem in Canada (Silver et al., 2004). Echoing findings elsewhere, they have also been associated with heightened psychological consequences, including long-term trauma (Schaffer, 1996), difficulty with daily activities and increased fear and distrust (Dauvergne et al., 2007). These psychological effects also have been found to extend into the victims' communities (Roberts, 1995) to the extent that 11 percent of visible minorities report being worried or very worried about being victims of hate crimes (Silver et al., 2004).

Conclusion

Members of certain racial minority groups are substantially over-represented in Canada's criminal justice system. Racism in the country's legal and justice systems, while perhaps less blatant than its United States counterpart, is no less insidious. With respect to the denial of racism on the part of legislators, criminal justice system officials and members of the media, Backhouse (1999: 274) notes 'To advocate "color blindness" as an ideal for the modern world is to adopt the false mythology of "racelessness" that has plagued the Canadian system for so long. Under current circumstances, it will only serve to condone the continuation of white supremacy across Canadian society.'

While suggestions for increased representation of minority groups in criminal justice system occupations (Stenning, 2003) as one strategy for ameliorating this problem need to be given serious consideration, we also maintain that Canada should implement a system to collect race-based crime (and other) statistics. As the Canadian Race Relations Foundation (n.d.) argued, 'Collecting regular, accurate, and reliable data on the relative socio-economic status of racial and ethnic groups and other dimensions of their identity, including gender, can be instrumental in confronting and eliminating racism and racial discrimination'. Similarly, the McMurtry and Curling (2008: 240) report noted 'The need for race-based data is overwhelming... The need should be obvious: without data we can neither prove nor disprove the extent of racism in any particular part of our society.' Interestingly, as we were writing this chapter, a joint statement from the Canadian Human Rights Commission and the Canadian Race Relations Foundation recommended that police, border guards and security agencies across the country systematically track their interaction with members of the public, a process that would include the collection of information on people's race (*Toronto Star*, 2009). In addition to the collection of race-based crime and socio-economic data, serious efforts to reduce the social and economic inequality experienced by minority groups must be initiated if their disproportional involvement in Canada's criminal justice system is to be curtailed.

Notes

1. Throughout history, the terms "Indian", "Native", "Aboriginal" and "First Nations" have been used to describe these groups in Canada. We use the terms interchangeably here (especially based on their use in original publications), while recognizing that for many in Canada, the term "Indian" is pejorative.
2. It is notable that in any given year the entire country of Canada typically has fewer homicides than several US cities.
3. Aboriginal homicide rates were much higher in the late 1970s, peaking at more than 30/100,000 Canadian Indians in 1978 and 1979 (Silverman and Kennedy, 1993).
4. Full provincial franchise for Natives was not obtained until 1949 in British Columbia and Newfoundland, 1952 in Manitoba, 1954 in Ontario, 1960 in Saskatchewan and the Yukon, 1963 in Prince Edward Island and New Brunswick and 1965 in Alberta. At the federal level, Indians' unconditional right to vote was not established until 1960 (Jefferson, 1994).
5. The right of Indians to consume alcohol off reserves was not established until 1969 in the *Drybones* case. Drybones was found passed out in the city of Yellowknife, and was charged with 'being an Indian' who was 'unlawfully intoxicated off a reserve, contrary to s. 94(b) of the Indian Act. In a Supreme Court of Canada decision, Justice Ritchie wrote 'I am therefore of the opinion that an individual is denied equality before the law if it is made an offence punishable at law, on account of his race, for him to do something which his fellow Canadian is free to do without having committed any offence or having been made subject to any penalty (*R. v. Drybones*, 1969). Tanovich (2006) argues that in many respects, the *Drybones* case represented Canada's symbolic *Brown* v. *Board of Education*.

6. Canada's *Youth Criminal Justice Act* (2003) also includes a similar provision in relation to young offenders.
7. The 2005 'Kelowna Accord' which pledged $5 billion to alleviate Native poverty and to improve their health and education offered some hope in this regard. However, the Liberal party lost the next federal election, and the plan was shelved (MacGregor, 2009).
8. In 2006, Canadian Prime Minister Stephen Harper issued a formal apology for this practice and announced financial redress of $20,000 to an estimated 50 living head tax payers and living spouses of deceased head tax payers (National Anti-Racism Council of Canada, 2007).
9. In addition to increases in profiling of these groups, in the 2-month period between September 11 and November 15, 2001, 115 incidents of various forms of hate crimes against Muslims in Canada were documented (National Anti-Racism Council of Canada, 2007).

References

Alberta. (1991). *The Task Force of the Criminal Justice System and Its Impact on the Indian and Metis People of Alberta*. Edmonton: Justice On Trial.

Amiel, B. (1992). 'Racism: An excuse for riots and theft.' *Maclean's*, May 18.

Amnesty International (2001). *Canada: Amnesty International Report*.

Assembly of First Nations (2006). *A First Nations Diabetes Report Card*. Ottawa: Assembly of First Nations.

Backhouse, C. (1999). *Color Coded: A Legal History of Racism in Canada*. Toronto: University of Toronto Press.

Ball, J. (2008). 'Promoting equality and dignity for Aboriginal children in Canada.' *Institute for Research on Public Policy Choices* 14(7): 1–27.

Beattie, K. (2006). *Adult Correctional Services in Canada, 2004/2005*. Ottawa: Canadian Centre for Justice Statistics.

Black, D. (2007). 'Maher Arar's wife calls for honest debate.' *Toronto Star*, October 17, Retrieved October 17, 2007, from http://www.thestar.com.

Berry, J. W. and Kalin, R. (1995). 'Multicultural and ethnic attitudes in Canada: An overview of the 1991 national survey.' *Canadian Journal of Behavioural Science* 27(3): 301–20.

Brozowski, J., A. Taylor-Butts and S. Johnson. (2006). *Victimization and Offending Among the Aboriginal Population in Canada*. Ottawa: Canadian Centre for Justice Statistics.

Byfield, L. (2001). 'If you wish Indians well, say a prayer for Mr. Nault.' *Alberta Report*, June 25.

Canada (1876–1902). 'Report of the Department of Indian Affairs.' *Sessional Papers*, 44(16): no. 25b–26a. Ottawa: Parliament.

Canada (Cohen Report) (1966). *Report of the Special Committee on Hate Propaganda in Canada*. Ottawa: Queen's Printer.

Canada (1996). *Royal Commission Report on Aboriginal Peoples*. Last retrieved on October 30, 2009, from www.ainc-inac.gc.ca.

Canadian Race Relations Foundation (n.d.) 'A national policy on the collection of race-based statistics.' Retrieved January 22, 2009, from http://www.crr.ca.

Cernetig, M. (2007). 'Inquiry called into death of native man.' *Vancouver Sun*, February 23, Retrieved February 23, 2007, from http://www.vancouversun.com.

Chansonneuve, Deborah (2007). *Addictive Behaviors Among Aboriginal People in Canada.* Ottawa: Aboriginal Healing Foundation.

Chui, T., Tran, K. and Flanders, J. (2005). 'Chinese Canadians: Enriching the Cultural Mosaic.' *Canadian Social Trends.* Catalogue No. 11–008. Ottawa: Statistics Canada.

CNW Group (2007). 'Tribunal rules racial profiling in case against Peel Police.' May 17, Retrieved March 30, 2009, from http://www.newswire.ca.

Correctional Services of Canada (1991). *Creating Choices: The Report of Task Force on Federally Sentenced Women.* Last retrieved October 30, 2009, from www.csc-scc.gc.ca

Curry, B., and Howlett, K. (2007). 'Natives died in droves as Ottawa ignored warnings.' *The Globe and Mail*, April 24, Retrieved March 9, 2009, from http://www.theglobeandmail.com.

Dauvergne, M., Scrim, K. and Brennan, S. (2007). 'Hate Crime in Canada, 2006.' *Canadian Centre for Justice Statistics Profile Series.* No. 17. Statistics Canada Catalogue no. 85F0033M. Retrieved May 15, 2009, from http://www.statcan.gc.ca/pub/85f0033m/85f0033m2008017-eng.htm.

Delaney, J. (2006). 'Asian organized crime thriving in Canada.' *Victoria Epoch Times*, December 8–14, p. 3.

Department of Justice Canada (2008). 'Justice minister announces additional $40 million to help support traditional Aboriginal justice.' Retrieved on August 18, 2009, from www.justice.gc.ca.

Diebel, L. (2008). 'Harper 'sorry' for Native residential schools.' *Toronto Star*, June 12, Retrieved March 15, 2009, from .http://www.thestar.com.

Edmonton Sun (1999). 'Editorial.' January 16.

Fantino, J. (2002). 'We do not do racial profiling.' *Toronto Star*, October 19, Retrieved March 10, 2009, from http://www.thestar.com.

Farnsworth, C. (1995). 'Black in Quebec: Escaping the streets.' *New York Times*, October 13, Retrieved March 10, 2009, from http://www.nytimes.com.

Fitzgerald, R. and Carrington, P. (2008). 'The neighborhood context of urban Aboriginal crime.' *Canadian Journal of Criminology and Criminal Justice* 50: 523–557.

Fromm, P. (2006). 'Toronto's gun crime: The Jamaican connection.' Retrieved January 17, 2009 from http://www.canadafirst.net/jamaicans.html.

Gabor, T. (2004). 'Inflammatory rhetoric on racial profiling can undermine police services.' *Canadian Journal of Criminology and Criminal Justice* 46: 457–466.

Gannon, M. (2004). *Crime Comparisons between Canada and the United States.* Ottawa: Canadian Centre for Justice Statistics.

Gannon, M. and Mihorean, K. (2005). 'Criminal victimization in Canada, 2004.' *Juristat* 25(7). Statistics Canada Catalogue no. 85-002-XPE. Ottawa.

Gannon, M. (2006). *Crime Statistics in Canada, 2005.* Ottawa: Canadian Centre for Justice Statistics.

Gladue Court (2001). *Gladue (Aboriginal Persons) Court – Fact Sheet.* Ontario: Ontario Court of Justice.

Globe and Mail Editorial (1996). 'Unanswered questions on race and crime.' Retrieved on January 18, 2009, from www.cfdp.ca.

Gordon, S. (2005). 'Native abuse victims to get $2 billion.' *Toronto Star*, November 11, Retrieved March 5, 2009, from http://www.thestar.com.

Grekul, J. and P. LaBoucane-Benson. (2008). 'Aboriginal gangs and their (dis)placement: Contextualizing recruitment, membership, and status.' *Canadian Journal of Criminology and Criminal Justice* 50: 59–82.

Hagan, J. (1998). 'Foreward.' in C. Mosher (ed.), *Discrimination and Denial.* Toronto: University of Toronto Press, pp. xi–xii.

Haig-Brown, C. (1991). *Resistance and Renewal: Surviving the Indian Residential School.* Vancouver: Tillacum Library.

Hainsworth, J. (2009). 'Ahead of 2010 Olympics, violence stalks Vancouver.' *Associated Press*, March 28, Retrieved March 28, 2009, from http://www.seattle times.com.

Hale, S. (1990). *Controversies in Sociology.* Toronto: Copp Clark Pitman.

Hansen, D. 2009 (February 25). 'Family claims racial profiling by police on night of son's death.' *Vancouver Sun.* Retrieved February 25, 2009, from http://www. vancouversun.com.

Harding, K. 2007 (July 16). 'Nunavut reeling from soaring suicide rate.' *Globe and Mail.* Retrieved July 16, 2007, from http://www.theglobeandmail.com.

Herek, Gregory M. and Berrill, K. T. (1992). *Hate Crimes: Confronting Violence Against Lesbians and Gay Men.* Newbury Park, CA: Sage Publications.

Herrnstein, R. and Murray, C. (1994). *The Bell Curve.* New York: The Free Press.

Janhevich, D. (2001). 'Hate Crime in Canada: An Overview of Issues and Data Sources.' Catalogue no. 85–551-XIE. Ottawa: Statistics Canada.

Jenness, D. (1932). *The Indians of Canada.* Ottawa: Department of Mines.

Johnson, S. (2005). *Returning to Correctional Services after Release: A Profile of Aborigi-nal and Non-Aboriginal Adults Involved in Saskatchewan Corrections from 1999/100 to 2003/04.* Ottawa: Statistics Canada.

Kobayashi, A. (1990). 'Racism and the law.' *Urban Geography* 11: 447–73.

Latimer, J. and Casey-Foss, L. (2004). *A One-Day Snapshot of Aboriginal Youth in Custody Across Canada: Phase II.* Ottawa: Department of Justice Canada.

Law Reform Commission of Canada (1991). *Report on Aboriginal Peoples and Canadian Justice.* Ottawa: Law Reform Commission.

Levin, Jack and McDevitt, J. (1993). Hate *Crimes: The Rising Tide of Bigotry and Bloodshed.* New York: Plenum Press.

Library of Congress (2003). *Asian Organized Crime and Terrorist Activity in Canada – 1999–2002.* Author.

Lindsay, C. (2001). *Profiles of Ethnic Communities in Canada.* Catalogue no. 89-621-XIE. Ottawa: Statistics Canada.

MacDonald, N. (2009). 'Northern blight.' *Maclean's*, March 23, p. 38.

MacGregor, R. (2009). 'A hand up, not a handout, for Canada's Natives after all.' *The Globe and Mail*, March 30, Retrieved March 30, 2009, from http://www. theglobeandmail.com.

MacQueen, K. (2009). 'The rankings: Canada's most dangerous cities.' *Macleans*, March 5, Retrieved March 31, 2009, from http://www2.macleans.ca.

MacQueen, K. and Treble, P. (2008). 'Canada's most dangerous cities.' *Macleans*, March 24, Retrieved March 30, 2009, from http://www2.macleans.ca.

Manitoba (1991). *The Report of the Aboriginal Justice Inquiry.* Winnipeg: Aboriginal Justice Implementation Commission.

McMurtry, R. and Curling, A. (2008). *The Review of the Roots of Youth Violence.* Toronto: ServiceOntario Publications.

Meadows, B. (2009). 'Secure custody facility opens.' *Thunder Bay Chronicle Journal.* Thunder Bay, Canada. Printed on March 24, 2009.

Mecredi, O. (2000). *Aboriginal Gangs: A Report to the Correctional Service of Canada on Aboriginal Youth Gang Members in the Federal Corrections System.* Ottawa: Correctional Service of Canada.

Meloff, W. and Silverman, R. (1992). 'Canadian kids who kill.' *Canadian Journal of Criminology* 24: 15.

Miller, J. R. (1996). *Shingwauk's Vision: A History of Native Residential Schools*. Toronto: University of Toronto Press.

Monture, G. (1967). *Indians and the Law*. Ottawa: Canadian Corrections Association.

Morris, R. (1985). 'One Indian as good as another – Native people and the Canadian justice system.' *Canadian Dimensions* 19: 7–8.

Mosher, C. and Hagan, J. (1994). 'Constituting class and crime in Upper Canada: The sentencing of narcotics offenders, circa 1908–1953.' *Social Forces* 72: 613–641.

Mosher, C. (1998). *Discrimination and Denial – Systemic Racism in Canada's Legal and Criminal Justice Systems, 1892–1961*. Toronto: University of Toronto Press.

National Anti-Racism Council of Canada. (2007). *Racial Discrimination in Canada*. Toronto.

Nielsen, M. (2003). 'Canadian Aboriginal healing lodges: A model for the United States?', *The Prison Journal* 83: 67–89.

Nova Scotia (1989). *The Royal Commission on the Donald Marshall Prosecution*. Nova Scotia: Royal Commission on the Donald Marshall, Jr. Prosecution.

Offman, C. (2008). 'Racism alive, but without measure.' *National Post*, November 22, Retrieved November 22, 2008, from http://www.nationalpost.com.

Ontario (1995). *Report of the Commission on Systemic Racism in the Criminal Justice System*. Toronto: Commission on Systemic Racism in the Ontario Criminal Justice System.

Ontario Human Rights Commission (2003). *Paying the Price: The Human Costs of Racial Profiling*. Toronto: Ontario Human Rights Commission.

Ontario Human Rights Commission. (2008). *Annual Report: 2007/2008*. Toronto: Ontario Human Rights Commission.

Organization for Security and Cooperation in Europe (OSCE) (2005). 'Combating hate crimes in the OSCE region: An overview of statistics, legislation, and national initiatives.' *Office for Democratic Institutions and Human Rights*. Warsaw, Poland.

Perraux, L. (2001). 'Constable's lawyer: Freezing deaths will taint trial.' *National Post*, September 10, Retrieved September 10, 2001, from http://www.nationalpost.com.

Porter, C. (2002). 'Police union blasts star.' *Toronto Star*, October 22, Retrieved October 22, 2003, from http://www.thestar.com.

Prison Justice Day Committee (2008). *Aboriginal Prisoners*. Vancouver: Author.

R. v. Drybones (1969). *Criminal Reports New Series* 10: 334–356.

R. v. Gladue. (1999). *Supreme Court Reports* 1.

Rankin, J. and Powell, B. (2008). 'The criminals among us.' *Toronto Star*, July 21, Retrieved July 21, 2008, from http://www.thestar.com.

Roberts, J. V. (1995). *Disproportionate Harm: Hate Crime in Canada – An analysis of Recent Statistics* (Working Document WD1995-11e). Ottawa: Department of Justice Canada.

Roberts, J. and Melchers, R. (2003). 'The incarceration of Aboriginal offenders: Trends from 1978 to 2001.' *Canadian Journal of Criminology and Criminal Justice* 45: 211–42.

Rogan, M. (2001). 'An epidemic of gas sniffing decimates Arctic Indian tribe.' *New York Times Magazine*, March 4, Retrieved March 10, 2009, from http://www.nytimes.com.

Royal Canadian Mounted Police (1997). *Understanding Asian Organized Crime*. Last retrieved on October 30, 2009, from www.rcmp-learning.org.

Indian Justice Review Committee (1992). *Reports of the Saskatchewan Indian and Metis Justice Review Committee*. Regina, Saskatchewan: The Committee.

Schmidt, J. (1959). 'Lo the poor, irresponsible, lazy Indian.' *Saturday Night*, November 21, p. 60.

Schaffer, M. (1996). 'Criminal responses to hate-motivated violence: Is Bill C-41 tough enough?' *McGill Law Journal* 41: 199–250.

Scott, J. (1900). 'Indians.' *Canadian Magazine*, p. 210.

Sillas, B. (1997). 'The new Indian wars.' *Alberta Report*, October 20.

Silver, W., Mihorean, K. and Taylor-Butts, A. (2004). 'Hate crime in Canada.' *Juristat* 24(4). Statistics Canada Catalogue no. 85-002-XPE. Ottawa.

Silverman, R. and Kennedy, L. (1993). *Deadly Deeds: Murder in Canada*. Scarborough: Nelson Canada.

Statistics Canada (2002). *Aboriginal Peoples of Canada*. Retrieved on August 12, 2009, from http://www.statcan.gc.ca.

Statistics Canada (2008a). 'Adult and youth correctional services: Key indicators.' Retrieved March 31, 2009, from http://www.statcan.gc.ca.

Statistics Canada (2008b). *Aboriginal Peoples in Canada in 2006*. Ottawa: Author.

Stenning, P. (2003). 'Policing the cultural kaleidoscope: Recent Canadian experience.' *Police and Society* 7: 21–87.

Tanovich, D. (2006). *The Color of Justice – Policing Race in Canada*. Toronto: Irwin Law.

Tator, C. and Henry, F. (2006). *Racial Profiling in Canada – Challenging the Myth of 'A Few Bad Apples*. Toronto: University of Toronto Press.

Toronto Star (2002). 'Analysis raises board hackles.' October 20, Retrieved March 10, 2009, from http://www.thestar.com.

Toronto Star (2006). 'True justice is not blind.' February 18, Retrieved February 18, 2006, from http://www.thestar.com.

Toronto Star (2008). 'Police plan to test racial profiling ruling.' January 18, Retrieved January 18, 2008, from http://www.thestar.com.

Toronto Star (2009). 'Learning from race data.' March 25, Retrieved March 25, 2009, from http://www.thestar.com.

Tyler, T. (2002). 'Judge dismisses suit against the *Star*.' January 25, Retrieved January 25, 2002, from http://www.thestar.com.

Trevethan, S. and Rastin, C. J. (2004). *A Profile of Visible Minority Offenders in the Federal Canadian Correctional System*. Ottawa: Correctional Service of Canada.

Wadden, M. (2006). 'Turning the tide of despair.' *Toronto Star*, November 26, Retrieved November 26, 2006, from http://www.thestar.com.

Walsh, P. and Dauvergne, M. (2009). 'Police-Reported Hate Crime in Canada.' *Juristat* 29(2). Statistics Canada Catalogue no. 85-002-XPE. Ottawa.

Welsh, A. and Ogloff, J. (2008). 'Progressive reforms or maintaining the status quo? An empirical evaluation of the judicial consideration of Aboriginal status in sentencing decisions.' *Canadian Journal of Criminology and Criminal Justice* 50: 491–517.

Wente, M. (2005). 'Is the real problem here crime or systemic racism?' *The Globe and Mail*, May 31, Retrieved May 31, 2005, from http://www.theglobeandmail.com.

Wortley, S. and Tanner, J. (2003). 'Data, denials, and confusion: The racial profiling debate in Toronto.' *Canadian Journal of Criminology and Criminal Justice* 45: 367–89.

Wortley, S. and Tanner, J. (2005). 'Inflammatory rhetoric? Baseless accusations? A response to Gabor's critique of racial profiling research in Canada.' *Canadian Journal of Criminology and Criminal Justice* 47: 581–609.

Wright, D. H. (2004). *The Report of the Commission of Inquiry into Matters Relating to the Death of Neil Stonechild*. Regina, Saskatchewan: The Queen's Printer.

12

Race, Crime and Criminal Justice in South Africa

Kgomotso Pearl Bosilong
CSIR – Defence, Peace, Safety and Security (DPSS), South Africa

Paulin Mbecke
CSIR – Defence, Peace, Safety and Security (DPSS), South Africa

Introduction

As a preamble, this chapter begins with a brief tour of South Africa's justice and political systems, demographics and discourses of race. The brief narrative, which will also allude to situations in Apartheid South Africa, is meant to aid understanding of contemporary issues in race, crime and criminal justice in South Africa.

South Africa is a republic consisting of nine provinces under a semi-federal system. The administrative capital is Pretoria, the legislative capital is Cape Town and the judicial capital is Bloemfontein. Post-Apartheid South Africa has a mixed legal system, a product of the interweaving of a number of distinct legal traditions: a civil law system inherited from its Dutch colonisers, a common law system from its English colonisers and indigenous law, often termed 'African customary law'. These traditions have had a complex interrelationship, with the English influence most apparent in procedural aspects of the legal system and methods of adjudication, and the Roman–Dutch influence most visible in its substantive private law.

As a general rule, South Africa follows English Law in the areas of Procedural Law, the Law of Contracts and the Law of Evidence, while Roman–Dutch Common Law is followed in areas such as the South African Law of Delict (Tort), Law of Persons, Law of Things and Family Law. Today, another strand has been added to this weave: the Constitution, which is the supreme law. In terms of Section 165 of the Constitution of the Republic of South Africa 1996, the judicial authority in South Africa is vested in the courts, which are independent and subject only to both the Constitution and the law. The Department of Justice and Constitutional Development (DoJ&CD) is responsible for the administration of the courts and constitutional development. The DoJ&CD is accountable to the public and the state in rendering accessible, fair, speedy and cost-effective administration of justice in the interests of achieving a safer and more secure South Africa. However, it performs these functions in conjunction with the judiciary, prosecuting authority and various role players such as the South African Police Services (SAPS), the Department of Social Development (DSD), the Department of Correctional Services (DCS) and legal representatives.

The Criminal Justice System (CJS), also known as the Integrated Justice System (IJS), is made up of a variety of processes and interdependent links and is in fact a 'virtual organisation'. The various participating departments cooperate and work together to achieve a common goal, namely the establishment of an integrated justice process for South Africa, premised on the 1996 Constitution of the Republic of South Africa. The Criminal Justice Process is one of four pillars (the other three pillars are the Social Crime Prevention Approach, Developing Institutional Arrangements and Encouraging Community Participation) of the CJS. This pillar aims to increase the efficiency and effectiveness of the CJS, improve access, forge the interdepartmental integration of policy and management in order to coordinate planning, coherent action and ensure effective use of resources [National Crime Prevention Strategy (NCPS) 1996].

South Africa is situated at the southern tip of the African continent. Covering 1.2 million square kilometers, most of the country lies in the sub-tropical region. A large part of the country is on a plateau that rises 1,000 meters above sea level. South Africa is a nation of more than 48 million people. Even though its population has increased in the past decade (primarily as the result of immigration), the country had an annual population growth rate of -0.501 percent in 2008, including immigration. South Africa is home to an estimated 5 million illegal immigrants, including some 3 million Zimbabweans (Statistics South Africa, 2008).

The country is known for its diversity in cultures, languages, and religious beliefs. It is ethnically diverse, with the largest Caucasian, Indian and racially mixed communities in Africa. Statistics South Africa (2008) provided five racial categories by which people could classify themselves, the last of which, 'unspecified/other' drew negligible responses, and these results were omitted. The 2006 midyear estimated figures for the other categories were Black African at 79.5 percent, White at 9.2 percent, Coloured at 8.9 percent and Indian or Asian at 2.5 percent. Although approximately 80 percent of the South African population is black, this category is neither culturally nor linguistically homogenous, as people within this classification speak a number of different Bantu languages, nine of which have official status. Eleven official languages are recognised by the South African Constitution. English is the most commonly spoken language in official and commercial public life; however it is only the fifth most spoken home language (Statistics South Africa, 2008).

South Africa's method of racial categorisation has its roots in the Apartheid law, which had two main components: petty Apartheid and grand

Apartheid. The first aspect – or petty laws – aimed to regulate everyday life in racist ways in order to create a racially divided and unequal way of life for South Africans. Examples of petty Apartheid laws are the Prohibition of Mixed Marriages Act 55 of 1949, which made marriages between whites and people of other races illegal. The Immorality Amendment Act 21 of 1950 went even further to forbid sex between a white and a black, Indian or coloured person. Grand Apartheid separated races on a large scale, by forcing people to live in different places according to their race. This was an outcome of the 1948 white majority vote for Afrikaner nationalism and the consequent series of restrictive laws that were introduced to benefit the white minority and ensure inferior amenities for Africans, Asians and coloureds.

Grand Apartheid required race classification and was achieved through the Population Registration Act 30 of 1950. According to this law, all South Africans had to be classified as white, black, coloured or Indian, and their race then recorded in their identity passes. Official teams or Boards were set up to decide the fate of those people whose race was considered uncertain. This caused much heartache especially for coloured people whose unique mixed race features often led to families being split up after members were assigned different races (South African History Book, Grade 9 [Sa]).

The second element of grand Apartheid was the Group Areas Act 21 of 1950. Until that time, in most towns the different races had coexisted peacefully. This act brought an end to racially mixed residential areas. It defined where people had to live and work as each race was allocated its own area. People had no choice but to move and this act provided the base for forced removals in later years. The Natives' Land Act 1952 divided South Africa into 'white' and 'black' areas, thereby forming the cornerstone of Apartheid. In addition, public facilities were divided along racial lines. Not only were there separate public hospitals, transport, recreation facilities and so forth for different races but these government services also varied in terms of both quantity and quality. Those built for white people were among the best in the world while the others were few and far between and were barely adequate. In government buildings there were different queues for different races (South African History Book, Grade 9 [Sa]).

In another significant development, the Bantu Education Act of 1953 created a separate educational system for black students under the management of the Department of Bantu Education. According to H.F. Verwoerd, who was the Education Minister at the time, the purpose of 'Bantu' Education was to prepare African people for a subordinate role under white minority rule. In the Afrikaans newspaper *Die Burger of 1953*, Verwoerd made the following statement about equality:

> When I have control of 'Native' education, I will reform it so that the 'Natives' will be taught from childhood to realize that equality with Europeans is not for them.

In Apartheid South Africa, white workers had control over the determination of which jobs to allocate to the four racial groups in South Africa. It showed that white workers allowed the desegregation of semi-skilled jobs in the late 1960s and 1970s to take place only because it was economically beneficial to them. The institutional arrangement in which job allocation was determined meant that whites had to explicitly support desegregation before it could occur. In the Industrial Conciliation (IC) Act of 1956, the government gave white workers the power to determine the level of segregation. In a final consolidation of Apartheid, the non-urban 'black' areas were patched together into 'homelands' to create separate 'nation states' for the different ethnic groups. Classification of the population into racial groups under Apartheid had profound economic and social impacts. The rights of African people were systematically stripped away while there was a corresponding growth in the political power of the Afrikaners (Mariotti, 2008).

The situation began to change in 1990, with the beginning of negotiations between the government and anti-Apartheid groups. These culminated in the first national election, which ushered in a full democracy in South Africa on 27 April 1994. The transition into a post-Apartheid republic also witnessed the transitioning of South Africa's race discourse. Race discourse has two particular turns: the Apartheid and post-Apartheid eras. In both contexts and in particular in the case of the former, 'race' has highlighted itself as a socially and legally constructed concept, which over time has served as key support for white-vested social and political interests. Embedded within the social construction process of 'race' is racism, which, according to Anthias and Yuval-Davis (1992), is not only an ideology or discourse. They argue that racism also concerns the ability of a group to impose their beliefs as hegemonic, and as the basis for a denial of rights and equality. This has been and still is the case in South African society, impacting negatively on the provision of criminal justice services.

Racial discrimination was institutionalised, legalised and internalised for the benefit of Whites. The institutionalisation of racial discrimination was intended to ensure that white people retained power and privileges. Segregation was designed in such a way that white people had no competition for land or employment from the black population (Africans, Indians and coloured). As Jennet and Stewart (1987) state, 'apartheid was introduced less as a result of prejudice or because people had to be separated but mainly to establish the superiority of whites over blacks'. The consequences of this, however, were to create and entrench prejudiced and racist beliefs in the white population, and to make 'race' one of the defining characteristics of identity in South Africa (Allen, no date). Also notable was the creation of 'race' as a mechanism for violence under the Apartheid regime. 'Race', in and of itself, was the social and psychological reality through which repression and violence functioned in South Africa. South Africans saw the world literally in 'black' and 'white' terms and violence was used commonly to maintain this status quo.

However, during the first post-Apartheid or Mandela era (1994–1999), a new vocabulary emerged to describe the social order. This vocabulary spoke in terms of nationhood, unity, racial harmony and reconciliation. South Africa became labelled as a 'rainbow nation'. Reference to 'race' entered a sensitive and delicate terrain (Fullard, 2004). The notion of the 'rainbow nation' was a positive attempt to give South Africans a new language for speaking about – and to – each other, but at the same time it rendered the real, often violent, consequences of 'race' invisible. During the Mandela era, there was little national debate about how 'race' had influenced past human rights violations. Research by the Centre for the Study of Violence and Reconciliation (CSVR) demonstrated that there was also little recognition that race continues to shape identity and interactions – violent or not – within the present (Harris, 2004).

Consequently, efforts made by the new South Africa are not yet maximal because race continues to be a powerful factor in determining which groups have access to resources and opportunities. The effects of past divisive social and political policies in South Africa continue to be felt, although in a more lenient way than during the Apartheid period.

Offending and criminal justice

South Africa has the highest levels of violent crime in the world. In 2007, South Africans were victims of more than 19,000 murders, 52,000 rapes and attempted rapes, 218,000 serious assaults and 126,000 robberies with aggravating circumstances, among a total of more than 2 million crimes (South African Institute of Race Relation (SAIRR), 2008). Loots (2005) maintain that for most South Africans, particularly the poor, crime, and in particular violent crime, is not a recent phenomenon. Extreme levels of inequality and decades of political conflict have produced a society prone to violent crime. Evidence indicates that crime rates in black townships have been high for years, but that racial segregation largely shielded or isolated whites from its effects. The indication here is that offending, to some extent, finds an explanation on the way non-whites (specifically blacks from townships) have behaved or perpetrated violent crimes.

In contrast to the Apartheid period, when inequality echoed the division between non-whites (especially blacks) and whites, the post-Apartheid period has seen rising levels of inequality within the black community. The breakdown of communal solidarity linked to the dissolution of Apartheid and the increased social mobility of sections of society not only undermines cohesion but also reinforces insecurity about personal worth (Bruce, 2006). According to Bruce (2006), these insecurities could contribute to gender and racial violence as well as to aggression against other men from within their own social group. For example, low self-esteem and status insecurity might take certain forms in the coloured community and might help to explain the high levels of violence in this community. Linked partly to the continuing internalisation of racist concepts, members of the coloured community might be prone to see themselves, in racist terms, as lacking worth simply because of the colour of their skin. There have been claims that certain communities are affected by high levels of violence and that members of such communities are more willing to use violence in their everyday lives. The theory is that these people exist on the fringes of society and create their own rules of behaviour. These subcultures see violence and are more willing to use violence in situations where other people would not (Thomson, 2004).

The coloured community would seem to represent the extreme of this violent culture. They have a long history of unemployment, inadequate housing and health care, along with high rates of alcohol abuse and family dislocation. The high number of gangs in the coloured community is a result of this phenomenon. Young people compose the majority of gang membership and they use the gang structure to exert some power over the often-chaotic and disadvantaged environment in which they live (Healey, 2000). The gangs fill the gaps in service provision and socio-economic opportunities in the community by giving young males a sense of identity as well as opportunities for economic improvement and for gaining a sense of power, acceptance and purpose. Gang formation and involvement in South Africa is inextricable from the history of Apartheid. As noted by the National Institute for Crime Prevention and Rehabilitation of Offenders (NICRO) and the Institute of Criminology (1990), Apartheid legislation contributed substantially to the growth of gangsterism in both the African and the so-called coloured urban communities. The Group Areas Act, the pass laws, the migrant labour system and the job reservation laws all played roles in disturbing the careful web of internal authority and control in these areas. Gangs use violence to achieve their goals and have normalised the carrying and use of weapons.

There are shocking statistics on the Department of Correctional Services Web site – at end of 2005, 3 percent of the South African 'coloured' population was in prison, compared to approximately 0.06 percent of any other race group (Black, White and Asian collectively). Coloured people represent only 9 percent of the national population, but make up 18 percent of the national prison population (Leggett, 2004). According to SAIRR (2008), members of the coloured population are incarcerated at a rate almost double that of black South Africans. Evidence suggests that the higher prison rate for the coloured population could be attributed to the prevalence of gangsterism, alcohol and drug abuse among this population group. The coloured community has a long history of alcohol abuse, which was encouraged through the 'Dop System' (paying employees with alcohol), and it is not surprising that this sector of the population suffers from high rates of violence (Thomson, 2004). In October 2007, some 80 percent of the South African prison population was made up of Africans who also made up 79 percent of the entire South African population. However, the coloured population was incarcerated at a rate of almost 651 per 100,000 people, almost twice the imprisonment rate of the African population (342 per 100,000). White and Indian populations were incarcerated at the same rate of around 60 per 100 000 people (SAIRR, 2008). Owing to the relatively greater incomes of the white and Indian populations and their greater levels of education it might well be the case that they enjoyed a superior standard of legal representation than did the other two population groups, and could thus avoid jail (SAIRR, 2008).

South Africa's crime problem is not a recent phenomenon. Levels of crime under the Apartheid regime were very high, although they often remained unseen and under-reported given their concentration among poor and black communities. Social exclusion as a result of Apartheid policies gave rise to conditions conducive to criminality. Sachs (1985) argued that there was no lack of law in Apartheid South Africa but the law that existed was a law that protected the racist state in its violence against the people. The law expressly denied fundamental rights and freedoms. It reserved 87 percent of the surface area of the country for the permanent ownership of the dominant racial minority; it forced the rest of the population to live in reserves, locations, compounds and ghettos; it allocated each individual to a particular racial group with differential rights and duties; it controlled the movement and residence of workers; and it denied to the voteless and dispossessed majority the right even to campaign for basic rights.

The Apartheid police created crimes in its concern to erect moral, economic and political boundaries between statutorily defined races. South Africa demonstrated that crime and injustice through the law could manifest in two ways: first, various official enactments 'legalised' the implementation of the cruel Apartheid programme, authorising state officials to dispossess and humiliate citizens on a massive scale as well as to use force to repress those who resisted; second, when state officials acted outside the wide authority given to them and indulged in massacres and torture, laws were passed to grant blanket indemnity to those responsible (Sachs, 1985). As a direct consequence, the privileged white minority was protected from the impact of crime by the system of policing which aimed to isolate violence in black areas and prevent its spread to wealthy and white localities. Other areas of the South African criminal justice system were affected by the 'race' factor. The history of Apartheid and its consequent racial and class variations in the respective compositions of the judiciary and the clientele of the criminal justice system had detrimental effects on the administration of justice and notably in the administration of the death penalty.

For over 40 years, the black majority suffered widespread, systematic human rights violations under white minority governments, with a hugely disproportionate percentage of Africans on death row. According to Mariotti (2008), Amnesty International (AI) reported in 2002 that between June 1982 and June 1983, 81 blacks were convicted of murdering whites and of these 38 were hanged. By contrast, of the 52 whites convicted of murdering whites, only one was hanged – and none of the 21 whites convicted of murdering blacks were hanged. There was an arbitrariness identified at every stage of the death penalty process: police investigation, prosecutor's presentation, defence's effectiveness, trial judges' personality and attitude to capital punishment and appeal judges selected. This combined with the social and cultural divides between defendants and the almost exclusively white middle-class judges before whom they appeared resulted in disparate justice (Fagborun, 2002). In addition, trial proceedings were conducted in either English or Afrikaans, which were spoken and understood by judges but of which many defendants had imperfect understanding, if any. Interpreters were often needed for witness evidence and discourse between judge and defendant, which also affected the fairness of the proceedings. Most defendants could not afford legal assistance and defence counsel under the pro deo system were often young, inexperienced and from a different race, hence the necessity of an interpreter. Pro deo counsel were paid a nominal fee, and lacked the financial resources to undertake necessary investigations and research, employ expert witnesses, gain advice on matters relevant to sentencing, trace witnesses and generally conduct an effective defence (ibid.). Poverty, race and chance influenced the outcomes of capital cases and the decision about who would live or die. Race affected every aspect of South African life thus Apartheid's history and differences in judges and defendants' cultural and class backgrounds detrimentally affected the judicial system, including the administration of the death penalty (ibid.).

In 1997, the Constitutional Court abolished the death penalty. One of the reasons cited for this abolition was that race and poverty affected the administration of the death penalty (Fagborun, 2002). The abolition of the death penalty may have eradicated one of the glaring and most violent forms of racism, but the thinking that created this racially based form of punishment is still reflected in other legitimised forms of penal responses in contemporary South Africa. Recent media coverage makes it clear that race is still playing a negative role in sentencing. In an article in the *Sowetan* newspaper (28 January 2009), a white senior public prosecutor was accused by her colleagues of playing the 'race' card when prosecuting minors. Carlette Muller was responsible for prosecuting criminal cases involving minors in the Johannesburg region. Social workers, police and prosecutors believed that Muller preferred to send black children to court while withdrawing cases involving their white counterparts. 'This leaves black children with criminal records for life,' said a concerned senior justice official. Muller's colleagues complained to the National Prosecuting Authority. They also approached the senior magistrate at the Johannesburg family court to deal with the matter.

In August 2008, Muller apparently decided to prosecute a 12-year-old black child despite recommendations by social workers that the child be sent to a rehabilitation programme. The minor was accused of stealing clothes worth R1,000 (70 British pounds). A month earlier Muller had recommended that a 16-year-old white girl arrested for the theft of clothes valued at R2,900 (200 British pounds) be sent to a rehabilitation centre. In this case the suspect's mother had testified that her daughter was a drug abuser and that she was stealing things from home in order to support her habit. Muller had also withdrawn theft charges against a 16-year-old white youth despite social workers requesting the boy be detained at a centre while they investigated his case. In the same newspaper report on the Muller case of January 2009, the chairman of the Parliamentary Portfolio Committee on Correctional Services was also reported as stating that social workers and other prison officials had complained that whenever a black child was arrested they were denied bail but when a white child was involved prosecutors went out of their way to get relatives or guardians so that the juvenile could be released. He stated: 'We have heard that some of the prosecutors are not consistent when they apply the law' (*Sowetan*, 28 January 2009).

Crime victimisation and criminal justice

Crime in South Africa, and in particular violent crime, is at exceedingly high levels and the risk of victimisation of citizens, residents and visitors is inordinately high. Available crime statistics and victim surveys explain the extent to which crime, as well as the nature and efficacy of the state's response to it, has become one of the focuses for policy and political debate in South Africa. The South African Law Commission argues that, with the possible exception of job creation and the economy, no single issue of governance comes close to the levels of attention and concern associated with the problems of crime, criminality and victimisation (South African Law Commission, 2001).

Whilst violent crime in South Africa is widespread, anecdotal and statistical evidence show that data on rates of crime victimisation in South Africa are inadequate for a variety of reasons:

- Police crime statistics are generally regarded as unreliable because they reflect only those crimes, which are: (a) reported to the police; and (b) recorded by them. This means that a large number of crimes go either unreported or unrecorded;
- Assessments of the South African Police Services (SAPS) systems continue to reflect concerns that the systems used by the SAPS for the gathering of crime statistics are either not properly understood or not properly utilised by police officers; and
- Victimisation surveys, which seek to assess levels of crime and to capture the extent of under-reporting, are relatively new initiatives. As such,

they cannot be used to measure trends over time (South African Law Commission, 2001).

Because of widespread crime and violence, everyone is forced to think of themselves as potential victims. Race, class and gender are significant determinants of the nature of victimisation in South Africa. The wealthy are victims of property crime; they are also victims of violent crime, many of them apparently gratuitous. While it is true that affluent neighbourhoods are targeted as providing rich pickings, poor communities are not immune to property theft. The poor are victims of violent crime as well as property crime and in line with Fattah's (1991 cited in Davis and Snyman 2005) observation, households with higher incomes are more likely to be victims of property crime rather than violent crime. Poverty increases the vulnerability to criminal victimisation and increases the impact of individual crimes on their victims. Often, socio-economically deprived victims have less access to support and assistance; they are, for instance, unlikely to have insurance or to be able to replace any stolen goods. Property crimes (where the victim will claim on the insurance) are believed to have some of the highest rates of reporting, since a police case number is usually a prerequisite for filing an insurance claim. It follows that where there is no likelihood of recovery from insurance, the reporting rate will be lower. This leads to a skewed perception that the more affluent members of society suffer higher levels of property theft.

However, if international experience holds true in South Africa, indications are that most crimes are committed within close proximity of the criminal's home. Poor criminals will seek out the closest 'attractive target' rather than seeking out more distant opportunities (Stanko, 2002). Given the historical perspective in which the majority of poorer people in South Africa were forced to live a considerable distance from more affluent communities and were not allowed access to such communities, it is likely that a similar pattern exists, once again reinforcing the vulnerability of poor people to not only interpersonal but also property crimes. The historical engineering of Apartheid South Africa served not only to increase the vulnerability of poor communities but also to create a false picture of crime trends and patterns, as it was unlikely that the majority of victims could expect to receive a positive or service-oriented response from the police, thus reducing the likelihood of reporting. Interpersonal crimes exhibit no demographic favouritism but, once again, poverty increases the levels of vulnerability and risk. The lack of privacy in shacks and shanties, or even in those houses built under the 'Reconstruction and Development Programme' (RDP), overcrowding, migration factors, the inadequate supervision of children, high levels of alcohol abuse and gang activity all bring with them increased vulnerability and victimisation (Council for Scientific and Industrial Research and U-Managing Conflict, 2003).

In Zedner's (1997 cited in Frank 2007) UK-based analysis of victimisation, she observes that the socio-economically marginalised and similar vulnerable social groups are not only more fearful of crime but are likely to suffer higher levels of stress when victimised. Zedner (ibid.) also states:

> Criminal damage, theft and burglary are all likely to place heavier burdens on those with fewer financial resources, particularly because these are the very groups least likely to be insured against such loss. Generalised feelings of vulnerability amongst groups such as women, ethnic minorities, and the elderly also appear to magnify the impact of crime. Lack of ability to resist or to defend oneself against an attacker may amplify pre-existing feelings of vulnerability.
>
> (Frank, 2007: 9)

Victim surveys conducted in South Africa between 1997 and 2000 show that the poor, the majority of whom are black or coloured and live in the townships, are at a greater risk of being victims of interpersonal violent crimes as well as violent property crimes like robbery. By comparison, wealthy people living in the suburbs are most at risk of property crimes, in particular vehicle theft and burglary (Schonteich and Louw, 2001). On the specific issue of criminal victimisation by race, a survey by the Institute for Security Studies (ISS) found that coloured people – who constituted 49 percent of the sample population – were victimised the most, followed by whites and blacks. Across crime types, it appears that both black and coloured people are disproportionately victimised in terms of the populations they represent while whites are slightly less at risk of victimisation. When analysed according to the type of crime, black and coloured people are disproportionately victimised by violent crimes while whites are largely victimised by property crime (Camerer et al., 1998). This racial disparity in experiences of crime victimisation includes murder. Research by the Medical Research Council (MRC) cited in News24 (2004) reported that blacks were 17 times more likely to be victims of murder than whites; whites were more likely to commit suicide than be murdered.

There are remarkable differences in the levels of repeat victimisation experienced by different races, with coloured people far more likely to become repeat victims than either blacks or whites – especially in relation to assault. This raises a number of questions about protection and lifestyle and points to the fact that in 37 percent of cases, victims of assault and their perpetrators were known to each other by name. The 2003 Victims of Crime Survey conducted by the Institute for Security Studies (ISS) (which focused on respondents aged 16 and above) indicated that 23 percent of South Africans were victims of crime between September 2002 and August 2003 (Burton et al., 2004). Almost 80 percent of violent crime victims in South Africa are black, which is highly above average considering that blacks make up

75 percent of the population (Davis and Snyman 2005). Davis and Snyman (ibid.) cites Mawby and Walklate's (1994) observation of a similar situation with reference to England. Therein, black people experience more personal and household crime than whites.

In South Africa, the disproportionate level of black criminal victimisation can be attributed to the fact that many black people live in areas where there are high levels of unemployment and poverty. This fact ties in with Fattah's (1991 cited in Davis and Snyman 2005) claim that the poorest people appear to be the most likely victims of crime because they live in crime-prone areas. In 'new' South Africa, the majority of black people still live under dire circumstances in the poorest areas, that is, in squatter camps or informal settlements where guardianship – in terms of effective security – is limited. Black and coloured residents of Cape Town are mostly affected by violent and property crime while white residents are affected by property crime. The aforementioned ISS victim survey indicates that those residents most at risk of crime are coloured men between the ages of 21 and 35 and their exposure to criminal victimisation is due to socio-economic factors such as long history of unemployment, inadequate housing and health care, high rates of alcohol use and family dislocation (Camerer et al., 1998).

Clearly, criminal victimisation does not affect people equally and a variety of social factors – race, class, age and gender – play individual and collective roles in determining who is most at risk of victimisation by crime and particular crime types. Such factors can determine how people respond to their feeling of vulnerability in terms of preventing crime victimisation. In South Africa, the rich and even the moderately well-off blacks and whites live behind barred windows, with guard dogs, security gates and electric fences. Because of the high level of victimisation and the violent nature of crime, the rich – whites and blacks – will resort to expensive security measures. However, a survey conducted by the Hunan Science Research Council (HSRC) in 2004 reveals that only 2 percent of blacks have a private security or armed response system in contrast to 45 percent of whites. This demonstrates that the preoccupation with criminal violence and victimisation plays out in racially, as well as economically, defined ways (Valji et al., 2004).

Policy and practice responses to criminal victimisation have also functioned along the lines of 'race' and related factors. The CSVR acknowledged that the historical engineering of Apartheid South Africa served not only to increase the vulnerability of poor communities. It also created a false picture of crime trends and patterns, as it was unlikely that the majority of victims (non-white) could expect a positive or service-oriented response from the police, thus reducing the likelihood of reporting. As already indicated, offenders with white victims were more likely to face the death penalty under Apartheid. Amnesty International report that a black defendant convicted of killing a white person had a greater chance of receiving the death penalty than in any other racial combination (Fagborun, 2002).

Prior to 1994, victimology under Apartheid was strongly political, and service delivery was left to feminists and activists. The government only provided compensation services to white victims of political violence through the Terrorism Fund, while anti-Apartheid organisations supported victims of the struggle. In some white communities, a Eurocentric approach towards service delivery was followed whereas in the townships the victims were simply ignored (Davis and Snyman, 2005). At the time, policing efforts in South Africa were aimed primarily at enforcing Apartheid legislation, not at preventing crime. This largely reactive approach to policing has meant that the police have little experience of preventive interventions regarding crime.

In sum, South Africa has only recently developed enough to be in line with international victimological trends. In the past, there were narrow legalistic and highly politicised victims of crime. Since 1994, the transformation of the police from Law and Order to Safety and Security has in effect changed the understanding of crime and of the levels of victimisation experienced by all communities in South Africa (Rauch, 1998). The South African Police Service Act 1995, the Victim Charter and other policies facilitate the understanding of crime and victimisation and the appropriate way of dealing with victims of crime (Rauch, 1998). The current Department of Safety and Security plays a crucial role in the process of societal transition through monitoring, evaluation and guiding the transformation of the police. The Department oversees the South African Police Service (SAPS) for crime investigation, combating and prevention through visible policing, and the Independent Complaints Directorate for all complaints against members of SAPS. The transformation process within the police, as well as the limited resources available for carrying out their duties, will of necessity induce a greater focus on preventive measures (Camerer, 1996). In this regard, South Africa's approach to the prevention, reduction of criminality and victimisation focuses on three fundamentals or 'basic elements' of crime as described in the South African Manual for Community Based Crime Prevention (National Crime prevention Centre, 2000: 4). They are:

- Victims: Crime prevention initiatives could consider what makes victims vulnerable and/or attractive targets.
- Offenders: Crime prevention initiatives could focus on what makes offenders both likely to commit, and also capable of committing, the crime.
- The environment: Crime prevention initiatives could focus on designing out factors in the environment that create the opportunities for crime or facilitate criminal intent.

Conclusion

The establishment of the post-Apartheid regime in South Africa has not led to the achievement of equality. Harris (2004) points out that within South Africa's transition to democracy, the issues of race, racism and violence have not remained static. Rather, these expressions of intolerance have found creative ways to change with the political order. The South African Constitution outlaws racism, yet racial prejudice is a clear feature of both Apartheid and post-Apartheid society. In post-Apartheid South Africa instances of 'old-style' actions of insensitive racism reflect continuity with the ideology of Apartheid. In other instances, 'newer' patterns of prejudice (for example, xenophobic actions against foreigners) suggest shifts in the targets and tactics of racism in South Africa. Race has continued to play a critical role in offending and criminal victimisation in South Africa, and addressing this fact consists of identifying and remedying to policies and practices that continue to advantage some social groups at the expense of others.

Effective law enforcement, education, poverty alleviation and the application of sound crime prevention practices can reduce the vulnerability of victims to crime and offer them better protection. There is an expectation that government should 'do something' to reduce crime, and while it is true that crime will not decrease without sustained improvements to the criminal justice system and more effective service delivery to the victims of crime, crime is everybody's business and requires a long-term, sustained effort by all South Africans to reject criminal behaviour.

References

Allen, D. (no date) *Race, Crime and Social Exclusion: A Qualitative Study of White Women's Fear of Crime in Johannesburg.* http://www.springerlink.com/content/vylrucphx4gcjjk7/fulltext.pdf. [O] (accessed on 26 July 2008).

Anthias, F. and Yuval-Davis, N. (1992) Rationalized Boundaries: Race, Gender, Color, Class and the Racism Struggle. http://www.omct.org/pdf/ESCR/2006/intl_conference2005/ii_b_4_violence_south_africa_profile.pdf. [O] (accessed on 26 July 2008).

Bruce, D. (2006)'Racism, Self-esteem and Violence in South Africa: Gaps in the NCPS' Explanation?', *Crime Quarterly*, no. 17.

Burton, P., Du Plessis, A., Leggett, T., Louw, A., Mistry, D. and Van Vuuren, H. (2004) National Victims of Crime Survey, South Africa, 2003, monograph 101. Institute for Security Studies, [O]: available http://www.iss.org.za/pubs/monographs/N0101.htm (accessed on 22 October 2008).

Camerer, L. (1996) *Policing the Transformation*, Monograph No. 3, April 1996. Cape Town South Africa: Institute for Security Studies (ISS).

Camerer, L., Louw, A., Shaw, A., Artz, L. and Scharf, W. (1998) *Results of a City Victim Survey*, Monograph vol. 23, April 1998. Cape Town, South Africa: Institute for Security Studies (ISS).

Council for Scientific and Industrial Research (2004) An Overview of Enclosed Neighbourhoods in South Africa. http://www.csir.co.za/plsql/ptl0002/PTL0002_PGE015PRODUCT? PRODUCT_NO=1600817 (accessed on 20 July 2004).

Council for Scientific and Industrial Research and U-Managing Conflict (2003) *Local Crime Prevention Toolkit: Strategic Planning Workbook*. Pretoria: Council for Scientific and Industrial Research and U-Managing Conflict.

Davis, L. and Snyman, L. (2005) *Victimology in South Africa*. Pretoria: van Schaik Publisher.

Fagborun, M. (2002) *Race and the Administration of the Death Penalty: An International Perspective*. http://www.wmin.ac.uk/law/pdf/Morayo%20Fagborun.pdf.

Fattah, E.A. (1991) *Understanding Crime Victimisation*. Scarborough, Ontario: Prentice Hall.

Frank, C. (2007) *Victimisation in South Africa and the Needs of Crime Victims: A Review of Victim Policy in South Africa*, Monograph no 137, July 2007,: Institute for Security Studies, Pretoria, South Africa.

Fullard, M. (2004) 'Dis-placing Race: The South African Truth and Reconciliation Commission (TRC) and Interpretations of Violence', in *Race and Citizenship in Transition Series*, Centre for the Study of Violence and Reconciliation, Braamfontein, South Africa.

Harris, B. (2004) *Arranging Prejudice: Exploring Hate Crime in Post-Apartheid South Africa*, http://www.csvr.org.za/docs/racism/arrangingprejudice.pdf. [O] (accessed on 22 July 2008).

Healey, S. (2000) *Finding Social Control in the Western Cape: The Role of Gangs in the Current Context*, University of Cape Town, Cape Town, South Africa.

Jennet, C. and Stewart, R. (eds) (1987) *Three Worlds of Inequality: Race, Class and Gender*. South Melbourne: Macmillan of Australia.

Leggett, T. (2004) Still marginal: Crime in the Coloured Community, ISS Monograph, *Crime Quarterly*, no.7. http://www.iss.co.za/pubs/CrimeQ/No.7/Leggett2.pdf. [O] (accessed on 20 October 2008).

Loots, C. (2005) *Violence in South Africa: The Human Rights Institute of South Africa*. South Africa: Human Rights Institute of South Africa, Pretoria, South Africa.

Mariotti, M. (2008) Desegregating Labor Markets during the Apartheid Regime. http://www.ekon.sun.ac.za/ehssa/Mariotti.pdf.

Mawby, R.I. and Walklate, S. (1994) *Critical Victimology*. London: Sage.

National Crime Prevention Centre (2000) South African Manual for Community Based Crime Prevention, [O], http://www.saps.gov.za/crime_prevention/community/crimeprevent.pdf (accessed on 22 October 2008).

National Crime Prevention Strategy (1996) Crime Prevention Strategy [O]available http://www.info.gov.za/otherdocs/1996/crime1.htm (accessed on 20 March 2008).

National Institute for Crime Prevention and Rehabilitation of Offenders, and the Institute of Criminology (1990) *Gangs: The Search for Self Respect*. University of Cape Town, Cape Town, South Africa.

News 24 (2004) Crime hits some harder, News 24[O]. http://www.news24.com/Content/SouthAfrica/DecadeofFreedom/1061/976dfff7fdda447eb02a4ebd946ea070/22-04-2004%2003-04/Crime_hits_some_harder (accessed, 22 October 2008).

Rauch, J. (1998) *The Role of Provincial Executives in Safety and Security in South Africa: A Policy Analysis*: Centre for the Study of Violence and Reconciliation, Braamfontein, South Africa.

Sachs, A. (1985) Apartheid as an International Crime: State Criminality in South Africa. http://www.anc.org.za/ancdocs/history/campaigns/legal/part3.html. [O] (accessed 16 September 2008).

Schonteich M. and Louw A. (2001) *Crime in South Africa: A Country and City Profile*, ISS Paper 49, April 2001.: Institute for Security Studies, Pretoria, South Africa.

South African Institute of Race Relations (2008) Fight against Crime is a Race against Race Hatred. http://www.sairr.org.za/press-office/institute-opinion/fight-against-crime-is-a-race-against-race-hatred.html. [O] (accessed on 22 October 2008).

South African Law Commission (2001) A Compensation Scheme for Victims of Crime in South Africa, Discussion Paper 97, Project 82, Sentencing. http://www.saflii.org/za/other/zalc/dp/97/97-CHAPTER.html (accessed on 02 October 2008).

South African History, Grade 9 [Sa] Apartheid in South Africa: How it Affected Peoples' Lives. [O]. http//www.sahistory.org.za/pages/hands-onclassroom/classroom/pages/projects/grade9/lesson6/03-effects-apartheid.htm (accessed on 02 October 2008).

Stanko, E.A. (2002). *Violence: The International Library of Criminology, Criminal Justice and Penology*. London: Royal Holloway, University of London.

Statistics South Africa (2008) South Africa Population, June 2008 [O]available: http://www.southafrica.info/about/people/population.htm (accessed on 20 March 2008).

Thomson, J. (2004) 'A Murderous Legacy: Coloured homicide trends in South Africa', Institute for Security Study Monograph', *Crime Quarterly*, no.7, Pretoria, South Africa.

Valji, N., Harris, B. and Simpson, G. (2004) Crime Security and Fear of the Other. http://www.csvr.org.za/wits/articles/artvhgs.htm. [O] (accessed on 14 September 2008).

Zedner, L. (1997). 'Victims', in M. Maguire, R. Morgan and R. Reiner (eds), *The Oxford Handbook of Criminology*, 2nd edition. Oxford: Oxford University Press.

13
Race, Crime and Criminal Justice in the United States of America

Daniel E. Georges-Abeyie
Texas Southern University, USA

Introduction

The Michael Hall article, 'Thirty-Seven Men', published in the November 2008 issue of *Texas Monthly* (Hall, November 2008, pp. 148–64), features short histories of 37 men, all but seven of whom were Non-White, who collectively spent 525 years in Texas Department of Corrections facilities for crimes they did not commit. The 37 DNA exonerations were a fraction of the 222 recent exonerations identified by the Innocence Project, a nonprofit advocacy group for the wrongly convicted (Hall, November 2008, p. 150). The June 12, 2000 issue of Phoenix, Arizona's premier news daily, the *Arizona Republic*, published two feature articles on capital punishment, which highlight serious concerns in regard to criminal justice in the USA. These are: 'AMA asked to endorse execution moratorium' (2000, June 12, p. A1) and 'Study: Flaws rife in capital cases' (2000, June 12, p. A1).

The article 'AMA asked to endorse execution moratorium' notes that 'A group of public health physicians is asking the American Medical Association to endorse a national moratorium on execution until some controversial questions, including the availability of DNA evidence, are resolved' (2000, June 12, p. A1). 'Study: Flaws rife in capital cases', which the *Arizona Republic* called 'The most far-reaching study of the death penalty in the United States has found that two out of three convictions were overturned on appeal, mostly because of serious errors by incompetent defense lawyers or over-zealous prosecutors who withheld evidence' (2000, June 12, p. A1). The disturbing error rates noted in 'Study: Flaws rife in capital cases'; i.e., the percentage of death penalty cases overturned on appeal because of serious errors, were as follows for the ten states most afflicted by that travesty of compromised due process: (1) Kentucky 100 percent; (2) Maryland 100 percent; (3) Tennessee 100 percent; (4) Mississippi 91 percent; (5) Wyoming 89 percent; (6) California 87 percent; (7) Montana 87 percent; (8) Idaho 82 percent; (9) Georgia 80 percent; and (10) Arizona 79 percent.

Although neither *Arizona Republic* article focuses on the issue of race and criminal justice or ethnicity and criminal justice, human rights, civil rights, ethnicity- and-race-based non-governmental organizations (NGOs) and constitutional rights organizations, such as Amnesty International USA, Human Rights Watch, the National Association for the Advancement of Colored People, the National Association for the Advance of Colored People Legal Defense Fund, the National Coalition to Abolish the Death Penalty, the American Civil Liberties Union and the Innocence Project, have for years been concerned about the overrepresentation of Non-Whites in US prisons and jails as well as the overrepresentation of Non-Whites on state and federal death rows.

This chapter analyzes the interface of race, crime and criminal justice in the USA, thereby sharing in the concerns of the aforementioned NGOs, in regard to the transmutation of discretion into discrimination, keyed by racial animus, and resultant social distance. The issue of racial animus and resultant social distance and petit apartheid processing of alleged criminal defendants, that is, discretional decisions that transmute into positive and negative discrimination, and their likely impact on municipal, county, state and federal adult and juvenile criminal justice agents and agencies, key on two of the least understood and most inconsistently utilized concepts in social science: race and ethnicity. The confusion, or inconsistency, in the utilization of the term race as a social-cultural or biological delineator is, in large part, the result of a lack of understanding of the terms 'race' and 'ethnicity' (see Georges-Abeyie 1992; Parrillo, 2003 ; Schaefer, 2004).

According to Georges-Abeyie (1992), social scientist Richard T. Schaefer notes that

'Race has many meanings for many people. Probably the only thing about race that is clear is that we are confused about the origins and proper use of the term... [Schaefer notes that] Race has a precise biological meaning. A biological race is a genetically isolated group characterized by a high degree of inbreeding that leads to distinctive frequencies. This distinctiveness is made most apparent by the presence of hereditary physical characteristics that differentiate members of a group from other humans... [Professor Schaefer notes that race is often confused for ethnicity, an essentially cultural delineator, that] There are three major areas of confusion over the biological use of the term race with respect to humankind. Disagreement arises over (1) the number and characteristics of human races, (2) the presence of pure races and their origin, and (3) the relationship of race to personality traits, such as intelligence... [that] Ethnic groups, therefore, are groups set apart from others because of their national origin or distinctive cultural patterns.'

(Schaefer, 2004, p. 8)

The Georges-Abeyie article 'Defining Race, Ethnicity, and Social Distance...' (1992) quotes the UNESCO Statement on Race as stating that 'Race has only one scientific meaning and that is a biological one. It refers to a subdivision of a given species, members of which inherit physical characteristics, which tend to distinguish that subdivision from other populations of the same species' (Montagu, 1972, p. 40).

In brief, the scientific definition of race refers to a biological reality rather than a social reality. 'Ethnicity', a much more complex term and a much less exact term, includes social, biological, cultural and spatial components in that most definitions of ethnicity, utilized in the West, are similar to that offered by Milton Gordon in his classic *Assimilation and American Life: The Role of Race, Religion, and National Origin* (Gordon, 1964), which included the biological (race), the social-cultural (religion) and the spatial (national origin). Unfortunately, for the study of Negroid ethnicity, much less for the study of crime commission by Negroids as a racial group as well as the criminal victimization and processing of Negroids, the standard definitions of ethnicity are better suited to studying easily identified European immigrants and their communities and neighborhoods (ghettoes) than Negroid immigrants and migrants whose original national origins were frequently eradicated by slavery. This comprehension of the differentiation between the cultural, social, spatial and the biological, that is, between race and ethnicity, is the key to comprehending the difference between (1) causation, that is, the criminogenic and (2) crime association.

This confusion in the usage of the concepts race and ethnicity results in the formulation of theories based upon inaccurate aggregated data, for example (1) data, which has confused ethnicity for race; for example, the aggregation of phenotypically Negroid Hispanics in the Caucasian category, as in the case of Florida Department of Corrections data or the simple discussion of various American aboriginal people, that is, Native Americans, as a racial and cultural monolith as well as the discussion of Antebellum and Post-Antebellum Negroid populations as a racial and cultural monolith; (2) the under count of Negroid, Hispanic, Caribbean and Native American offenders; and (3) the over count of Caucasian offenders, possibly distorting the impact of discretion (actually positive and negative discrimination) upon sentences within racial and ethnic categories. The aforementioned differentiation also necessitates the revision of classic definitions of ethnicity currently incognizant of the unique experience of specific Negroid identity groups in the Americas before realistic theories of Negroid criminogenics and crime associations can be developed. Thus, analysis and findings on distinct Negroid ethnic groups in the Americas have been presented as if the Negroid Diaspora in the Americas constitutes a racial monolith. The similar tendency by social scientists to view aboriginal people, so-called 'Indians'/'Native Americans' and Hispanics as racial monoliths confuses race for ethnicity and vice versa.

In any case, the self-declaration of racial and ethnic identity utilized in the US Census are suspect for many reasons, including issues of social distance toward one's own personal identity group or toward other racial and ethnic personal identity groups as well as the possibility of biracial or bi-ethnic parentage or multiracial or multiethnic heritage. The issue of self-hatred or social distance toward one's own ethnic or racial identity grouping, a manifestation of petit apartheid in the US criminal justice system, has been noted by social scientists, including Georges-Abeyie (1984) and Regoli and Hewitt (2010), who note resultant increased rates of excessive use of force by minority law enforcement officers against minorities as well as elevated rates of minorities reporting minority officers for excessive use of force, corruption and other criminal wrongdoing. Thus, minority social distance toward minority personal identity groupings, including toward their own personal identity grouping, probably impacts crime offense data reported to the police as well as self-report data and victimization data.

It is common knowledge that darker-complexioned *homo sapiens* of African, Asiatic, European and Hispanic 'racial' origin, and/or parentage, have phenomenological and objective life experiences that are different from those of their so-called lighter-complexioned racial counterparts in terms of a wide range of events, including morbidity, mortality in general, infant mortality, wealth, income, status, prestige, self-conceptualization of phenotypic attractiveness, educational achievement, criminality, juvenile delinquency, custody, incarceration and detention. It is also common knowledge or at least common belief that specific African, Asiatic, European and Hispanic ethnic groups offend at different rates, although they share national origin and so-called shared racial 'origin' and identity; e.g., Miami's Little Havana disproportionately houses self-declared White and pale-complexioned Cubans while Alapata and Liberty City houses darker-complexioned and mixed-race Cubans, that is, mulattos, morenos and Negros who are allegedly more crime prone than their lighter-complexioned 'White' nation-state compatriots.

This issue of differential offending by Hispanics with different skin color, phrenology, physiognomy and somatotype is also commonly raised among Mexican American [Chicano] and Mexican national personality identity groups as well as other Latin American and Caribbean personal identity groupings. It is also common knowledge and belief in the Southwestern border states that different Hispanic nationality and ethnic groups offend at different rates and achieve the 'American Dream' and are assimilated into the greater so-called 'American Melting Pot' at different rates, for example, "White" Cubans, Chileans, Paraguayans, Uruguayans have a much lower offense rate and are assimilated into the 'American Dream' and 'American Melting Pot' more readily than Puerto Ricans, Dominicans, Panamanians, Virgin Islanders, Nicaraguans and Guatemalans, perhaps due to phenotypic racial and ethnic characteristics (Parrillo, 2008). It is also common knowledge and belief that Japanese and Japanese American, and even Chinese and Chinese American, adults and juveniles criminally offend and are incarcerated at a lower rate than Vietnamese, Filipino, Cambodian, Hmong, Laotian and South Pacific Islanders. It is also common knowledge that various nationality groups with shared racial characteristics form distinct ethnic-based adult and juvenile street gangs and prison gangs, for example, the Mexican Mafia and Nuestra Familia are predominantly Chicano, whereas the New Mexican Mafia is predominantly Mexican national and MS-13 Guatemalan. So-called Negroid or African American street criminals, street gangs and prison gangs are frequently ethnically distinct, yet racially 'monolithic', for example, African American Antebellum and Post-Antebellum African immigrants, such as West Indian, Maroon (Gullah and Geechee in the North Caroline barrier islands south of Cape Fear, the South Carolina and the Georgia Sea Islands and Lowland/Low Country), Delaware Whites, Louisiana Creoles, the North Carolina and South Carolina Lumbee and Post-Antebellum Africans, especially Nigerians and Liberians. Nonetheless, unincorporated area, county, state and federal crime data are frequently only race-based, rather than ethnicity-based, although many of these groups manifest distinct linguistic, dialect and other cultural characteristics, that is, role-sets (mores and related folkways and norms), including language, importance of the nuclear and/or the extended family, personal and family honor and concepts of machismo, which may act as a criminogenic.

The most comprehensive recent census is the 2000 Census – the US Bureau of the Census (USBC) conducts a comprehensive census every 10 years. However, the USBC (2000a) also provides non-census year population estimates and population projections. The USBC recognizes five racial identity groups as 'One race' identity groups, noting Hispanic as an ethnic identity grouping, which may include persons from the 'One race' identity groupings; i.e., White, Black, American Indian and Alaskan Native [AIAN], and Native Hawaiian and Other Pacific Islander [NHPI] or the 'Two or More' racial identity groups. The USBC also recognizes that a respondent may have two or more self-declared racial identities, regardless of Hispanic or Non-Hispanic ethnic identity. In brief, the 2000 USBC (2000b) Summary of Modified Race, based on Census 2000 Race Distributions for the United States prepared by the USBC, 2002, is as follows for Modified Race with the Hispanic Population estimated at 35,797,250 [12,72 percent of the US population] in 2002 (US Bureau of the Census, 2002):

One Race

- White 228,104,485   [81.05%]
- Black or African American 35,704,124   [12.69%]
- American Indian and Alaskan Native 2,663,818   [0.95%]
- Asian 10,589,265   [3.76%]
- Native Hawaiian and Other Pacific Islander 465,534   [0.16%]

Two Races

- Specified Race Only 3,578,053   [1.27%]
- Specified Race and Non-Specified Races (X)   [X]

Three or More Races

- Specified Race Only 319,627   [0.11%]
- Specified Race and Non-Specified Races (X)   [X]

Hispanic or Latino and Race
One Race

- White 32,529,000   [92.13%]
- Black or African American 1,391,117   [3.94%]
- American Indian and Alaskan Native 566,378   [1.60%]
- Asian 232,461   [0.66%]
- Native Hawaiian and Other Pacific Islander 95,430 [0.27%]
- Specified Race Only 34,814,386   [98.61%]
- Non-Specified Race Only (X)   [X]

Two Races

- Specified Race Only 433,726   [1.23%]
- Specified and Non-Specified Races (X)   [X]

Three or More Races

- Specified Race Only 57,706   [0.16%]
- Specified and Non-Specified Races (X)   [X]

The USBC also provides 'Annual Estimates of the Population by Sex, Race, and Hispanic Origin for the United States: April 1, 2000 to July 1, 2007' with estimates of population for July 1, 2007; July 1, 2006; July 1, 2005; July 1, 2004; July 1, 2003; July 1, 2002; July 1, 2001; and July 1, 2000. The further from the 2000 Census, the more speculative the estimates of population. Thus, prolific population data are provided by the USBC, although its accuracy and reliability is suspect, in part, due to self-declaration of racial and ethnic identity and confusion or misunderstanding of the terms race and ethnicity, much less Hispanic, Black and African American. Any demographic compilation, much less discussion of demographic data, which includes the category Hispanic is at best suspect and lacking in validity when millions of phenotypically Non-White or phenotypically Negroid Hispanics self-declare as Whites, a racial identity grouping, not an ethnic grouping, for example, Dominicans, Puerto Ricans, Venezuelans, Columbians and upper-middle social-economic class and upper social-economic class Cubans frequently self-declare as White, regardless of their racial phenotype. Social distance realities by Non-Whites toward Non-Whites, including toward 'their own' phenotypic racial identity group likely result in an overestimate of the White population; i.e., the act of 'passing' or identifying culturally, socially, politically and emotionally with Whites. Simply stated, it is this author's belief that Non-Whites of 'mixed racial parentage' or of 'mixed race' phrenology, physiognomy and somatotype are more likely to self-identify as White than as any other racial identity; note the social science videos *A Question of Race: Assignment Discovery* (Discovery Channel, 2001) and *A Question of Color: Color Consciousness in Black America* (Sandler, 1980). Thus, analyses of offending by Non-Whites and Whites as well as victimization of Non-Whites and Whites are at best suspect, if not overtly unreliable and therefore lacking in validity.

The USBC data, regardless of the year compiled and presented to the public, mirror the findings of its northern neighbor, Canada, that is, the Non-White population:

- Is younger on average, their unemployment rates are higher and incomes lower than that of the White population.
- Lives in more crowded conditions than their White counterpart.
- Is more mobile residentially than their White counterpart.
- Is more likely to be members of a lone-parent family than their White counterpart.
- Has a lower level of educational achievement than their White counterpart.

Criminality and criminal justice practices

Key problems with the analysis of offending by Non-Whites and Whites, in addition to self-declaration of race and ethnicity, are the lack of comprehensive spatial analysis; much less spatial analysis correlated with race and the perception of White, Non-White, Negroid, Hispanic and Native American people as racial or ethnic monoliths. In reality many, if not most, Negroid, Hispanic, White and Native American North Americans, live in spatially segregated residential neighborhoods in regard to race and frequently ethnicity, that is, ghettos, slums and slum-ghettos. However, the extent of ghettoization may vary by race, ethnicity and eth-class, that is, not only by one's ethnicity and visible minority racial identity but also by one's social-economic class. Most North American criminological and criminal justice studies view Negroid, Hispanic, White and Native American North Americans as racial and ethnic monoliths, thereby ignoring their ethnic heterogeneity, although different ethnic groups of shared racial identity likely have very distinct social, cultural and economic histories. The treatment of the North American Negroid and the North American Negroid slum-ghetto as ethnic and racial monoliths is especially egregious. Such studies usually also view the Negroid slum-ghetto as a spatial monolith (Georges-Abeyie, 1978, 1981, 1984, 1989, 1990a, 1990b, 1992, 2009a), when in fact,

North American Negroids have distinct ethnicities and racial manifestations, while the aforementioned slum-ghettos are just that, slum-ghettos not simply ghettos, and exhibit distinct urban morphologies with distinct land use patterns and internal social–cultural dynamics.

The term 'ghetto' is classically utilized to denote an area of disproportionate residence by one or more ethnic or racial groups. It implies nothing about the economic status of the residents (Forman, 1971; Georges-Abeyie, 1978, 1981, 1989, 2002, 2009a; Wirth, 1956). The ghetto morphology includes: (1) a Zone of Transition (spatial units in which 30 percent to 49 percent of the resident population is of the lower-status ethnic or racial group represented in the ghetto core; this is not a permanent ghetto manifestations in that the spatial unit is rapidly expanding); (2) a Fringe (spatial units in which 50 percent to 74 percent of the resident population is of the lower status ethnic or racial group represented in the ghetto core); and (3) a Core (spatial units in which 75 percent to 100 percent of the resident population is of the lower status ethnic or racial group (Georges-Abeyie, 1978, 1981, 2009a)). It is also important to note that ghetto morphology is constantly changing, with the tipping point approximating 20 to 30 percent residence by the low status racial or ethnic identity group ushering in the mass exodus of the higher status racial or ethnic group, for example, the phenomenon of 'White flight' (Rose, 1971). The term 'ghetto' also implies that the low status resident population has limited residential choice.

The term 'slum' classically refers to a spatial entity demarcated by poverty and related characteristics, such as high morbidity and high infant mortality rates, mixed land use, extreme high or low population densities within the same spatial entity, dilapidated housing and elevated crime offense and criminal victimization rates (Forman, 1971; Georges-Abeyie, 1978, 1981, 2009a; Rose and McClain, 1990). Thus, the term 'slum-ghetto' is symbolic of dynamic spatial units in which both slum and ghetto conditions exist. Georges-Abeyie (2009a) discusses in detail the dual myth of the black racial monolith with its implied slum-ghetto devoid of distinct zones of transition, fringe and core, although he introduced the concept of black ethnic heterogeneity in his previous articles cited above.

Thus, when one speaks of the Negroid ghetto or slum-ghetto, one is noting a residential area inhabited by a residentially segregated people, or peoples with low status and rather limited residential choice. The Negroid ghetto or slum-ghetto can be representative of one or more racial and/or ethnic neighborhoods with the African–American neighborhood, just one of several Negroid neighborhoods, demarcated by distinct social–cultural and biological boundaries. The African–American resident is distinct from other Negroid and non-Negroid Hispanic, Francophone, Anglophone, Lusophone, Anglophone Caribbean people and Post-Antebellum African immigrants and migrants by a host of identifiable genetic, social, cultural and economic traits, some of which may be crime associative or criminogenic. The distinguishing genetic traits, and attribute of geographic race, and sometimes ethnic identity, often result in visible phenotypes due to distinct migratory streams from Africa and distinct assimilation interactions with distinct Caucasoid nationality groups and distinct tribal groups of indigenous Americans of the Western Hemisphere, that is, so-called Native Americans.

One should note that distinct racial or ethnic ghetto and slum-ghetto morpholoes may exhibit distinct P.O.E.T.s ['P' – the demographics in regard to race and ethnicity; 'O' – the organization and manifestation of criminal role-sets, including the *modus operandi*; 'E' – the environs, the situational and site factors in regard to the alleged perpetrator, victim and criminal defendant, and 'T' – the time of the occurrence of the alleged criminal event, the *actus reus*] (Georges-Abeyie, 1978, 2002, 2009a). It is also important to note that Native American ghetto and slum-ghetto morphologies, similar to Negroid ghetto and slum-ghetto morphologies, may exhibit distinct rates of criminal offending behavior not only by tribe/nation/nationality grouping but also by zone, for example, one Native American or Negroid ethnic group/'visible minority' identity grouping may offend at a higher rate than another, yet local, state and federal data are usually collected on the basis of race, not ethnicity. Thus, aggregated crime rate data analysis is also conducted on the basis of race rather than ethnicity, which may mask differential rates of offending within racial categories. For example, although the black racial identity grouping includes numerous ethnic groups, a factorial analysis which controls for income, population density, rental property and ownership of residential units and other related variables, which partials (controls for) head of household by ethnic group or ethnicity, or the arrestee by ethnic group or ethnicity may indicate that all black ethnic groups have, or do not have, similar crime rates. Thus, 'important/key' life experiences or crime rates may vary not only by race but also by ethnic group and perhaps actual or phenomenological life experiences, and reactions to actual and phenomenological life experiences.

It is also possible for the crime offense or crime victimization rate to vary by the racial or ethnic ghetto and slum-ghetto Core, Fringe and Zone of Transition. Differentials in the rate of offending and of victimization by Negroid and Native American people, as the result of shared group experience, that is, racial and ethnic identity group history, is also likely to be true for Hispanics and Whites or any of the USBC race identity groupings, including European Americans, some of whom have extensive histories of spatial isolation and discrimination/victimization, that is, ghettoization, for example the Irish and various Southern, Eastern and Central European identity groupings, including Poles, Greeks, Italians, Ukrainians, Jews, Armenians and Russians. Thus, differential offense and victimization rates may also manifest in the morphology of Non-Negro and Non-Native American ghettos and slum-ghettos, that is, within the ghetto and slum-ghetto Core, Fringe and Zone of Transition.

Macro-level [large-scale] demographic data and crime data with ethnic and racial components have been provided by Uniform Crime Program data, Hate crime statistics and the US Department of Justice, Bureau of Justice Statistics for various years. Arrests information by charge, age group and race for 2002 is provided as follows by the *Sourcebook of Criminal Justice Statistics 2003* (State University of New York – US Department of Justice (2003a, pp. 358–60):
Total of 446,356 violent crimes with arrestee demographics:

- White 266,681 [59.7%]; White % of population in 2002 [81.9%].
- Black 169,525 [38.0%]; Black % of population in 2002 [13.3%].
- American Indian/Alaskan Native 4895 [1.1%]; American Indian/Alaskan Native % of population in 2002 [1.5%].
- Asian/Pacific Islander 5255 [1.2%]; Asian/Pacific Islander % of Population in 2002 [4.5%].

Total of 1,167,778 property crimes with arrestee demographics:

- White 791,165 [67.7%]; White % of population in 2002 [81.9%].
- Black 345,244 [38.0%]; Black % of population in 2002 [13.3%].
- American Indian/Alaskan Native 13,593 [1.2%]; American Indian/Alaskan Native % of population in 2002 [1.5%].
- Asian/Pacific Islander 17,776 [1.5%]; Asian/Pacific Islander % of Population in 2002 [4.5%].

Thus, Black violent crime commission as estimated by arrest data notes an elevated violent crime rate in 2002. The Black property crime commission as estimated by arrest data is also elevated in comparison to its percent of the population in 2002. Similar representation of Black arrest rates for violent and property crimes is reproduced in 2006 (State University of New York – US Department of Justice, 2006a).

Death row constitutes an outcome of petit apartheid sentencing decisions where the over representation of Blacks is probably most problematic. The percentage of Blacks under sentence of death in 2002 as well as in 2006 is greater than the percentage of Blacks in the population for either year (see State University of New York – US Department of Justice 2003b, 2006b, p. 537), which is true regardless of the year examined. For example, Death Penalty Information Center data on the Race of Death Row Inmates as of April 17, 2009 (Death Penalty Information Center, 2009) reveal that Blacks constitute 35 percent of those held on death row, Whites 56 percent, Hispanics 7 percent and Others 2 percent.

Social scientists have argued endlessly whether the disproportionate arrest, incarceration and execution of juvenile offenders and adult offenders is racially disproportionate, or has been the result of overt or covert racism and ethnocentrism, that is, grand apartheid or petit apartheid within the US criminal justice and juvenile systems, especially at those opportunities for discretion to transmute into discrimination (Becker, 1963; Gabbidon, Greene, and Young, 2002; Georges-Abeyie, 1989, 1990, 2002, 2006; Greene and Gabbidon, 2000; Lemert, 1951; Lynch and Patterson, 1991; MacLean and Milovanovic, 1990; Milovanovic and Russell, 2001; Penn, Greene, and Gabbidon, 2006; Tannenbaum, 1938; Wright, 1987). Other social scientists have posited the belief that the disproportionate arrest, processing, conviction, incarceration and execution of Non-White racial identity groupings is the result of simple disproportionate offending by racial and ethnic minorities as well as the aggravation in their offense behavior (Hirschi, 1969; Cohen, 1955; Curtis, 1975; Merton, 1938; Miller, 1958; Sellin, 1938; Shaw and Mckay McKay, 1942; Sutherland, 1947; Wilbanks, 1987). It has also been argued by social scientists such as Wilbanks (1987) that the differential, disadvantaging discriminatory treatment of Non-Whites by and within the US criminal justice system is a myth; a non-discrimination thesis vigorously rejected by other social scientists (Georges-Abeyie, 1990a, 1990b; MacLean and Milovanovic, 1990; Milovanovic and Russell, 2001).

It is worth mentioning at this point that the US criminal justice system, unlike many of the world's other criminal justice systems, is not a unitary justice system. The US criminal justice system is actually comprised of many systems concerned with juvenile and adult offenders, that is, components of the juvenile and adult 'criminal justice system' function on the unincorporated, municipal, county, state and federal level. Municipalities, counties, state and federal agencies manifest initiatives unique to their level of governance, impacting offending by Non-Whites and Whites. The demographics within each of these levels of governance may vary dramatically, as may their voting and non-voting constituencies. Crime fighting initiatives also vary wildly based upon economic resources and electoral politics, which impact policing/law enforcement, detention/jails, courts and corrections.

Dissimilar to its neighbor to the north, agencies at all levels of governance in the US compile, analyze and act upon comprehensive information based on race and ethnicity. The US Department of Justice, Bureau of Justice Statistics as well as various federal agencies, such as the Federal Bureau of Investigation, are engaged in the politically incorrect act of data compilation and analysis resulting in societal and individual, private and public sector, finger pointing and race and ethnic scapegoating. Most of these data lack ethnic specificity and uses race as a pseudonym for ethnicity, or ignores ethnicity altogether. State and federal government response to offending by Non-Whites and Whites has resulted in the disproportionate arrest, incarceration and execution of Non-White racial and ethnic minorities, most of whom are economically disadvantaged. The US criminal justice system is championed as a social distance-bias-free review of offenders as exemplified, that is symbolized, throughout the USA, by the statue or ornate facade of the blindfolded 'lady liberty' holding a balanced scale at countless courthouses throughout the USA. However, numerous Supreme Court cases document the long arduous march for justice and equal due process within courts too frequently impacted by racial and ethnic bigotry, for example, *Batson* v. *Kentucky; Georgia* v. *McCollum; Furman* v. *Georgia; Gregg* v. *Georgia*; and *McCleskey* v. *Kemp*.

Regardless of the long arduous march toward racial and ethnic justice in the courts, more needs to be done in regard to the recognition of race-and-ethnicity-based mitigation and exculpatory realities associated with *mens rea* in that culture conflict and ignorance of fact and of the law ['mistake of fact' and 'mistake of law'] may play a role, however limited, in reference to criminally offending behavior by indigenous as well as immigrant and migrant offenders of various races and ethnicities. The why of offending by the native-born offender and the immigrant/alien offender may be lost in the data compilation, which may mask differential rates of offending by same race offenders of different ethnicities. What currently appears beyond doubt is that Non-Whites offend and are victimized at a higher rate than Whites except for hate crimes (discussed below), where Whites may actually offend at a higher rate than Non-Whites, after controlling for the over count of Whites by noting the inclusion of self-declared phrenologically Non-Whites as Whites and those declared White on criminal justice forms by their processors, when the cataloged individuals are usually considered Non-White in daily life.

Crime and victimization

The US Department of Justice annually publishes voluminous crime victimization data sets as does the *Sourcebook of Criminal Justice Statistics*, based at the State University of New York. This section utilizes bias motivated victimization data sets; i.e., data noting ethnic and racial bias were the motivation for victimizing; e.g., the *Sourcebook of Criminal Justice Justices Online* crime victimization data sets, and National Crime Victimization Survey data sets for 2002 and 2006. Crime Victimization data for 2002 is utilized due to the comprehensive US Census 2002; the availability of 2002 crime victimization data, in general; and the more likely accuracy of 2002 population estimates than population projections for later years. Crime victimization data for 2006 is utilized due to its availability, including bias motivation data. It is also utilized because 2006 is near the census midpoint and data reliability and validity degenerations with each year after 2000. The perusal of available demographic and crime victimization data for the years 2000–2005 and 2006–2008 reveals demographic characteristics and crime victimization patterns similar to that noted for 2002 and 2006.

The Sourcebook of Criminal Justice Statistics (State University of New York – US Department of Justice 2003c, p. 201) provides the following estimated number and rate information (per 1000 households) of property victimizations by type of crime and race of head of household, United States, 2002:

Property Crimes All Races 17,539,220; Rate 159.0:

- White 14,527,440; Rate 157.0.
- Black 2,434,780; Rate 173.7.
- Other 576,990; Rate 139.8.

Property crime rate data by race of victims for 2002 show that Blacks have the most elevated rate of property crime victimization. Also, property crime rate data for 2006 shows elevated property crime rate victimization for Blacks and even more so for Others with Two or More Racial Identities (State University of New York – US Department of Justice, 2008). For personal criminal victimization of those aged 12 and older, data for 2002 note that Blacks exhibit the highest criminal victimization rate, although not dramatically higher than that for Whites the Black personal crime victimization rate for 2006 is similarly elevated (State University of New York – US Department of Justice, 2003d, p. 193; 2006c). Of greater significance is the dramatically elevated personal victimization rate for Other with Racial Identity of Two or More Races. The lack of micro-level ethnic specific and site and situational specific data does not allow for reasoned speculation as to why the Other with Two or More Racial Identities is so dramatically elevated. Again, it is prudent to note that data on Black victims are presented as if Blacks are an ethnic monolith when Black ethnic groups may vary in regard to membership within social–economic class categories and spatial domains and therefore within victimization categories.

Federal government statistical data online provided by the *Sourcebook of Criminal Justice Statistics* (State University of New York – US Department of Justice, 2003e, p. 194) and the *Sourcebook of Criminal Justice Statistics* (State University of New York – US Department of Justice, 2006d) provide macro-level ethnic data limited to the categories Hispanic and Non-Hispanic in reference to personal crimes. This macro-level statistical source on ethnic referenced personal crime data for 2002 and 2006, similar to race referenced date, lacks specificity (in reference to ethnic identity and eth-class identity within the Hispanic and Non-Hispanic categories) as well as site and situational specificity in reference to spatial data, thereby limiting reasoned data-based speculation. Macro-level data show no appreciable difference in personal victimization rates when the categories Hispanic and Non-Hispanic are utilized; Hispanic is an inaccurate pseudonym for race when a Hispanic can be of any race. However, race-specific census data, which in themselves are quite macro level, indicate differences in educational achievement, income, residential mobility, whether the household is headed by one parent, et cetera, for the various race-specific census categories, which are also likely to be true for the various Hispanic nationality groupings. For example, White Cuban immigrants and White Cuban American nationals exhibit higher income and higher levels of educational achievement, and less residential mobility and lower crime rates than other Hispanic identity groupings (Parrillo, 2008). Thus, one might speculate, without comprehensive race and ethnic data that different ethnic groups within specific racial identity categories manifest differences in educational achievement, income, residential mobility, whether the household is headed by one parent, et cetera, and thus, likely, different rates of victimization and criminal offense data.

It is known that property crime and personal victimization can be inter-racial or intra-racial (or inter-ethnic or intra-ethnic), with the latter exemplified in gang violence in certain inner cities across the country. Inter-racial personal victimization is probably best illustrated with reference to hate crime. Hate crime, also known as bias crime, is defined by the US Department of Justice online (2002) as 'a criminal offense committed against a person, property, or society which is motivated, in whole or in part, by the offender's bias against a race, religion, disability, sexual orientation, or ethnicity/national origin'. The US Department of Justice online (2002) notes that in 2002, Blacks and Hispanics were grossly disproportionately targeted as victims of hate crime. Of the 49.7 percent victims of all single-bias hate crime motivated by racial prejudice, 62.7 percent were Black and 19.9 percent were White. Hate crime victims targeted because of ethnicity/national origin bias made up 15.3 percent (of the 49.7 percent victims of all single-bias hate crime) and Hispanics comprised 45.4 percent of this figure. Data from the US Department of Justice also show that Blacks and Hispanics were grossly disproportionately targeted as hate crime victims in 2006 (US Department of Justice, 2006a, 2006b). Blacks made up 66.4 percent of the 5020 victims of racially motivated hate crime, and the figures for Whites, Asian/Pacific Islander and American Indian/Alaskan Native were 21 percent, 4.8 percent and 1.5 percent, respectively. Hispanics comprised 62.8 percent of the 1305 victims of ethnicity/national origin-based hate crime (ibid.). The lack of comprehensive site and situational spatial data as well as the lack of micro-level race and ethnic spatial-related data limits rational data-based speculation in regard to whether some Black and Hispanic ethnicity identity groups were, or were not, disproportionately the victims of bias crimes; in that Blacks can manifest varied ethnicity while Hispanics can manifest varied ethnicity as well as racial identity in any of the US Bureau of the Census race categories.

State and federal governments have enacted hate crime/bias crime sentence enhancement in reference to the specific targeting of victims based on specific group identity characteristics, including that of race and ethnicity.

However, limited resources are directly allocated toward the study and/or comprehension of race- and-ethnic based victim precipitation, much less toward the study, comprehension and eradication of non-race and non-ethnic-based criminogenic factors, such as low income and extensive inter-generational poverty, high morbidity rates, high rates of residential mobility, low rates of educational achievement, high population density, mixed commercial and residential land use and elevated levels of legal drug use, much less drug abuse, including the consumption of alcohol. These crim-inogenic factors can also explain the perpetration of hate crime by Whites.

Bias motivation data for 2002 indicates that White offenders are the most common category of offenders, although they are not out of proportion for their percentage of the total US population. The US Department of Justice, Federal Bureau of Investigation Incidents, Offenses, Victims, and Known Offenders by Bias Motivation 2002 (US Department of Justice, 2002) notes the following:

Total offenders 7314:

- White Offenders 4517 [62%]; White % of population in 2002 [81.9%].
- Black Offenders 1592 [22%]; Black % of population in 2002 [13.3%].
- American Indian/Alaskan Native 43 [6/10%]; American Indian/Alaskan Native % of population in 2002 [1.5%].
- Asian/Pacific Islander 87 [1%]; Asian/Pacific Islander % of Population in 2002 [4.5%].
- Multiple Races, Group 355 [5%]; Two or more races % of Population in 2002 [1%].
- Unknown Race 720 [10%].

The offender categories Black and Multiple Racial Group are the most ele-vated when compared to their percentage of the total US population. Bias motivation data for 2006 indicates the same for White Offenders, and the Black and Multiple Racial Group, although the elevation for the latter two is not grossly disproportional (State University of New York – US Department of Justice, 2006e). However, the Black and Multi Racial Group categories provide impetus for fascinating speculation, especially when one examines other victimization data presented above. The macro-level monolithic racial presentation, devoid of micro-level ethnic data, prevents rational specu-lation as to whether certain ethnic groups, due to their ethnic identity group history in the USA or abroad, engage in bias motivated crimes more commonly than their ethnic counterparts. One must again be cautious in regard to bias motivation speculation based on race, due to an inability to note the spatial dynamics of the offending in terms of site and situ-ation as well as possible 'faulty' self-declaration of racial identity due to social distance factors toward one's own racial identity grouping as well as general lack of comprehension of the term 'race', much less one's own racial identity.

Law enforcement initiatives in specific ghettos or within specific sectors of specific ghettos as well as the bias of law enforcement officers may impact who is formally arrested. Thus, speculation in reference to the race of the offender is at best speculative and likely to be unreliable, and thus lacking in validity, while data-based offense speculation in reference to ethnicity is totally lacking. The lack of site-specific data and micro-level spatial analysis correlated with race or ethnicity may result, for example, in the erroneous correlation of race with property offenses, when factorial analysis utilizing partial correlations, zero order correlation and multiple regression may reveal a greater association with poverty, strip mall economy, ethnicity or unique land use than with race.

One must also question if the US Department of Justice, Office of Civil Rights more vigorously recorded and pursued offenses by Non-White offenders than by White offenders, resulting in the over-reporting of Non-White offenders and the under-reporting of White Offenders, especially if the offender–victim dynamic involved an alleged Non-White assailant and an alleged White victim, that is, selective prosecution during the George W. Bush administration implied on Wednesday February 18, 2009, by the newly appointed US Attorney General, Eric Holder appointed by the newly elected US president Barack Obama.

Conclusion

There is no debate as to whether property crimes and crimes against the person are elevated in the USA. They are. There is no debate as to whether racial and ethnic minorities, especially Blacks, are disproportionately included among the ranks of victims and offenders. They are. What is necessary for rational data-based policy analysis of offending and victimization, cognizant of the role of race and ethnicity, is the more comprehensive analysis of spatial factors cognizant of site and situation [the P.O.E.T.], and ghetto and slum-ghetto racial and ethnic morphology, that is, cognizant of if, when, and why, crimes occur within the zone of transition, the fringe and/or the core. Race is at best a 'social–cultural construct', which focuses on some biological characteristics while ignoring others. Nonetheless, it purports to be an essentially biological concept. Ethnicity stresses the social and the cultural, that is, role-sets, which include folkways and related mores and norms, although ethnic constructs frequently include a biological component. Nonetheless, more consistency in the use of the terms 'race', 'ethnicity' and 'eth-class' are sorely needed, if the dynamics of criminal offending and criminal victimization is to be better understood. It is also important that demographic data recognize the ethnic diversity within racial categories utilized by the US Bureau of the Census and the US Department of Justice in that different ethnic groups have experienced, and continue to experience, different social, cultural, political, and economic realities, which may also be true for Antebellum and Post-Antebellum Negroid ethnic groups. It is also important to note that different identity group histories, within racial and ethnic categories, likely result in:

- Different levels of oppression.
- Different rates of recognition of oppression.
- Different levels of alienation.
- Different rates of victim precipitation.
- Different experience within and by the varied criminal justice agencies.
- Different manifestation of criminogenic factors.
- Different rates of criminal offending.
- Different rates of criminal victimization.

The Canadian and European policy of political correctness, for example, that of France, in regard to the compilation and analysis of race- and-ethnicity-based crime and criminal justice data, has resulted in a dearth of reliable crime and criminal justice and juvenile justice data. The US policy of vigorous compilation of adult crime and criminal justice data and juvenile justice data is commendable but misguided, due to the limited spatial, site and situational data and the unfortunate treatment of racial and ethnic identity groups as monoliths, and the terms 'race' and 'ethnicity' as pseudonyms.

References

Becker, H. S. (1963). *Outsiders*. New York: The Free Press of Glencoe.

Cohen, A. K. (1955). *Delinquent Boys*. New York: The Free Press.

Curtis, L. A. (1975). *Violence, Race, and Culture*. Lexington, MA: D. C. Health.

Forman, R. E. (1971). *Black Ghettos, White Ghettos, and Slums*. Englewood Cliffs, NJ: Prentice Hall.

Gabbidon, S. L., Greene, H. T. and Young, V. D. (eds) (2002). *African American Classics in Criminology and Criminal Justice*. Thousand Oaks, CA: Sage Publications.

Georges-Abeyie, D. E. (1978). *The Geography of Crime and Violence: A Spatial and Ecological Perspective*. Washington, DC: Association of American Geographers.

—— (1981). Studying black crime: A realistic approach. In P. J. Brantingham and Brantingham, P. L. (eds). *Environmental Criminology* (pp. 97–107). Beverly Hills, CA: Sage Publications.

—— (ed.) (1984). *Criminal Justice System and Blacks*. New York: Clark Boardman, Ltd.

—— (1989). Race, ethnicity, and the spatial dynamic: Toward a realistic study of black crime, crime victimization, and criminal justice processing of blacks. *Social Justice*, 16: 35–54.

—— (1990a). Criminal justice processing of non-White minorities. In B. D. MacLean and D. Milovanovic, D. (eds). *Racism, Empiricism, and Criminal Justice* (pp. 25–34). Vancouver, Canada: The Collective Press.

—— (1990b). The myth of a racist criminal justice system? In B. D. MacLean and D. Milovanovic (eds). *Racism, Empiricism, and Criminal Justice* (pp. 11–14). Vancouver, Canada: The Collective Press.

—— (1992). Defining race, ethnicity, and social distance: Their impact on crime, criminal victimization, and the criminal justice processing of minorities. *Journal of Contemporary Criminal Justice*. May, 8, (2), 100–13.

—— (2002). Race, ethnicity, and the spatial dynamic: toward a realistic study of black crime, crime victimization, and criminal justice processing of blacks. In S. L. Gabbidon, H. T. Greene and Young, V. D. (eds). *African American Classics in Criminology & Criminal Justice* (pp. 227–42). Thousand Oaks, CA: Sage Publications.

—— (2006). Race, ethnicity, and social distance severity. *The Western Journal of Black Studies*, 30(2), Spring: 103–17.

—— (2009a). Black ethnic monolith. In H. Greene, E. Penn and S. Gabbidon (Eds). *Encyclopedia of Race and Crime* (vol. 1, pp. 61–3). Thousand Oaks, CA: Sage Publication.

—— (2009b). Petit apartheid in the US criminal justice system. In H. Greene, E. Penn and Gabbidon, S. (eds). *Encyclopedia of Race and Crime* (vol. 2, pp. 619–21). Thousand Oaks, CA: Sage Publication.

Gordon, M. M. (1964). *Assimilation and American Life: The Role of Race, Religion, and National Origin*. New York: Oxford University Press.

Greene, T. H. and Gabbidon, S. L. (eds) (2000). *African American Criminological Thought*. Albany, NY: State University of New York Press.

Hirschi, T. (1969). *A Control Theory of Delinquency*. Berkeley, CA: University of California Press.

Lemert, E. (1951). *Social Pathology: A Systematic Approach to the Theory of Sociopathic Behavior*. New York: McGraw-Hill.

Lynch, M. J. and Patterson, E. Britt (eds) (1991). *Race and Criminal Justice*. Albany, NY: Harrow and Hesston Publishers.

MacLean, B. D. and Milovanovic, D. (eds) (1990). *Racism, Empiricism, and Criminal Justice*. Vancouver, Canada: The Collective Press.

Merton, R. K. (1938). Social structure and anomie. *American Sociological Review*, 3 (October): 672–87.

Miller, W. B. (1958). Lower class culture as a generating milieu of gang delinquency. *Journal of Social Issues*, 14(3): 5–19.

Milovanovic, D. and Russell, K. K. (eds) (2001). *Petit Apartheid in the U.S. Criminal Justice System: The Dark Figure of Racism*. Durham, NC: Carolina Academic Press.

Montagu, A. (1972). *Statement on Race*. New York: Oxford University Press.

Parrillo, V. N. (2003). *Strangers to These Shores*. Boston: Allyn and Bacon.

Parrillo, V. N. (2008). *Strangers to These Shores*. New York: John Wiley & Sons.

Penn, E. V., Greene, H. T., and Gabbidon, S. L. (eds) (2006). *Race and Juvenile Justice*. Durham, NC: Carolina Academic Press.

Regoli, R. M. and Hewitt, J. D. (2010). *Exploring Criminal Justice: The Essentials*. Sudbury, MA: Jones and Bartlett Publishers.

Rose, H. M. (1971). *The Black Ghetto: A Spatial Behavioral Perspective*. New York: McGraw-Hill.

Rose, H. M. and McClain, P. D. (1990). *Race, Place, and Risk: Black Homicide in Urban America*. Albany, NY: State University of New York Press.

Schaefer, R. T. (1988). *Racial and Ethnic Groups*. Glenview, IL: Glenview Press.

Schaefer, R. T. (2004). *Racial and Ethnic Groups*. Upper Saddle River, NJ: Pearson-Prentice Hall.

Sellin, T. (1938). Culture conflict and crime. *Social Science Research Council, Bulletin No. 4*, 63–70.

Shaw, C. R. and McKay, H. D. (1942). *Differential Systems of Values*. Chicago: University of Chicago Press.

Sutherland, E. (1947). *Principles of Criminology*, 4th edn. Philadelphia: J. B. Lippincott.

Tannenbaum, F. (1938). *Crime and the Community*. New York: Ginn.

Wilbanks, W. (1987). *The Myth of a Racist Criminal Justice System*. Monterey, CA: Brooks/Cole Publishing Company.

Wirth, L. (1956). *The Ghetto*. Chicago: University of Chicago Press.

Wright, B. (1987). *Black Robes, WWhiteWhite Justice: Why Our Legal System Doesn't Work for Blacks*. New York: A Lyle Stuart Book.

Internet References

Death Penalty Information Center (2009). *Facts about the Death Penalty*. Retrieved June 27, 2009, from Death Penalty Information Center via http://www.deathpenaltyinfo.org/facts/death/penalty.

Federal Bureau of Investigation. (2002). *Crime in the United States 2002*. Retrieved December 26, 2008, FBI Uniform Crime Report Online via http://www.fbigov/ucr/cius_02/html/web/offreported/02-nhatecrime12.html retrieved.

State University of New York – US Department of Justice (2003a). *Sourcebook of Criminal Justice Statistics Online – Arrests by Charge, Age Group, and Race 2003*. Retrieved December 27, 2009, from Sourcebook of Criminal Justice Statistics via http://www.albany.edu/sourcebook/pdf/t322.pdf.

State University of New York – US Department of Justice (2003b) *Sourcebook of Criminal Justice Statistics 2003* Prisoners Under Sentence of Death December 31, 2002. Washington, DC: US Government Printing Office, 537.

State University of New York – US Department of Justice. (2003c). *Sourcebook of Criminal Justice Statistics Online – Property Victimizations by Crime and Race of Head of Household 2003*. Retrieved December 27, 2009, from Sourcebook of Criminal Justice Statistics via http://www.albany.edu/sourcebook/pdf/t322.pdf.

State University of New York – US Department of Justice. (2003d). *Sourcebook of Criminal Justice Statistics Online – Personal Victimizations by Type of Crime and Race of Victim 2003*. Retrieved December 27, 2009, from Sourcebook of Criminal Justice Statistics via http://www.albany.edu/sourcebook/pdf/t322.pdf.

State University of New York – US Department of Justice. (2003e). *Sourcebook of Criminal Justice Statistics Online – Hispanic and Non-Hispanic Personal Crimes 2003*. Retrieved December 27, 2009, from Sourcebook of Criminal Justice Statistics via http://www.albany.edu/sourcebook/pdf/t322.pdf.

State University of New York – US Department of Justice. (2006a). *Sourcebook of Criminal Justice Statistics 2006 Online – Violent Crime Commission*. Retrieved December 27, 2009, from Sourcebook of Criminal Justice Statistics via http://www.albany.edu/sourcebook/pdf/t382006.pdf.

State University of New York – US Department of Justice. (2006b). *Sourcebook of Criminal Justice Statistics Online – Prisoners by Race Under Sentence of Death*. Retrieved December 27, 2009, from *Sourcebook of Criminal Justice Statistics* via http://www.albany.edu/sourcebook/pdf/t6802006.pdf.

State University of New York – U.S. Department of Justice. (2006c). *Sourcebook of Criminal Justice Statistics Online – Personal Victimizations by Type of Crime and Race of Victim 2006*. Retrieved December 27, 2009, from Sourcebook of Criminal Justice Statistics via http://www.albany.edu/sourcebook/pdf/t382006.pdf.

State University of New York – US Department of Justice. (2006d). *Sourcebook of Criminal Justice Statistics Online – Hispanic and Non-Hispanic Personal Crimes 2006*. Retrieved December 17, 2008, from Sourcebook of Criminal Justice Statistics via http://www.albany.edu/sourcebook/pdf/t392006.pdf.

State University of New York – US Department of Justice (2006e). *Sourcebook of Criminal Justice Statistics 2006 Online – Type of Bias Motivation, United States 2006*. Retrieved December 26, 2009, from Sourcebook of Criminal Justice Statistics via http://www.albany.edu/sourcebook/pdf/t4102006.pdf.

State University of New York – US Department of Justice. (2008). *Sourcebook of Criminal Justice Statistics Online – Property Victimizations by Crime and Race of Head of Household 2006* (2008). Retrieved December 27, 2009, from Sourcebook of Criminal Justice Statistics via http://www.albany.edu/sourcebook/pdf/t3222006.pdf.

US Bureau of the Census (USBC). (2000a). *Projections Online*. Retrieved December 24, 2009, from Census Government Population Estimates Archives via http://www.census.gov/population/www/projections/aboutproj.html.

US Bureau of Census (USBC). (2000b). *Summary of Modified Race Based on Census 2000 Race Online*. Retrieved December 24, 2008, from US Bureau of Census via http://www.census.gov/popest/archives/files/MRSF-01-USl.html.

US Bureau of Census. (2002). *Projections Online*. Retrieved December 24, 2009, from Census Government Population Estimates Archives via (http://www.census.gov/popest/archives/files/MRSF-01-USl.html retrieved.

US Department of Justice. (2002). *FBI Uniform Crime Report Hate Crime Data* 2002. Retrieved December 29, 2008, from Hate Crime Statistics 2002 via http://www.fbi.gov/ucr/hc2002victims.html.

US Department of Justice. (2006a). *FBI Uniform Crime Report Hate Crime Data 2006*. Retrieved December 29, 2009, from FBI Uniform Crime Report Hate Crime via http://www.fbi.gov/ucrhc2006/victims.html.

US Department of Justice. (2006b). *FBI Uniform Crime Report Hate Crime Data 2006*. Retrieved December 29, 2009, from Victims – Hate Crime Statistics 2006 via http://www.fbi.gov/ucr/hc2006/victims.html.

Video/DVD References

Bishop, Charles and Donavan, Michel (Producers), and Moore, Michael (Director) (2002). *Bowling for Columbine* (Documentary). Available from Metro Goldwyn Mayer, USA.

Discovery Channel (2001). *Assignment Discovery: A Question of Race* (Documentary VHS). Available from Discovery Communications, Inc., Bethesda, Maryland.

Sandler, Kathe (Producer and Director) (1980). *A Question of Color: Color Consciousness in Black America* (Documentary). Available from ITVs, USA.

Supreme Court Cases

Batson v. Kentucky, 476 U.S. 79 (1986).
Furman v. Georgia, 408 U.S. 238 (1972).
Georgia v. McCollum, 505 U.S. 42 (1992).
Gregg v. Georgia, 428 U.S. 153 (1976).
McCleskey v. Kemp, 481 U.S. 279 (1987).

Part IV
Conclusion

14
In Conclusion: Comparative Assessment of Race, Crime and Criminal Justice in International Perspectives

Anita Kalunta-Crumpton
Texas Southern University, USA

Introduction

This book opened with a focus on race using two broad categories – white (European descent) and non-white (non-European descent) – for emphasis. Whites are identifiable by their physical characteristics. Non-whites compose a range of racial groups that can be visually categorized according to similarities of physical appearance shared by each racial group. The above few lines of a description of 'race' may seem elementary since common knowledge of this fact about human variations may seem to render this basic tutorial unnecessary. But I deem this piece of information important because it points to the role of marked physical features – primarily skin color – as a crucial starting point in the negotiation of interactions between people who share similar or different physical characteristics. Within this framework, the purpose of the book was to use visible physical characteristics as a base for assessing any differentials or similarities in how crime is interpreted and responded to in the various countries covered in this book.

But as we have seen from Chapters 2 to 13, this purpose marks a key point of divergence in the book in light of the fact that racial grouping is detectable in the narratives of some chapters and not wholly so in others. A key reason for this disparity seems straightforward: racial grouping can be detected in those countries where race in its own right is categorized in crime data or identified in other influential sources of crime information; and it may not be clearly detected in others where the variable is not recognized in crime data. In the latter case, it may seem that defining identities through the use of terms such as 'immigrant', 'nationality' and 'foreigners' has become an acceptable form of freely classifying groups and perhaps expressing stereotypical viewpoints about them without the seemingly forbidden overt reference to their racial group. What is striking about this method of creating demarcations between peoples is its extension to white ethnicities so that the visibility of race appears to be shadowed by the use of collective terms that seemingly cut across white and non-white racial groups. In this sense, the terms 'immigrant', 'non-citizens', 'foreigners', 'migrant', 'ethnic minorities', 'foreign nationals' and so forth are represented in all-encompassing official data irrespective of differences in racial background. Presumably, these forms of identity evoke similar connotations when applied to immigrants from Asia, Africa, Europe, the Middle East, the Americas and so forth. Thus if immigrants are criminalized, it is assumedly a collective experience shared by them regardless of their racial differences. This is a perception that may sit comfortably in the absence of race (or ethnicity) in official crime data and the incognizance of the concept in discourse.

For ease of accessibility and clarity, later on in the discussion I use the terms 'Race Code' and 'No Race Code' to distinguish countries where race or ethnicity is coded systematically in official data from countries where they are not.

What does race absenteeism in official data tell us about race, crime and criminal justice?

Law (1996: 6) states that dismissing '... the explicit use of the race idea in policy making, for example in France, has not stopped racism permeating significant areas such as immigration policy, urban policy and labour market policies'. This is a viewpoint that some of the chapters did not mince words in highlighting. In the case of Italy, race or ethnicity is not recorded in official crime statistics. In discourse, race debates are hardly evident because, as Ruggiero states, such debates would attract allegations of racism. Yet as Ruggiero notes, the use of 'nationality', 'Italian and non-Italian' as variables for categorizing residents does not mean that racial/ethnic differences and the negative stereotypes that accompany those differences are buried and forgotten. I reiterate this very important point by quoting Ruggiero's captivating statements that:

> Even those who are indeed racist, therefore, prefer to adopt terms such as foreigners or immigrants, while most would designate the newcomers by their country of origin. This does not mean that stereotypes are avoided. On the contrary, naming people by nationality may become a shortcut leading to their faster labeling. Thus, 'Romanian' may evoke theft, 'Albanian' violence, and 'Nigerian' prostitution ... Nationalities, in brief, may become synonymous of specific illegal activities ... Nationality, therefore, incorporates race and ethnicity, namely embarrassing variables through which racism would immediately transpire.

The above quote sums up my thoughts on some of the complexities in debating the race effect on crime and criminal justice from an international perspective. Being the first manuscript in the collection to be submitted, I was keen to see race debated blatantly in the chapter. However, the chapter's ingenious approach to the issue of human diversity and crime was illuminating, and in addition it prepared me for subsequent manuscripts on other countries where the race or ethnicity variable is not recorded systematically. In these cases, the authors' acknowledgment of the missing piece of the race variable in the crime data puzzle is much appreciated. According to Mosher and Mahon-Haft, 'the release of race-based crime statistics in Canada' is informally prohibited and data on offenders' racial background are not collected systematically by law enforcement agencies. Albrecht identifies the fascist genocide regime of the 1930s and 1940s as the causal explanation for the removal of race and ethnicity from official data in Germany. In the absence of these variables in Germany, the populations of racial or ethnic groups border significantly on estimates, gleaned from the nationality variable used in the recording of such statistics. This, Albrecht acknowledges, limits our calculation of racially or ethnically based disparity in relationship between the offender/victim and the criminal justice system. In the Netherlands, crime data are recorded according to nationality, which means that the racial/ethnic origins of migrants who have Dutch nationality are not identifiable. Like Albrecht, Junger-Tas gives informative reason for the absence of race/ethnicity in present-day Dutch official data: such variables, previously part of Dutch official data, were used by Nazis to identify Jews during the Second World War.

In France, it is illegal to record ethnicity; rather residents are classified into two broad groups: citizens and non-citizens. Thus ethnicity/race does not inform crime data. Instead, crime data are reported only by the nationalities of non-citizens (that is, *étrangers*) and not French citizens who also include non-natives. Spain and Portugal tell the same story. Goode notes that in Spain 'crime data that detail race and ethnic factors' are generally relegated to the 'internal domain of official agencies', and related to this is that the term race or ethnicity is not used in Spain's crime discourse. In Portugal, the law prohibits racially/ethnically coded official data in order to avoid racial stereotyping; only nationality is registered in official data and crime statistics record foreigners as a collective regardless of whether they have resident or non-resident status.

In sum, the general picture is that non-white groups not only contribute to the populations of 'non-nationals' of these countries, but also contribute to their populations of 'nationals'. And in the absence of a statistical breakdown of racial or ethnic groups in the non-national and national populations – particularly the latter – it is difficult to make an accurate estimate of the contributions of racial groups to official data, including crime figures. Despite this limitation, each of the authors of the 'No Race Code' chapters was able to draw on available data, literature and research to unveil, albeit to varying degrees, elements of ethnicity and race in their analyses of crime and criminal justice. It is worth noting that the pattern of nego- tiating differences based on 'non-race' variables has allowed access to the circumstances of some white ethnicities. Perhaps, these ethnicities would not have featured otherwise in discourses of race in *black* and *white* as is tra- ditionally the case in countries such as Britain and the United States where there is a relatively defined categorization of differences based primarily on racial groups, and where debates on race and crime have tended to focus on minority racial groups while limiting our knowledge of the white racial group. In the uniqueness of the 'No Race Code' chapters, we learn not only of ethnic groups within non-white racial groups, as exemplified in the dis- cussions of Moroccans and Surinamese, but also, albeit minimally, of the position of white ethnicities – for example, former Yugoslavian and ethnic Germans – in crime discourses. And based on their position as immigrants and a minority, certain white ethnicities, like their non-white counterparts, seem to suffer the consequences of what immigrant, foreign nationality, ethnic minority and related connotations stand for in popular reactions to crime.

In France, Germany, Italy, Canada, the Netherlands, Spain and Portugal, immigrants or minorities, broadly speaking, seem to have certain experiences in common: they experience various forms of socio-economic disadvantage, and they are prominent in crime discourse and criminal jus- tice practices. In France, immigrant marginalization (particularly of *étrangers*) is seen in overcrowded housing, high levels of concentration in social hous- ing, segregated and run-down residential areas, segregated schools, language barriers and so forth. These variables are associated with high crime and vic- timization rates among France's immigrant population. In Germany, high unemployment rates, low incomes, high levels of dependency on social security and educational underachievement are among the indices of socio- economic deprivation found among immigrants. Also, Germany's foreign nationals are over-represented in police crime data. Spain's minority pop- ulation is socio-economically segregated and marginalized, and this factor identifies minority communities with certain ethnic groups, skin color, culture, criminality and victimization. In Canada, minorities are socio- economically disadvantaged, have high rates of both offending and criminal victimization and are over-represented in the criminal justice system. In the Netherlands, certain immigrant groups are concentrated in disadvan- taged localities, dependent on social security, have low levels of educational achievement and high offending rates. Portugal's cohort of foreigners tends to be situated in menial jobs, substandard housing and deprived residential areas, and to be over-represented in the criminal justice system, includ- ing the prison establishments. Features of socio-economic deprivation are applied to the analysis of offending among Italy's migrant population in the sense that they can foster exposure to certain criminal activities, often acquisitive criminal opportunities, which, despite their low levels of economic benefit, are extremely prone to surveillance and detection. Similarly, Albrecht notes that immigrants are disadvantaged by stricter immigration controls and changes in the labor market in which demands for a highly skilled labor force continue to push immigrants away from the conventional labor market into 'shadow economies, black markets and low paid jobs'. Under such structural changes, risks of criminalization are high as reflected in the popular association of immigration with crime and young immigrants as potential chronic offenders.

While the above description summarizes some of the situations generally shared by those designated as immigrants or minorities or foreigners and so forth in each of the countries where race/ethnicity is not officially coded, there is evidence that certain minority groups stand out in the narratives of crime and criminal justice. And underlining the conspicuousness of such minorities is the visibility of their ethnic grouping and their racial identity.

Goode identifies sub-Saharan Africans, Moroccans, South Americans and the Roma/Gitana as part of Spain's main ethnic minorities most racially profiled by the police. The Roma/Gitana are Spain's historical gypsy population, perceived as the 'enemy within'. Like the Roma/Gitana, Spain's 'old' immigrants of Jewish and Muslim backgrounds and her 'new' immigrants, the majority from Africa and South America, are racialized and criminalized in ways that initiate and rationalize racist attacks upon them. Findings from a Spanish survey identify Moroccans, Muslims and Jews as Spain's main immigration threats. Portugal has her share of immigrants from Brazil and her former colonies in Africa. In Portugal, immigrants from Lusophone Africa (and the gypsy population) are particularly socio-economically disadvantaged; the African immigrants make up the majority of foreigners in prison, and have featured in the criminalization process, particularly in the 1980s.

The Aboriginal and black populations of Canada are structurally disadvantaged. The level of structural disadvantage is more severe for Aboriginals, who have lower levels of life expectancy because of health problems, higher rates of unemployment and residence in substandard housing and lower levels of average income than non-Aboriginals. Rates of substance abuse, suicide, single-parent households, children in foster care, offending, violence and criminal victimization are high among Aboriginals whose adult and juvenile populations also have disproportionate rates of incarceration. Like Aboriginals, blacks have a higher and disproportionate incarceration rate than whites. Blacks have high levels of police stops and arrests, and are less likely to be granted bail; they are also more likely than Aboriginals and other visible minority groups to be victims of racially motivated hate crime. Unlike Aboriginals and blacks, Canada's Asian population is under-represented in prison figures, however, they fall victim to hate crime, racialization, stereotyping and discriminatory policy and practice at national and law enforcement levels relating to, for example, organized crime and immigration. There is evidence of racial attacks on Muslims and Arabs who began to be noticed in law enforcement profiling practices following the incidents of 9/11 in the USA and the subsequent introduction of anti-terrorism legislation in Canada.

The process of racialization within the realm of religion is very significant in France. Therein, race underscores discourses of crime as well as criminal justice policy and practice; it is crucially integrated with religion and immigration whereby 'visible ethnicity' intersects with non-Christianity to generate racialized 'immigrant others'. This category of 'immigrant otherness' contains populations from Turkey, and former French colonies in North Africa – Algerians, Tunisians and Moroccans – whose allegiance to Islam and perceived detachment from mainstream France render them ever more visible in political rhetoric on crime problems and related social concerns such as terrorism. Regardless of whether or not they are French citizens, their foreignness is identifiable by virtue of their skin color and their Muslim religion. This is particularly relevant in the case of the populations from North Africa. Jackson notes that of the 14 million resident population with foreign ancestry, 21 percent have a North African background, and this group is portrayed as the 'crime problem' and subjected to racist violence and harassment, including the desecration of their mosques and tombs. North Africans and Turkish are over-represented in the criminal justice system. They are more likely to be unemployed than French citizens, and this disparity is somewhat attributed to employment discrimination. 'Anti-minority sentiments', Jackson argues, are demonstrated in exclusionary immigration policies targeted at non-Europeans. The effects of the application of those policies are seen in the high numbers of foreigners in the prison population. Jackson notes how the attack on immigration and immigrants has culminated in indiscriminate criminalization and the incarceration of non-Western foreigners (including the legally resident) mainly from North and sub-Saharan Africa for non-immigration offenses such as drug possession.

Like the situation in France, in the Netherlands a distinction is drawn between Western (largely from the new EU member states and former Yugoslavia) and non-Western migrants, which can help to throw some light on the issues of ethnic and racial grouping. The majority of the non-Western migrants comprise Surinamese, Antilleans, Moroccans and Turkish. Other non-Western migrants have originated from places such as Egypt, Somalia, India, Pakistan, China and the Middle East. Unlike Western migrants and the Dutch, non-Western migrants tend to reside in disadvantaged localities of acute socio-economic deprivation, including substandard schools; they are more likely to be reliant on social security benefits; they are younger and have lower levels of educational achievement, meaning that their employment opportunities are often limited. Among migrant parents, the highest levels of unemployment are to be found among Africans, Moroccans and Antilleans; these groups also reside in the most disorganized areas. In contrast, the unemployment level is lowest among Dutch and West European parents. Various forms of socio-economic disadvantage, especially residence in areas of acute deprivation among non-Western youths, interact with their offending behavior and experiences of criminal victimization. Police statistics show that delinquency is highest among Moroccans and Antilles, followed by Somalian and Surinamese males; former Yugoslavians and Turkish (who are under-represented in the youth justice system and youth protection system) show lower rates. Also, self-report data show a higher rate of delinquency amongst the three main ethnic groups: Surinamese/ Antilleans, Moroccans and Turkish than the Western migrants, the Dutch and other non-Western migrants.

In some of the 'No Race Code' countries, particularly Canada, France and the Netherlands, we see the prominence of non-whites in the analyses of crime. In some others, this is not the case. In comparison to the other 'No Race Code' countries, Germany and Italy are relatively silent on the exact location of visible racial/ethnic groups in the rhetoric of and reactions to immigrants and crime. We know, on the basis of estimates, that there are sizeable communities of both Africans and Asians within the German immigrant population. It is evident that indices of immigrant socio-economic deprivation are highly pronounced in the case of Africans and Asians. But the implications of these for offending may only be deduced from the general analytical framework within which Albrecht discusses immigration and crime with reference to, for example, immigrants' disadvantaged socio-economic position, their young age profile, the over-representation of foreign nationals in police crime data and immigrants' similarity with non-immigrants in experiences of personal and property criminal victimization based on findings from the 2005 European Crime Survey.

It is from this general approach to the issue of human variation and crime in Germany that we can allude to the situation in Italy. Ruggiero notes that non-Italians are over-represented in crime statistics from offending to prison population, and have a high rate of criminal victimization, especially for violent crimes. In the absence of official statistics to glean how certain social variables guide police actions, Ruggiero makes the logical assumption that the visibility of certain migrants by way of skin color or attire and the association of specific localities with specific migrants render certain ethnic groups more open to police surveillance for deviant features associated with them. One might see this viewpoint aligning with Albrecht's note that in Germany there are crime types that attract ethnic profiling. Drug distribution exemplifies such crime types and illustrates the hidden economies through which the unemployed and illegal immigrants of African (Nigeria, Senegal, Morocco, Algeria), Turkish, Lebanese and Arab descent are more likely to come into contact with law enforcement agencies.

Relative to non-whites, the visibility of whites is limited in the discussions. Despite Turkey's geographical affiliation to Europe, it is designated as non-Western and non-European. Furthermore, its association with Islam situates Turkish migrants in a position somewhat similar to immigrants from beyond the borders of Europe. In Germany, this externalization of Turkish immigrants can be seen in their portrayal as being apathetic toward integration into mainstream Germany and as forming a "parallel society" with its own culture and language. It is with reference to Eastern Europeans that we begin to see some explicit incorporation of white ethnicity in the human variation and crime debate. Cunha relates the increase in Portugal's prison population in the early 21st century to an increase in the numbers of Eastern European prisoners, particularly those from Russia, Ukraine and Moldavia. In Germany, the specific inclusion of white ethnicity is apparent with reference to former Yugoslavia and may be consistent with the fact that immigrants from this country (and Turkey) constitute almost half of the immigrant population of Germany. Young migrants from former Yugoslavia (and Turkey) are shown in German self-report studies to be over-represented in violent crime, an observation which tallies with Junger-Tas' findings that show violence or violent-related crimes to be associated with Yugoslavian (and Turkish) youths in the Netherlands.

In the following section, we review the 'Race Code' countries for their contribution to our comprehension of race, crime and criminal justice in international perspectives.

Is the race variable in official crime data telling us something different about race, crime and criminal justice?

The breakdown of crime statistics – from offending to prison population – according to race is a key factor distinguishing Britain, Australia and New Zealand, South Africa, United States and Brazil from those countries discussed above. On the basis of the racially defined categorization of crime data, it is presumed that we can make clearer and more informed assessment of trends in the involvement of different racial groups in offending and criminal victimization as well as their contact with agencies in the criminal justice system. In this regard, the racial classification unveils, in explicit terms, any disparities or similarities in the circumstances and experiences of whites and non-whites on the basis of which one can debate the presence or absence of race-specific influences. In contrast, such debate may not find significance in countries that do not operate racially coded data perhaps for the self-explanatory reason that the invisibility of race in official data seemingly erases its significance in any crime debate. But as preceding discussions have shown, it is difficult to suggest that human physical differences are not pertinent to the conceptualization and contextualization of crime in the 'No

Race Code' countries more so in some than others. It will also be difficult not to locate similarities in perspectives shared by both the 'No Race Code' and 'Race Code' countries based on what we can deduce from the various labels used by the former to classify people. Indeed, those labels have offered specifics on ethnic groups in a way that may not be found in 'Race Code' countries where a discussion of, for example, Asians as a racial group may not signify the specific circumstances of ethnic groups such as Indians and Pakistanis (this point is rehearsed by Georges-Abeyie in his chapter on the United States). Yet, it is through those labels that areas of agreement with 'Race Code' societies can be noticed.

There are discussions about visible minorities, especially Aboriginals and blacks in Canada, non-Western migrants in the Netherlands, foreigners in Portugal, non-European immigrants in France and Spain, all of which echo discussions that are familiar to Australia and New Zealand with reference to Aboriginals and the Maori; to South Africa with reference to blacks and coloreds; to Brazil with reference to blacks and mulattos; to Britain with reference to blacks and Asians in particular; and to the United States with reference to blacks in particular.

Australia and New Zealand, and South Africa – similar to Canada – share experiences of colonization which understandably place the non-white natives of these countries at the center of the authors' discussions, despite the fact that there are other non-white groups that contribute to the populations of these countries. Similar to the circumstances of Canadian Aboriginals, Jeffries and Newbold's account of Australian Aboriginals show a range of socio-economic and health-related disadvantages. A higher percentage of Australian Aboriginals than non-Aboriginals are unemployed and even when they do find employment they are concentrated in low-paid jobs, such as manual laboring. In contrast, the non-indigenous populations are to be found predominantly in professional jobs. The disadvantaged circumstances of Aboriginals also extend to other areas, including housing, residential area, health and political position. Existing data show a disproportionate presence and higher rates of Aboriginals than non-Aboriginals in offending and criminal victimization statistics, notably in relation to violence, crimes of disorder and drug use. Australian Aboriginals are more likely to be arrested than non-Aboriginals, and they are over-represented in the prison population. Similarly, but to a lesser extent than Aboriginals, New Zealand Maori are socio-economically marginalized, with the community experiencing a high unemployment rate and predominance in manual employment. They are also over-represented in arrest figures for almost all major crimes, and are more likely to be arrested and convicted for such crimes than non-Maori; they are also over-represented in prison figures. South Africa's black and colored communities, especially the latter, have higher incarceration rates than whites and Asians; they reside mostly in townships where various indications of poverty are apparent. Criminal victimization, particularly in relation to violent crime, is disproportionately high amongst black and colored South Africans.

In Brazil, non-whites are over-represented in prison figures and have higher homicide victimization rates than whites. Specifically, the Brazilian black and mulatto populations are far more socio-economically disadvantaged than whites, and in line with their low position in the socio-economic strata, are more likely to come into contact with the criminal justice system. In Britain, the urban areas – where the highest proportions of non-whites reside – record the highest crime rates. These urban areas are located in major cities popular for non-whites. High-crime urban areas also experience multiple socio-economic deprivations such as substandard housing, high unemployment rates and poverty, school exclusion, low levels of educational achievement and health problems. Prison statistics indicate that non-whites of black and Asian origins in particular are more likely than whites to come into contact with the criminal justice system. Presumably, they have a higher offending rate than their white counterparts in England and Wales, and Scotland. Similar picture is mirrored in the youth justice system with black, mixed heritage, Asian and Chinese youths receiving harsher or less lenient sentencing and pre-sentencing disposals than white youths. In the United States, the non-white population experience higher levels of unemployment and similar forms of socio-economic disadvantage than whites; in terms of offending and criminal victimization rates, we particularly notice the over-representation of blacks who are also disproportionately represented in death row statistics.

In ways relative to each country in the 'No Race Code' and 'Race Code' categories, reasons are provided for any differences in the representation of the different broad groups of people – be they non-whites and whites, citizens and non-citizens, immigrants and non-immigrants, ethnic minority and ethnic majority and so forth – in crime and the criminal justice system. Nevertheless, the range of explanations converges at some points to offer similar accounts to what seems to be a similar situation. Significantly, I see in both the 'Race Code' and 'No Race Code' countries two key issues: socio-economic disadvantage and discrimination, debated in relation to their contributory influence on how diverse human groups feature in crime and criminal justice. I have identified experiences of socio-economic disadvantage of minority (and majority black South African) groups, notably non-white groups. There is some indication that this factor intermingles with experiences of criminal victimization and offending rates.

In her analysis of delinquency, Junger-Tas crucially locates non-Western migrants' experience of criminal victimization in negative socio-economic circumstances that create risks of victimization. For example, Junger-Tas relates this experience to the quality of geographical area rather than ethnicity: those who live in disadvantaged and high-crime localities are victimized in line with the characteristics of those areas regardless of ethnicity. A range of chapters will concur with Junger-Tas' viewpoint on criminal victimization. Cole notes that in Britain, higher risks of criminal victimization, notably violent and acquisitive crimes, are consistent with urban areas and disadvantaged inner-city neighborhoods than in less disadvantaged, and rural/affluent suburban areas. Likewise, unemployment as opposed to employment is an indicator of higher risks of victimization, which is more likely to be experienced by non-whites and in their local areas than whites. According to Jeffries and Newbold, criminal victimization in Australia and New Zealand seems to exhibit similar racial/ethnic and geographical characteristics. In addition, violent crimes in Aboriginal and Maori communities tend to be intra-racial and within the family, and also – in the case of the Maori – in gang conflicts. In regards to Canada, Mosher and Mahon-Haft show that Aboriginal and black populations have high rates of offending and victimization for violent crime which tends to be intra-racial. The intra-racial/ethnic nature of crime including violent crime may seem implicit in Ruggiero's observation that Italians are likely to perpetrate crimes against fellow Italians, and non-Italians (or migrants) against non-Italians. Intra-racial crime perpetration/victimization is explicit in Bosilong and Mbecke's account of the South African situation. The authors depict violent crimes to be notably intra-racial in black and colored communities. Criminal victimization, particularly violent crime, is disproportionately high amongst black and colored South Africans, and, according to Bosilong and Mbecke, this situation may be attributed to their residence in urban areas with high levels of social disorganization and high risks of criminal victimization. The importance of geography to our understanding of criminal victimization is endorsed by Georges-Abeyie with reference to the United States.

Although in both manifest and latent ways, both the 'Race Code' and 'No Race Code' countries have situated offending rates in the context of socio-economic marginalization, there are instances of mixed viewpoints over the extent to which socio-economic disadvantage accounts for offending rates by differing human groups. At this point, we begin to see other explanatory tools, primarily racialization and criminalization or racial discrimination, finding importance in the debate. From the standpoints of Jackson and Goode in particular, it seems that the intersection between socio-economic disadvantage and non-white offending (and criminal victimization) must not be separated from the influential role and consequences of the processes of racialization and criminalization experienced by minorities in France and Spain, respectively. Cole acknowledges in detail the link between socio-economic marginalization and criminality in Britain. Simultaneously, he questions the usefulness of the socio-economic factor in explaining non-white offending rates. In his argument, whites who reside in disadvantaged urban areas are vulnerable to the same criminogenic factors as non-whites. Cole also notes that the link between non-whites, socio-economic disadvantage and offending is not reflected in the findings from the 2003 self-reported Offending Crime and Justice Survey, and figures from the British Youth Offending Teams, which generally point to a higher offending rate for whites than non-whites in the adult and youth populations. Consequently, Cole draws attention to claims of racial bias in the criminal justice process as another possible explanation for non-white offending rates.

Other chapters also share the 'racial bias' perspective. Georges-Abeyie recognizes the possible influence of racial discrimination in encounters between non-whites and the US criminal justice system where blacks, in particular, are over-represented. Across the US border, the role of racial bias and racialization is given a relatively prominent position in Mosher and Mahon-Haft's account surrounding the over-representation of blacks in the Canadian criminal justice system. Also, in explaining the disproportionate representation of Canadian Aboriginals in the criminal justice system, Mosher and Mahon-Haft highlight the contributory influences of historical colonization on Aboriginal structural disadvantage alongside racial discriminatory practices of the criminal justice structures. Racial discrimination is apparent in South Africa. According to Bosilong and Mbecke, it was overt in the Apartheid regime and covert in the post-Apartheid era. Although the authors are modest on the issue of white/non-white relations in contemporary South African criminal justice, they are assertive in illustrating how the legacy of Apartheid is seen in high levels of violent crime, socio-economic inequality, a lack of community cohesion and so forth in black and colored communities. The authors also note that racism still permeates the criminal justice system, although it is not as apparent as the racist death penalty policy and practice instituted in Apartheid South Africa. Similar to the authors of the 'South Africa' and 'Canada' chapters, Jeffries and Newbold acknowledge the impact of historical colonization on the marginalized and offending situations of the indigenous populations of Australia and New Zealand, especially the Aboriginals. They attribute Aboriginal and Maori offending rates to their higher levels of involvement in criminal activity. However, the authors note that Aboriginal offending rate is also linked to police racial profiling of this group of people and their residential areas. But unlike the Aboriginals, the Maori offending rate is not connected to racial discrimination by criminal justice agencies. Rather, the over-representation of the Maori in prison figures is associated with their involvement in violent crimes which attract longer prison sentences.

Indeed, the 'no racial discrimination' account is not unique to the Maori situation. In some of the chapters, this approach is clearly identified. Those chapters emphasize notably the central influences of legally provided criteria and/or socio-economic disadvantage – as opposed to the race or ethnicity factor – in determining contact and outcomes of interactions between non-whites and the criminal justice system. After controlling for a range of legal variables in their research on sentencing in Brazil, Cano, Ribeiro and Meireles concluded that racial bias played no part in sentencing, even though they noted that this finding did not mean that it did not exist at earlier stages of the criminal justice process. For Junger-Tas, ethnicity cannot be viewed as a predictor of either offending or criminal justice practices. Instead, non-Western migrants' delinquency is linked to socio-economic disadvantages that create the opportunity to commit offences. This observation calls to mind evidence from the Netherlands' self-report data presented by Junger-Tas. The data show that the main non-Western ethnic groups (Surinamese/Antillean, Moroccan and Turkish) report the highest number of offenses. While the self-report findings are consistent with evidence from the Netherlands police crime statistics about these ethnic groups, they are in conflict with the aforementioned British self-report findings, which, according to Cole, show lower offending rates for non-white youths than white youths. Nevertheless, in her view on the insignificance of ethnicity in criminal justice practices, Junger-Tas observes that policing is not guided by racial discrimination but by 'powerful constraints derived from the police organization, the particular local situation in which they find themselves and the prevailing values and norms, all of which oppose racial discrimination'. Junger-Tas argues that decisions at other stages of the criminal justice process such as pretrial detention and sentencing may be determined by seriousness of offence, nationality, residence status, plea status and so forth. These factors may work against minorities or foreigners who, for example, are more likely to commit drug and violent offenses, have no fixed abode and enter a plea of 'not guilty'.

Junger-Tas' viewpoint on the socio-economic factor and offending nexus assigns support to findings from Cunha's study of a Portuguese prison facility for women. Her study shows that participants in the Portuguese retail drug economy and drug offenders in prison are drawn largely from deprived urban localities. Cunha argues that class takes precedence over ethnicity in determining offending and contact with the criminal justice system. Although Cunha notes that in Portugal, foreigners are more likely than their Portuguese counterparts to attract more severe punishment in the criminal justice system in similar circumstances, she recognizes the impact of legal criteria in the treatment of foreigners and Portuguese nationals. Seriousness of offense and/or perceived risk of absconding impacts negatively on foreigners. Foreigners are charged with offenses (such as those related to drugs) that are more likely to attract a conviction and a harsher sentence, and they are more likely to be remanded in custody pending trial. Such legal influences are relevant to Albrecht's viewpoint that prosecutorial, pre-trial and sentencing decision-making is affected less by nationality or ethnicity than by offence seriousness and similar offence characteristics as well as other legally provided criteria such as prior convictions and community ties. Ruggiero's recognition of the significance of legal variables in Italy's criminal justice system is identified in his note that migrants in comparison to Italian citizens may be sentenced more harshly for reasons that are suggestive of elements of institutional racism. These are reflected, for example, in the exclusionary criteria used in criminal justice decisions such as community ties, the absence of which may foster judicial decisions to give a custodial rather than a non-custodial sentence. Some of these legally provided elements also evoke the social and economic explanatory factor for differentials in dispositions by the criminal justice system. For example, a lack of adequate legal representation can be a consequence of unemployment and socio-economic marginalization, and thereby not being financially able to afford a good lawyer. This point is endorsed by Bosilong and Mbecke in their claim that white and Asian South Africans share similar incarceration rates (lower than the rates for blacks and coloreds). The authors claim that this fact is linked to some extent to their relatively advantaged socio-economic position – higher income and levels of education – and possibly their ability to afford adequate legal representation to avoid incarceration.

In these frameworks for making a critical assessment of the impact of race or ethnicity on offending rates, other social variables such as age and gender have featured as a predictor of offending or the criminal justice response to offending. Age is a significant example. Portugal's immigrant population has an over-represented proportion of young men; in Germany, immigrants have a younger age profile than their German counterparts, as do both non-whites in Britain and non-Western migrants in the Netherlands. This fact arguably indicates proneness to offending, especially in combination with socio-economic disadvantage.

Conclusion

This collection presents different geographical settings and different combinations of human populations. Nonetheless, this fact does not overshadow the commonalities that run through the chapters at points of agreement and disagreement on the position of visible physical differences in our comprehension of crime and criminal justice. We now know that the absence of systematic race-specific quantitative crime data in many of the countries is a major factor that may seem to differentiate the analyses pertaining to them from those countries where the race variable is central to the quantitative recording of crime data. While I would respect criticisms that may arise around this fact, I simultaneously advocate that whatever lessons we learn from the 'Race Code' countries should not blind us to at least the subtleties of such lessons that may be picked out in the discussions relating to the 'No Race Code' countries.

I have already raised eyebrows over the neglect of this important variable in crime data, not necessarily because such omission minimizes our awareness of its contextual application but principally because of its usefulness in presenting a foundation needed to facilitate forward-looking debates and interventions on the issue. Albrecht refers to a recent critical attack on

Germany by the Committee on the Elimination of Racial Discrimination for neglecting the race or ethnicity variable in official data, including censuses. The importance of such data collected in detail and systematically should not be underestimated, not least for their purpose in monitoring one of the most problematic areas of victimization. Herein, I am referring to racially motivated hate crime, which is internationally recognized as a problem given its devastating implications for people who by virtue of their visible association to a certain group are vulnerable to physical and/or psychological attack and abuse. We learn that in Germany, the 2005 European Crime Survey showed that a significant proportion of immigrants perceived their general experiences of victimization to be hate-motivated; however, we do not know how this proportion is distributed across racial/ethnic groups. In Italy, hate crimes are absent from records of criminal victimization on non-Italians – an anomaly criticized by Ruggiero who cited England and Wales as an example of European countries where hate crimes are monitored. Cole's analysis on the issue of victimization in Britain provides a statistical detail of experiences across non-white groups and white British. According to the British hate crime data, whites are disproportionately represented as perpetrators and non-whites as victims – especially the Chinese and, in recent years, Muslims. We also learn from the US statistical information that perpetrators of racially/ethnically aggravated hate crimes are mostly white, with blacks and Hispanics disproportionately represented as victims.

Of course, my expression of concern over the absence of race in some countries' official statistics is not to claim that racially coded crime data tell us every piece of information we need to know about crime perpetration and victimization according to racial groups. Far from it. After all, crime data in general have their limitations, ranging from problems of crime reporting/non-reporting and recording/non-recording that amount to the 'hidden figure' of crime to the underestimation/overestimation of certain crime types and situations. Some of the limitations of crime data and official data in general are acknowledged in this collection – for example, by Georges-Abeyie, Albrecht, Cole, Jeffries and Newbold, Junger-Tas and Cano and colleagues. Racially coded quantitative crime data neither tell us how and why negative stereotypes such as "wetbacks"' are used to describe African immigrants accosted by coastguards while trying to enter Spain from the Mediterranean (see Goode's chapter), how and why certain discourses of black people and Asians in contemporary Canada are situated in negative biological and cultural explanations (see Mosher and Mahon-Haft's chapter), nor do they reveal the subtle but powerful role of subjective influences in the creation of quantitative crime data (see Kalunta-Crumpton 1998, 1999, 2000). The point is that we do not need to rely solely on a statistical breakdown of offending rates according to race to make sufficient sense of the representation of certain human groups in crime discourses and their encounters with the criminal justice system.

As shown in the narratives expressed in this collection, non-whites seem to feature most in rates of crime and contact with the criminal justice system. As also demonstrated in this collection, there are reasons for this and they do not all suggest racial discrimination within the criminal justice system. However, all the chapters acknowledge, in one form or another, the socio-economic factor as an important explanatory ingredient for offending or non-offending. The latter scenario can be exemplified with reference to Asians. Asians are non-white, and in some of the chapters where they are featured, it is clear that they have a lower offending rate. Linked to this is the finding that in general they do not suffer the level of structural disadvantage experienced by blacks, for instance. In the socio-economic disadvantage and offending account, certain white ethnicities of Eastern European origin seem to be incorporated – for example, former Yugoslavians in Germany and the Netherlands. Yugoslavians (and other Eastern Europeans) are a relatively new breed of immigrants in Western Europe and like 'new' migrants from non-Western countries, their country of origin suffers relative poverty. In this respect, their visibility in crime discourse and its consistency with their socio-economic status may be a reflection of how the dynamics of global socio-economic (and political) stratification shape human relations within affluent Western countries.

In these human relations, non-Western peoples have been the traditional subordinate in the stratification system. Nevertheless, former Yugoslavian immigrants in Western Europe may illustrate a case of the white ethnic victim of the dynamics of economic and political power – a situation that somewhat echoes the historical experiences of the Irish, for example. That said, it may be the case that the whiteness of former Yugoslavians and other Eastern Europeans will, over time, make it easier for them to assimilate fully into their host country in line with West-European migrants who appear to be inconspicuous in crime concerns. In contrast, full assimilation may not be available to non-whites who in general are more likely to continue to experience structural disadvantage and its wider implications for offending rates and criminal victimization. This is particularly the case for those non-white groups who are still experiencing the legacies of historical slavery and colonization. Whether structural disadvantage propels non-whites to commit crime or makes them a target of or vulnerable to criminal justice policies and practices or all of the above, we see a framework that is consistent with their obvious physical contrast to people of European descent. The contributory role of racial discrimination to this setup may remain a contentious issue particularly in the absence of the background benefits of systematic racially coded crime data in many of the countries covered in this book.

At this juncture, I must add that upon close reading of the chapters in this collection I am inclined toward the observation that for the purpose of crime data in the differing countries, there is a need for a narrower and systematic classification of human diversity by ethnic grouping (irrespective of residency or nationality status in the host country) in order to produce detailed and comprehensive background information for the race, crime and criminal justice debate. This is principally because certain ethnic groups may be much more likely to offend, experience criminal victimization and come into contact with the criminal justice system than other ethnic groups within their disparate racial groups. Likewise, the reasons for any ethnicity-based disparities and similarities in crime data in different countries may vary according to country-specific factors and situations that affect differ-ent white and non-white ethnic groups in different ways. Ultimately, in attempts to assess the effects of race-based discrimination on crime figures, it appears important that we differentiate between the possible role of *ethnicity* (that is, ethnicity-based discrimination which may be experienced by certain white ethnic groups and may not be experienced by all non-white ethnic groups) and the possible role of *race* (that is, discrimination that cuts across all ethnic groups of a particular race). Ethnicity-based crime data would allow for an examination of how much, for example, people of Pakistani origin (not Asian), Ivorian origin (not Black) and English origin (not White) contribute to offending and victimization statistics, and why. At the same time, ethnicity-based crime data would provide access to the same pieces of information as they apply to racial groups in their monolithic form. I there-fore conclude by yielding to Georges-Abeyie's call for crime data based on differentiated ethnic groups. I view his observation as the starting point of reference for examining critically and comparatively the significance of eth-nic and racial differences or similarities in crime statistics both nationally and cross-nationally.

References

Law, I. (1996) *Racism, Ethnicity and Social Policy*. London: Prentice Hall.

Kalunta-Crumpton, A. (1998) 'The Prosecution and Defense of Black Defendants in Drug Trials: Evidence of Claims-making', *British Journal of Criminology*, 38(4): 561–591.

——— (1999) *Race and Drug Trials: The Social Construction of Guilt and Innocence*. Aldershot: Ashgate.

——— (2000) 'Black People and Discrimination in Criminal Justice: The Message from Research', in A. Marlow and B. Loveday (eds), *After MacPherson*. Dorset: Russell House Publishing.

Index